An Introduction to 3D Studio Max for Windows 95

An Introduction to 3D Studio Max for Windows 95

A. Yarwood

Registered Developer

LONGMAN

Addison Wesley Longman Limited
Edinburgh Gate, Harlow
Essex CM20 2JE, England
and Associated Companies throughout the world

First published 1998

British Library Cataloguing in Publication Data
A catalogue entry for this title is available from the British Library

ISBN 0-582-31744-4

Set by 24 in 10/13pt Melior
Produced by Longman Singapore Publishers (Pte) Ltd
Printed in Singapore

Contents

List of plates

Colour plates are between pages 116 and 117.

Preface

3D Studio Max is a world class graphics, design, rendering and animation software package designed to run in either Windows NT (Release 1 onwards) or in Windows 95 (Release 1.1 onwards). This book deals with Release 1.2 of the package running in Windows 95. The contents of the book are just as suitable for those using the package running in Windows NT, except for the differences in some of the icons and windows in NT.

It must be emphasised that this book is only an introductory text, suitable for those wishing to start learning how to use what is an extremely complex graphics, rendering and animation package. There is no way in which such a complex software package could be fully described in a book of this size. It is hoped however that the student or beginner will, by following the descriptions of the comparatively simple examples given throughout the book, be encouraged to experiment and practise with the more advanced aspects of the use of the software.

I have been encouraged to write this book because my book *An Introduction to 3D Studio* first published in 1995 and reprinted in 1996 has been well received. Although the contents of that book could, in part, be suitable when working in Max, the differences between 3D Studio and Max demands another book.

3D Studio Max supersedes 3D Studio. Although the practised user of 3D Studio should have little difficulty in learning how to create scenes in Max, there are considerable differences between the methods of working the two packages. Whereas 3D Studio could only be run in MS-DOS, Max runs in either Windows NT or Windows 95, with all the advantages those two systems offer. The four separate programs 2D Shaper, 3D Lofter, 3D Editor and Keyframer in 3D Studio are combined into a single work face in Max. The addition of the Command panel in Max, with its extensive system of rollouts, more than meets the requirements previously covered in 3D Studio by the four separate programs.

The computer used for producing the illustrations in this book was equipped with a 120 Mhz Pentium CPU, more than a gigabyte of hard disk space and a 17 inch monitor equipped for SVGA. I found the CPU to be sufficiently fast for my purposes, mainly because I was not rendering very complicated scenes. If the reader wishes to render scenes containing a mass of detail, it will be necessary to use a computer equipped with a faster Pentium chip, or to be patient while a rendering develops.

Hardware requirements

1. PC fitted with a 90 MHz Pentium CPU, or better.
2. A minimum of 32 Mbytes memory (RAM), preferably more.
3. Hard disk, with at least 100 Mbytes of free space to allow for disk swap space, preferably more.
4. At least an SVGA monitor and video card supporting 800 × 600 with 256 colours, ideally better.
5. A mouse.
6. A 3D Studio Max specific hardware lock ('dongle') is necessary. 3D Studio or AutoCAD Release 13 hardware locks cannot be used in place of the 3D Studio Max hardware lock.
7. Windows 95 or Windows NT.

Aims of the book

To provide a text covering sufficient details of the use of 3D Studio Max for Windows 95 to make it suitable for students in Further Education or in Higher Education or for beginners in the use of 3D Studio Max wishing to learn how to use the software for design purposes.

A. Yarwood
Salisbury 1997

World Wide Web

I have prepared 12 sample *.max files which may be downloaded from

ftp://awl.co.uk/pub/awl-he/engineering/yarwood/studio_max

These can be opened within 3D Studio Max and will give the reader a variety of objects and settings to experiment with. Addison Wesley Longman Higher Education's homepage web address is:

http://www.awl-he.com

Acknowledgements

The author wishes to acknowledge with grateful thanks the help given to him by members of the staff at Autodesk Ltd.

Trademarks

The following trademarks are registered in the US Patent and Trademark Office by Autodesk Inc:

Autodesk®, AutoCAD®.

The following are trademarks of Autodesk Inc:

ACAD™, DXF™, 3D Studio Max™.

IBM® is a registered trademark of the International Business Machines Corporation.

MS-DOS® is a registered trademark, and Windows™ is a trademark of the Microsoft Corporation.

A. Yarwood is a Master Developer with Autodesk Ltd.

CHAPTER 1

Introduction

Introduction

Autodesk 3D Studio Max is a modelling/rendering/animation software package which is primarily designed to work in Windows NT. However, 3D Studio Max Release 1.1 (and later) also functions in Windows 95. The package is worked in a manner similar to its predecessor 3D Studio, which works in MS-DOS. Because 3D Studio Max functions within Windows 95 (or NT), full advantage is taken of Windows' graphical user interface – menus, tools, icons, windows, etc. Max has many enhancements over 3D Studio, including a completely new screen layout, the merging of the 3D Studio programs (3D Editor, 2D Shaper, 3D Lofter and Keyframer) into a set of tools, menus and icons which are fully Windows 95 compliant. With the aid of 3D Studio Max:

1. 3D models can be constructed.
2. Surfaces and materials can be added to 3D solid models.
3. Lighting of 3D solid models can be included in scenes to produce a whole range of lighting effects, including colour.
4. The resulting 3D models in scenes including the lighting can be rendered to produce realistic photolike representations of solid models with the aid of cameras incorporated within 3D scenes.
5. 3D Models can be realistically animated as can the lighting and cameras associated with the scenes.
6. 2D and 3D models can be imported from CAD packages in DXF format and in AutoCAD *.DWG format. Such models can have materials, cameras and lighting added for realistic rendering and/or animation.
7. 3D Studio files in the form of mesh files (*.3DS), project files (*.PRJ) and shape files (*.SHP) can be imported into 3D Studio Max.

System requirements

1. PC fitted with a Pentium or Pentium Pro computer processing chip (CPU) – at least a Pentium 90, or faster chip. The software will function in a PC fitted with a 30836 or 30846 chip, but the systems will work very slowly.
2. At least 32 Mbytes of RAM. More will produce faster rendering of very large models.
3. A hard disk with at least 200 Mbytes free – up to 100 Mbytes for the program with a further 100 Mbytes for a swap disk.
4. Super Video Graphics Array (SVGA) monitor with 800×600 display showing a range of 256 colours. If available a higher display up to 1280×1280 with full colour video card. The larger the monitor, the better.
5. Windows 95 or Windows NT. In this book, all illustrations are from Windows 95 screens.
6. A mouse.
7. A hardware lock ('dongle') supplied with the software is essential. The software will not function without the dongle.
8. It is an advantage to have a CD-ROM drive fitted to take advantage of libraries of material and texture maps and files which are available for 3D Studio and Max.

Start-up of 3D Studio Max from Windows 95

Assuming the 3D Studio Max program files have been loaded onto the hard disk of the PC, to startup the software programme from Windows 95, *left-click* on the **Start** button of the Task bar of the Windows 95 screen, followed by another *left-click* on **Program** in the **Start** menu list which appears. Then another *left-click* on **Kinetix** in the program pop-up list, brings to screen the icons in the Start list for 3D Studio Max. *Left-click* on **3D Studio Max** (or icon) in the list (Fig. 1.1) and after the programme loads into memory, the 3D Studio Max window will appear (Fig. 1.2).

Note: It might well be that 3D Studio Max has been loaded under another start-up name than **Kinetix**, depending upon the person who originally loaded the software files onto the hard disk, but the most likely name will be Kinetix.

Viewport configurations

As shown in Fig. 1.2 the start up window for 3D Studio Max contains four viewports, usually named **Top**, **Front**, **Left** and **Perspective**, usually with grids in each viewport. The number of viewports

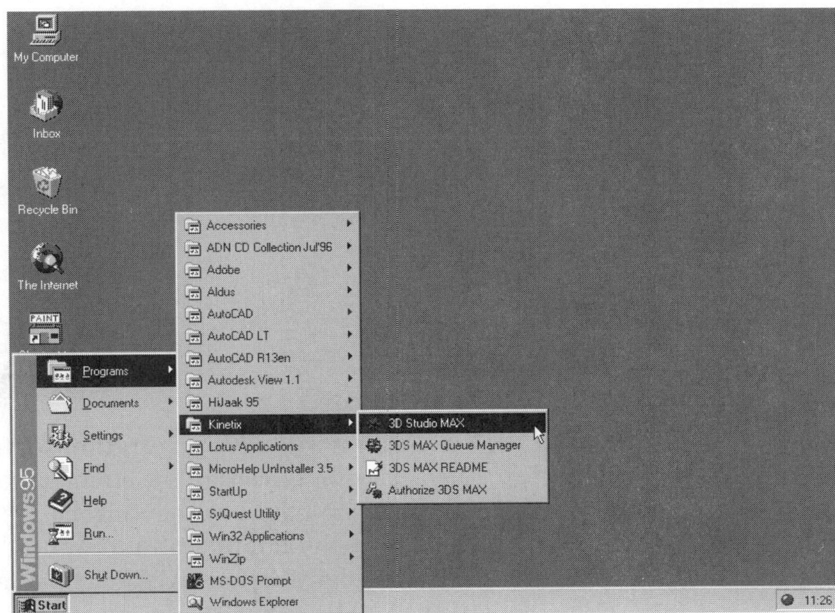

Fig. 1.1 The Windows 95 Start-up screen

available can be varied and their positions relative to any 3D model showing in the window can also be varied. To change the viewport configuration, *left-click* on the name **Edit** in the menu bar of the 3D Studio Max window, followed by another on **Viewport Configuration** in the pulldown menu which appears (Fig. 1.3).

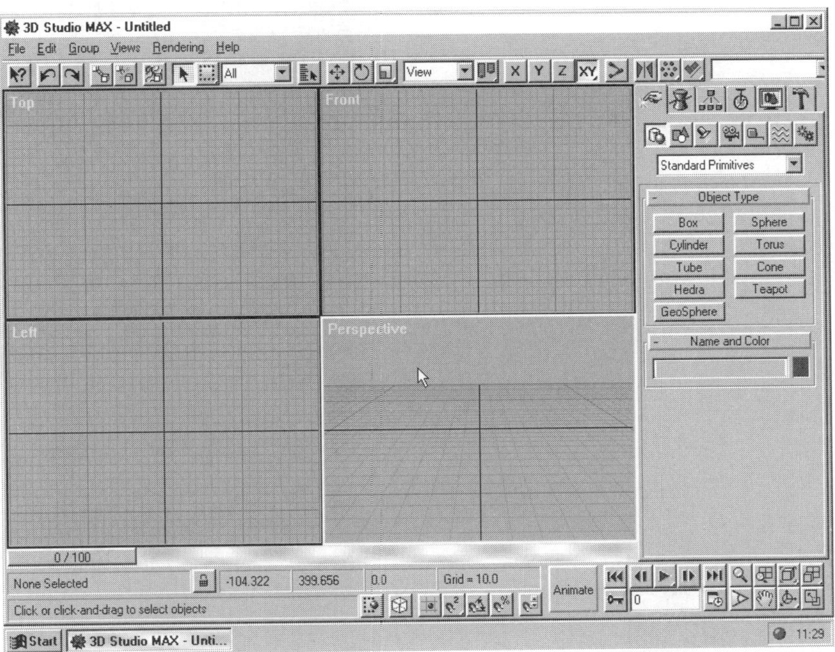

Fig. 1.2 The 3D Studio Max window on start-up

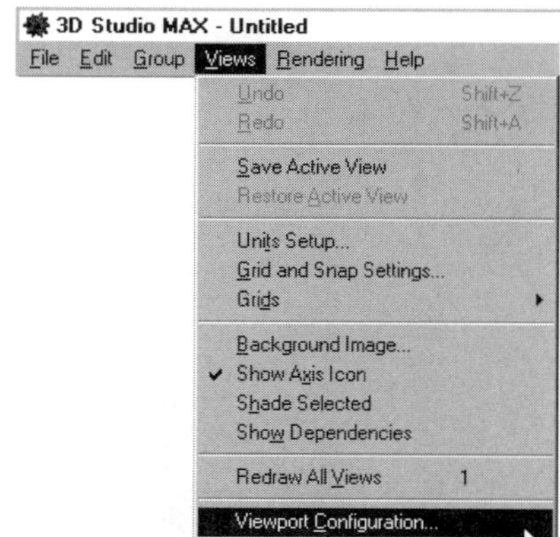

Fig. 1.3 Selecting **Viewport Configuration** from the **View** pulldown menu

The **Viewport Configuration** dialogue box appears on screen. *Left-click* on **Layout** in the menu bar of the dialogue box to bring up a second dialogue box showing the possible viewport configurations. To select the configuration required, *left-click* again in the icon showing the required layout, in this case a four-viewport layout with three small viewports on the left of the window and a larger one showing a **Perspective** view on the right (Fig. 1.4). A *left-click* on the **OK** button of the dialogue box and the Max window appears with the selected viewport layout (Fig. 1.5). In this book a number of different layouts will be shown.

Terms used throughout this book

The following terms are used to describe items from the 3D Studio Max window, together with terms used to describe some operations when constructing models in 3D Studio Max.

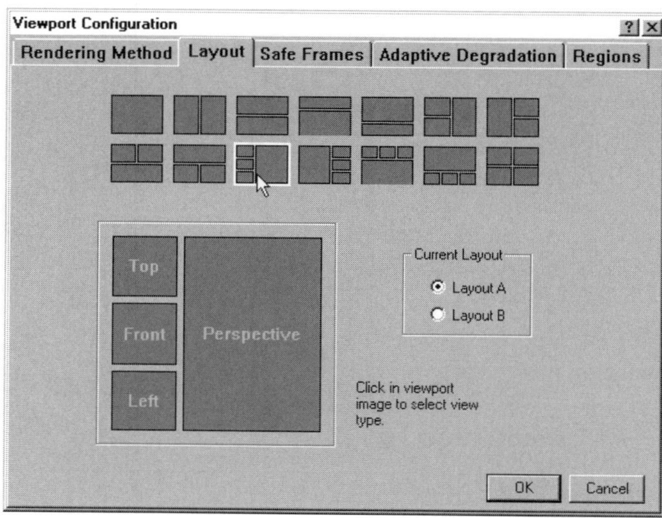

Fig. 1.4 The **Layout** dialogue box of the **Viewport Configuration** dialogue box

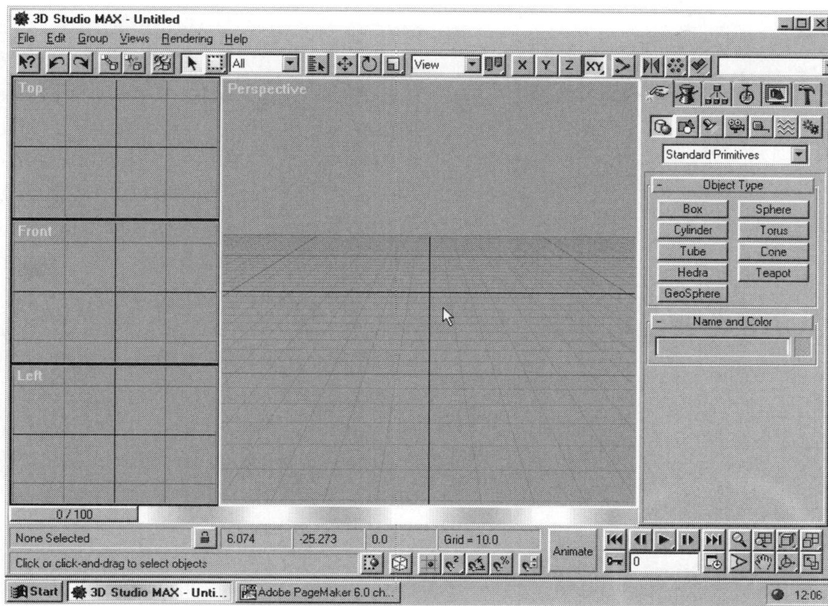

Fig. 1.5 The viewport configuration resulting from the selection in Fig. 1.4

Tool icons: Many of the tools (commands) in Max are called to screen from tool icons. Figure 1.6 shows the **Select and Move** tool icon when it has been selected. A *left-click* on the icon causes it to *highlight*, showing it has been selected.

Fig. 1.6 Selecting a tool icon

Tool tip: If the cursor under mouse control is placed over a tool icon, the tool icons tool tip appears in which the name of the selected tool is shown. Figure 1.7 shows the tool tip for the **Select and Move** tool. Note that the tool does not have to be selected in order for the tool tip to show – moving the cursor on to the icon is sufficient to display the tool tip.

Highlight: An example of highlighting was given with Fig. 1.6. When the tool icon was selected with a *left-click* on the icon, its background changed from grey to near white. Similarly a name from a menu highlights when selected. The background under the selected name in this case turns to black.

Fig. 1.7 The tool tip of the **Select and Move** tool icon

Dropdown menus: A *left-click* on any of the names **File**, **Edit**, **Group**, **Views**, **Rendering** or **Help** in the menu bar at the top of the 3D Studio window will bring a dropdown menu on screen. Figure 1.8

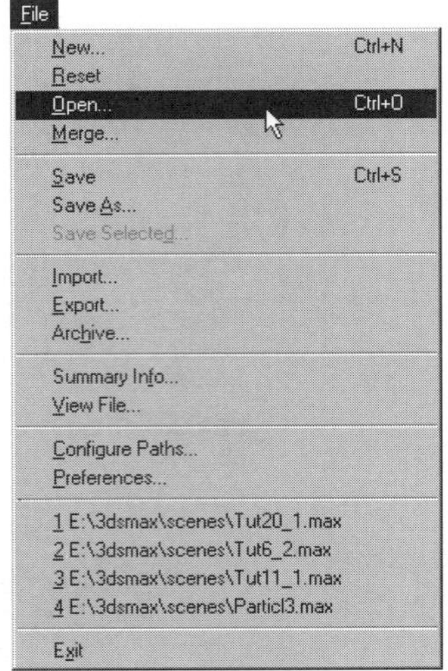

Fig. 1.8 The **File** dropdown menu with **Open...** selected

shows the result when **File** is selected from the menu bar. The command **Open...** has been selected from the **File menu** in Fig. 1.8. Note the three full stops (...) after some of the names in the **File** menu. When any of the names with **...** are selected, a dialogue box will appear. Note also some names are 'greyed-out', which shows they are not (at the moment) available.

Dialogue boxes: Two types of dialogue box will be seen in 3D Studio Max – *modal* which must be closed before any further actions can be taken with a construction under way and *modeless* which remain visible while constructions take place. Figure 1.9 is a *modeless* dialogue box. Figure 1.10 is an example of the more common dialogue box – a *modal* dialogue box. Figure 1.10 includes the names of the various parts of a dialogue box.

Left-click: Move the cursor under mouse control onto an icon, a name, or an element and press the left-hand button of the mouse.

Right-click: Move the cursor under mouse control onto an icon, a name, or an element and press the right-hand button of the mouse.

Double-click: Press both buttons of the mouse at the same time.

Fig. 1.9 An example of a *modeless* dialogue box

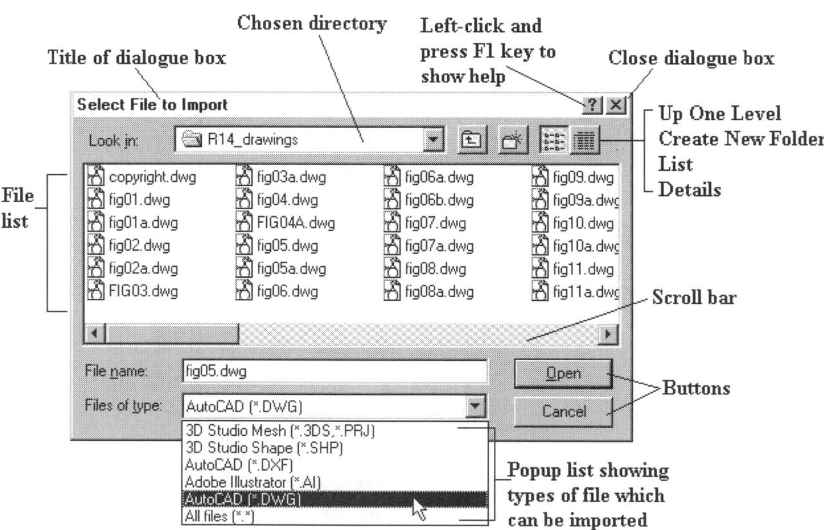

Fig. 1.10 A *modal* dialogue box showing the names of its parts

Drag: Move the cursor under mouse control onto an object to be moved, hold down a *left-click* or a *double-click*. Move the mouse and the object moves under mouse control.

Rollouts: In the panel on the right-hand side of the 3D Studio Max window, if the whole of a set of tools cannot be seen, hold down the left-hand button (or both buttons) of the mouse in an area of the panel which does not contain a button, and a pan icon (a hand) appears. *Drag* the pan icon upwards towards the top of the screen and a further part of the panel appears. This is a rollout. This panning can take place either upwards or downwards as needed.

Cursors: A large variety of different cursors will be seen when using 3D Studio Max. These will be shown as they need to be described.

Flyouts: Some tool icons will show a small arrow in the bottom right corner of the button holding the icon. Holding a *left-click* on such icons will bring a flyout onto the screen, showing more tool icons associated with the tool icon from which the flyout originated. Figure 1.12 shows the flyout which appears with a *left-click* held on the **Select and Uniform Scale** tool icon.

Fig. 1.11 A **rollout**

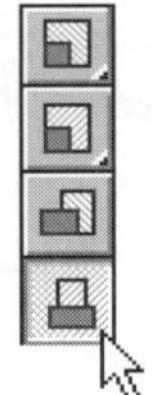

Fig. 1.12 A flyout

Viewports

Viewport configuration was mentioned in Chapter 1. Further features of viewports are included in this chapter. When **Viewport Configuration** is called from the **View** pulldown menu, followed by the selection of **Layout** from the **Viewport Configuration** dialogue box, **Layout B** under **Current Layout** is always the same, no matter which of the possible other layouts has been selected. In the selected viewport

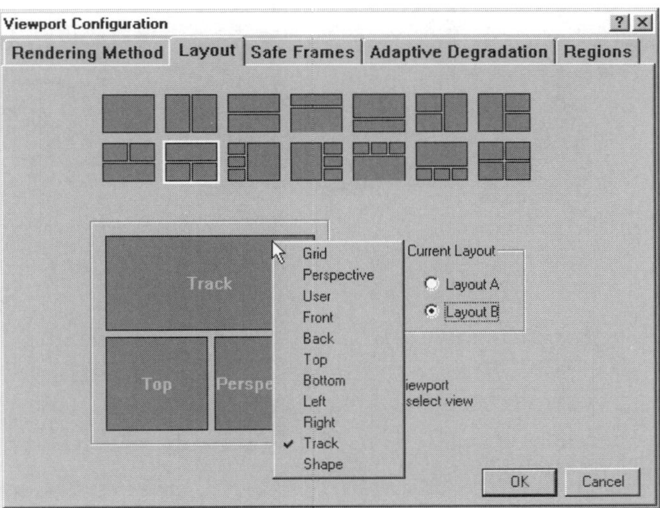

Fig. 1.13 Setting viewports in the **Viewport Configuration (Layout)** dialogue box

showing in the dialogue box, *click* in one of the viewports. A popup list appears with names of the views possible in the viewports (Fig. 1.13). If any of the names are chosen the selected view appears in the viewport in which the *click* was made.

The other dialogue boxes in which settings may be made from the **Viewport Configuration** set of dialogue boxes will be discussed in later chapters.

The 3D Studio Max window

The viewport configuration most often used will be the 4-viewport window normally appearing on start-up – **Top**, **Front**, **Left** and **Perspective** views. Figure 1.14 shows not only this configuration, but the names of the parts of the window. Details of the main features of the Max window are given below.

The toolbar

The toolbar contains icons of tool and buttons, together with some dropdown menus. Some of the icons appear only on the toolbar. Others will be repeated elsewhere as will be seen as you go through this book. Selecting some of the icons will result in flyouts appearing. See Fig. 1.14. The whole toolbar is too wide to fit across the screen. If the mouse cursor is placed on an empty part of the toolbar, a pan

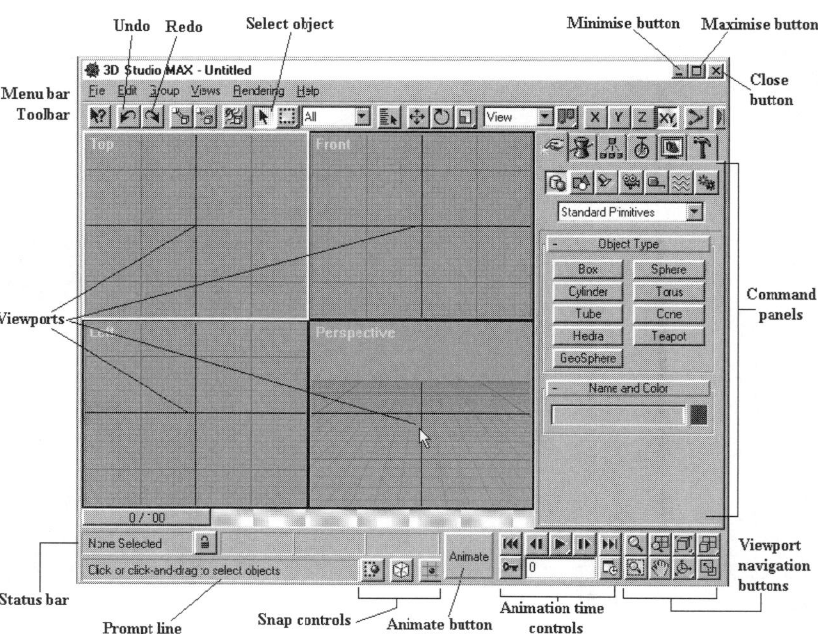

Fig. 1.14 The names of some parts of the 3D Studio Max window

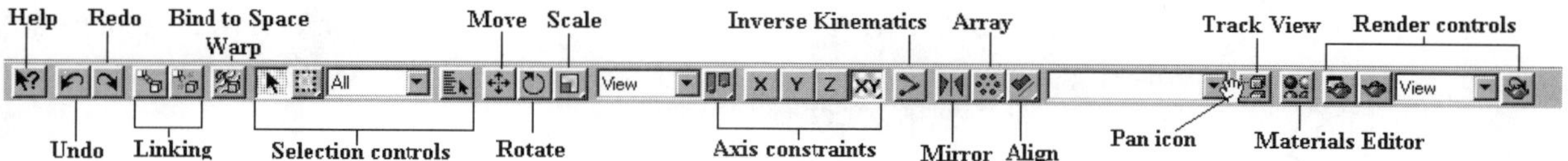

Fig. 1.15 The tools, buttons, popup lists and flyouts in the toolbar

icon appears. Hold down the left button on the pan icon and *drag* the icon sideways and the hidden parts of the toolbar come onto the Max window.

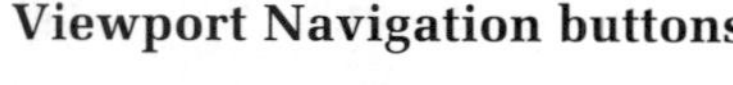

Viewport Navigation buttons

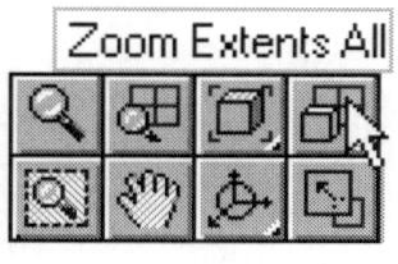

Fig. 1.16 The viewport navigation buttons

These are placed in a cluster in the bottom right-hand corner of the Max window. There are eight tool buttons in the cluster (Fig. 1.16), three of which have flyouts and all of which have tool tips. Figure 1.17 shows the names of the buttons.

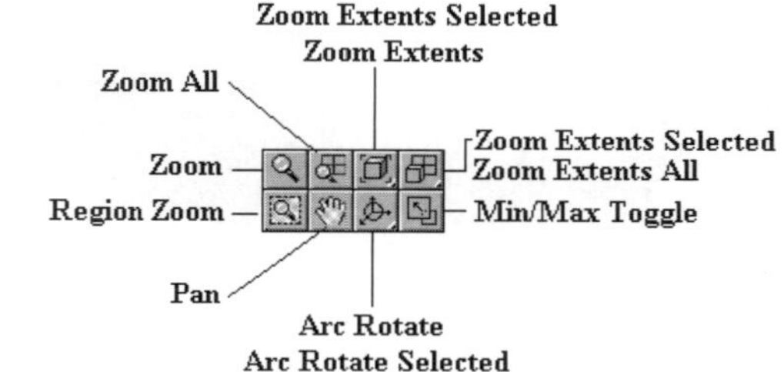

Fig. 1.17 The names of the buttons in the Viewport Navigation cluster

Even without a model in the viewports it is advisable to experiment with the navigation button. When one of the buttons is selected note the prompt explaining the use of the button appearing at the Prompt Line. A viewport is selected by *clicking* in its area.

Zoom: Move the cursor in a viewport up to zoom in (enlarges detail in the viewport) or down to zoom out (reduces detail in the viewport).

Zoom All: Zooms all viewports in response to any single one being zoomed

Zoom Extents and **Zoom Extents Selected:** Work in conjunction with **Zoom Extents All** and **Selected**. If **Zoom Extents Selected** is used, only a selected object is zoomed.

Min/Max Toggle: Switches between a single selected viewport and all viewports. Thus if the **Top** viewport is in current use, a *left-click* on the **Min/Max Toggle** button toggles between a single **Top** viewport and all viewports being used.

Arc Rotate: A circular icon appears in the selected viewport. Holding down the left mouse button and rotating of the mouse rotates the viewport or a selected object.

Pan: Pans a selected viewport in any direction without any zoom action.

Field of View: As the mouse is moved in the **Perspective** viewport, so the field of view changes. Its action is different to a zoom. Non-active in other viewports.

Notes

1. The viewport navigation buttons show their own icons, all with movements under mouse control.
2. A *right-click* or pressing the **Esc** button of the keyboard cancels the action of a tool or command.

Prompt line

When any tool or command is selected a prompt appears in the Prompt line informing the operator of the action he/she is to take. Figure 1.18 shows an example.

Fig. 1.18 The Prompt line when the **Field of View** button is selected

Command Panels

At the top of the Command Panels are two rows of buttons. The names of the commands controlled by these buttons are given in Fig. 1.19. The uses of the commands controlled by these buttons will be explained in a later chapter.

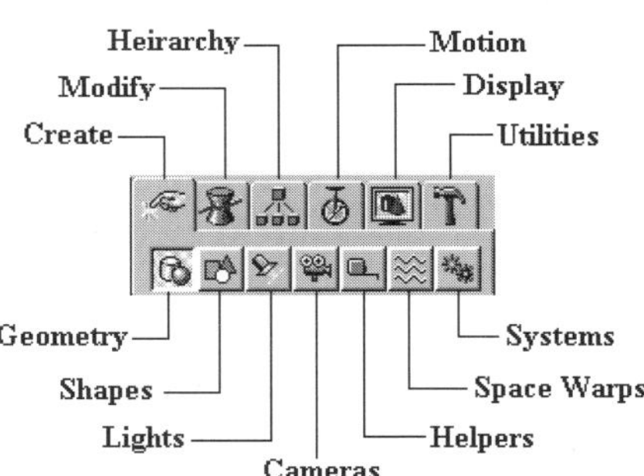

Fig. 1.19 The buttons at the top of the Command Panels

Maximise, Minimise and Close buttons

At the top right-hand corner of the 3D Studio Max window are these three buttons common to all Windows 95 windows. A *left-click* on the **Maximise** button and the screen is filled with the application window. A *left-click* on the **Minimise** button and the application window is reduced in size taking up only part of the monitor screen.

A *left-click* on the **Close** button closes the application. As with other applications these three buttons should prove of value when using Max.

Other features in the 3D Studio Max window

Other features of the 3D Studio window will be described in later chapters when their uses are involved in constructions.

Questions

1. Part of the toolbar cannot be seen in the 3D Studio Max window. How can the hidden part of the toolbar be brought on screen?
2. What advantages do you think 3D Studio Max has over 3D Studio?
3. What is the procedure to start-up 3D Studio Max?
4. How many viewports show in the 3D Studio Max window on start-up?
5. What is meant by the term 'tool icon'?
6. What is a 'tool tip'?
7. Two types of dialogue box are in use with 3D Studio Max. Can you name them?
8. If a name in a pull-down menu is followed by three full stops (...) what would you expect to happen when the name is selected with a *left-click*?
9. What is meant by the term 'flyout'?
10. What happens with a *left-click* on the **Max/Min Toggle** button at the bottom right-hand corner of the 3D Studio Max window?

CHAPTER 2

Create Geometry – Primitives

Selecting object(s)

When objects have been constructed in 3D Studio Max, they may have to be acted upon by other tools. Before such actions can take effect, the object(s) must first be selected. Selection can be made when the **Select object** tool icon in the toolbar is active (the icon is highlighted) as shown in Fig. 2.1. When another tool or command is in action, the **Select object** tool becomes inactive (it is no longer highlighted).

Each object created has its own default colour, which changes to white when it is selected. If objects are acted upon by a Boolean operative (see below), then all single objects in the group formed by

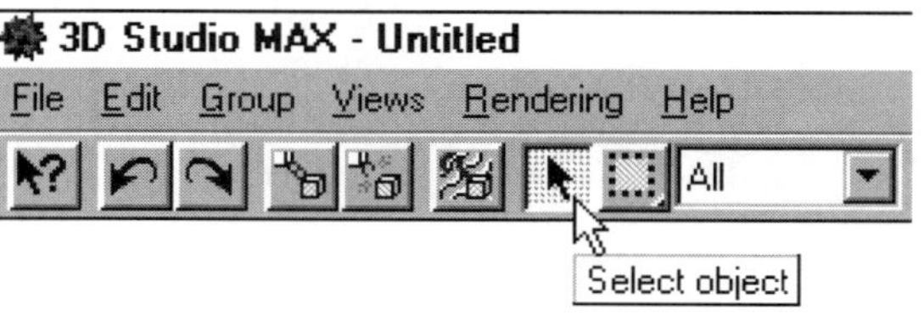

Fig. 2.1 The **Select objects** icon

the Boolean operative change to the same colour, the colour of the first of the objects in the Boolean group. The colour of an object can be changed if desired from the **Object Color** dialogue box.

Objects are selected either by placing the cursor onto an object, followed by a *left-click* , or by selection of one of the select options from the **Edit** pull-down menu (Fig. 2.2). A *left-click* on one of the options in the **Edit** menu and the selection takes place. When an object has been selected its colour changes to white.

After an object has been selected, to deselect an object, *left-click* in a viewport. The object resumes its colour.

When an object has been selected (its colour has changed to white), a *right-click* on the object brings the menu shown in Fig. 2.3 on screen. As can be seen in the menu, the object can be moved, rotated or scaled according to the selection from the menu.

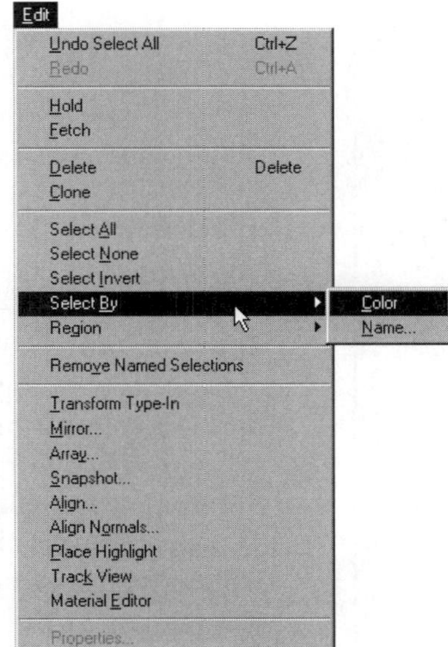

Fig. 2.2 The **Select** options from the **Edit** pull-down menu

The Standard Primitives

Left-click on the **Geometry** button in the upper part of the Command panel and the nine Standard Primitive buttons appear under the **Object Type** button (Fig. 2.4). Note there is a – symbol at the left-hand end of the **Object Type** button. *Left-click* on the button and the Primitive buttons disappear and the – symbol changes to a +.

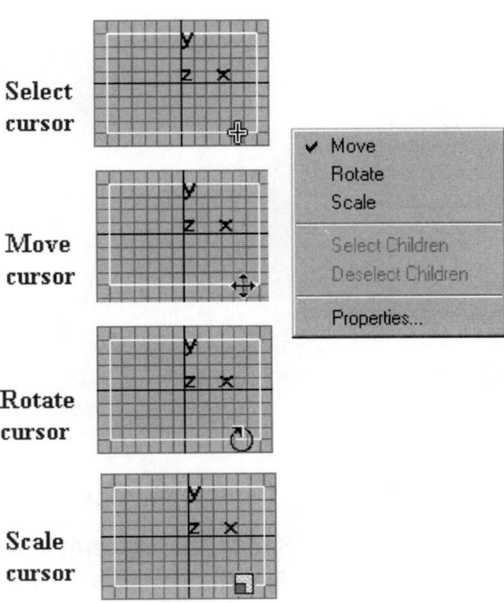

Fig. 2.3 The menu appearing with a *right-click* on a selected object and the cursors for each of the commands in the menu

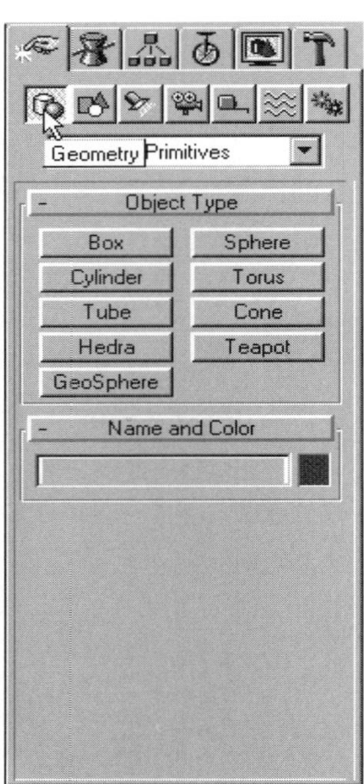

Fig. 2.4 The Command panel showing the set of Standard Primitives

Box

Left-click on the **Box** button. The Command panel changes as shown in Fig. 2.5. *Left-click* on the **Keyboard Entry** button in the Command panel. *Enter* the figures for **Length:**, **Width:** and **Height:** as shown in Fig. 2.5, followed by a *left-click* on the **Create** button. The box appears in the viewports as in Fig. 2.6. *Left-click* on the **Select object** icon and again on the box and it adopts its default colour.

Now, without *entering* any figures in the **Keyboard Entry** boxes, *left-click* on the **Box** button again and by movement of the mouse create a box in any viewport. This requires holding down the left-hand mouse button to obtain length and width, releasing the button and moving the mouse up or down it again to determine height. Figures will appear in the **Parameters** boxes of the Control panel.

Now practise *entering* figures in the **Length Seg:**, **Width Seg:** and **Height Seg:** boxes of the **Parameters** boxes followed by pressing the **Return** key of the keyboard after each entry.

Practise like this with both *entering* figures and mouse movement until satisfied you can create boxes in any of the viewports.

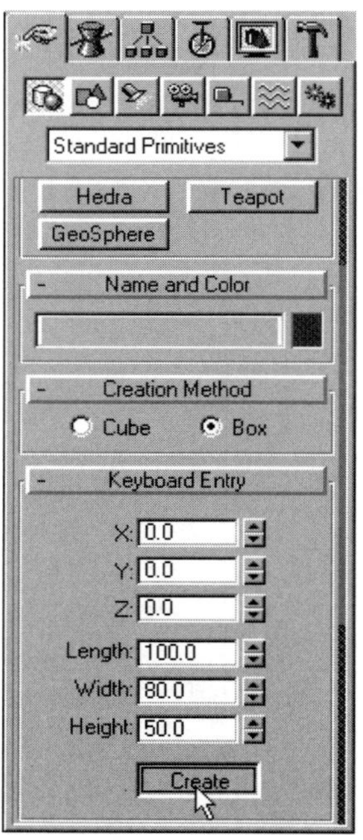

Fig. 2.5 Creating a box 100 × 80 × 50

Cylinder

Select the **Cylinder** button from the Standard Primitive buttons. Select the **Keyboard Entry** button again and create a cylinder of

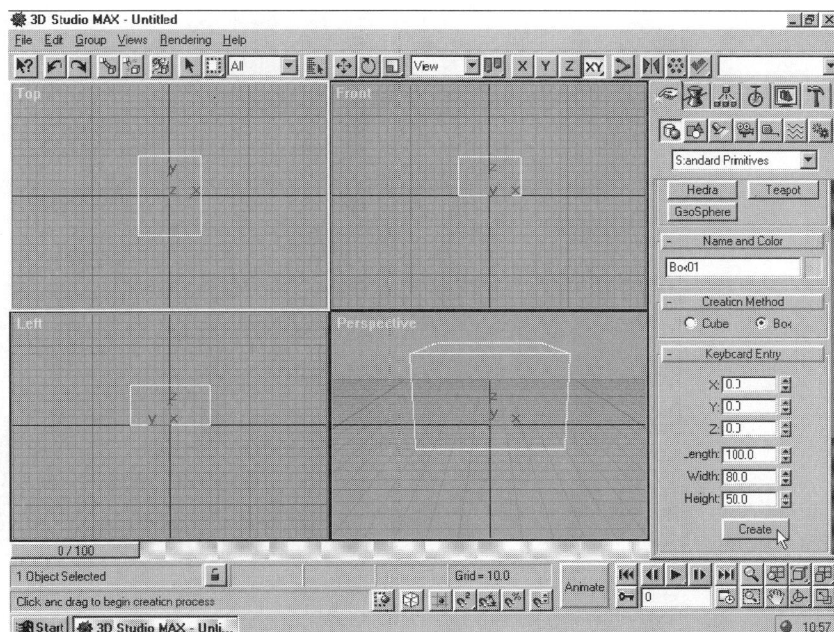

Fig. 2.6 The resulting box appearing in a four-viewport window

Radius: 50 and **Height:** 80. Pan the Command panel up until the **Parameters** button appears and *left-click* on it. Examine the panel which appears and experiment with further cylinders with different parameter settings *entered* in the various boxes of the **Parameters** panel (Fig. 2.7). Before deselecting the cylinder, experiment with changing its parameters, followed by pressing the **Return** key of the keyboard as each parameter is *entered*, noting the changes taking place in the cylinder in the viewports. Also try forming cylinders created under mouse control.

Parameters
Radius: 50.0
Height: 80.0
Height Segments: 1
Cap Segments: 1
Sides: 24
Smooth
Slice On
Slice From: 0.0
Slice To: 0.0
Generate Mapping Coords.

Fig. 2.7 The **Parameters** panel for cylinders

Tube

Select the **Tube** button from the Standard Primitive buttons. Select the **Keyboard Entry** button again and create a tube of **Inner Radius:** 50; Outer **Radius:** 30 and **Height:** 100. Then experiment with constructing tubes under mouse control without *entering* radii or height.

Boolean operators

Create a box, a cylinder and a tube to the sizes given above. Then **Move** the cylinder and box away from the tube as indicated in Fig. 2.8.

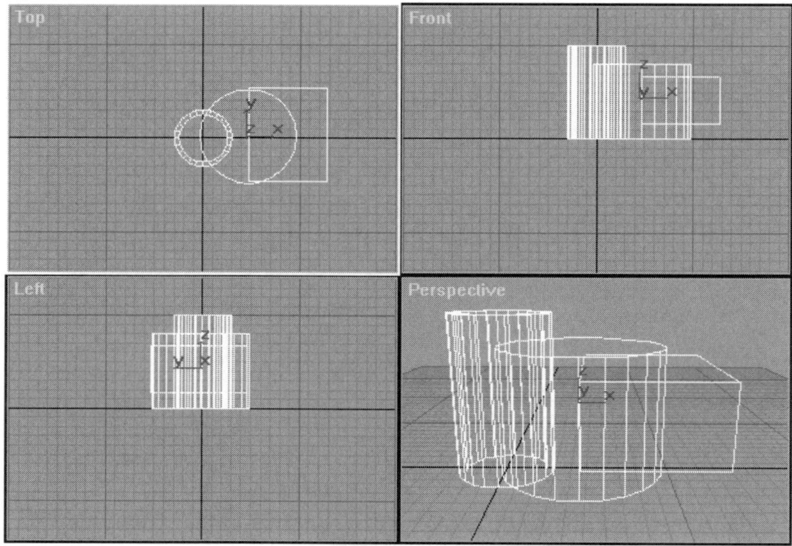

Fig. 2.8 The three objects showing in all four viewports

Boolean Union

Left-click on the name **Standard Primitives** to bring down the popup list associated with the name. In the popup list *left-click* on **Compound Objects** (Fig. 2.9), and on the **Boolean** button (Fig. 2.10). With the primitive box selected (white):

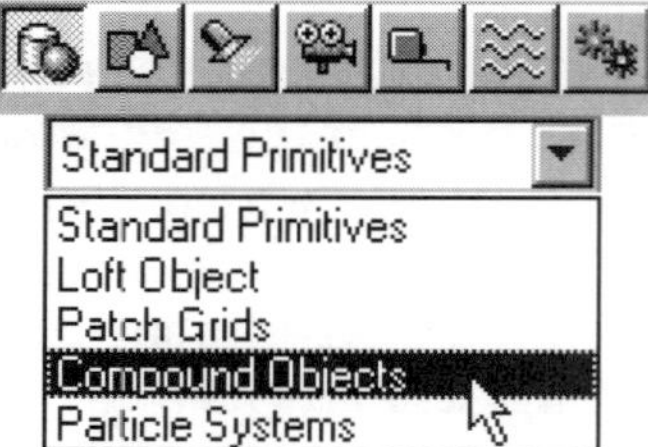

Fig. 2.9 Selecting **Compound Objects** from the popup list

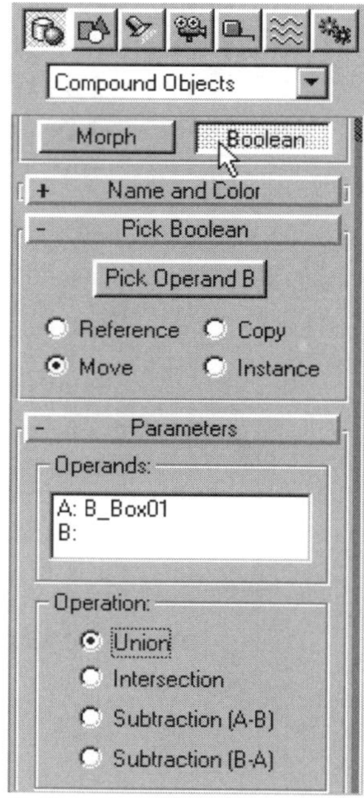

Fig. 2.10 Select the **Boolean** button, **Union** and the **Pick Operand B** button

1. In the Command panel, *click* in the **Union** check circle to set it on (black dot in circle).
2. *Left-click* on the **Pick Operand B** button.
3. *Left-click* on the cylinder. The cylinder is now a union with the box and the union is selected (white).
4. *Left-click* on **Pick Operand B** again, followed by another on the tube. The three primitives are now combined as a single object as a Boolean union.
5. *Left-click* in the **Perspective** viewport to make it the current viewport.
6. Pan the toolbar to the left and *left-click* on the **Quick Render** tool icon. The scene renders as shown in Fig. 2.11.

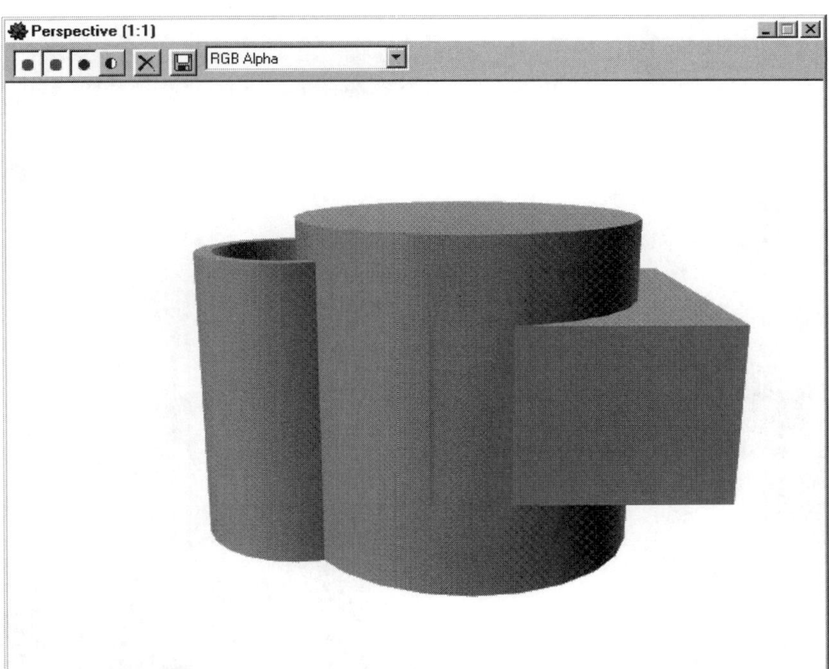

Fig. 2.11 A rendering of the three primitives after rendering

Boolean Subtraction

Create three primitives – a box, a cylinder and a tube – to any convenient size similar to those shown in Fig. 2.12. Then:

1. Select the box (changes to white colour).
2. *Left-click* on **Compound Objects** in the popup list.
3. *Left-click* on the **Pick Operand B** button.
4. *Left-click* on **Subtraction (A-B)** in the **Operation** part of the Command panel.

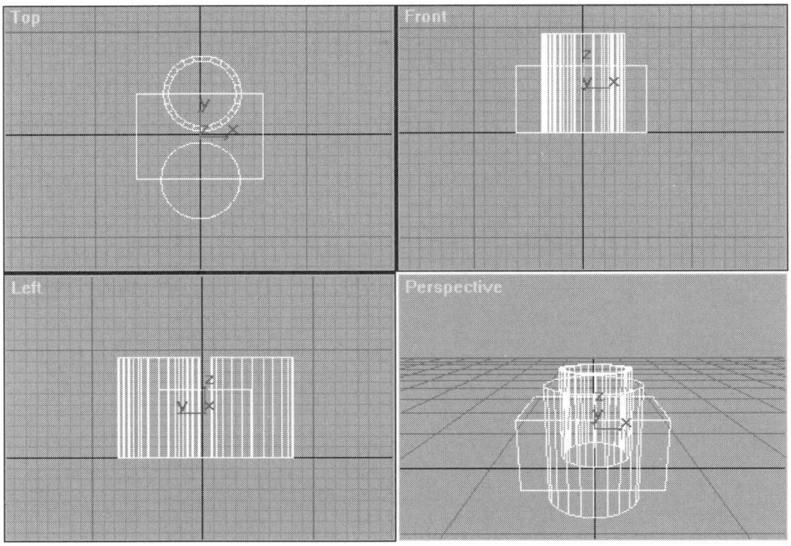

Fig. 2.12 Three primitives created ready for a Boolean subtraction

Fig. 2.13 A rendering of the three primitives after the action of Boolean subtraction

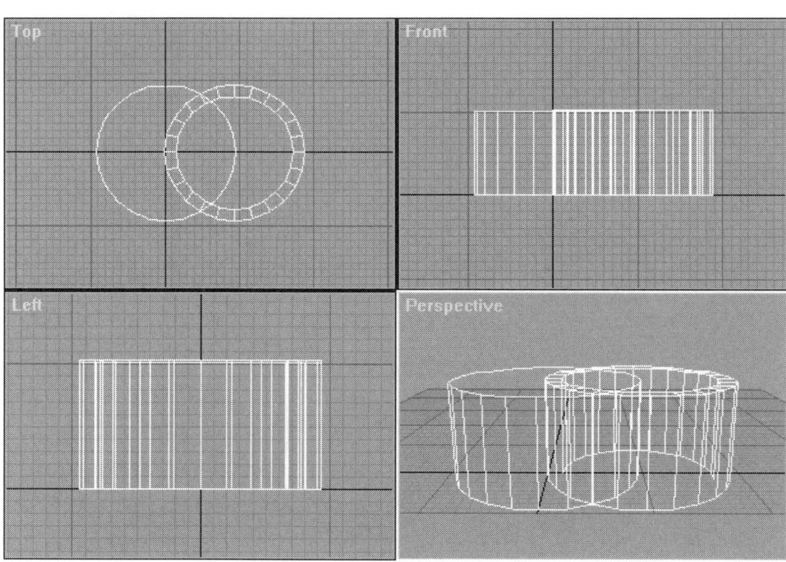

Fig. 2.14 The cylinder and tube created in the viewports

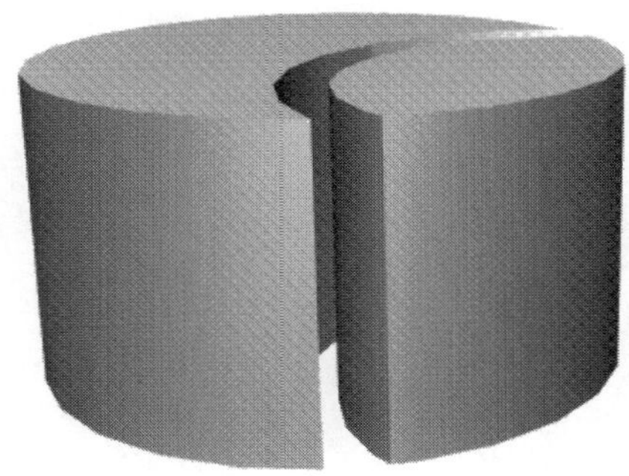

Fig. 2.15 A rendering of the resulting Boolean intersection

5. *Left-click* on the cylinder. It is subtracted from the box.
6. Select the subtraction of box-cylinder (changes to white colour).
7. *Left-click* on the **Pick Operand B** again.
8. *Left-click* on the tube. It is subtracted from the box/cylinder subtraction.

The result is shown in a rendering of the new object in Fig. 2.13.

Boolean Intersection

Now try using the **Intersection** operand. Start by creating a cylinder and a tube of about the same heights as in Fig. 2.14. Then, following the same procedures as indicated above, form the intersection between the two primitives. Figure 2.15 is a rendering of the resulting Boolean intersection.

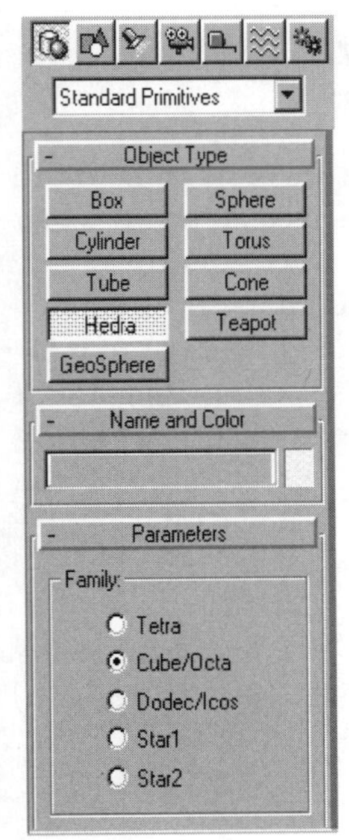

Fig. 2.16 The Command panel when **Hedra** is selected

Hedra

Hedra form a group of solids having a specified number of surfaces. When the **Hedra** button is selected from the **Standard Primitives** group, the Command panel opens as in Fig. 2.16. The panel lists the following hedra:

Tetrahedron: A tetrahedron has four faces.
Cube/Octahedron: An octahedron has 8 faces.
Dodecahedron: A dodecahedron has 12 faces.
Icosahedron: An Icosahedron has 20 faces.

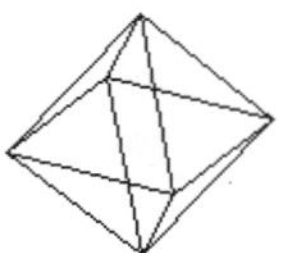
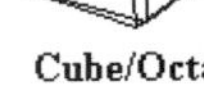
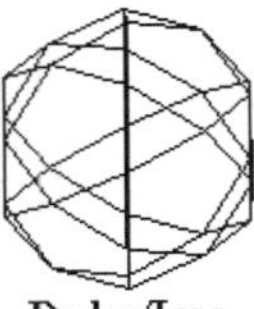
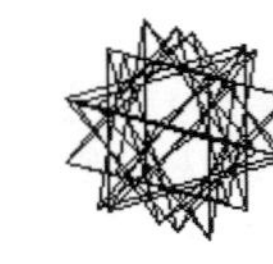
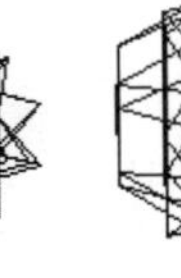

Fig. 2.17 The outlines of hedra as seen in the **Perpective** viewport

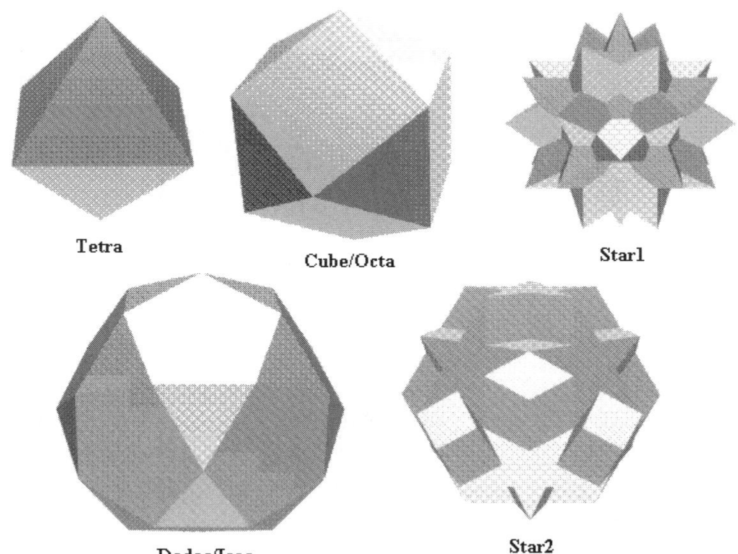

Fig. 2.18 Renderings of the five types of hedra

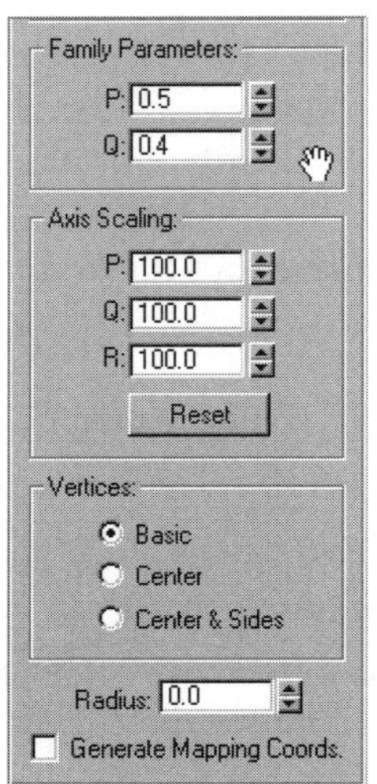

Fig. 2.19. The **Family Parameters** of the **Hedra** group of primitives

In addition two further hedra – **Star1** and **Star2** are included. Figure 2.17 shows the outlines produced in the **Perspective** viewport when each of the hedra are created in the 3D Studio Max window.

Figure 2.18 shows renderings of the five types of hedra created in 3D Studio Max window with **Parameters P and Q** both set to **0.0**.

Left-click on the **Parameters** button after selecting **Hedra** and *drag* the Command panel downwards with the pan icon. The **Family Parameters** settings can then be seen (Fig. 2.19). *Enter* figures in the **P** and **Q** boxes as shown. If the P + Q figures add up to a total greater

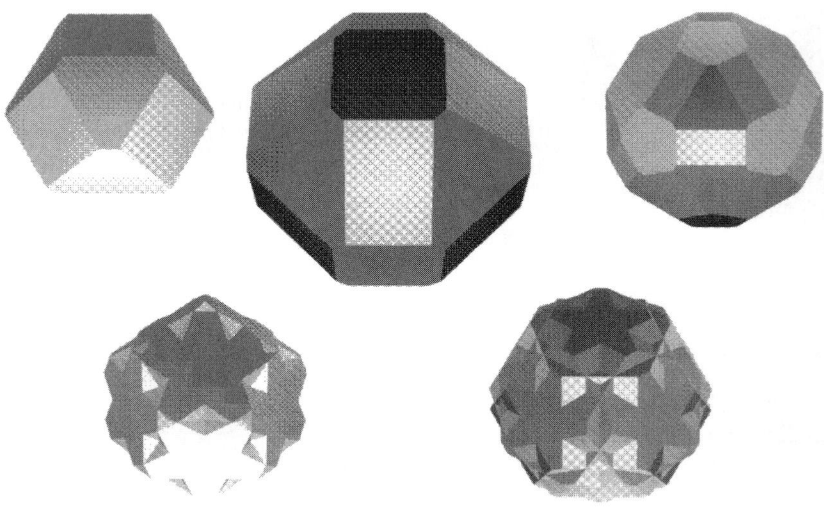

Fig. 2.20 Renderings of the five types of hedra with **P** set to 0.5 and **Q** set to 0.4

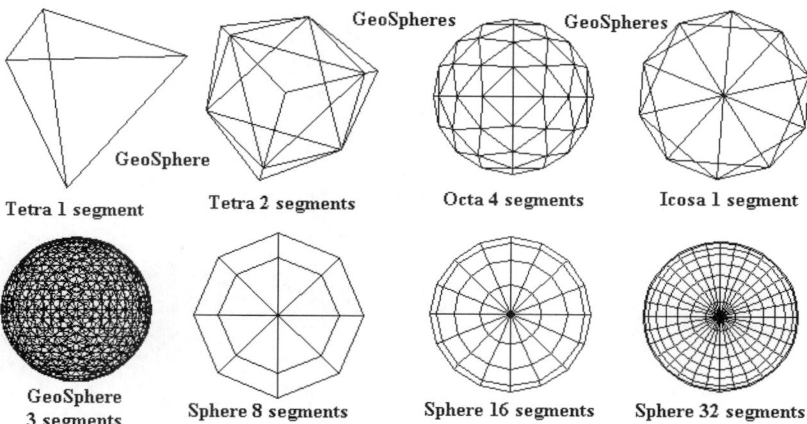

Fig. 2.21 **GeoSpheres** created with different **Geodesic Base Types** together with **Spheres** with different **Segments**

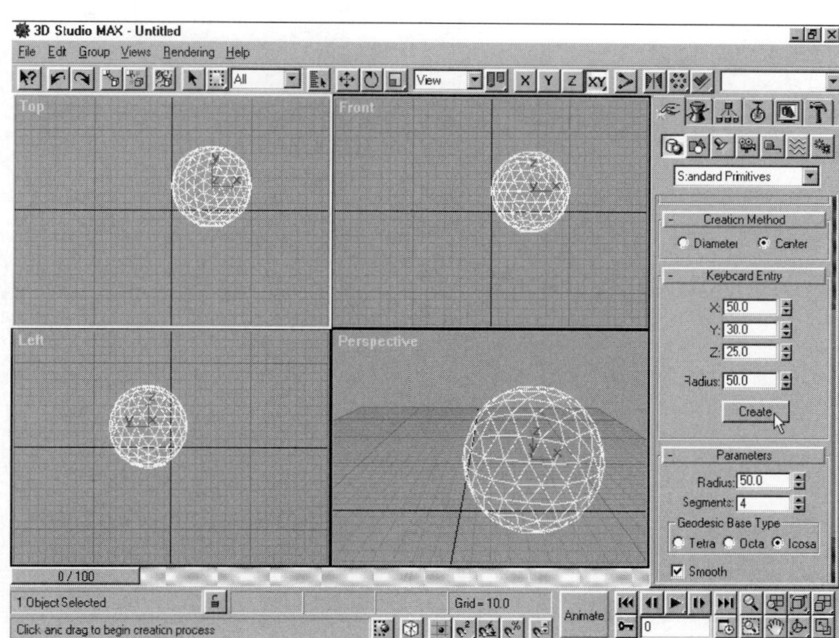

Fig. 2.22 An example of a **GeoSphere** created to *entered* parameters

than unity (1.0) the figures will not be accepted. Try it and check for yourself that this is so.

Figure 2.20 shows rendering of a set of the five types of hedra with the **P** setting at 0.5 and the **Q** setting at 0.4.

Practise creating a variety of hedra in the 3D Studio Max window.

GeoSpheres and Spheres

Figure 2.21 gives examples of GeoSpheres and Spheres created in Max. Figure 2.22 is an example of a **GeoSphere** of base type **Icosa**

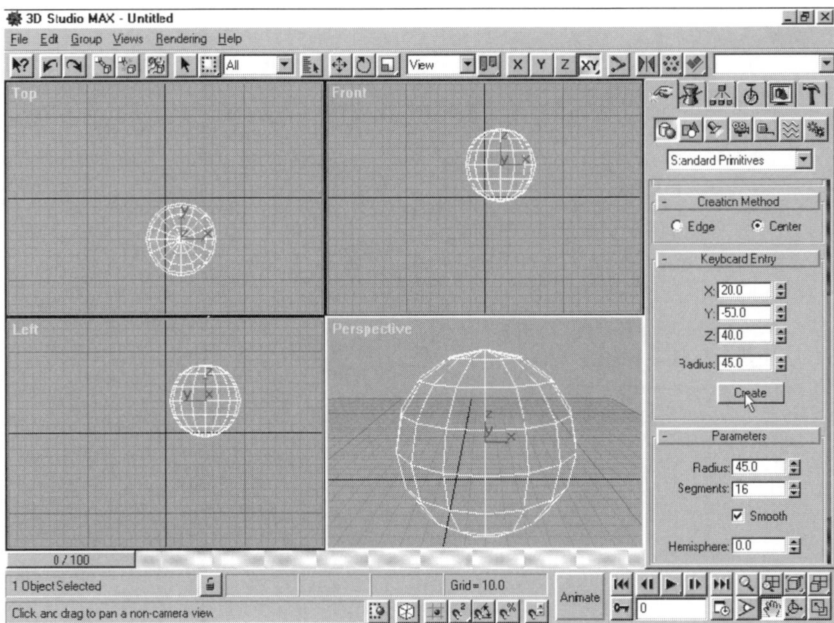

Fig. 2.23 An example of a **Sphere** created to *entered* parameters

created according to the parameters *entered* into the boxes of the **Keyboard Entry** part of the Command panel and Fig. 2.23 is an example of a **Sphere** created according to the parameters *entered* into the boxes of the **Keyboard Entry** part of the Command panel.

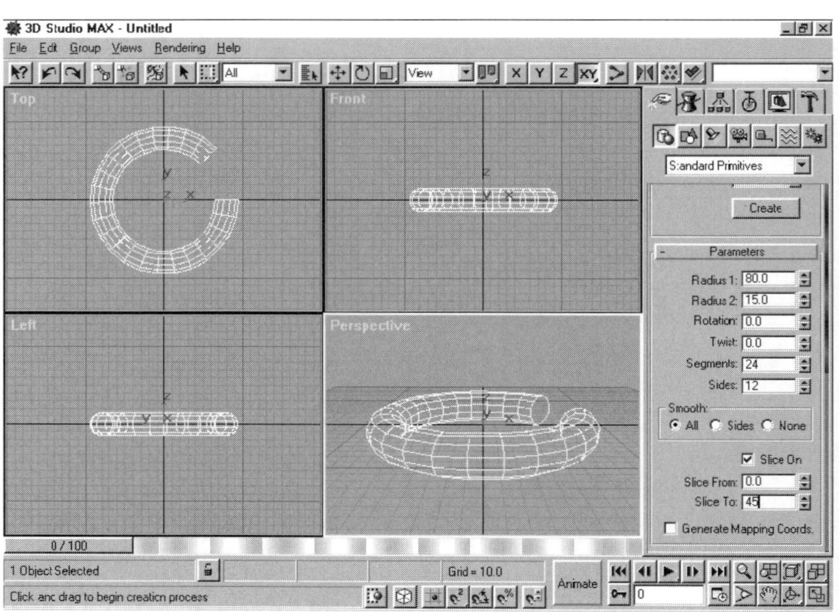

Fig. 2.24 An example of a torus created in Max

Torus

Figure 2.24 shows a torus created in Max to the parameters shown in the Command panel of the screen in the illustration. Figure 2.25 shows a number of different tori created to a variety of parameters.

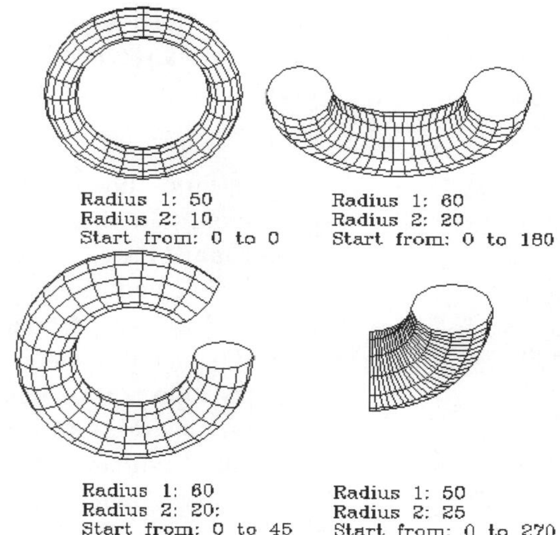

Fig. 2.25 A number of tori created to different parameters

Cone

Figure 2.26 shows a number of different cones created to a variety of parameters.

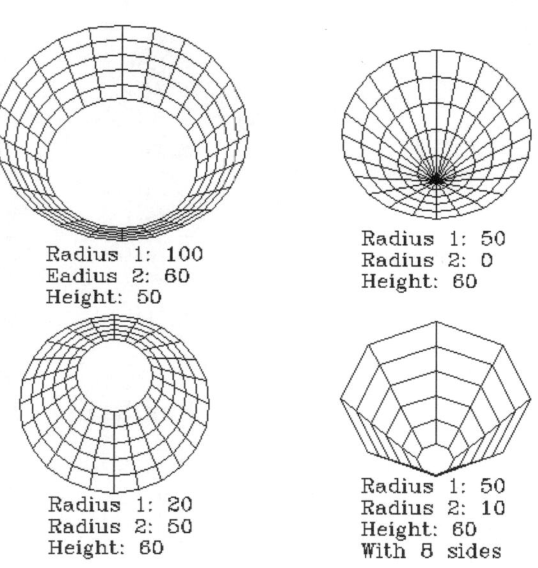

Fig. 2.26 A number of cones created to different parameters

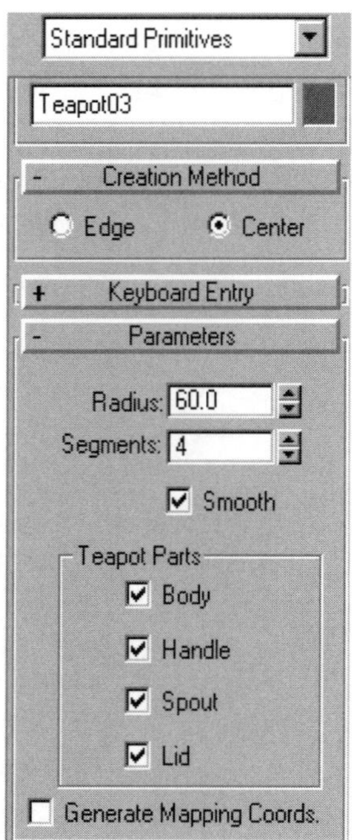

Fig. 2.27 The **Teapot Parts** area of the Control panel when teapots are being created

Teapot

Left-click on the **Teapot** button in the Standard Primitives and create the primitive to any size – by *dragging* the cursor in any viewport. This creates a standard 3D Studio Max 3D primitive. Note the **Teapot Parts** area of the Command panel (Fig. 2.27), showing that if check boxes are on (tick) or off (no tick), parts of the teapot can be created on screen as required. This is shown in the outlines of teapots or their parts in Fig. 2.28.

Notes

1. Sizes and the position of primitives can be *entered* from the keyboard in the boxes of that part of the Command panel for **Keyboard Entry**. An example of a cylinder created from keyboard *entry* is given in Fig. 2.29.
2. In the **X:**, **Y:** and **Z:** boxes, entered figures are relative to the position in 3D space shown by the intersections of the thick lines of the grids in the viewports. The intersecting points are where X,Y,Z = 0,0,0.
3. When positions and sizes are made by keyboard *entry*, a *left-click* on the **Create** button at the foot of the **Keyboard Entry** part of the Command panel is necessary to place the primitive on screen.
4. The Control panel must usually be panned in order to be able to make *entries* of position and size of the primitive being constructed.
5. Note the **Creation Method** part of the Command panel for each of the primitives. The size and position of a created primitive relies in part on the selected method – e.g. **Edge** or **Center**; **Diameter** or **Center** and so on.

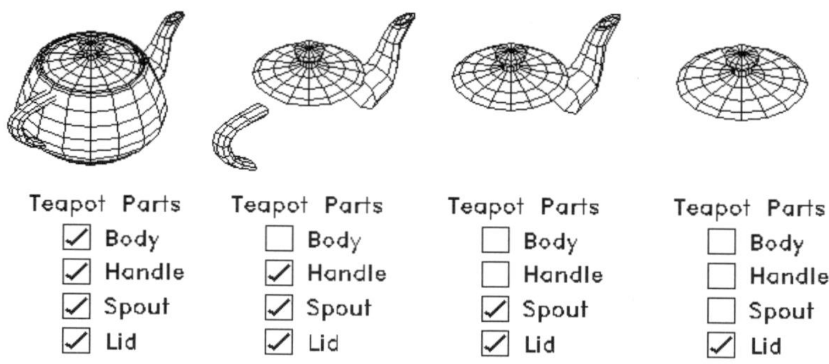

Fig. 2.28 Examples of outlines of teapots with different parts included

Rendering

A fuller description of rendering of 3D models created in 3D Studio Max will be given in a later chapter (Chapter 9). For the time being, it is suggested that the examples of the creation of 3D models which

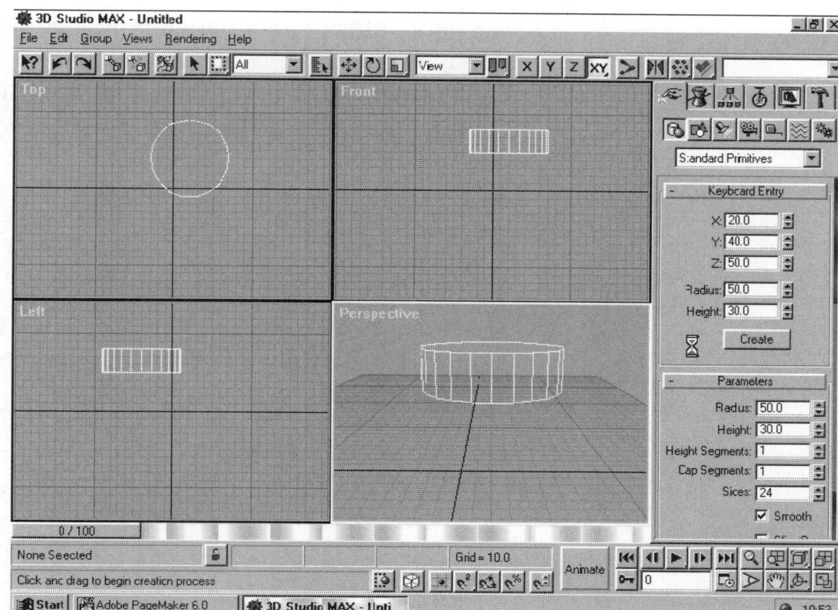

Fig. 2.29 An example of a primitive created with parameters *entered* in the **Keyboard Entry** area of the Control panel

follow can be rendered using the default lighting and camera available when any of the **Render** tools are selected.

Pan the toolbar to the left until the right-hand end of the toolbar is seen. Three rendering tools and a popup list are available in this right-hand end of the toolbar. The tool icons, their tool tips and the popup menu are shown in Fig. 2.30.

The rendering tools **Render Scene** and **Quick Render** produce the same result, the difference lying in that, when **Render Scene** is selected, a dialogue box appears on screen in which parameters for rendering can be *entered*, whereas **Quick Render** uses the parameters already loaded, or if any are not loaded, uses the default rendering

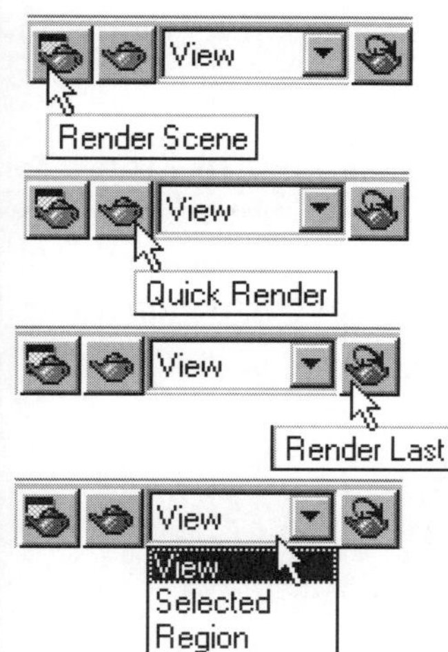

Fig. 2.30 The rendering tools and popup list at the right-hand end of the toolbar

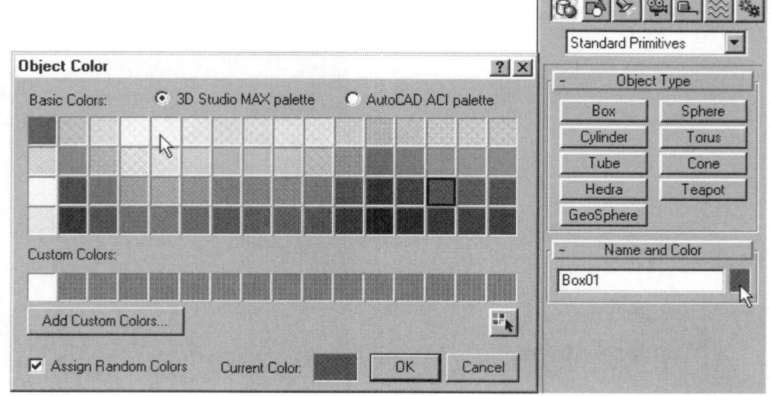

Fig. 2.31 Changing the colour of an object

parameters. As its name implies **Render Last** renders the last scene to be rendered. In all examples in this chapter we will be using the **View** scene. The settings for rendering parameters and the uses for the other parts of the popup list will be left until rendering is more fully explained in Chapter 9.

Changing the colour of an object

Select the object. The name and colour of the object appears in the **Name and Color** area of the Command panel. *Left-click* in the colour box to the right of the name and the **Object Color** dialogue box appears (Fig. 2.31). A new colour can be selected from the dialogue box.

Grid and Snap settings

Left-click on **View** in the menu bar, bringing down a menu. Then *left-click* on **Grid and Snap Settings...** to bring a dialogue box on screen (Fig. 2.32). Ensure that the **Home Grid** settings are as shown in Fig. 2.32, then *left-click* on **Snap** to bring up another dialogue box as in Fig. 2.33. Set the various check circles as shown and *enter* figures in the various boxes of the dialogue box as shown. Then *left-click* on the **OK** button.

Now from the **View** menu select **Units Setup...** to bring the dialogue box of this name on screen (Fig. 2.34). In this menu units can be set for **Metric** units – centimetres, metres or kilometres; **US Standard** in feet and inches; **Custom** – as required by the operator;

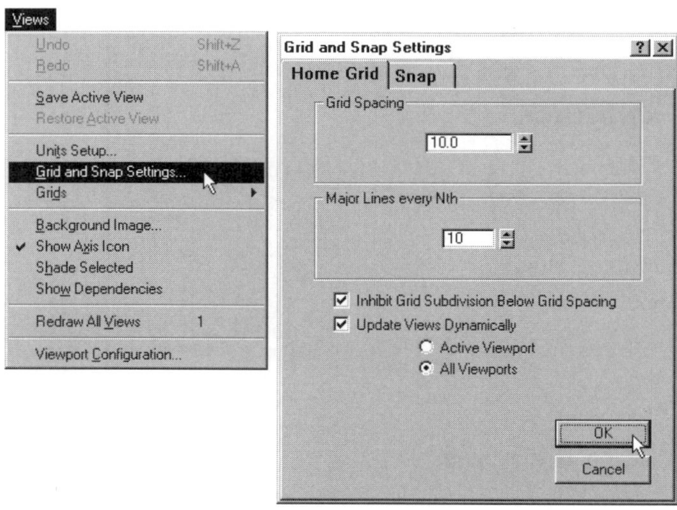

Fig. 2.32 The **Home Grid** dialogue box

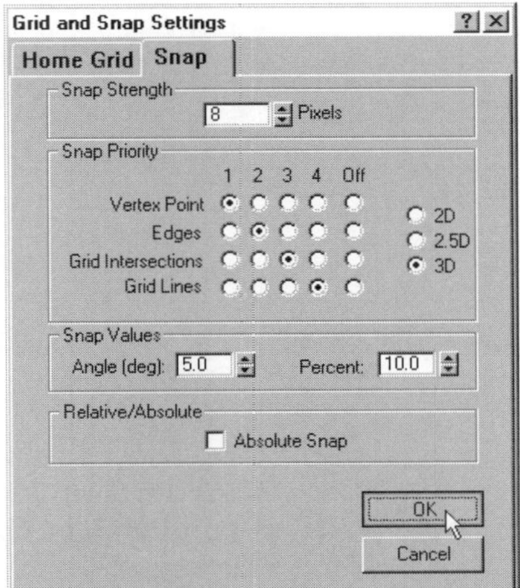

Fig. 2.33 The **Snap Settings** dialogue box

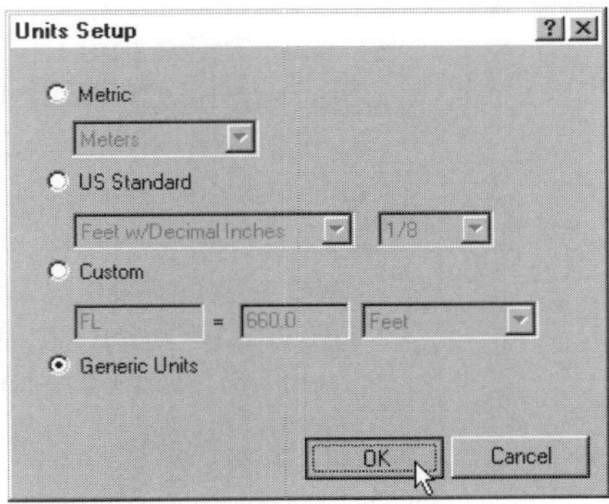

Fig. 2.34 Settings in the **Units Setup** dialogue box

Generic – which is the set of units we will normally be using throughout this book. When using **Generic** setting, the grids, which we have set at 10, give sizes in units, which we can assume to be to any system of measurement (metric, Imperial or other) as desired by the operator.

Snaps

Hold a *left-click* on the **3D Snap Toggle** icon in the Status bar (Fig. 2.35) and note that three types of snaps are available: **2D**, **2.5D** and **3D**. We will be mostly using the **3D** snap. A *left-click* on the **3D Snap Toggle** icon sets the 3D snap until it is closed again with another *left-click* on the icon. When any of the **Snaps** are set on, the cursor, under mouse control, will only move from grid intersection to grid intersection points. Set the **3D Snap Toggle** on and create a box. It will be seen that with the toggle on, when the box is created under mouse control, its sizes will be in grid multiples. This can be seen by watching the

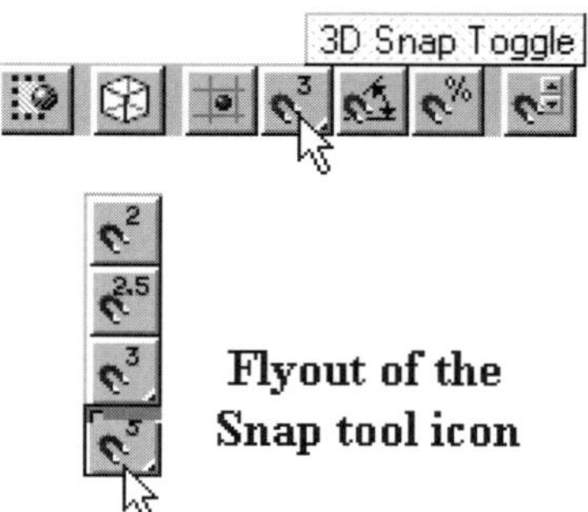

Fig. 2.35 The **Snap** tools in the Status bar

Parameters area of the Control panel as the box is created. **Length**, **Width** and **Height** sizes will be in multiples of 10.

X,Y,Z coordinates

It is assumed that the system of 3D Cartesian geometry as used when constructing 3D models in CAD systems is reasonably well understood. In this form of coordinate geometry, it is normal to assume that the **X** axis is horizontal, the **Y** axis vertical on the computer monitor and the **Z** axis is as if at right angles to the screen towards the operator. Upon start-up in 3D Studio Max the positions on screen where the coordinate position *x,y,z* 0,0,0 is situated is at the centre of each viewport, except in the **Perspective** viewport. This means that in the **Top** viewport:

1. +**X** is to the right of the viewport centre;
2. –**X** is to the left of the viewport centre;
3. +**Y** is above the viewport centre;
4. –**Y** is below viewport centre.

In the **Left** and **Front** viewports:

1. +**Z** is above the centre of the viewports;
2. –**Z** is below the centre of the viewports.

When an object has been, or is being, constructed three lines with arrows and letters (**x**, **y** and **z**) appear with the object. The position of this triad of lines and letters depends upon the position in which the object is being constructed. When constructing 3D solids, the x,y,z triads can be of good value in assisting the operator to determine the positions of objects in relation to the coordinate geometry of the whole 3D solid under construction. The triads disappear when an object is deselected, and reverts to its default colour.

Examples of 3D solids created from Standard Primitives

Example 1

1. *Left-click* on the **3D Snap Toggle** to set it on.
2. Select the **Box** button from the **Object Type** of the **Standard Primitives** part of the Command panel.
3. In **Keyboard Entry** make the following *entries* – **Z:** –50 (minus 50); **Length:** 100; **Width:** 100; **Height:** 100. *Left-click* on the **Create** button.
4. Pan the Command panel down so as to be able to select **Tube**.
5. In **Keyboard Entry** make the following *entries* – **X:** 0; **Y:** 0; **Z:** 0; **Inner Radius:** 15; **Outer Radius:** 25; **Height:** 200. *Left-click* in the **Left** viewport to make it the current active viewport. *Left-click* on the **Create** button.
6. In the **Top** viewport *right-click* on the tube and from the menu which appears select **Move**. Move the tube to a central position within the cube. The **3D Snap Toggle** being on can ensure exact positioning of the tube.
7. In the **Front** viewport, repeat items 5, and move the second tube to the centre of the cube in the **Top** viewport.
8. Select **Compound Objects** from the **Standard Primitives** popup list, *left-click* on the cube (turns white). *Left-click* on the **Boolean** button and **Union**. *Left-click* on the **Boolean B** button, followed by another on one of the tubes. A Boolean union forms between the cube and the tube.
9. Repeat item 8 with the second tube.
10. *Left-click* on the **Quick Render** icon to render the scene. The result is as shown in Fig. 2.36.

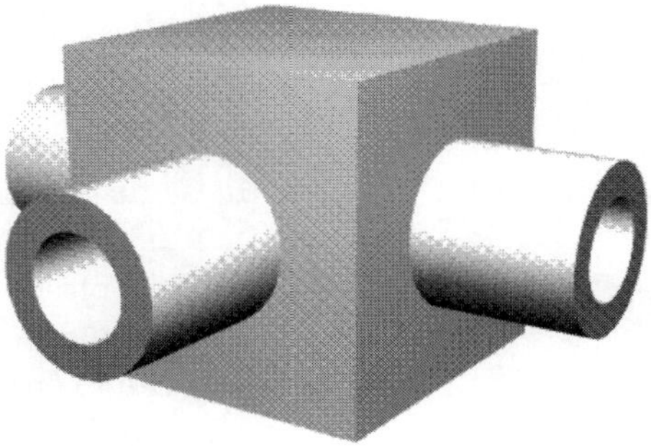

Fig. 2.36 Example 1 – a rendering

Example 2

1. In the **Left** viewport create **Cylinder01** of radius 25 and length 140.
2. In the same viewport, create **Cylinder02** of radius 10 and length 130.

3. Boolean subtract **Cylinder 02** from **Cylinder01**.
4. In the same viewport create **Box01** of length and width both 80 and height 20.
5. In the **Top** viewport move **Box01** to the left-hand end of the solid of two cylinders.
6. Boolean union the existing solid with **Box01**.
7. In the **Left** viewport, create **Tube01** of inner radius 20, outer radius 30 and height 5.
8. In the **Top** viewport, move **Tube01** so that it is 20 units from the left-hand end of the combined solid.
9. Boolean subtract **Tube01** from the solid so far created.
10. In the **Top** viewport, rotate the solid so that it appears in the **Perspective** viewport in a convenient position for rendering.
11. Using the **Quick Render** tool, render the solid in the **Perspective** window. The result should appears somewhat like Fig. 2.37.

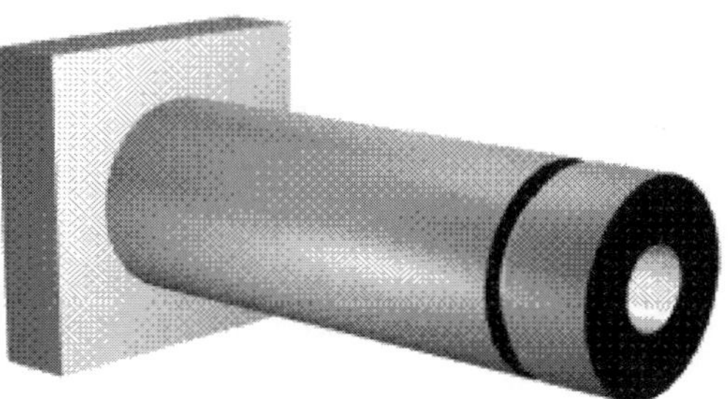

Fig. 2.37 Example 2 – a rendering

Example 3

1. Set the **3D Snap Toggle** on.
2. In **Front** viewport create **Box01** – length 120, Width 200 and height 5.
3. In the same viewport, create **Cylinder01** of radius 40 and height 5, with **X** set to –100 and **Y** and **Z** set to 0.
4. In the same viewport, create **Cylinder02** of radius 40 and height 5, with **X** set to 100 and **Y** and **Z** set to 0.
5. Boolean subtract **Cylinder01** from **Box01**.
6. Boolean subtract **Cylinder02** from the Boolean subtraction.
7. Still in the **Front** viewport create **Cylinder03** of the same radius and height, but with **X**, **Y** and **Z** all set to 0.
8. Boolean subtract **Cylinder03** from the solid so far created.
9. In the **Top** viewport, rotate the solid to obtain a good viewing position in the **perspective** viewport.
10. With **Quick Render**, render the resulting solid. The result should be similar to the rendering shown in Fig. 2.38.

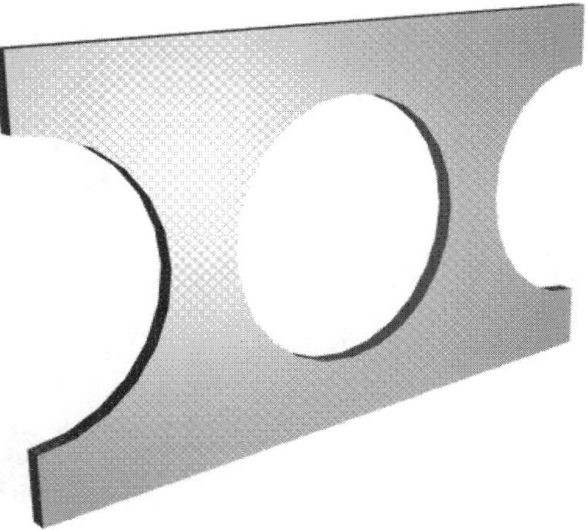

Fig. 2.38 Example 3 – a rendering

Fig. 2.39 Example 4 – a rendering

Example 4

1. **Top** viewport. **Cylinder01**: **X** and **Y** set at 0; **Z** set at –60; radius 50, height 120.
2. **Top** viewport. **GeoSphere01**: **X** and **Y** set at 0; **Z** set at 60; **Icosa**, **Hemisphere**; radius 50.
3. Boolean union **Cylinder01** and **GeoSphere01**.
4. **Top** viewport. **Torus01**: **X** and **Y** set at 0; **Z** set at 40; major radius 50, minor radius 10.
5. Boolean subtract **Torus01** from the union.
6. **Top** viewport. **Cone01 X** and **Y** set at 0; **Z** set at –70; radius 1 60, radius 2 50, height 10.
7. **Top** viewport. **Cylinder03**: **X** and **Y** set to 0; **Z** set at –90; radius 60, height 20.
8. Boolean union the last two primitives, one after the other to the remainder of the solid.
9. With **Quick Render**, render the resulting solid in the **Perspective** viewport. The result should be similar to the rendering in Fig. 2.39.

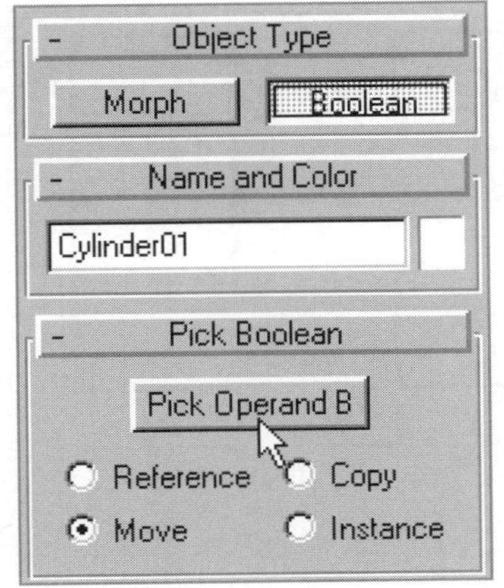

Fig. 2.40 The four check circles which can be set when using Boolean operators

A warning when using Boolean operands

When the **Boolean** button is pressed, under the button **Pick Operand** there are four check circles (Fig. 2.40). Unless a copy of the operand being picked is required, make sure the **Move** check circle is on (black dot in circle). Otherwise a copy of the picked operand will appear with the Boolean operation. See Fig. 2.41.

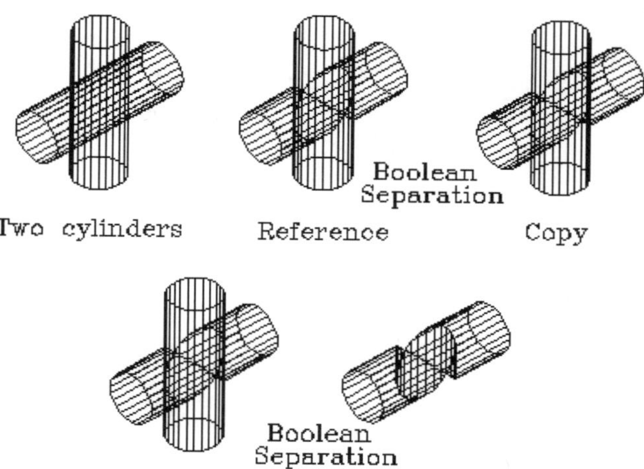

Fig. 2.41 Examples of the action resulting from the choice of check circles

Exercises

Before attempting the exercises detailed below, create the 3D solids described in the four examples given above. Then try creating the 3D solids given in the following six exercises.

1. A two-view orthographic projection of a 40 mm steel plate is shown in Fig. 2.42 and a rendering of the solid given in Fig. 2.43. Create the solid and, using the **Quick Render** tool, render the solid you have created.

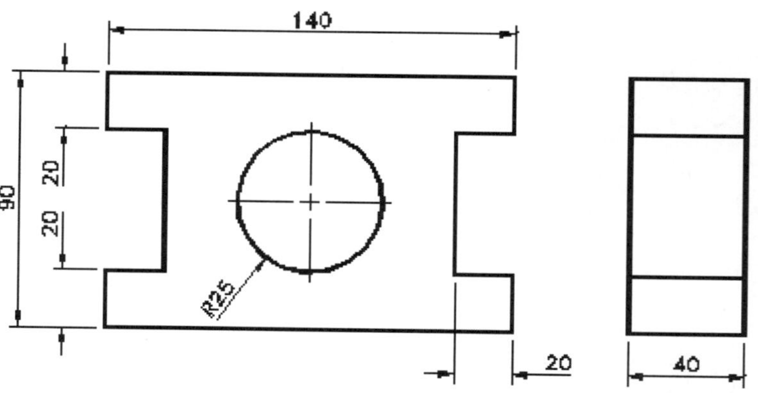

Fig. 2.42 Exercise 1

2. Figure 2.44 shows a two-view, third angle orthographic projection of a bar made from plastic. Construct the bar to the given sizes and then render your solid. Figure 2.45 shows a rendering of the solid.

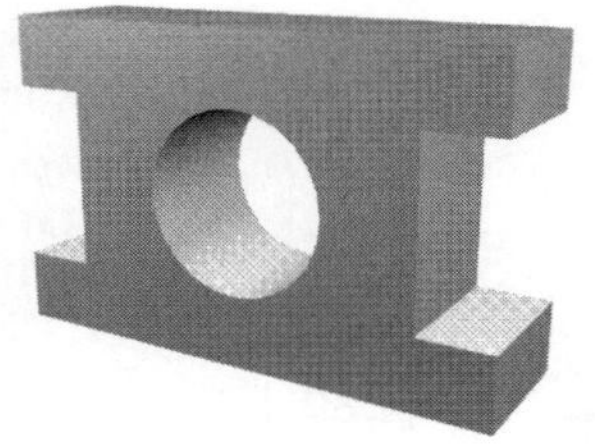

Fig. 2.43 Exercise 1 – a rendering

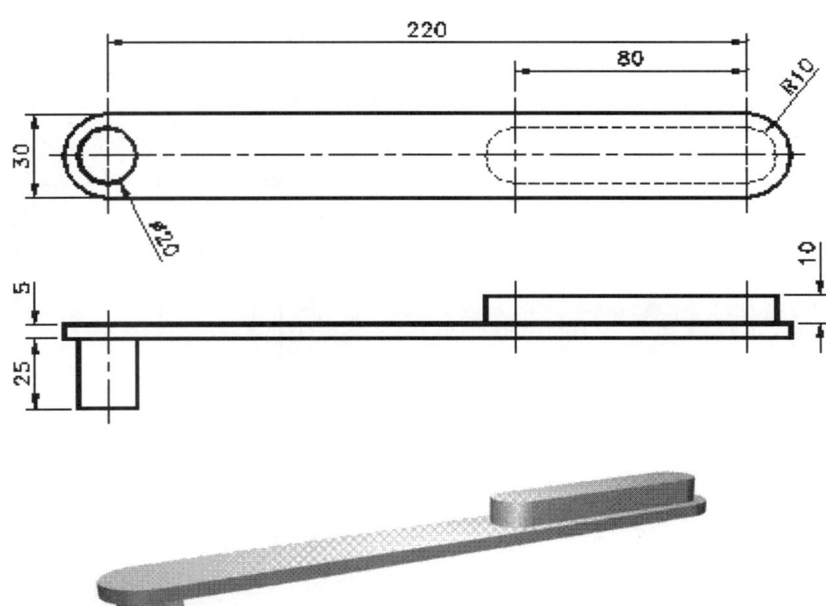

Fig. 2.44 Exercise 2

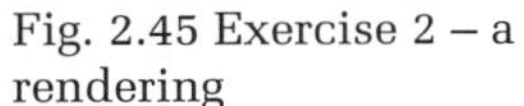

Fig. 2.45 Exercise 2 – a rendering

3. Figure 2.46 is a front view of a part from a switch of a cooking oven. Create a 3D model to the given dimensions and render the result. Figure 2.47 shows a rendering of the 3D solid.

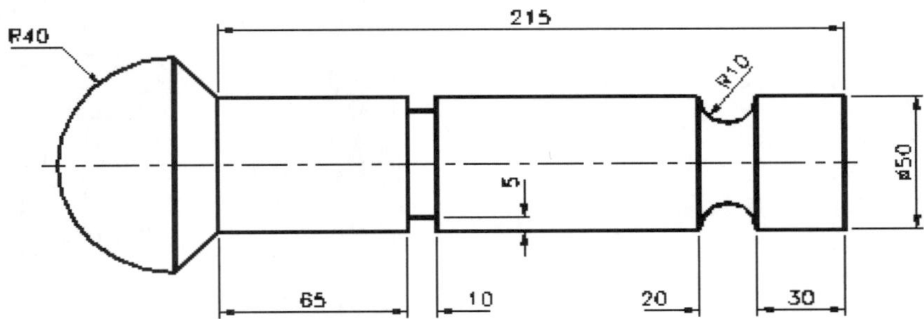

Fig. 2.46 Exercise 3

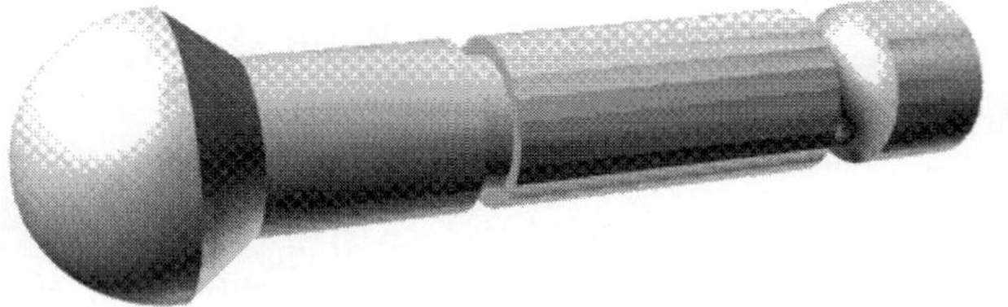

Fig. 2.47 Exercise 3 – a rendering

4. Figure 2.48 is a two-view orthographic projection of a plate of thickness 20. Create the plate to the given dimensions and render the resulting 3D solid. Figure 4.49 shows a rendering of the solid.

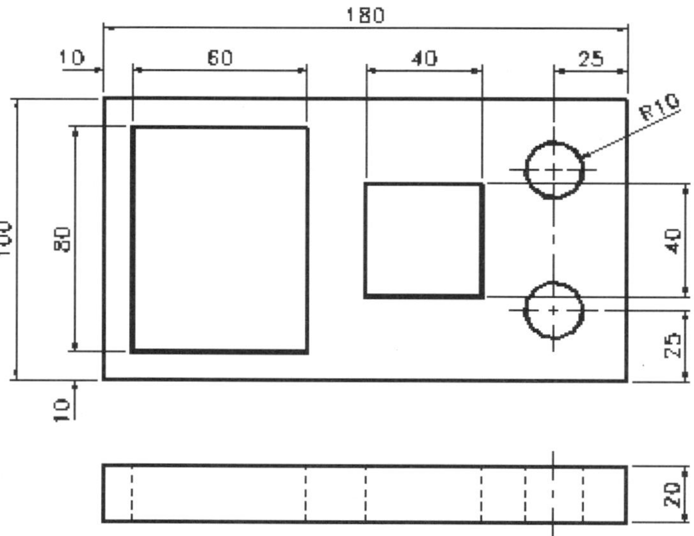

Fig. 2.48 Exercise 4

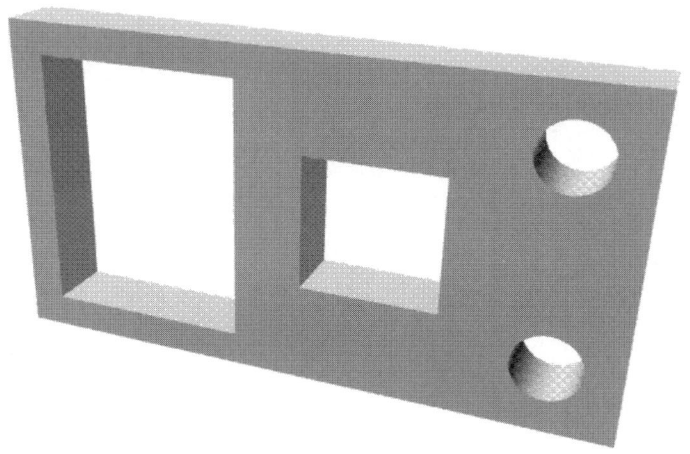

Fig. 2.49 Exercise 4 – a rendering

5. Figure 2.50 is a front view and plan of a base for a lamp. Create a 3D solid of the base and render the solid. Figure 2.51 shows a rendering of the resulting 3D solid.

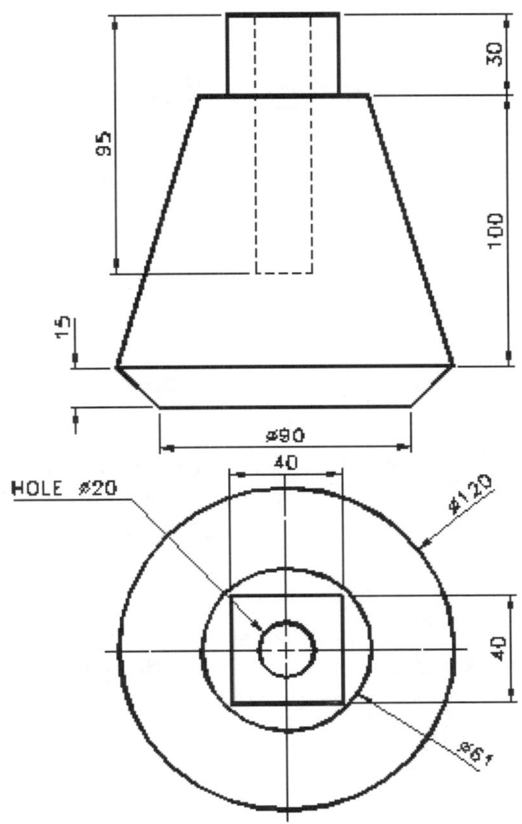

Fig. 2.50 Exercise 5

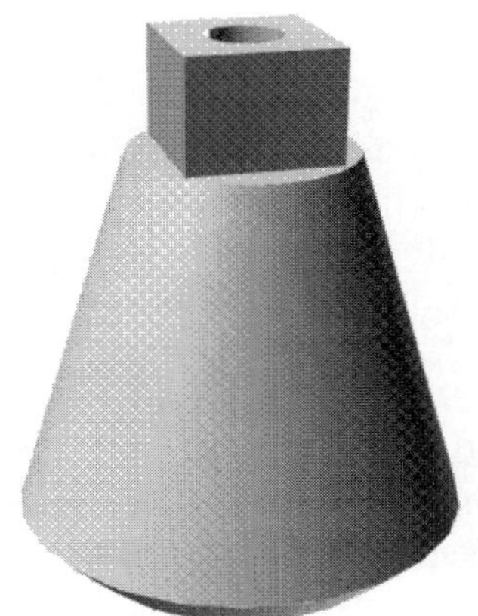

Fig. 2.51 Exercise 5 – a rendering

6. Figure 2.52 is a rendering of a box 160 long by 100 deep and 60 high, with a lid 20 high. All parts of the box are 10 thick. Create a solid to these dimensions, then render your answer.

Fig. 2.52 Exercise 6

CHAPTER 3

Create Shapes and Modifiers

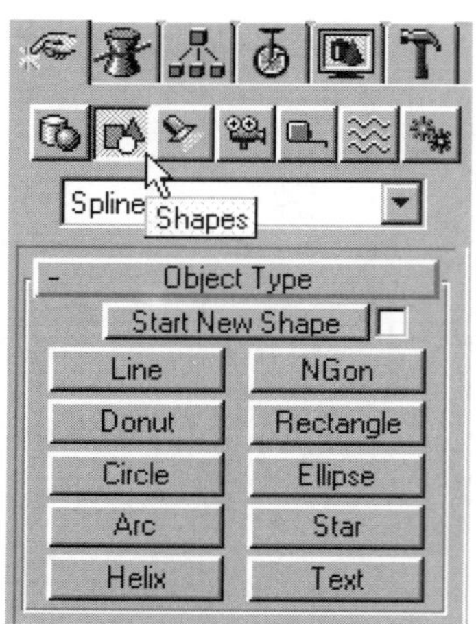

Fig. 3.1 The **Object Types** from a *left-click* on the **Shapes** icon

Shapes

Left-click on the **Shapes** icon in the Command panel and the types of shapes buttons appear (Fig. 3.1). The shapes are all based on spline curves, hence the word **Splines** at the head of the popup list appearing under the **Shapes** icon in the Command panel.

Examples of shapes are given in Fig. 3.2. All the shapes other than the **Helix** are two-dimensional (2D). The **Helix** is three-dimensional (3D) – it has height as well as length and width.

When a **Shape** has been created, it can be modified in a variety of ways. Modification possibilities will be seen with a *left-click* on the **Modify** button at the top of the Command panel (Fig. 3.3).

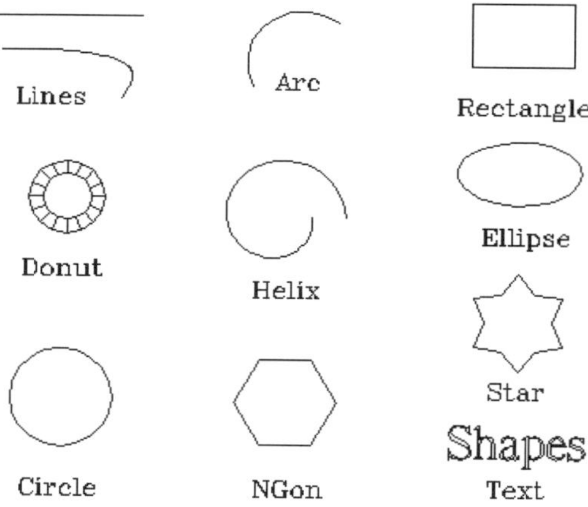

Fig. 3.2 The shapes produced from the use of the **Object Types**

Examples of modified Shapes

Example 1

1. *Left-click* on the **3D Snap Toggle** to make it active.
2. *Left-click* on **Line.** Pan the Command panel down until **Initial Type**

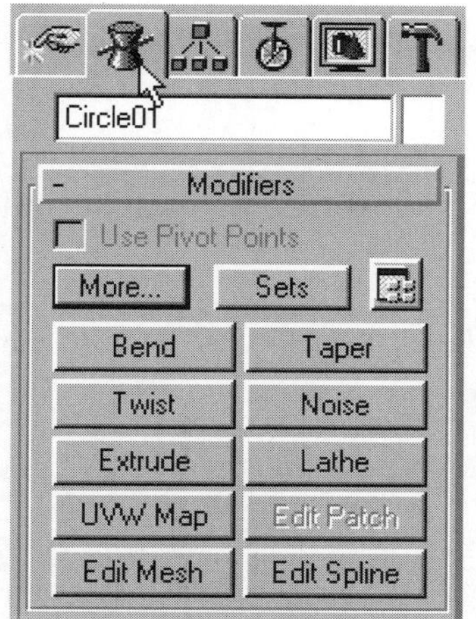

Fig. 3.3 The **Modifiers**

and **Drag Type** appear and under **Creation Method** set the check circles on against both **Corner** circles in both areas.

3. In the **Top** viewport, create an outline similar to that shown in Fig. 3.4. This involves *left-clicking* at each corner, followed by a *right-click* when all lines have been created.
4. *Left-click* on **Modify**, followed by another on **Extrude**. Pan the Command panel up until the **Parameters** area is visible. Set the check circle against **Morph**. *Enter* 50 in the **Amount** box and press the Return key of the keyboard.
5. Figure 3.5 shows the model as it will appear in the **Perspective** viewport.

Fig. 3.4 Example 1. The outline created from lines in the **Top** viewport

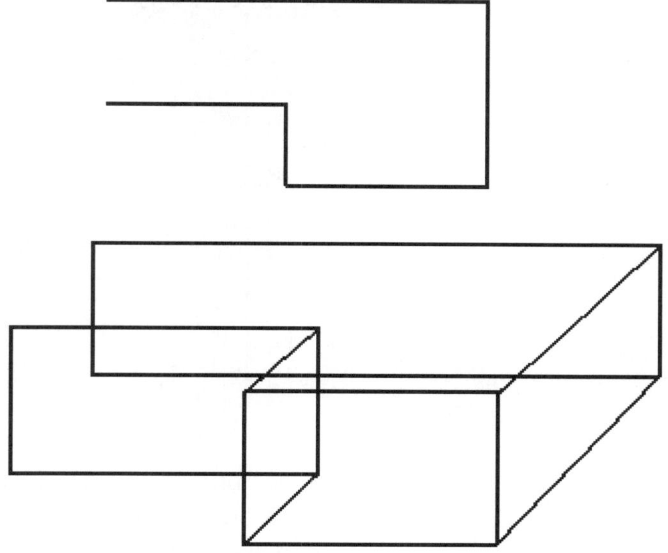

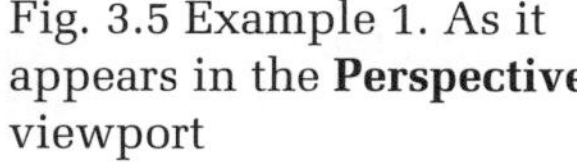

Fig. 3.5 Example 1. As it appears in the **Perspective** viewport

Example 2

1. Make the **3D Snap Toggle** active.
2. *Left-click* on **Line**. In the **Creation Method** part of the Command panel, set the check circles against **Smooth** and **Bezier** on.
3. In the **Top** viewport:
   (a) *left-click* at the point –100,50.
   (b) watch the coordinate numbers in the Status bar. It may not show exactly when the cursor is at the *x,y* point –100,50, but the **Snap** toggle being on will enable exact positioning.
   (c) *drag* the line which appears to the coordinate point 0,50 and *left-click*.

(d) *drag* the line to 50,0 and *left-click*.
(e) *right-click* to complete the line.

4. In the **Top** viewport:
   (a) *left-click* at the point -100,-50.
   (b) *drag* the line which appears to the coordinate point 0,-50 and *left-click*.
   (c) *right-click* to complete the line.
5. Note that the 'lines' are Bezier curves. Figure 3.6 shows the resulting two lines in the **Top** viewport.

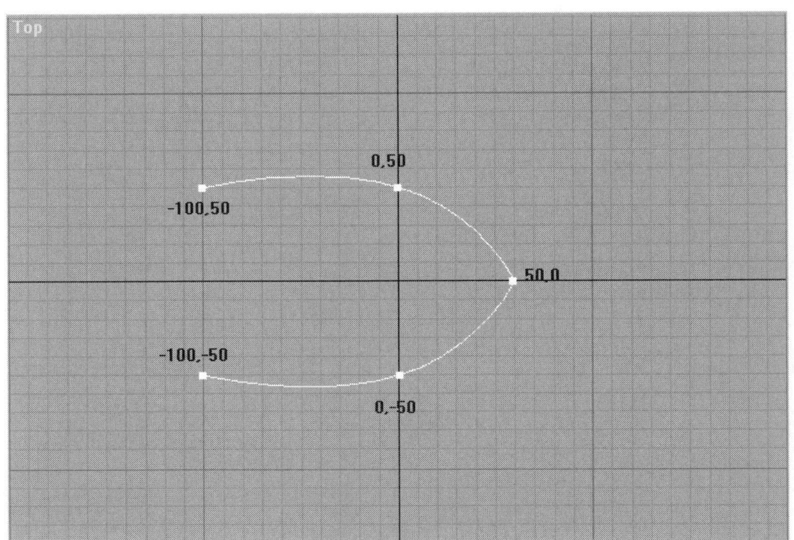

Fig. 3.6 Example 2 – the two lines created in the **Top** viewport

6. Select one of the lines. It turns white. *Left-click* on **Modify**, followed by another on **Extrude**. Pan the Command panel up until the **Parameters** area is visible. Set the check circle against **Morph**. *Enter* 50 in the **Amount** box and press the Return key of the keyboard.
7. Repeat item 6 for the second line. The two lines have extruded as shown in the rendering in Fig. 3.7.

Example 3

1. Select the front of the two lines (i.e. the lower line in the **Top** viewport);
2. Using the second example as a base, *left-click* on the **Bend** button in the **Modify** list of modifiers.
3. In the **Parameters** part of the Command panel, *enter* 10 in both the **Bend** and the **Direction** boxes. Note the changes which take place, particularly the red box surrounding the bend action area.

Fig. 3.7 Second example – a rendering

Fig. 3.8 Example 3 – a rendering

4. Experiment with different **Bend** and **Direction** figures.
5. Figure 3.8 shows a rendering of the example after the bend has taken place.

Example 4

1. Create a **Donut** of **Radius 1:** 50 and **Radius 2:** 40. **Extrude** the donut 50 units high.
2. Select the **Twist** button of the **Modify** set and *enter* 60 in the **Angle** box of the **Parameters** section of the Command panel. Note the changes within a red outline.

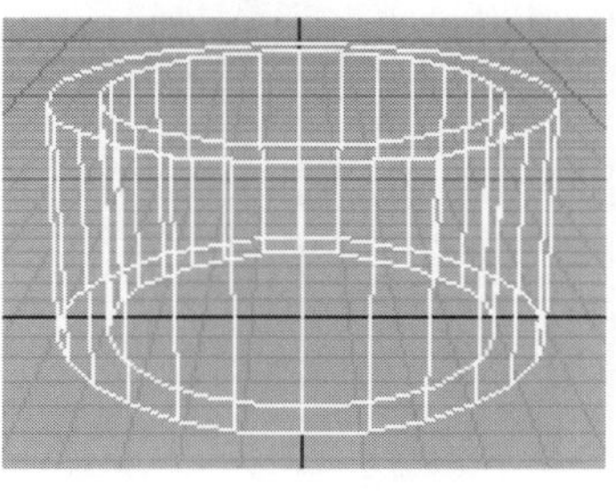

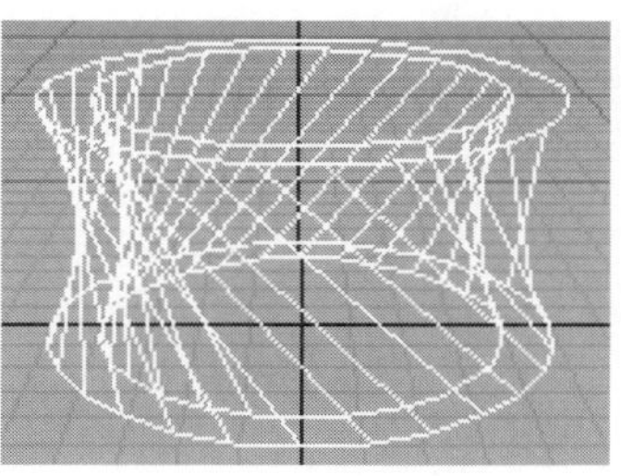

Fig. 3.9 Example 4

3. *Right-click* to complete the twist.
4. Figure 3.9 shows the donut both before the twist and after as seen in the **Perspective** viewport.

Example 5

1. Create a **Circle** of **Radius:** 50. **Extrude** it to a height of 100. When extruding make sure the two **Capping** check circles **Cap Start** and **Cap End** are set on. Also set the **Grid** check circle on.
2. Select the **Taper** modifier and in the **Parameters** area of the Command panel *enter* 1 in the **Amount** box.
3. Figure 3.10 shows the extruded circle before and after using the **Taper** modifier.

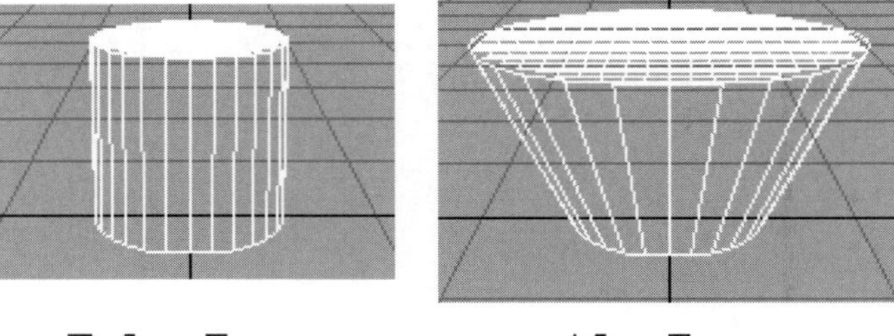

Fig. 3.10 Example 5

Before Taper **After Taper**

Example 6

1. Create a **Helix** to the following **Parameters**:
   Radius 1: 20; **Radius 2:** 20; **Height:** 200; **Number of Turns:** 6;
2. Extrude with **Parameters** set to:
   Amount: 4; **Cap Start**, **Cap End** and **Grid** set on.
3. Figure 3.11 shows the helix before and after the extrusions in the **Perspective** viewport.

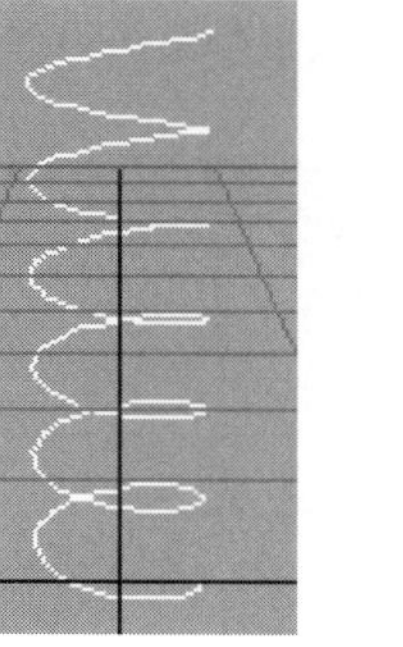

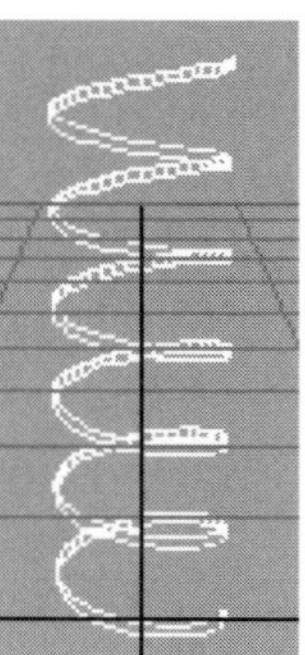

Fig. 3.11 Example 6

After Extrude

Example 7

1. Using Example 6 as a base, apply a bend of **Angle:** 60 to the extruded helix.
2. Figure 3.12 shows the result.

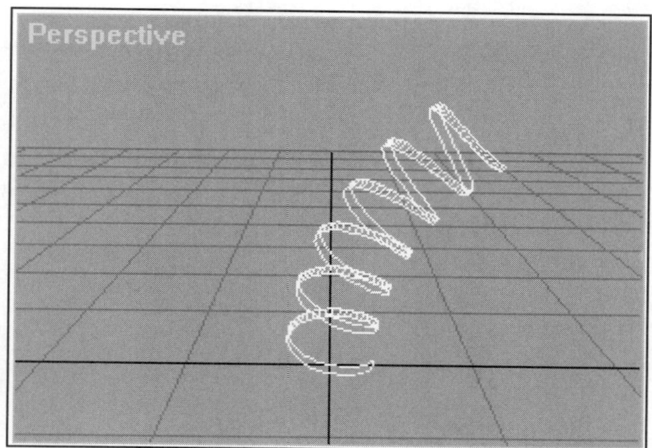

Fig. 3.12 Example 7

Example 8

1. Create a **Star** with **Parameters**:
   Radius 1: 80; **Radius 2:** 30; **Points:** 6.
2. **Extrude** to a height of 120.
3. **Bend** to an **Angle:** 20.
4. **Twist** to an **Angle:** 30.
5. The result is shown in Fig. 3.13.

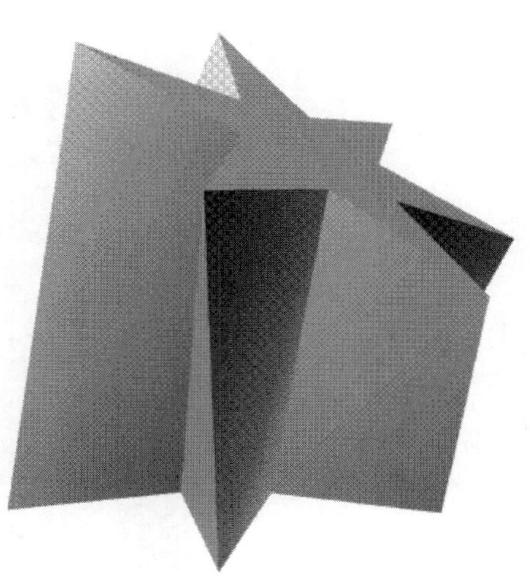

Fig. 3.13 Example 8 – a rendering

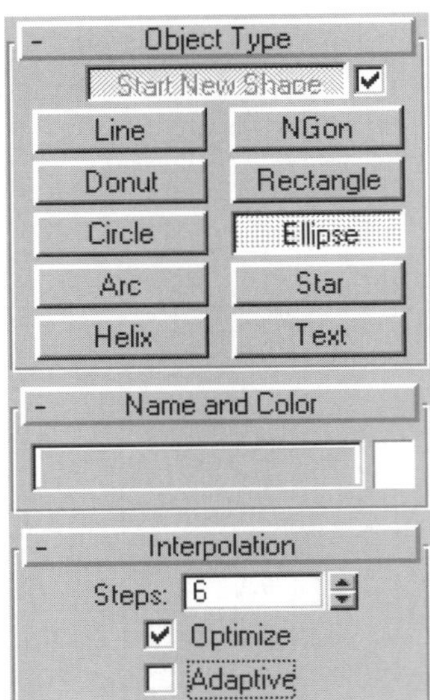

Fig. 3.14 The **Interpolation** figure for an **Ellipse**

Example 9

1. Create **Ellipse** to **Parameters**: **Length:** 80; **Width:** 120.
2. *Drag* the Command panel down until the **Interpolation** part of the panel is seen (Fig. 3.14). The default figure of 6 will be seen in the **Interpolation** box.
3. **Move** the ellipse to a different position in the **Top** viewport.
4. Create a second ellipse with **Interpolation** set at 4 and **Move**.
5. Create a third ellipse with **Interpolation** set at 2 and **Move**.
6. Create a fourth ellipse with **Interpolation** set at 1 and **Move**.
7. The four ellipses are shown in Fig. 3.15.

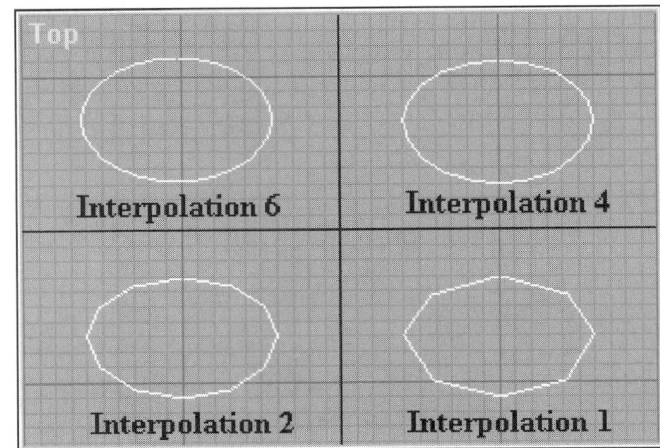

Fig. 3.15 Example 9

Example 10

1. Experiment with **Interpolation** settings when creating a **Circle**.
2. Experiment with settings when creating a **Star**. Figure 3.16 shows

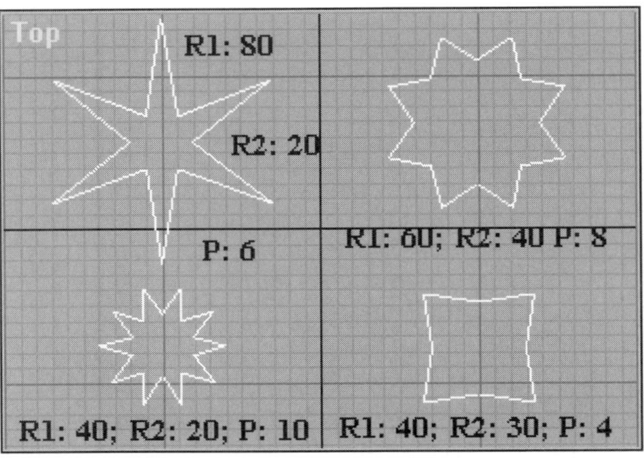

Fig. 3.16 Example 10 – Stars

a number of stars with different **Radius 1:**, **Radius 2:** and **Points:** settings (Fig. 3.16).

3. Repeat item 2, but with the creation of **NGons** (Fig. 3.17).

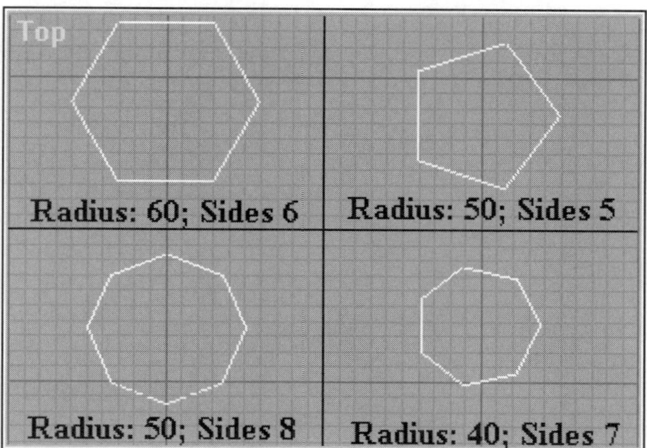

Fig. 3.17. Example 10 – NGons

Notes

1. The **Modify** commands can equally as well be used with the **Standard Primitives**.
2. A number of other **Modify** commands are available. To see the whole set, *left-click* on the **Object** icon (Fig. 3.18). The **Configure Button Sets** dialogue box appears (Fig. 3.19). To add **Modify** buttons to the set:

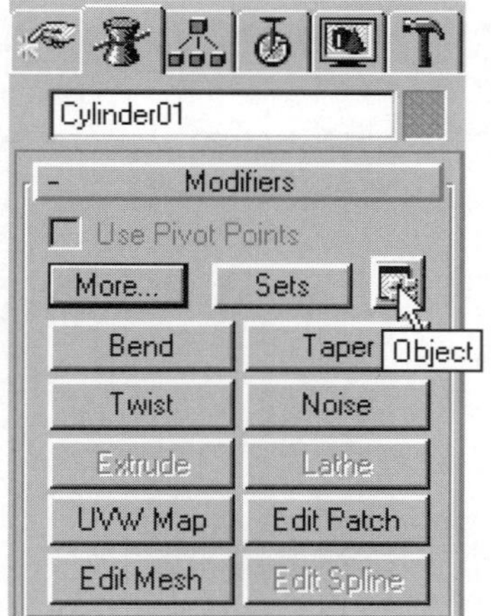

Fig. 3.18 *Left-click* on the **Object** icon

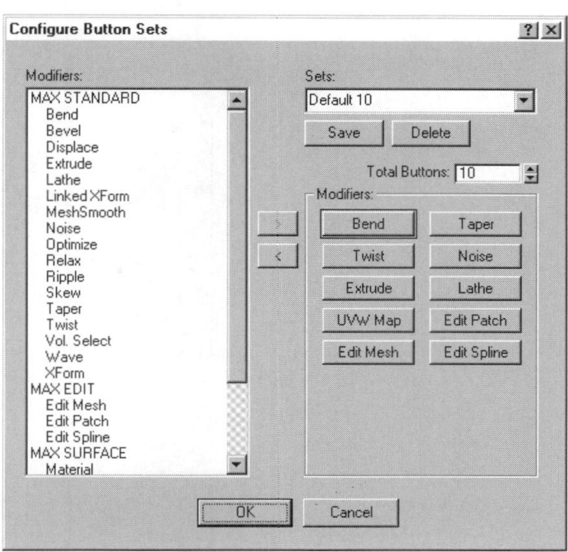

Fig. 3.19 First stage of adding modifiers to the Command panel

(a) *Enter* the number of buttons required. In the example given in Fig. 3.20, the figure 16 has been so *entered*.
(b) *Left-click* on the required modifier in the **Modifiers:** list. The selected name is higlighted.
(c) *Left-click* on an empty button, followed by another on the > arrow button. The modifier name appears in the button.

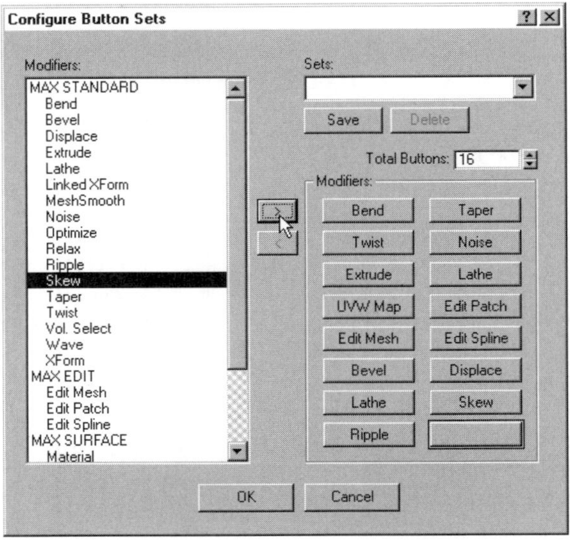

Fig. 3.20 Second stage of adding modifiers to the Command panel

The Lathe modifier

One of the more commonly used modifiers is **Lathe**. An example of the use of this modifier is shown in Figs 3.21 – 23.

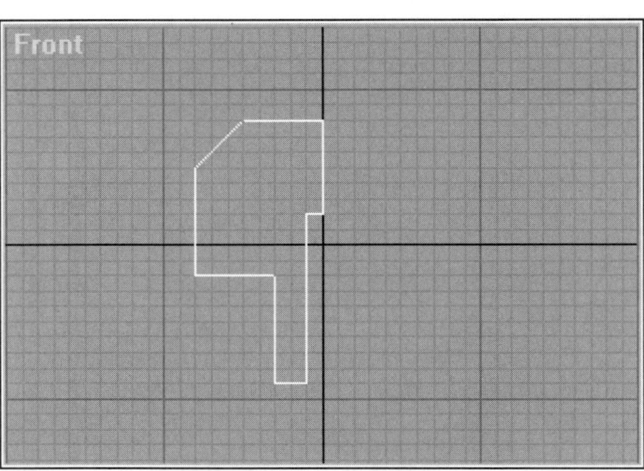

Fig. 3.21 The **Line** created in the **Front** viewport

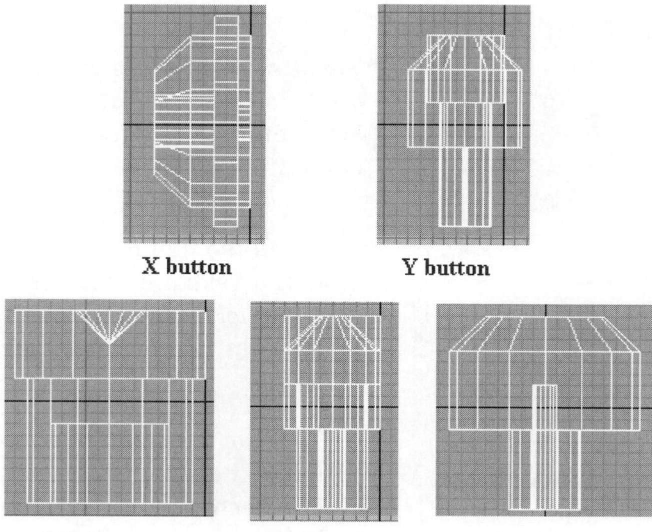

Fig. 3.22 Various settings from the **Creation Method** buttons

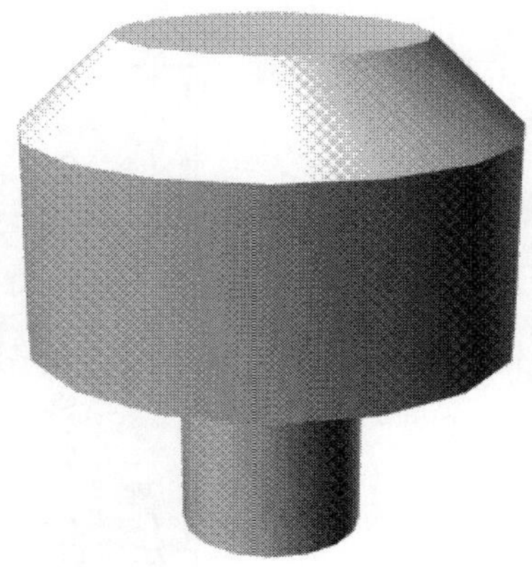

Fig. 3.23 A rendering of the 3D solid with **Y** and **Max** active

1. In the **Front** viewport using **Line** with **Creation Method** settings both set to **Corner**, create the line shown in Fig. 3.21.
2. With the line selected, *left-click* on the **Lathe** in the **Modifier** set. The line is revolved into a 3D solid. Its shape depends upon settings in the **Lathe Parameters** area of the Command panel.
3. The results of different settings are shown in Fig. 3.22, in which first the **X** button is *clicked*, then the **Y** button, followed by the **Min**, **Cen** and **Max** buttons with the **Y** button setting active.
4. Figure 3.23 is a rendering of the 3D solid resulting from using **Lathe** on the line with settings **Y** and **Max**.

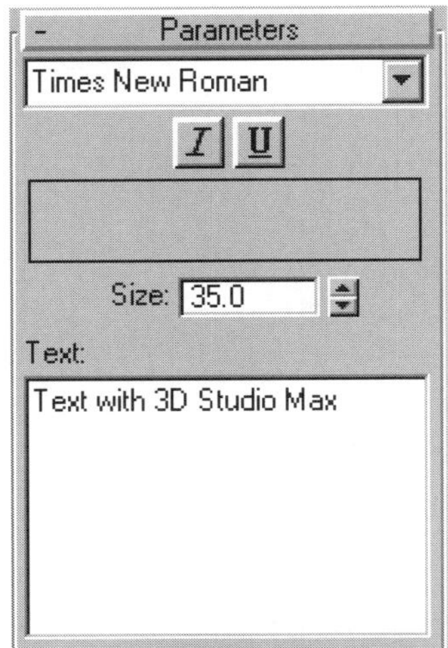

Fig. 3.24 Selecting fonts from the Text popup list

Text

Text can be acted on by the modifiers if wished. To create text, *left-click* on the **Text** button under the **Shapes** list. In the **Parameters** area of the Command panel, choose the text from the popup menu containing the names of the fonts available (Fig. 3.24). The selection is also shown in Fig. 3.25. To create text:

1. Select the font required. *Enter* figures for the **Size:**.
2. In the **Text:** area *enter* the required text.
3. *Left-click* in the viewport in which the text is to be placed. In Fig. 3.26, the text has been placed in the **Front** viewport.

Notes

1. Text can be acted upon by a modifier if wished. Figure 3.27 shows the text created in the **Front** viewport and then rendered in the **Perspective** viewport, after it has been acted upon by **Extrude** to a height of 50.
2. In the **Parameters** area for **Text** two buttons marked **I** (Italic) and **U** (Underline) can be used to produce italic or underlined text if required.

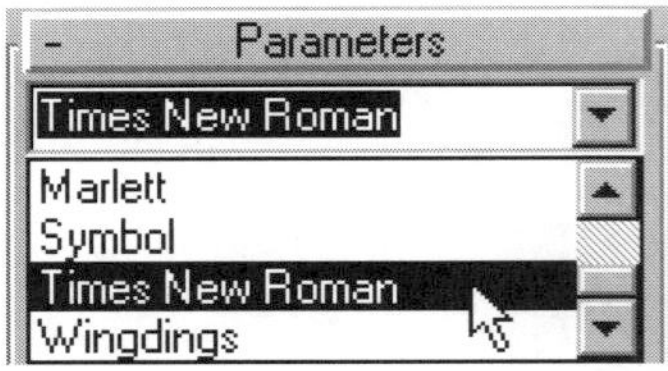

Fig. 3.25 The fonts popup list in the text **Parameters** area of the Command panel

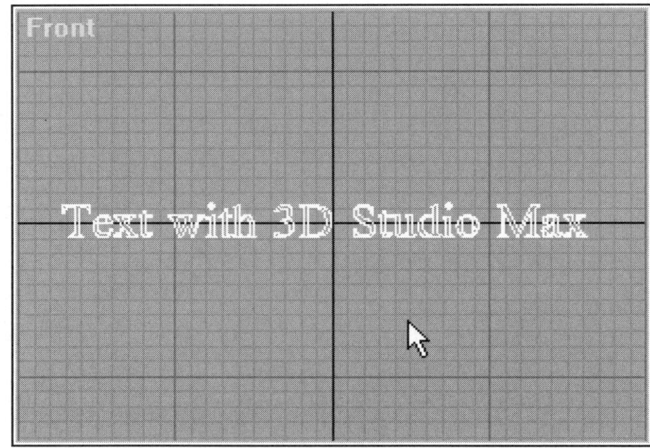

Fig. 3.26 Text *entered* in the **Front** viewport

Examples of 3D solids created from Shapes

Example 1

1. In the **Front** viewport draw the outline shown in Fig. 3.28. Use **Line** with **Corner** and **Corner** set in the **Creation Method** area of the Command panel.
2. Select the outline and *left-click* on the modifier **Lathe**. *Left-click* on the **Direction** button **Y** and the **Align** button **Max**.

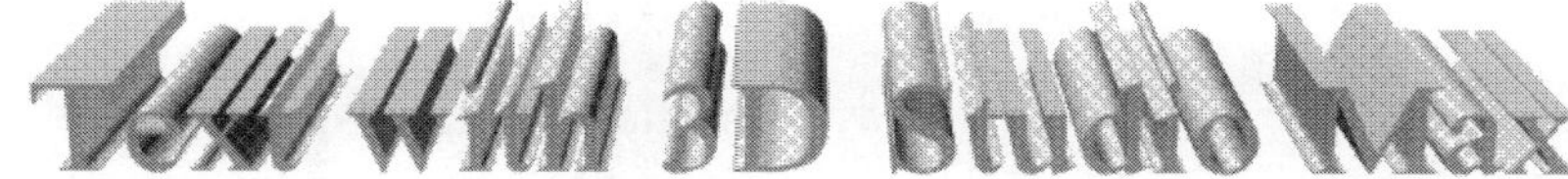

Fig. 3.27 Text can be acted upon by a modifier

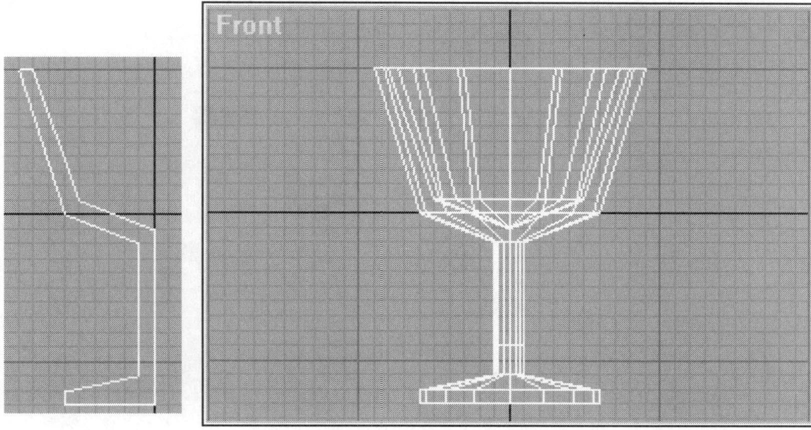

Fig. 3.28 The outline and the resulting **Lathe** solid in the **Front** viewport

3. Pan and zoom the **Perspective** viewport to obtain a good perspective view of the resulting solid and render the viewport. The result should be similar to that shown in Fig. 3.29.
4. Experiment with the **X** and **Z** buttons under **Direction** and with the **Min** and **Cen** buttons under **Align**. Then *left-click* in the **Sub-Object** button and move the **Axis** in various directions and observe the results.

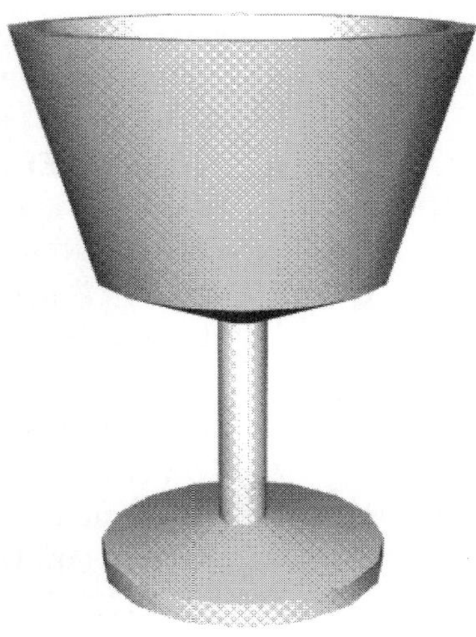

Fig. 3.29 Example 1 – a rendering

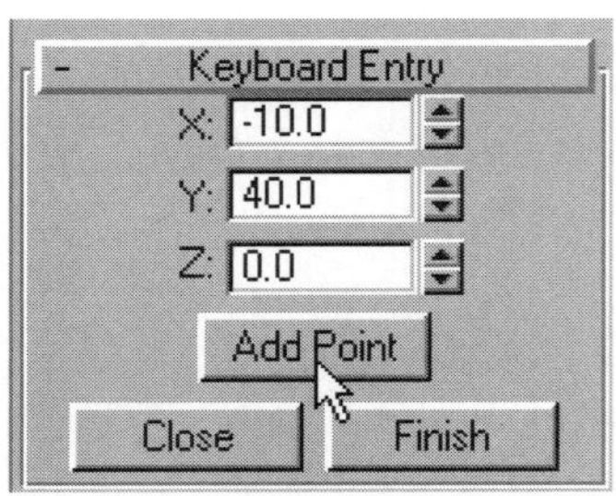

Fig. 3.30 Making *entries* in the **Keyboard Entry** of **Line**

Example 2

1. Set the **3D Snap Toggle** on.
2. In the **Top** viewport, create a **Donut** at X = 0, Y= 185 of **Radius 1** = 35 and **Radius 2** = 40.
3. In the **Top** viewport, create a **Donut** at X = 0, Y= 60 of **Radius 1** = 20 and **Radius 2** = 25.

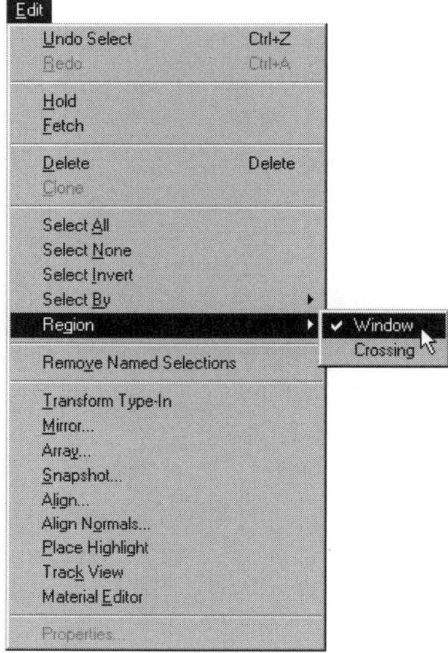

Fig. 3.31 Selecting **Group** , **Region**, **Window** from the **Edit** pulldown menu

4. In the **Top** viewport, create a **Line** from X,Y = –10,40 to 10,40 to 20, –150 to –20, –150 to –10,40 by positioning the cursor under mouse control and watching the coordinates figures in the Status bar.
5. In the **Top** viewport, create a **Line** from X,Y = –10,80 to 10,80 to 0,160 to –10,80 using the **Add Point** and **Close** buttons in the **Keyboard Entry** area of the **Line** command panel – see Fig. 3.30 – as each X,Y point is entered, *left-click* on the **Add Point** button. To close all the points, *left-click* on the **Close** button.
6. *Left-click* on **Edit** in the menu bar, on **Region** in the resulting pull-down menu, then on **Window** in the sub-menu (Fig. 3.31). Then window all the objects so far created – the two donuts and the two line outlines;
7. *Left-click* on **Group** in the menu bar and on **Group** in the pull-down menu (Fig. 3.32). When the **Group** dialogue box appears, *left-click* on **OK** to accept the name of the group (**Group01**). See Fig. 3.33. The four objects can now be treated as one.

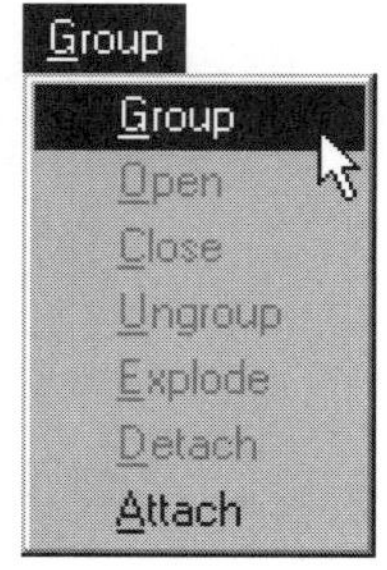

Fig. 3.32 The **Group** pull-down menu

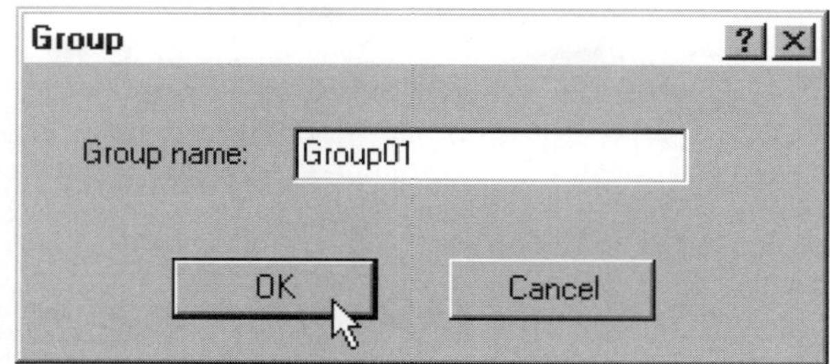

Fig. 3.33 The **Group** dialogue box

8. **Extrude** the group to 5 units high. In the **Parameters** area of the Control panel, make sure the **Grid** and **Mesh** check circles are set on. The result is shown in Fig. 3.34.
9. **Rotate** the resulting solid to obtain a good viewing position in the **Perspective** viewport.
10. In the **Perspective** viewport **Quick Render** the 3D solid (Fig. 3.35).

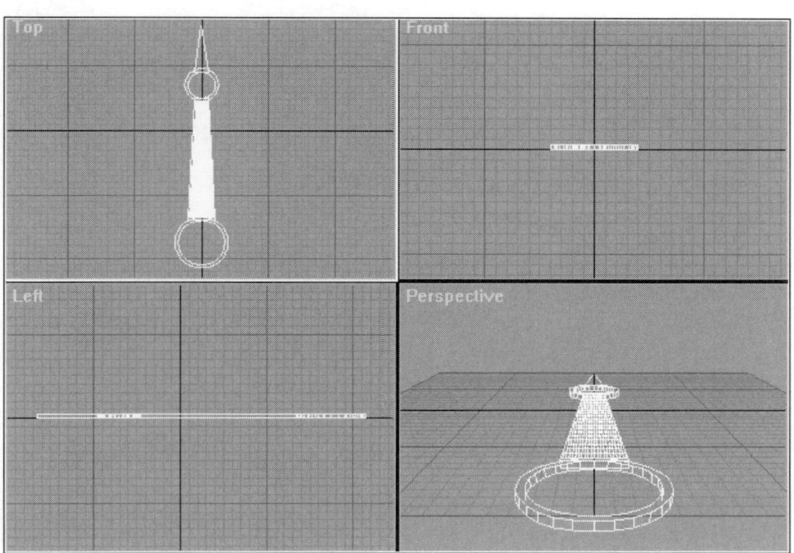

Fig. 3.34 Example 2

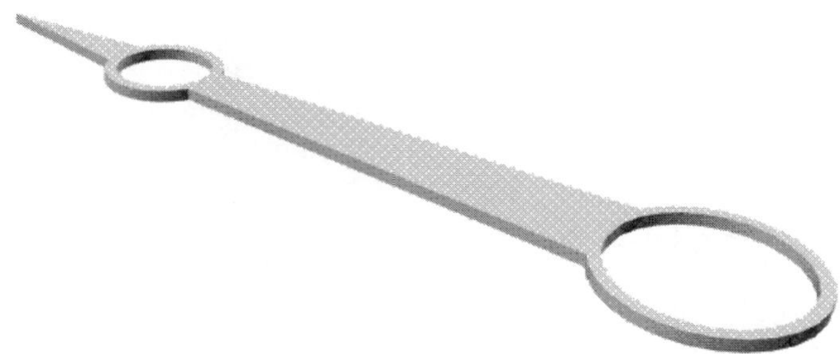

Fig. 3.35 Example 2 – a rendering

Example 3

1. Set the **3D Snap Toggle** on.
2. In the **Top** viewport create a **Line** outline for the top of the table. Use the cursor under mouse control and work to sizes of your own choice.

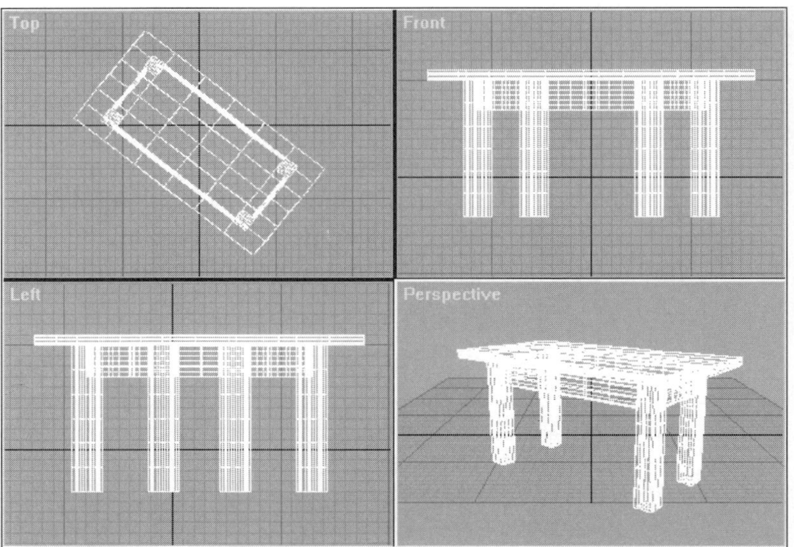

Fig. 3.36 Example 3

3. **Extrude** the **Line** outline by an **Amount:** of 10.
4. **Move** the top to a suitable position in the **Front** viewport.
5. In the **Front** viewport, with **Line** draw one leg of width 20 units and of a height of your own choice.
6. **Extrude** the leg by an **Amount:** of 20.
7. Repeat item 6 for a second leg.

Fig. 3.37 Example 3 – a rendering

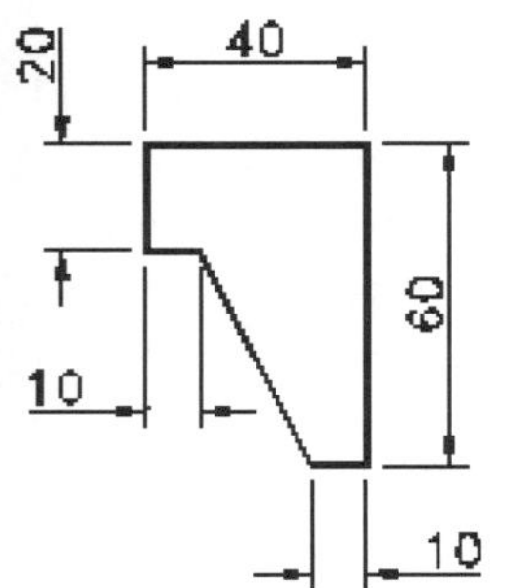

Fig. 3.38 **Line** outline to be created in two viewports

8. In the **Left** viewport **Move** each leg to a suitable position of your own choice.
9. Repeat items 5 to 8 to create the other two legs.
10. **Window** and **Group** all objects created in the **Top** viewport.
11. **Rotate** the group so as to achieve a good viewing position in the **Perspective** viewport. The result will be similar to that shown in Fig. 3.36.
12. **Quick Render** the resulting 3D model. Figure 3.37 shows the rendering.

Example 4

1. Set the **3D Snap Toggle** on.
2. With **Line** create the outline given in Fig. 3.38 in both the **Top** and the **Front** viewports.
3. In the **Top** viewport **Extrude** the outline to 800.
4. In the **Front** viewport **Extrude** the outline to 500.
5. In the **Top** viewport, select the extrusion and *left-click* on the **Mirror Selected Objects** icon in the toolbar (Fig. 3.39). This brings the **Mirror: Screen Coordinates** dialogue box onto the screen. Set up the dialogue box as shown in Fig. 3.40, followed by a *left-click* on the **OK** button of the dialogue box.
6. Repeat item 5 in the **Front** viewport. You should now have the four sides of a picture frame.
7. **Move** each frame member into position making full use of the **Zoom** tools in the Status bar to move the ends of the members into their exact positions.

Fig. 3.39 The **Mirror Selected Objects** icon in the toolbar

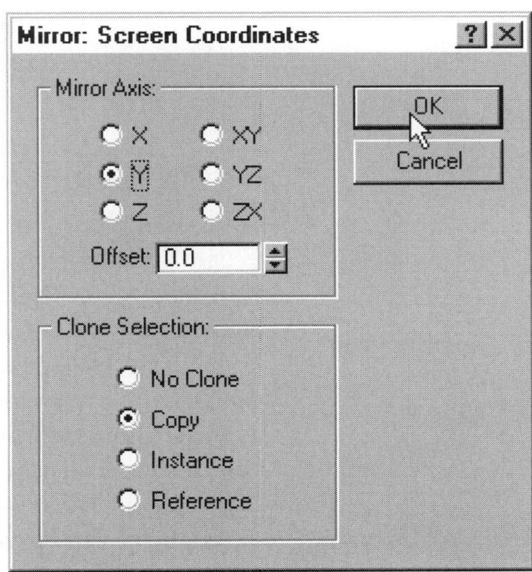

Fig. 3.40 The **Mirror: Screen Coordinates** dialogue box

8. **Window** and **Group** the four members of the frame.
9. *Left-click* on **Text** in the **Object Type** part of the Command panel. Select the font named **Arial**, set its size to 130 and *enter* the lines of text as shown in Fig. 3.41 one after the other in the **Text:** window of the Command panel. As each line of text is *entered* a *left-click* in an appropriate position in a viewport places the line of text at the selected position. If necessary each line can be moved in the same way as any other object.
10. **Window** and **Group** the frame and all the text.
11. **Rotate** the new group so that a good viewing position is obtained in the **Perspective** viewport.
12. With **Quick Render**, render the viewport. Figure 3.41 shows such a rendering.

Fig. 3.41 Example 4

Example 5

1. Set the **3D Snap Toggle** on.
2. Create a **Helix** to the following **Parameters:**
   Radius 1: =20; **Radius 2:** = 20; **Height:** = 200; **Turns:** = 10.
3. **Extrude** the helix by **Amount:** = 5.
4. *Left-click* on the **Array** icon in the toolbar (Fig. 3.42). The **Array** dialogue box appears (Fig. 3.43). Make settings in the dialogue box as shown and *left-click* on the **OK** button. A second helix appears.
5. **Window** and **Group** the two helices.
6. *Left-click* on the **Array** button again and in the **Array** dialogue box *enter* 280 in the **Move X** box and 0 in the **Y** box. *Left-click* on **OK**.

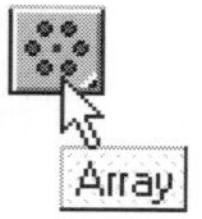

Fig. 3.42 The **Array** icon in the toolbar

Array

Array Transformation: World Coordinates (Use Pivot Point Center)

	X	Y	Z		
Move	0.0	200.0	0.0	units	
Rotate	0.0	0.0	0.0	degrees	Re-Orient
Scale	100.0	100.0	100.0	percent	Uniform

Type of Object

Copy

Instance

Reference

Total in Array: 2

Reset OK Cancel

Fig. 3.43 Settings in the **Array** dialogue box

7. **Window** and **Group** all four helices.
8. **Create** an **Ellipse** with **Keyboard Entry** settings:
   X: = 140; **Y:** = 100; **Z:** = 200; **Length:** = 500; **Width:** = 400.
9. **Extrude** the ellipse by **Amount:** = 10.
10. Create a **Rectangle** to fit snugly around the base of the helices and **Extrude** it by **Amount:** = 10. The result is shown in Fig. 3.44.
11. **Quick Render** the resulting 3D model in the **Perspective** viewport.

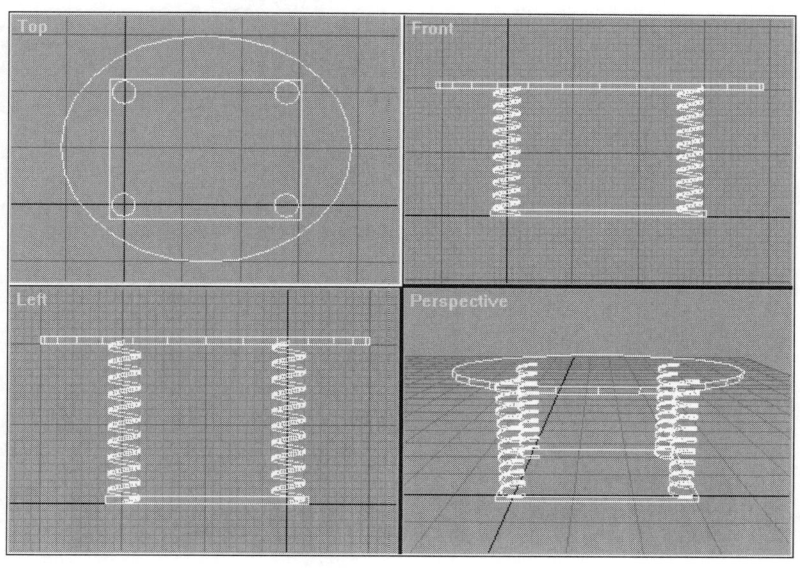

Fig. 3.44 Example 5

Keyboard shortcuts

3D Studio Max employs keyboard shortcuts for some operations. Many of these can be seen from the pull-down menus. As an example the upper part of the **File** pull-down menu (Fig. 3.45) shows that pressing the **Ctrl** key and the **N** key brings up a new screen; **Ctrl/O** brings up the **Open File** dialogue box on screen. **Ctrl/S** saves the screen to its current filename.

Two keyboard shortcuts which will be frequently in use are **Ctrl/Z** for undoing the last operation and pressing the **Esc** key which stops the action of the tool currently in use.

Fig. 3.45 The upper part of the **File** pull-down menu

You can assign your own keyboard shortcuts

Select **Preferences** from the **File** pulldown menu and the **Preference Settings** dialogue box appears (Fig. 3.46). *Left-click* on **Keyboard** at the top of the dialogue box, followed by another on any of the **Command** names in the list that appears. A note under the list shows

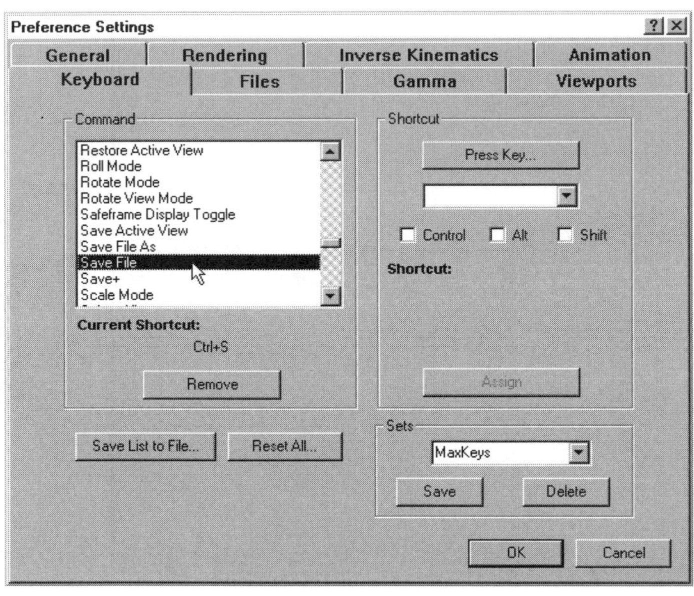

Fig. 3.46 The **Keyboard** box from the **Preference Settings** dialogue box

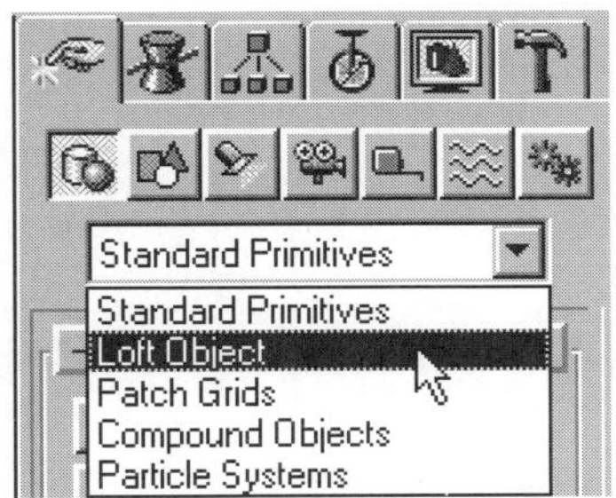

Fig. 3.47 Setting **Loft Object** in the **Standard Primitives** popup list

the shortcut already assigned to that command (if one has been assigned). If an attempt is made to assign a shortcut to any of the commands, a warning will appear in the **Shortcut:** area of the box telling you the shortcut already assigned to that command.

Thus if you wish to make your own assigned keyboard shortcuts, do so with care as to those already assigned. This is particularly important if you are not the only person to be using the computer at which you are working. Changing the keyboard shortcuts may confuse other users. If you are the only one using the computer, then by all means assign your own shortcuts.

Lofting

Shapes can be **Lofted** to form 3D models as shown in the following examples.

Example 1

1. Set the **3D Snap Toggle** on.
2. In the **Top** viewport create a **Circle** of radius 70.
3. In the **Front** viewport, create a **Line** vertically central to the circle and 100 long.
4. Set **Loft Objects** in the **Standard Primitives** popup list (Fig. 3.47).
5. Select the **Circle**.
6. *Left-click* on **Loft** in the Command panel.
7. *Left-click* the **Skin Parameters** in the Command panel and set the check box against **Skin** on (tick in box) (Fig. 3.48).

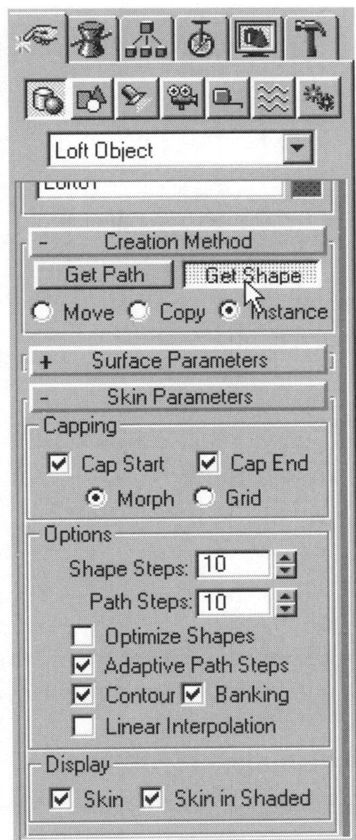

Fig. 3.48 Setting **Skin Parameters** in the Command panel

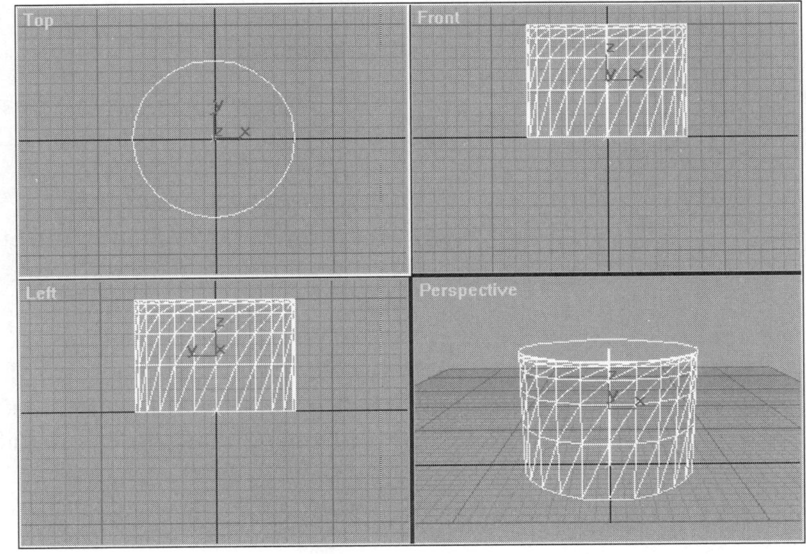

Fig. 3.49 Example 1

8. *Left-click* on the **Get Path** button, followed by another on the **Line**. The loft is created (Fig. 3.49).

Example 2

This example follows the same procedure as for the Example 1.

1. Figure 3.50 shows a **Circle** as the shape and an **Arc** as the path for the object to be lofted.
2. Figure 3.51 shows a rendering of the lofted model.

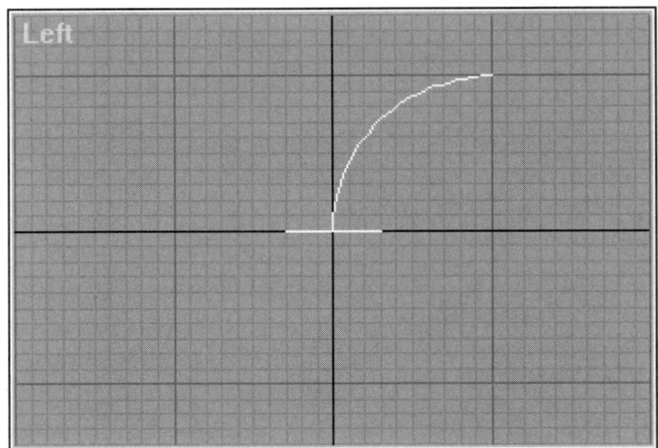

Fig. 3.50 Shape and path for Example 2

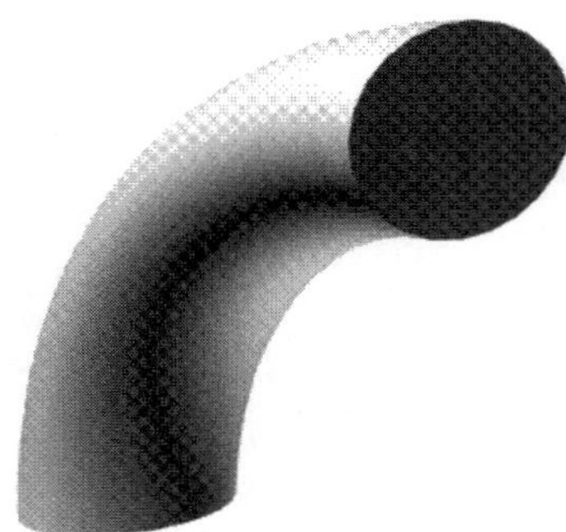

Fig. 3.51 Example 2

Example 3

1. In the **Top** viewport create a **Star** of **Radius 1:** = 50 **Radius 2:** = 20.
2. In the **Front** viewport create a **Line** as shown in Fig. 3.50.
3. Create the loft following the procedure given with Example 1.

Example 4

1. In the **Top** viewport create a **Circle** of radius 5.
2. In the **Front** viewport create an **Ellipse** of **Length:** = 80 **Width:** = 100 with the left-hand end of the major axis passing through the centre of the circle (Fig. 3.52).
3. Figure 3.53 shows a rendering of the lofted model.
4. **Loft** with the circle as the shape and the ellipse as the path (Fig. 3.52).
5. With **Array** (**X:** = 90 and **Copy** set on, with **Scale:** = 100%) create an array of five of the model (Fig. 3.54).
6. **Rotate** each other 'link' in the set of five into the vertical (select in **Front** viewport and **Rotate** in **Left** viewport).
7. Figure 3.55 shows a rendering of the chain so formed.

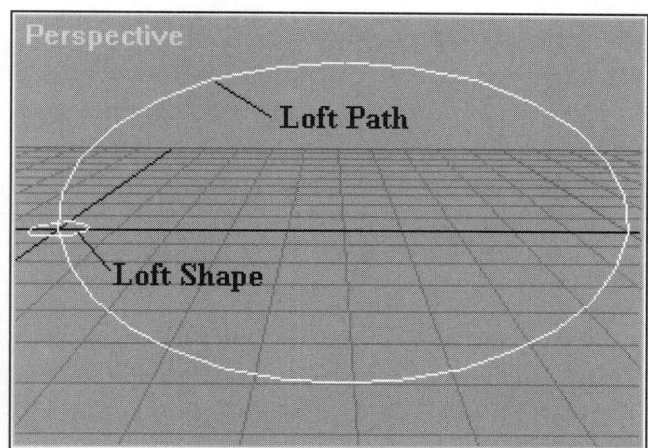

Fig. 3.52 The Shape and Path for Example 4

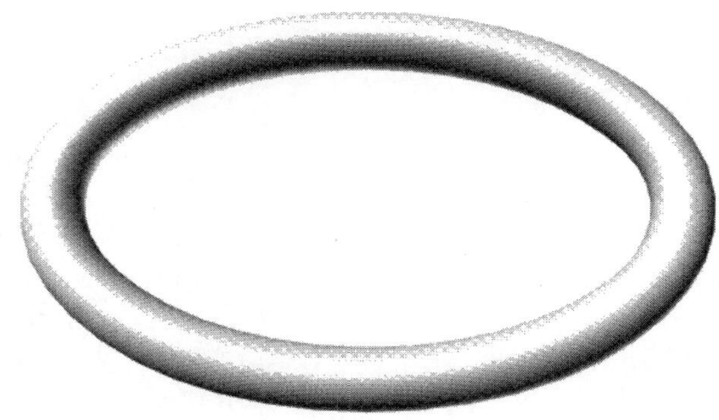

Fig. 3.53 A rendering of the loft for Example 4

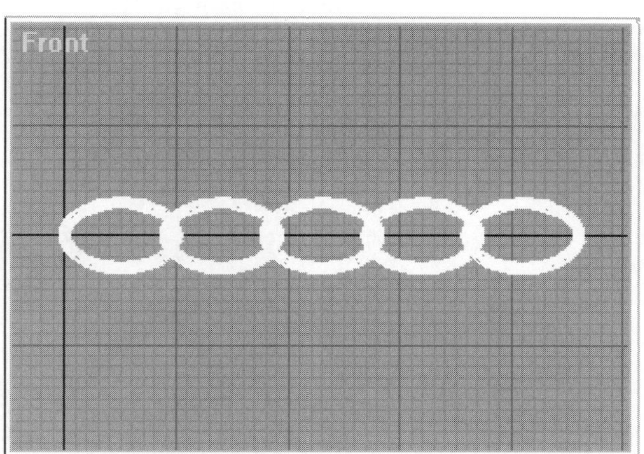

Fig. 3.54 **Array** the model five times

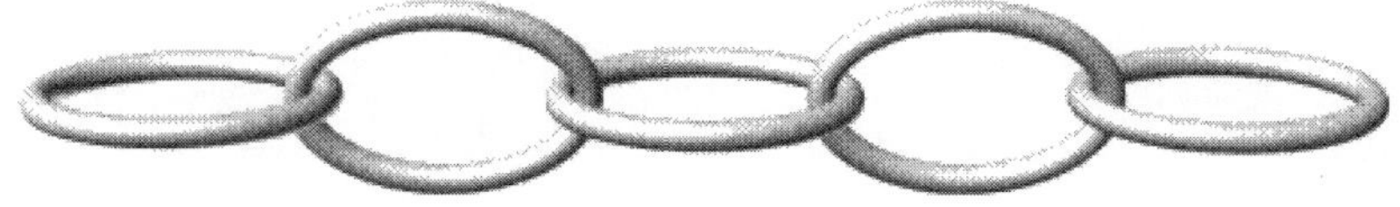

Fig. 3.55 A rendering of Example 4

Exercises

1. Figure 3.56 shows a rendering of a bobbin. Working to any convenient sizes and proportions create a similar rendering.

Fig. 3.56 Exercise 1

2. Figure 3.57 shows a rendering of a pair of pins. One pin was created with the aid of **Line** and the modifier **Lathe**. The single pin was then **Mirrored** and rendered in the **Perspective** viewport.

   The **Perspective** viewport was then changed to a **User** viewport with the aid of **Viewport Configuration** and rendered again.

   Working to any convenient sizes and proportions create the single pin, then using **Mirror** bring up a copy on the screen and render your view, first in a **Perspective** viewport and then in a **User** viewport.

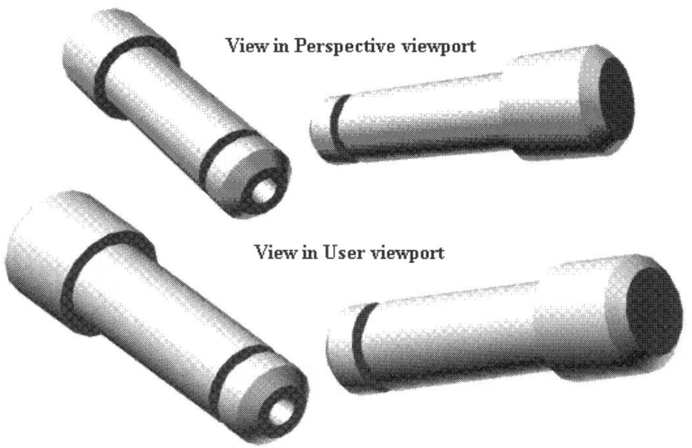

Fig. 3.57 Exercise 2

3. Figure 3.58 is a rendering of a plate in the form of a 3D solid model created with a variety of tools. Figure 3.59 is a dimensioned view of the plate.

   Working to the dimensions given in Fig. 3.59 create and render the plate.

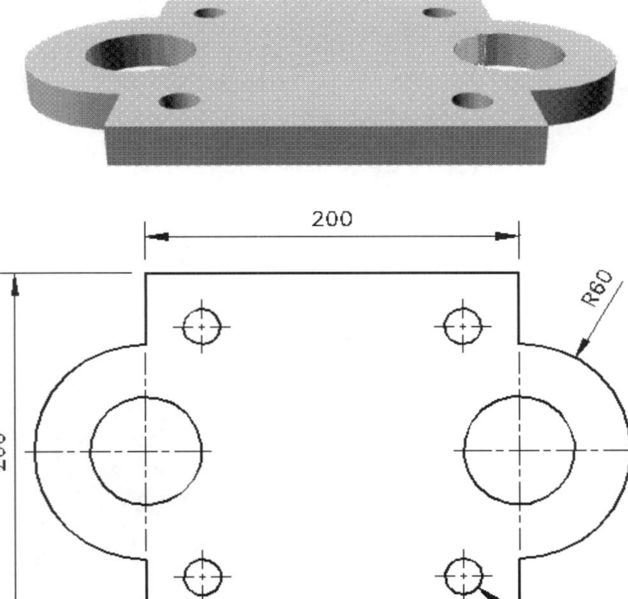

Fig. 3.58 Exercise 3

Fig. 3.59 Dimensions for Exercise 3

4. Working to the sizes given in Fig. 3.60 create and render the model of a clip given in Fig. 3.61.

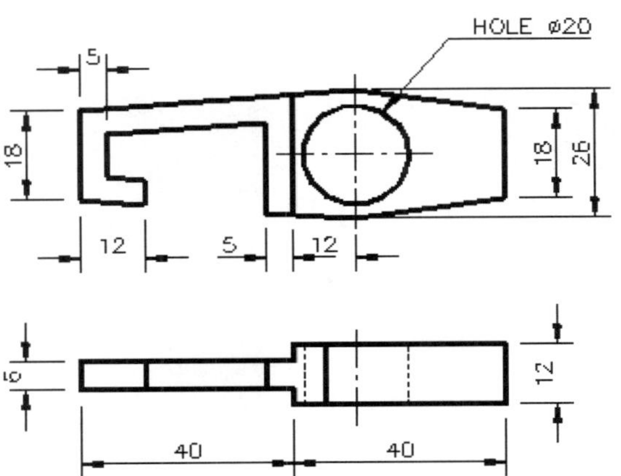

Fig. 3.60 Sizes for Exercise 4

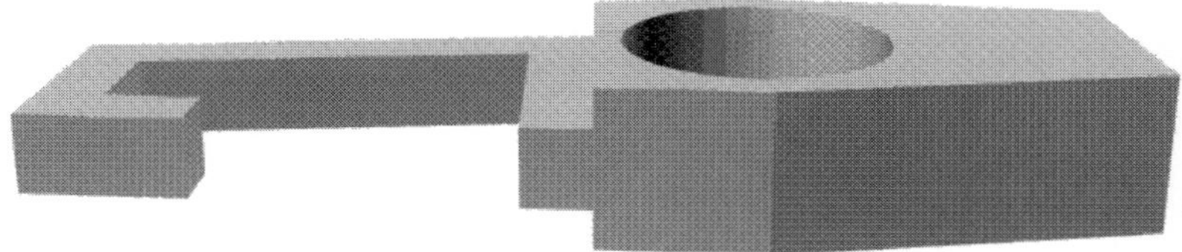
Fig. 3.61 Exercise 4

5. Figure 3.62 is a rendering of two elliptical pipes fitted to an elliptical base. The modifier **Bend** and the tool **Mirror** were used to obtain the model. Working to sizes of your own choice, create the model shown in Fig. 3.62.

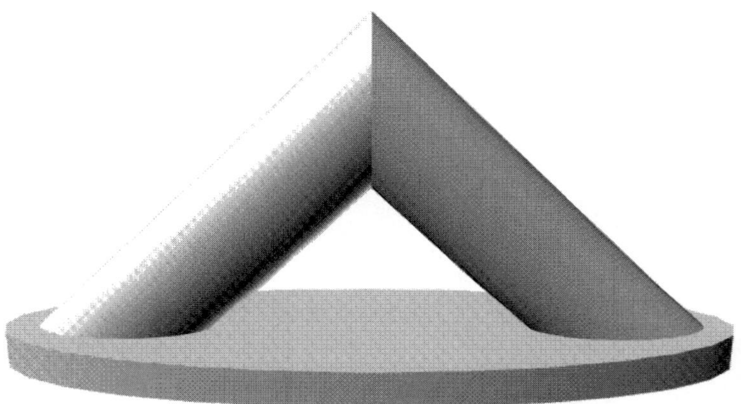
Fig. 3.62 Exercise 5

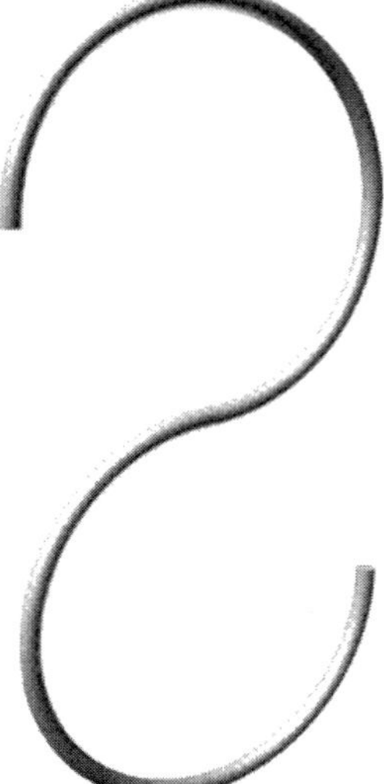
Fig. 3.63 Exercise 6

6. Figure 3.63 is a rendering of a hook lofted from a shape (a circle) and a path (a semi-circle created with **Arc**). The loft was then acted upon with **Mirror**. Create a similar 3D solid.
7. Figure 3.64 is a rendering of a U-shaped girder. The model required the use of the **Loft Object** command. Create a similar U-shaped item.

Fig. 3.64 Exercise 7

CHAPTER 4

Some tools from the toolbar

The toolbar

The toolbar is a series of icons and popup menus arranged horizontally in a bar just below the menu bar. The toolbar is too long to fit into the width of the 3D Studio Max window, so it is necessary to *drag* the bar to the left in order to allow the tools in the right-hand end of the toolbar to be used. Figure 4.1 shows the toolbar as it appears in the 3D Studio Max window upon startup and Fig. 4.2 the right-hand end of the toolbar when it has been *dragged* to the left with the **Pan** tool icon which automatically appears when the mouse cursor is placed in any space in the toolbar not occupied by tool icons.

Fig. 4.1 The left-hand end of the toolbar

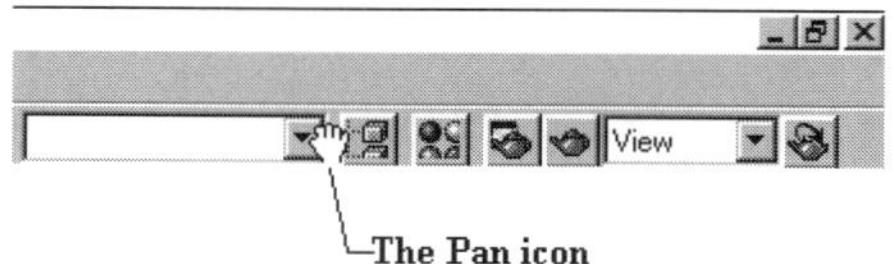

Fig. 4.2 The right-hand end of the toolbar

The tool icons in the toolbar

Help Mode

Fig. 4.3 The **Help Mode** icon

Double-click on the **Help Mode** icon (Fig. 4.3) and the **Using 3D Studio Max Help** dialogue box appears (Fig. 4.4). This gives information on using the **Help** facilities available in the software. Experiment with *left-clicks* on the buttons and the icons in the dialogue box to see the help available. Note that when any tool is in action, pressing the **F1** key of the keyboard brings a **Help** screen relating to that tool.

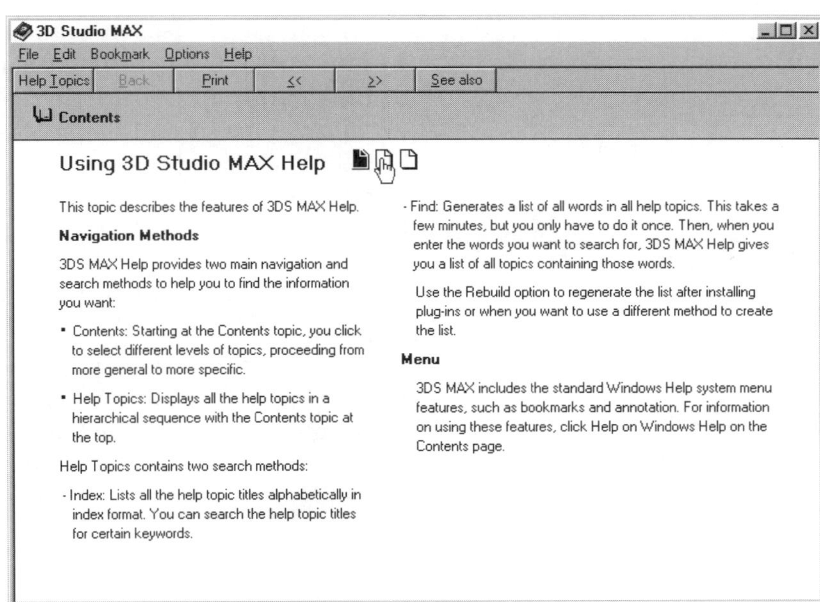

Fig. 4.4 The **Using 3D Studio Help** dialogue box

Undo

Fig. 4.5 The **Undo** icon

Left-click on the **Undo** icon (Fig. 4.5) and the last action taken by the operator is undone. The number of times **Undo** can be used is set in the **General** dialogue box of the **Preferences** dialogue box. To see this setting *left-click* on **Preferences...** in the **File** pull-down menu, followed by another on **General** in the resulting dialogue box. The figures showing in the **Undo Levels:** box of the **General** dialogue controls the number of times **Undo** can be used by repeated *left-clicks* on the **Undo** button.

Note that pressing **Ctrl+Z** keys has the same action as a *left-click* on the **Undo** icon. It is often quicker to use the keyboard shortcut than the *left-click* on the **Undo** icon when an error has been made.

Redo

Left-clicks on the **Redo** icon redoes any action performed by the use of the **Undo** button up to the full number of times set in the **Preferences** dialogue box.

Note that pressing **Ctrl+A** keys has the same effect as a *left-click* on the **Redo** button.

Fig. 4.6 The **Redo** icon

Select and Link

To demonstrate the effect of using the **Select and Link** tool (Fig. 4.7), create three shapes such as those shown in Fig. 4.8. Then:

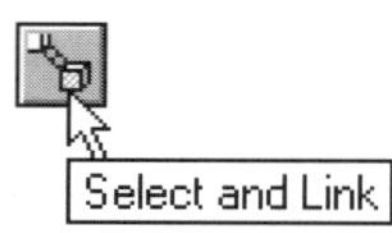

Fig. 4.7 The **Select and Link** icon

1. *Left-click* on the **Select and Link** icon to activate the tool.
2. *Drag* the cursor from one of the shapes to another. A link line and the **Link** cursor appears as the *drag* takes place.
3. *Left-click* on the second shape. The second shape is now linked to the first. The second shape is said to be the **child** of the first (which is its **parent**).
4. Now move the child of the link. It will be seen that the parent moves as well.
5. Now move the parent of the link. The child does not move with the parent.
6. Now link the third shape with the child. It, in turn, becomes the child of the original child. Check again by moving the second child. All three shapes will move together. But the first child will move with its parent independently of the second child.

The **hieratical linking** produced by the use of **Select and Link** is of value when animating parts of 3D models.

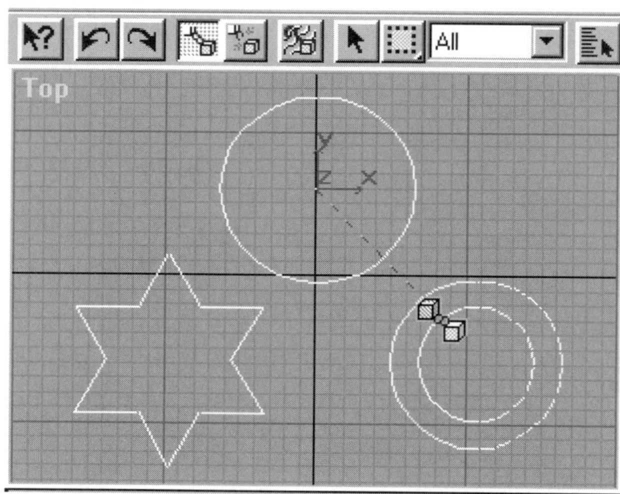

Fig. 4.8 Using **Select and Link**

Unlink Selection

Select one of the parents in a linkage, followed by a *left-click* on **Unlink Selection** (Fig. 4.9). The linkage becomes broken. Check by moving the child.

Fig. 4.9 The **Unlink Selection** icon

Bind to Space Warp

To demonstrate the use of this tool:

1. Create **Standard Primitive** – say a **GeoSphere**.
2. *Left-click* on the **Wave** button in **Space Warps** (Fig. 4.10) and create a wave – in much the same way as one would create a **Standard**

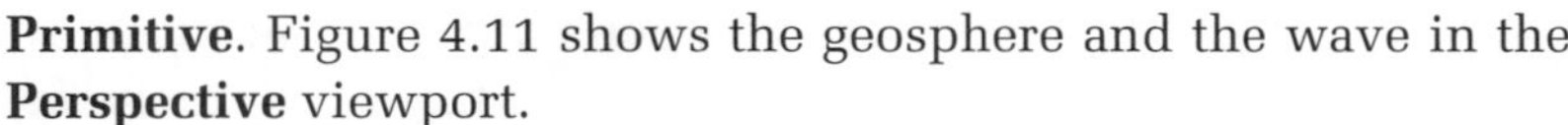

Primitive. Figure 4.11 shows the geosphere and the wave in the **Perspective** viewport.

3. Select the **Bind to Space Warp** tool icon (Fig. 4.12). Select the geosphere and *drag* the **Space Warp** icon to the wave. Figure 4.13 shows the geosphere modified to a wave form. Figure 4.13 also shows the cursor appearing when the **Bind to Space Warp** tool is in use.

Fig. 4.10 The **Space Warps**

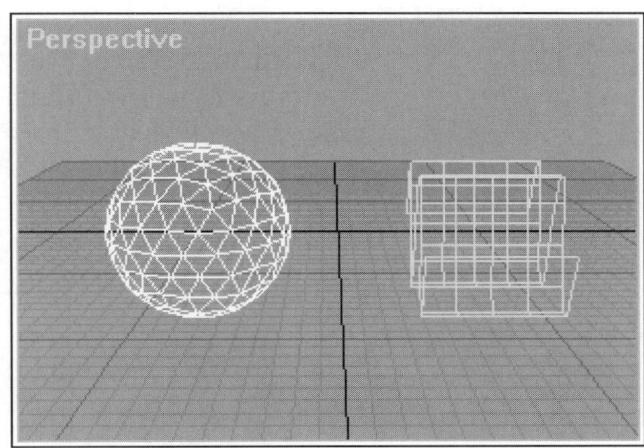

Fig. 4.11 A **GeoSphere** and a **Wave** in the **Perspective** viewport

Fig. 4.12 The **Bind to Space Warp** icon

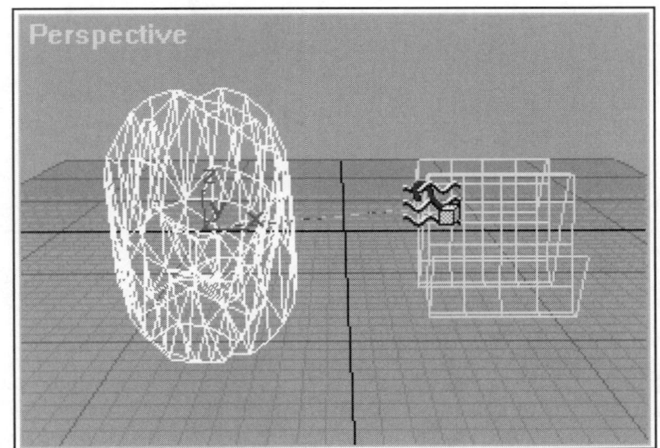

Fig. 4.13 The modified geosphere and the wave cursor

Select object

This is liable to be the tool icon most frequently used. A *left-click* on the icon, followed by another on an object and the object changes colour to white, showing that it has been selected.

When some tool icons are selected, such as **Select and Move**, **Select and Rotate**, **Select and Scale**, **Bind to Space Warp**, the **Select**

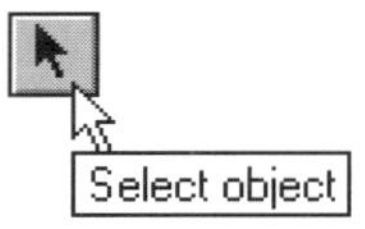

Fig. 4.14 The **Select Object** icon

object icon becomes deselected (it is no longer highlighted). This can cause confusion at times, easily overcome by a *left-click* on the **Select object** icon.

Rectangular, Circular and Fence selection icons

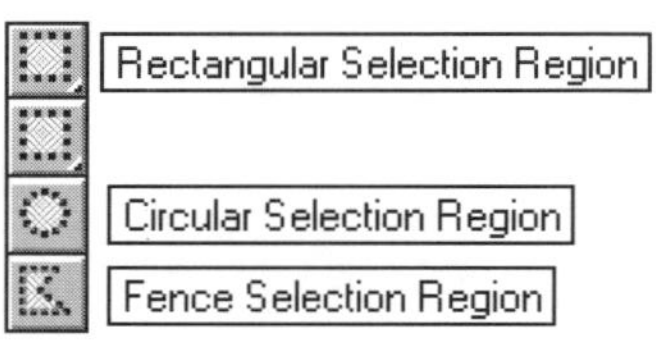

Fig. 4.15 The selection popup list

A number of objects can be selected with the aid of this group of tools (Fig. 4.15). A *left-click* on the **Rectangular Selection Region** icon allows a rectangular window to be *dragged* around the group of objects, which all turn white in colour showing they have been selected. A *left-click* on the **Circular Selection Region** allows a circle to be *dragged* around a group of objects. The **Fence Selection Region** makes use of line after line crossing or surrounding the objects. The crossed or surrounded objects become highlighted.

Fig. 4.16 The **Select by Name** icon

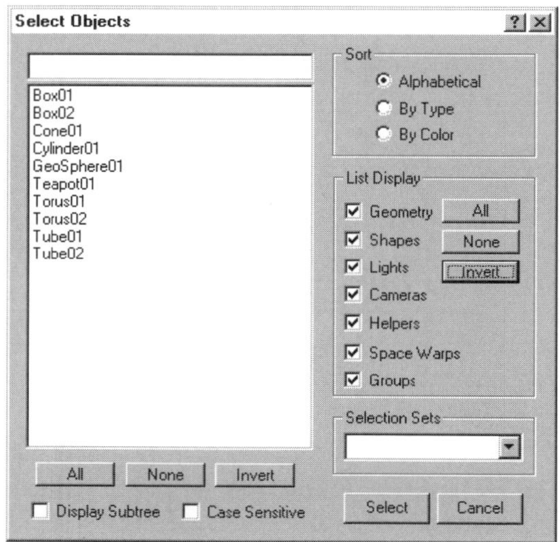

Fig. 4.17 The **Select Objects** dialogue box

Select by Name

A *left-click* on the icon (Fig. 4.16) brings up the **Select by Name** dialogue box (Fig. 4.17), from which the names of objects (and other features) can be chosen for selection by name.

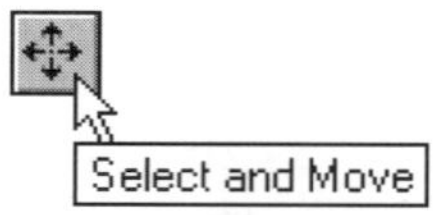

Fig. 4.18 The **Select and Move** icon

Select and Move and Select and Rotate

The two tool icons **Select and Move** and **Select and Rotate** have the same function as the **Move** and **Rotate** commands from the popup menu which appears with a *right-click* on a selected object. Each of these two tools has its own cursor type.

Fig. 4.19 The **Select and Rotate** icon

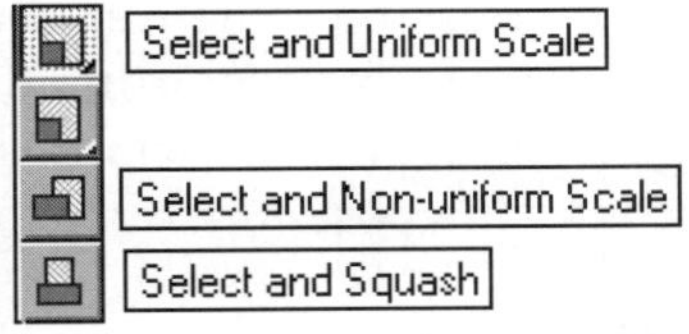

Fig. 4.20 The **Select and Scale** icons

Select and Scale

It will be remembered (see page 13) that the popup menu which comes on screen with a *right-click* on a selected object has a **Scale** command. This may be either one of the three scale tools shown in the icon flyout in Fig. 4.20. Depending upon which of the three icons has been selected, so the popup list from the *right-click* will show a uniform, a non-uniform or a squash scale. The popup list reflects the choice from the scale flyout.

It is therefore necessary to make one of the scale tools active with a *left-click* on the required tool icon if any other than the default **Select and Uniform Scale** is to be used.

Use Selection Center

Holding a *left-click* on the **Use Selection Center** icon brings down the flyout as shown in Fig. 4.21. To demonstrate how the tools on the flyout function:

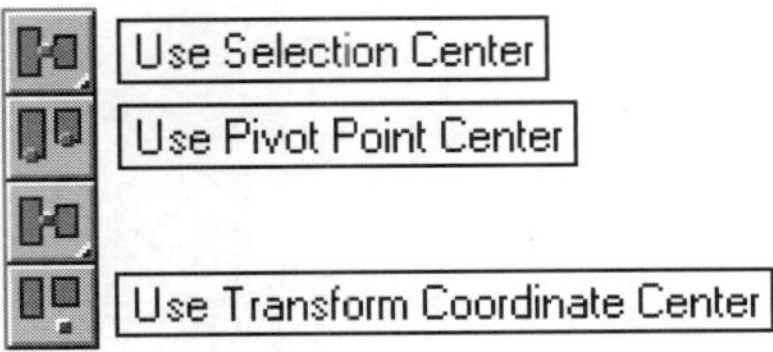

Fig. 4.21 The flyout from **Use Selection Center**

1. Create a **Line** – any length, any position.
2. Using the **Rotate** command, select the **Use Selection Center** icon and rotate the line, noting where the centre point of the rotation is.
3. Repeat item 2, but with **Use Pivot Point Center** selected, again noting where the centre point of the rotation lies.
4. Repeat item 2, but with the **Use Transfer Coordinate Center** tool active. Again note the centre of rotation.

Restrict to X (Y or Z)

Fig. 4.22 The **Restrict to X** icon

Left-click on the **Restrict to X** icon (Fig. 4.22) and then on any object in each viewport in turn, noting the changes which take place in the triads showing the directions of the X, Y and Z axes.

Repeat with the **Restrict to Y** tool active and also with the **Restrict to Z** tool active.

Restrict to XY Plane

Hold a *left-click* on the **Restrict to XY Plane** icon. A flyout appears as in Fig. 4.34.

Fig. 4.23 The **Restrict to Planes** flyout

Experiment with the four tools on the flyout in the same way as with the experiments with the **Restrict to X** and other coordinate direction tools, noting the changes to the X, Y and Z triads denoting the directions of the coordinate axes in each viewport.

Inverse Kinematics On/Off Toggle

The uses for this tool will be discussed later in connection with animation of 3D models.

Mirror

Create a simple 3D model such as that shown in Fig. 4.24. Then select the model, followed by a *left-click* on the **Mirror** icon (Fig. 4.25). The **Mirror Screen Coordinates** dialogue box appears as shown. In the example given the model was mirrored with **Copy** along the **X** axis **Offset** by 100 units

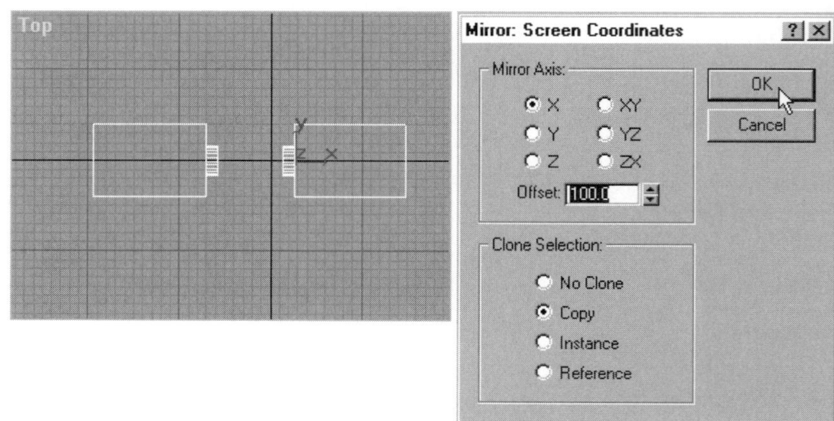

Fig. 4.24 An example of the action of **Mirror**

Array

Fig. 4.25 The **Mirror** icon

Figure 4.26 shows the flyout from holding a *left-click* on the **Array** icon. The **Snapshot** tool is concerned mainly with animations, so does not concern us at the moment. With **Array** in action objects can be arrayed in rows along coordinate axes at predetermined distances from the object being arrayed. In order to create an array:

1. Select the object (or group) to be arrayed and *left-click* on the **Array** icon.
2. The **Array** dialogue box appears. Make entries as required in the dialogue box and *left-click* on its **OK** button (Fig. 4.27).
3. The array configured in the **Array** dialogue box is created (Fig. 4.28).

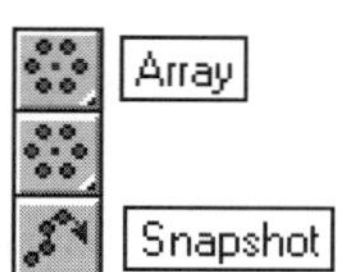

Fig. 4.26 The **Array** icon

Array

Array Transformation: Screen Coordinates (Use Pivot Point Center)

X Y Z

Move 50.0 50.0 50.0 units

Rotate 0.0 0.0 0.0 degrees Re-Orient

Scale 100.0 100.0 100.0 percent Uniform

Type of Object

Copy

Instance

Reference

Total in Array: 4

Reset OK Cancel

Fig. 4.27 The **Array** dialogue box as configured for Fig. 4.27

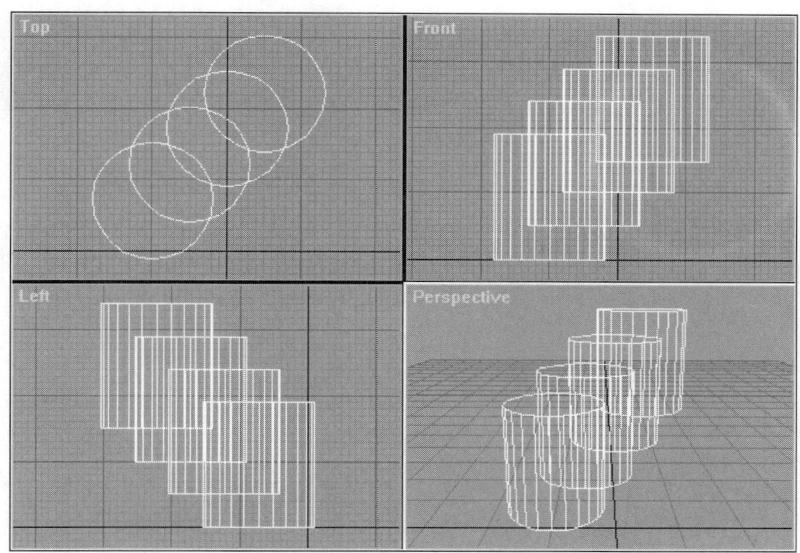

Fig. 4.28 An example of the use of the **Array** tool

Align

Experiment with the **Align** tool (Fig. 4.29) as indicated in Fig. 4.30.

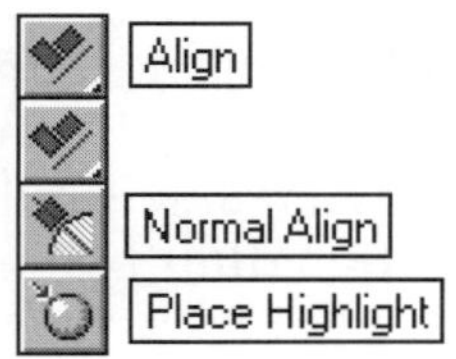

Fig. 4.29 The **Align** icon and flyout

1. Create a **Tube** and a **Cylinder** to any size as shown.
2. Select the cylinder.
3. *Left-click* on **Align**. The **Align** cursor appears. *Drag* it onto the cylinder and *left-click*. The **Align Selection** dialogue box appears.
4. Experiment with the check circles and check boxes, watching the position of the cylinder as the experimentation proceeds. It will be seen that the cylinder can be aligned with respect to any of the coordinate axes.

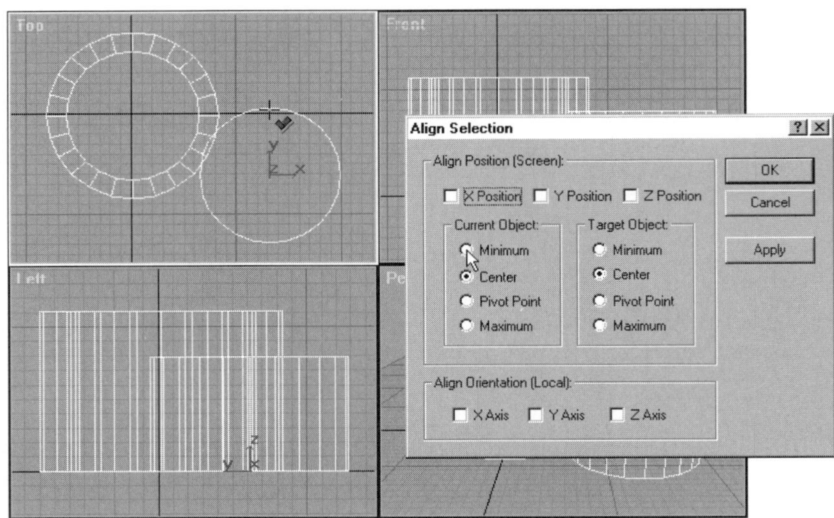

Fig. 4.30 Experimenting with **Align**

Normal Align

Selecting this icon allows the operator to change the directions of the coordinate axes of an object. The cursor (Fig. 4.31) comes on screen when the icon is selected.

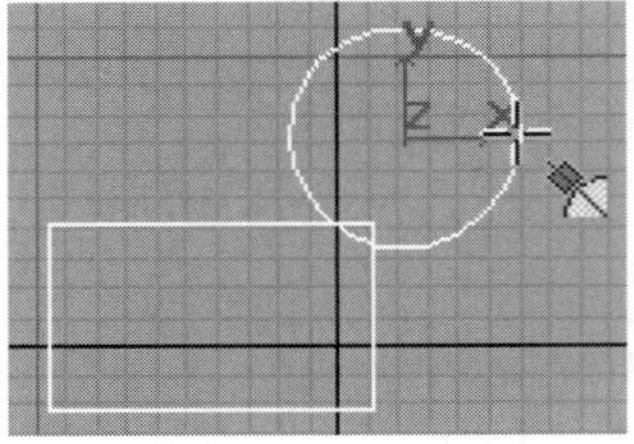

Fig. 4.31 The **Normal Align** cursor

Place Highlight

Select the icon and move the cursor onto an object in a viewport and *click* and the object highlights – changes to white.

Track View

A *left-click* on the icon (Fig. 4.32) brings a **Track View** dialogue box on screen. Because this tool and its dialogue box are available in connection with animations, the uses of the tool will be described in the chapter dealing with animations (Chapter 10).

Fig. 4.32 The **Track View** icon

Material Editor

A *left-click* on the **Material Editor** icon (Fig. 4.33) brings up the **Material Editor** dialogue box (Fig. 4.34). With the aid of the dialogue box, new materials can be created, existing materials amended and existing materials examined. More about the **Material Editor** in the chapters on rendering (Chapters 9 and 11).

Fig. 4.33 The **Material Editor** icon

The Render icons

We have already used **Quick Render** for rendering of examples from previous chapters. The only difference between **Render Scene** and

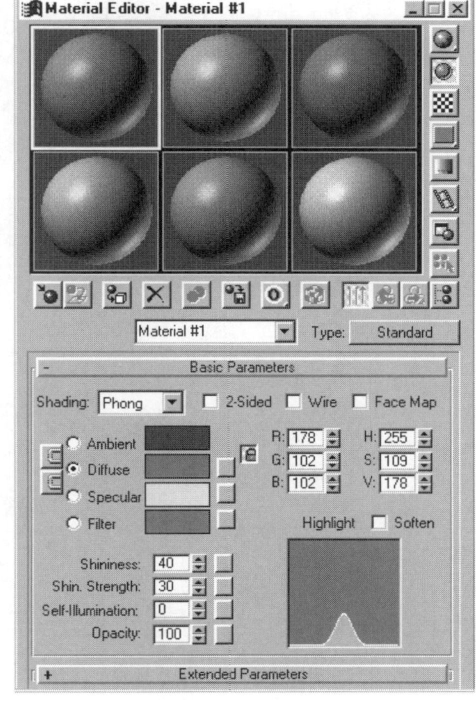

Fig. 4.34 The **Material Editor**

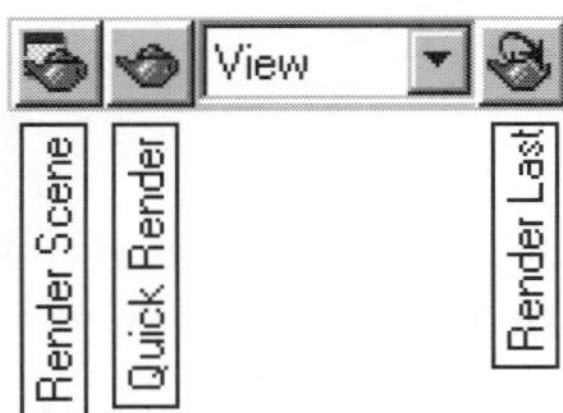

Fig. 4.35 The set of **Render** icons

Quick Render is that a *left-click* on **Render Scene** brings up the **Render Scene** dialogue box (Fig. 4.36) in which parameters for the rendering are set. **Quick Render** does not bring the dialogue box on screen, but renders to parameters previously set, or accepts the default settings. The default settings have been accepted in the renderings shown in previous chapters.

Render Last, as its name implies brings back the last scene to be rendered onto the screen.

The View popup list

Lying between the **Render Scene** and **Quick Render** icons is the popup list shown in Fig. 4.37. When any other than **View** or **Selected** of the choices in the list are made, the **Render Scene** dialogue box does not come on screen when the **Render Scene** icon is selected until a broken line window delimiting the area to be a **Region** or **a Blowup** has been made. The broken line window comes up when either of these two choices is made. The window can be manipulated with the aid of the mouse to cover the **Region** or **Blowup** to be rendered. Then pressing the **Return** key of the keyboard brings up the **Render Scene** dialogue box.

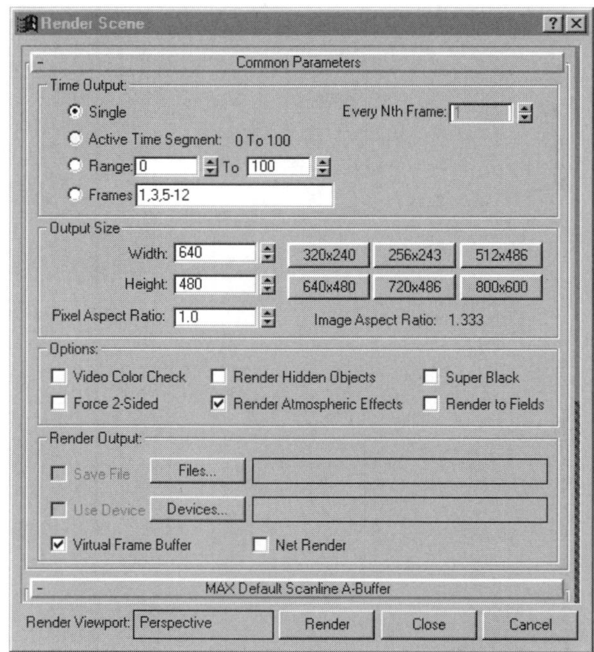

Fig. 4.36 The **Render Scene** dialogue box

Fig. 4.37 The **View** popup list

Exercises

1. Figure 4.38 is a rendering of a steel gate. Create the gate to the dimensions given in Fig. 4.39 and render the resulting 3D model.

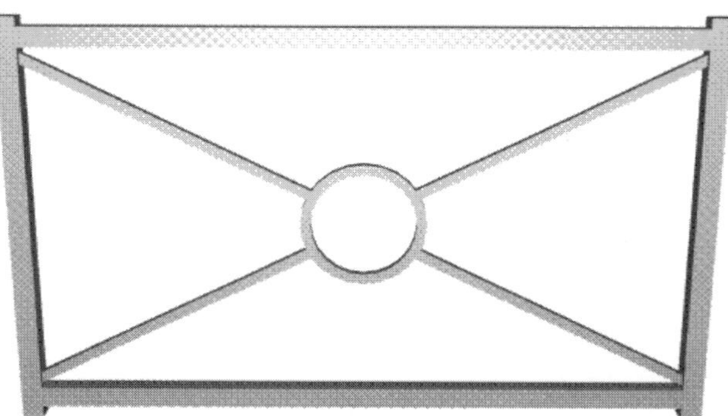

Fig. 4.38 Exercise 1

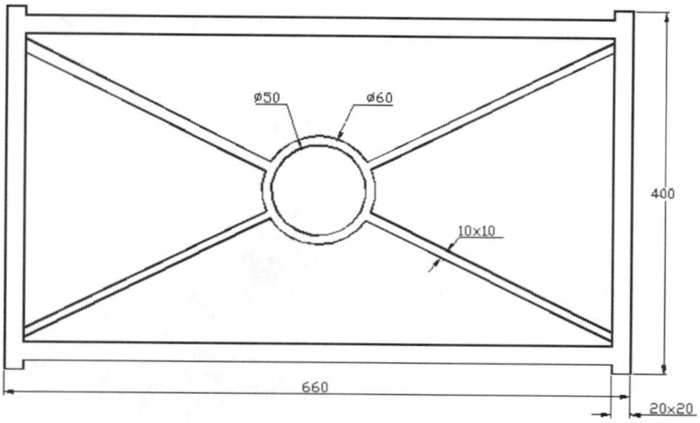

Fig. 4.39 Dimensions for Exercise 1

2. Figure 4.40 is a rendering of a model of a wall light. Figure 4.40 includes dimensions to which the wall light was created. Create and render the model.

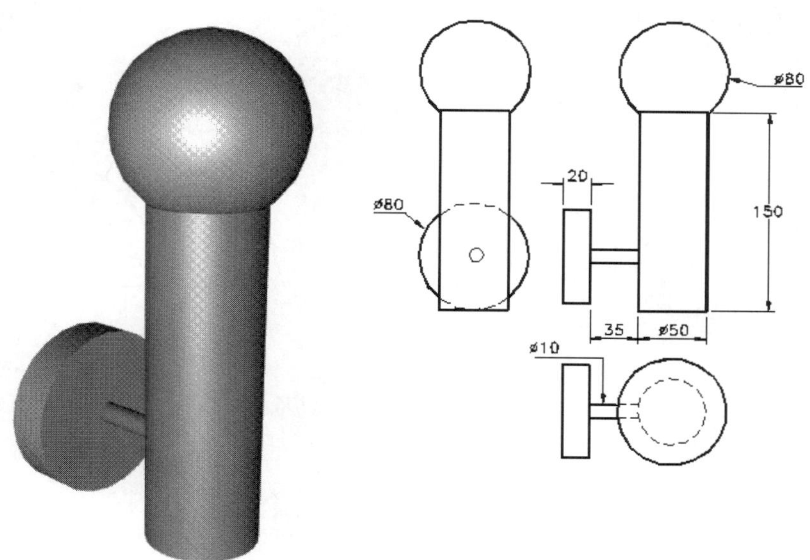

Fig. 4.40 Exercise 2 and the dimensions for Exercise 2

3. Working to the dimensions given in Fig. 4.42 construct the model, a rendering of which is given in Fig. 4.41.

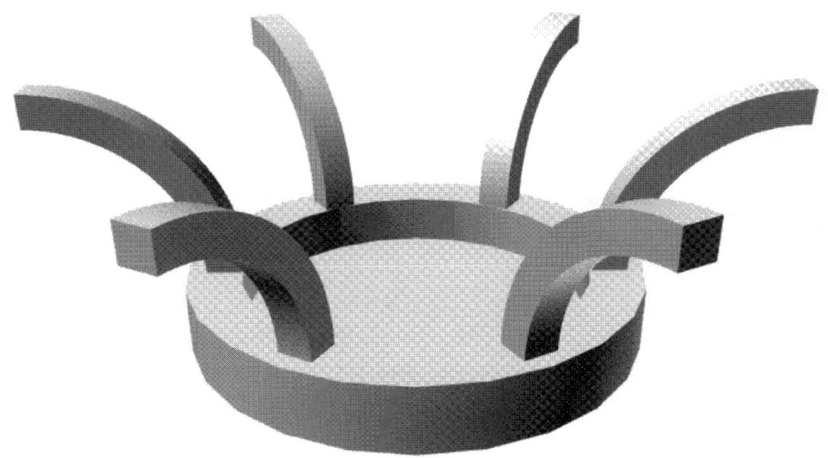

Fig. 4.41 Exercise 3

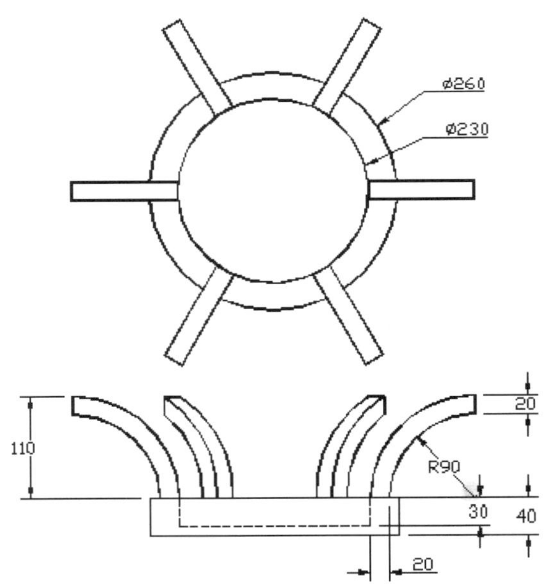

Fig. 4.42 Dimensions for Exercise 3

4. Figure 4.43 is a rendering of a model of a plastic box with lid created and rendered in 3D Studio Max. Create the model to the dimensions given in Fig. 4.44 and render your completed model.

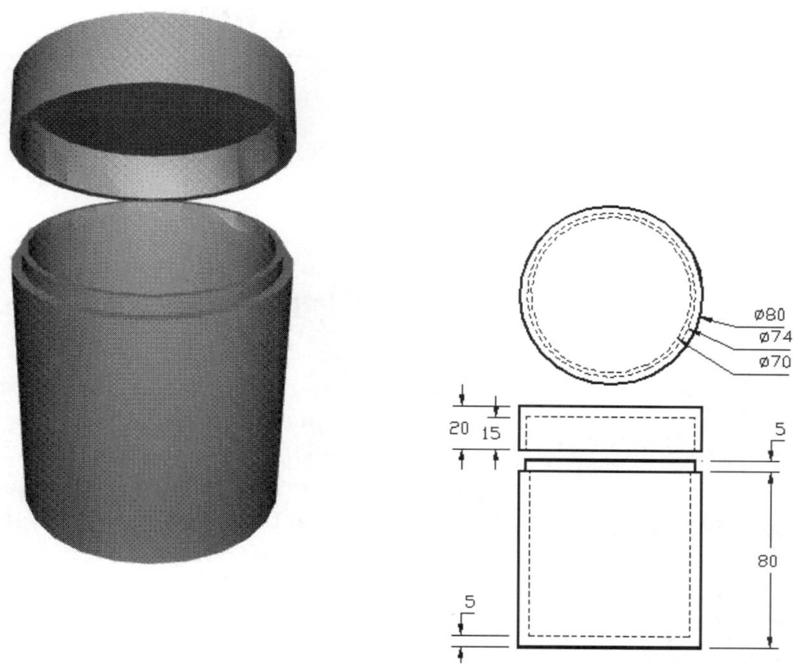

Fig. 4.43 Exercise 4

Fig. 4.44 Dimensions for Exercise 4

5. Figure 4.46 is a rendering of five cups created and rendered in 3D Studio Max to the dimensions given of the one cup in Fig. 4.45. Create and render the group of cups.

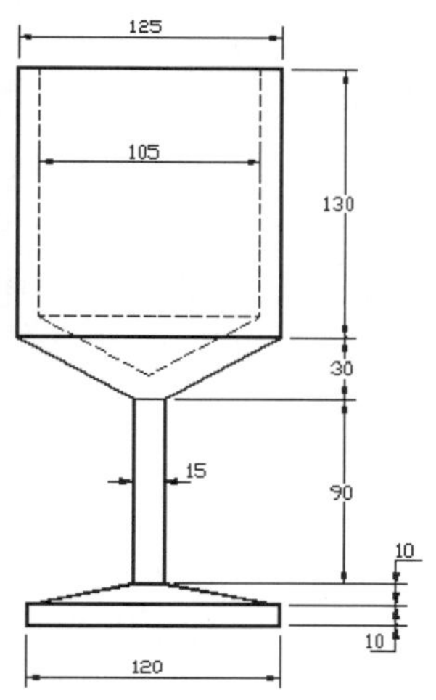

Fig. 4.46 Dimensions for Exercise 5

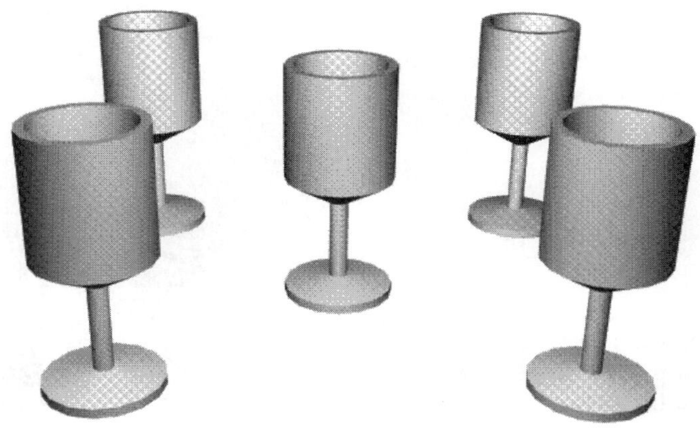

Fig. 4.45 Exercise 5

CHAPTER 5

Importing, viewing and exporting

Imports

A number of different file types can be imported into 3D Studio Max. Select **Import...** from the **File** pull-down menu (Fig. 5.1). The **Select File to Import** dialogue box comes up (Fig. 5.2). The types of file it is possible to import are seen with a *left-click* on the arrow button in the box opposite **Files of type:**. The **Files of type** popup list appears (Fig. 5.3). In these last two illustrations the AutoCAD drawing type (***.dwg**) has been selected. Once the type of file has been chosen from the popup list, followed by selection of the directory from which the file is to be imported, a file list appears in the dialogue box as indicated in Fig. 5.2.

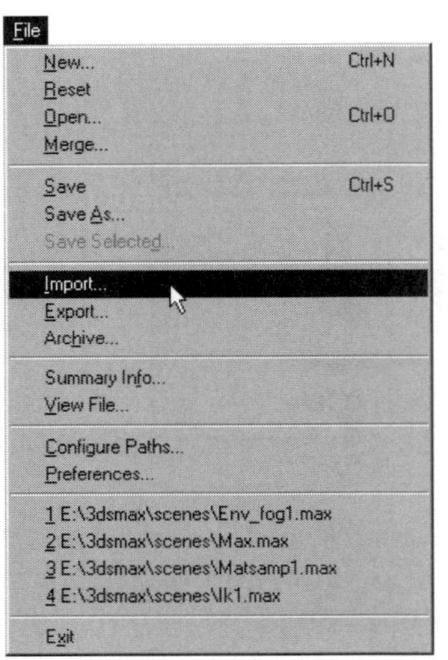

Fig. 5.1 Selecting **Import...** from the **File** pull-down menu

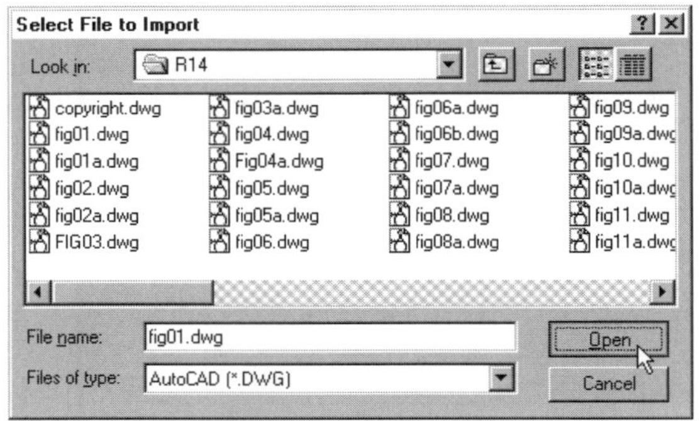

Fig. 5.2 The **Select File to Import** dialogue box

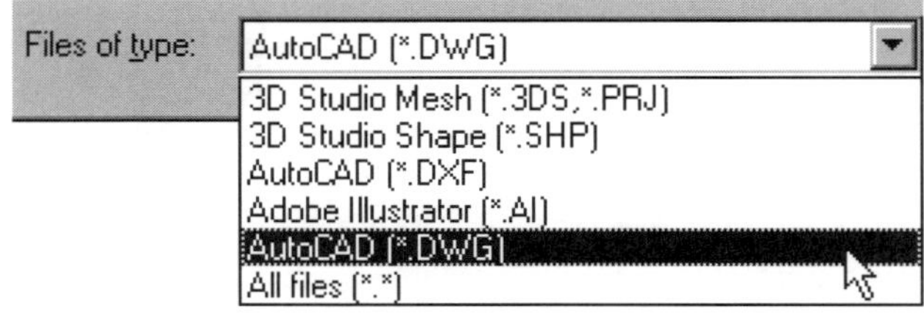

Fig. 5.3 The **Files of Type:** popup list from the **Select File to Import** dialogue box

Importing a file

In the example given in Fig. 5.2 the file **c:\R14\fig01.dwg** has been selected. *Left-click* on the **OK** button of the dialogue box and a second dialogue box, **Import Options** (Fig. 5.4), appears. Set check circles for the options within the dialogue box and *left-click* on **OK**. The drawing file loads into 3D Studio Max. Figure 5.5 shows the drawing as it is seen in 3D Studio Max.

The AutoCAD drawing was of a solid model which has AutoVis lights and material included. The lights show up in the 3D Studio Max screen and if the model is rendered, it will be seen that the lights

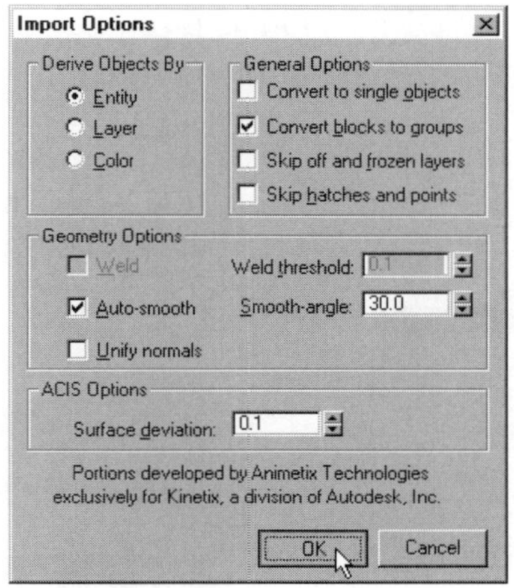

Fig. 5.4 The **Import Options** dialogue box

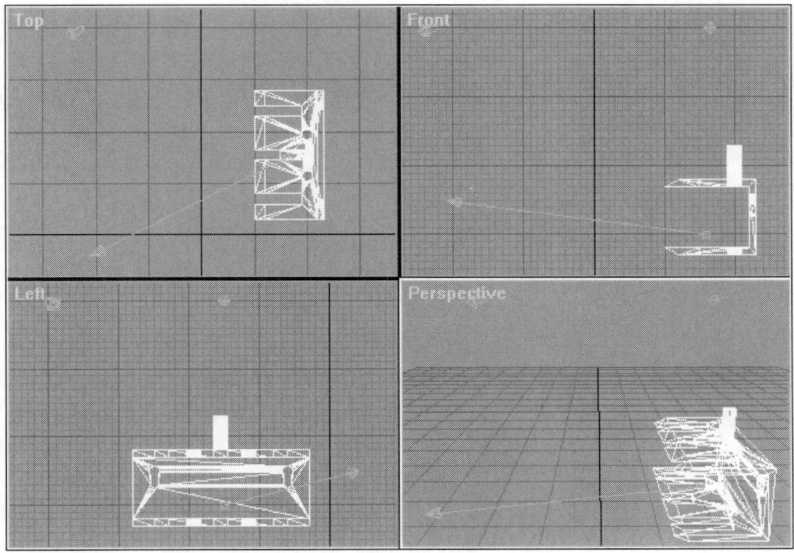

Fig. 5.5 The 3D Studio Max viewports when an AutoCAD drawing has been imported

are operative. Materials have, however, been lost. If required, materials can be added to the model from the material libraries in 3D Studio Max.

Note: The only files that can be imported are 3D Studio files, Adobe Illustrator files, AutoCAD drawing files or Data Exchange files of the DXF type. Most CAD systems will allow the saving of drawing files to a DXF format and these can be imported into 3D Studio Max. Once imported the data can be saved in the 3DS Studio Max format – ***.max.**

Fig. 5.6 Selecting **View File...** from the **File** pull-down menu

Viewing a file

Other types of graphic files can be viewed in 3D Studio Max, but only viewed – they cannot be saved. If an attempt to save is made, the resulting file will not carry any usable data.

To view a graphic file select **View File...** from the **File** pull-down menu (Fig. 5.6). The **View File** dialogue box appears (Fig. 5.7). The **List files of type** popup list (Fig. 5.8) shows the types of graphics files which can be viewed.

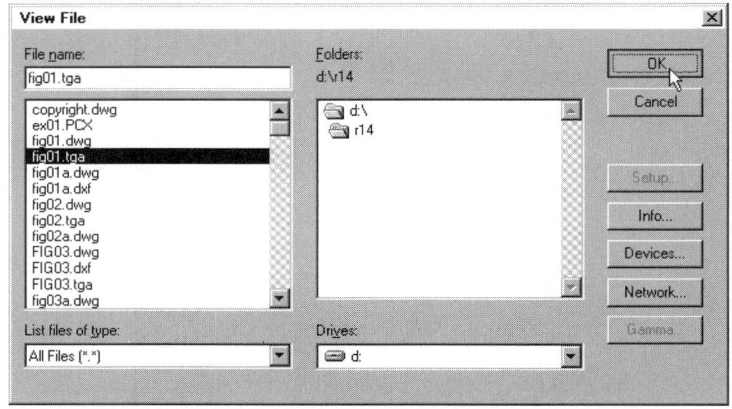

Fig. 5.7 The **View File** dialogue box

Figure 5.9 shows the rendering of the same 3D solid model which was used to show the importing of an AutoCAD drawing file (Fig. 5.5). The model was created in AutoCAD Release 13, then in AutoVis, the solid was rendered after lights and material had been added to the scene containing the model and then saved as a file of the ***.tga** type in AutoVis. Because the file is of a **Targa Image File** type, the colours of the AutoVis lighting and materials is retained when viewed in 3D Studio Max.

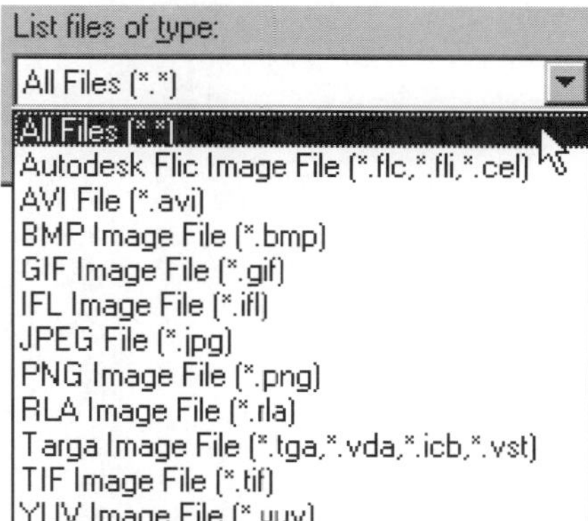

Fig. 5.8 The **List files of type:** popup list of the **View File** dialogue box

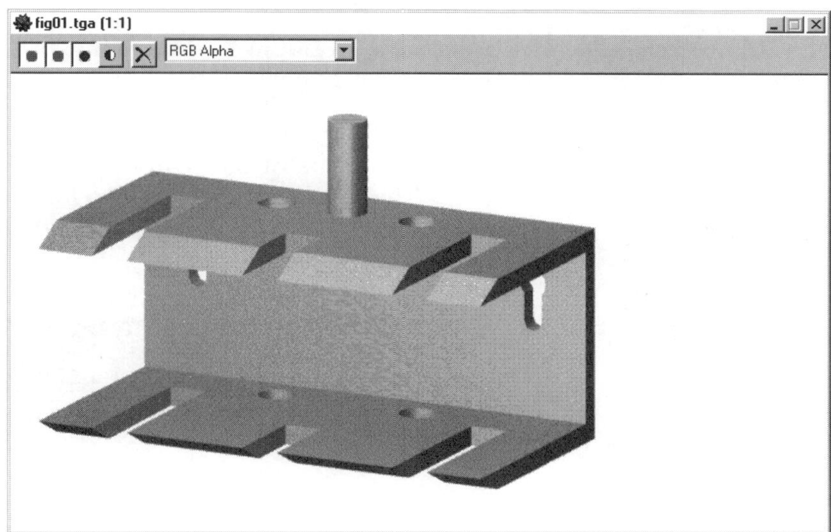

Fig. 5.9 The *.tga file viewed in 3D Studio Max

Importing 3D Studio files

3D Studio files of the type ***.3ds** can be imported into 3D Studio Max. This allows those operators who have a number of 3DS files to continue using them when working with Max. After importing ***.3ds** files, they can be saved to the Max format ***.max** for further use or modification.

To import a ***.3ds** file, proceed in the same manner as when importing an AutoCAD ***.dwg** file, except that the **3D Studio Mesh (*.3DS,*.PRJ)** file type is chosen from the **File of type** popup list. Before the mesh can be imported, selection of replacing or adding to the current scene must be made from the **3DS Import** dialogue box (Fig. 5.10) which appears when a 3DS file has been selected from the **Import** dialogue box.

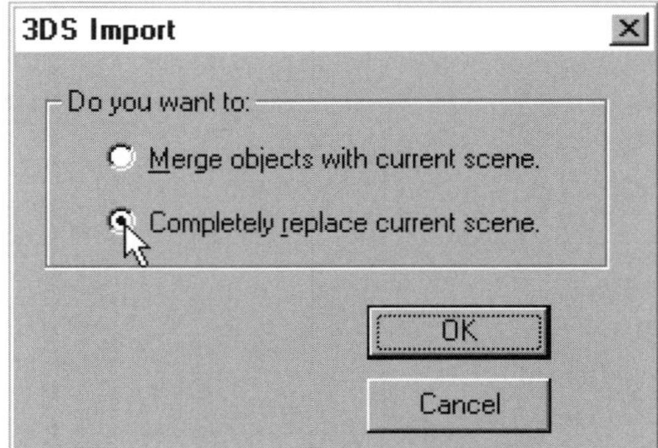

Fig. 5.10 The **3DS Import** dialogue box

Examples of importing files

Example 1 – importing an AutoCAD outline drawing

1. Construct the outline. Figure 5.11 shows the outline for this example as constructed in AutoCAD Release 13. The outline has been constructed with the tools **Polyline**, **Fillet**, **Trim** and **Array**. The whole outline was then formed into a single polyline with the aid of the tool **Polyline Edit** (Pedit). The file was saved to the filename outline05.dwg.

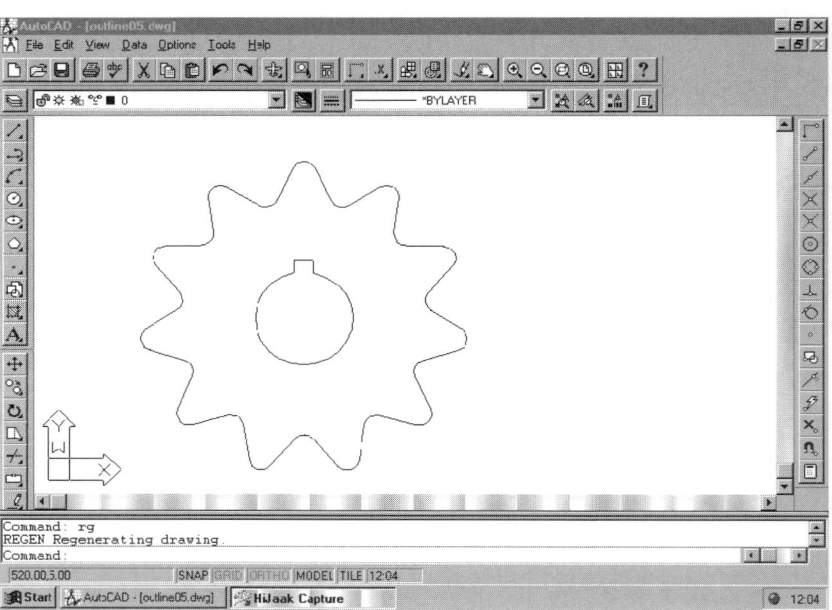

Fig. 5.11 Example 1 – the outline constructed in AutoCAD Release 13

2. In 3D Studio Max, import the file using the **AutoCAD *.DWG** file type.

3. In the **Import Options** dialogue box ensure that the two check circles against **Layer** and **Weld** are set on (dot in circles) – Fig. 5.12. If these parameters are not set, the outline, with its many vertices, cannot be acted upon by the modifiers in 3D Studio Max to give correct results.

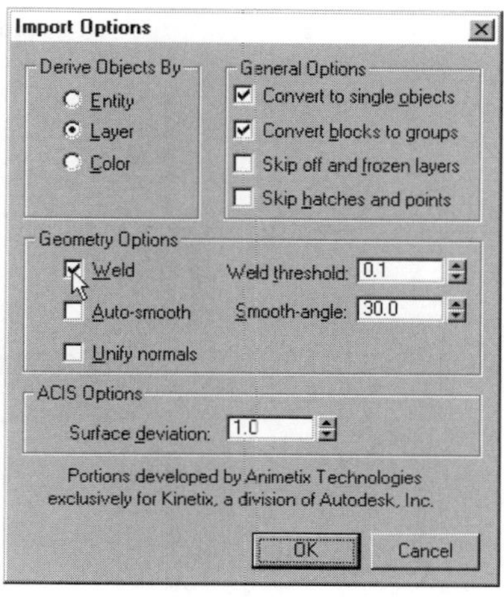

Fig. 5.12 Example 1 – settings in the **Import Options** dialogue box

4. The outline appears in the viewports of Max (Fig. 5.13).
5. Select the modifier **Extrude** and set parameters as shown in Fig. 5.13.
6. Set the viewport configuration to show a **User** viewport in place of the **Perspective** viewport – in the **View** pull-down menu, select **Viewport Configuration....** This changes the perspective view into a parallel isometric view. This was carried out for this example

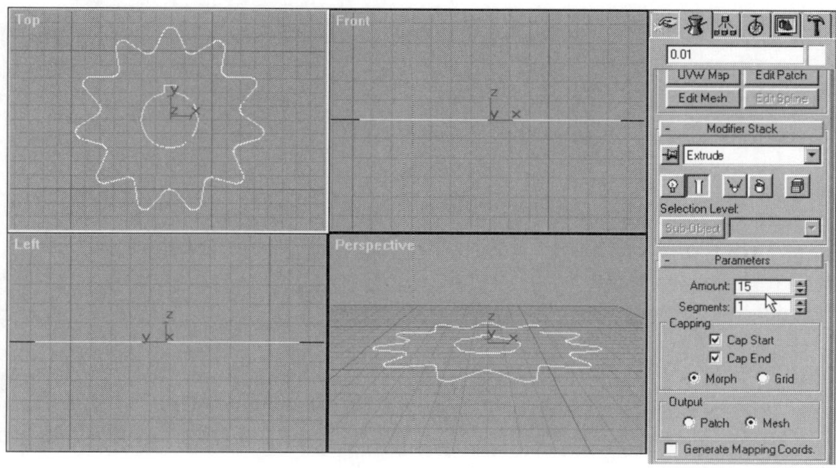

Fig. 5.13 Example 1 – the AutoCAD outline as it appears in 3D Studio Max when imported

because it shows the shape of the 3D model more clearly than in a perspective view.

7. Render the **User** viewport with **Quick Render**. The result is shown in Fig. 5.14.

Fig. 5.14 Example 1 – a rendering

Example 2 – importing an AutoCAD 3D solid model

1. The 3D solid model is first constructed in AutoCAD and saved to the filename **trailer_pin.dwg**.
2. Using **Import...** from the **File** pull-down menu import the file into 3D Studio Max – Fig. 5.15.

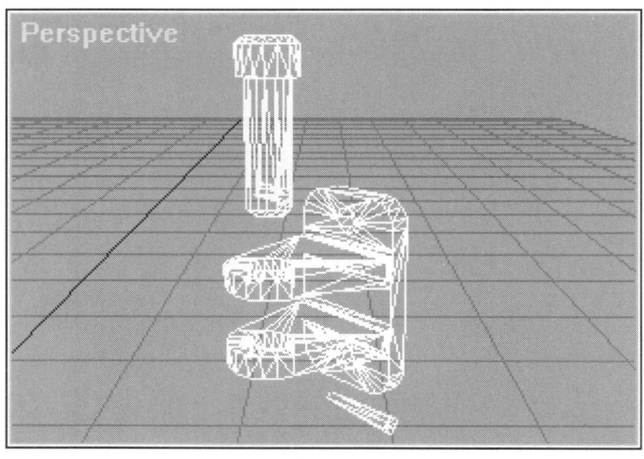

Fig. 5.15 Example 2 – the AutoCAD solid model drawing as seen in the **Perspective** viewport

3. The model can now be rendered as required. No modification was required before this example could be rendered.

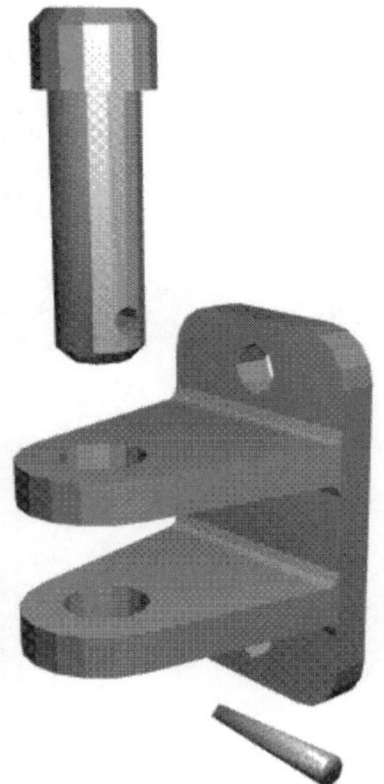

Fig. 5.16 Example 2 – a rendering of the solid model

Example 3 – importing a 3D Studio file

1. This example is of a group of objects which had been created in 3D Studio and saved as a ***.3DS** file. The file was imported as such into 3D Studio Max.
2. Figure 5.17 shows the objects of this import in the **Top** viewport of Max. Figure 5.18 shows a rendering with **Quick Render** (using default lighting etc.) of the objects in the **Perspective** viewport.

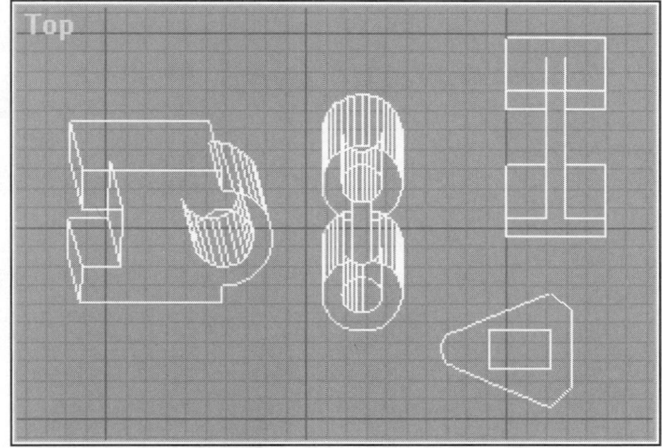

Fig. 5.17 Example 3 – the **Top** viewport view of the 3DS file imported into 3D studio Max

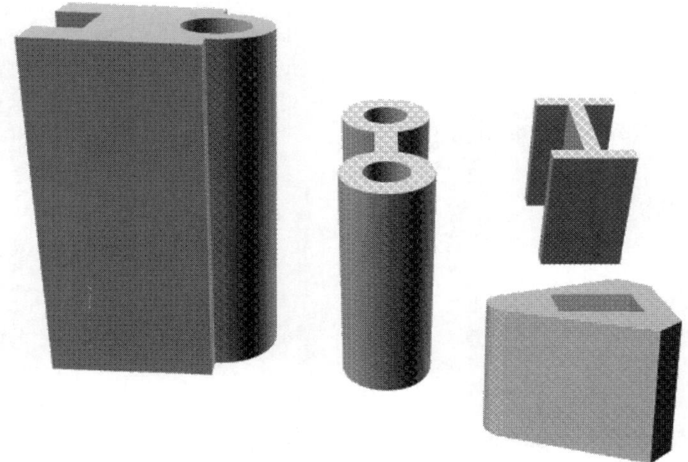

Fig. 5.18 Example 3 – a rendering in the **Perspective** viewport

Example 4 – importing a shape file (*.shp)

3D Studio *.SHP files are 2D outline only files constructed in the **Shaper** program of the software. When imported into 3D Studio Max, they can be acted upon by the modifiers as required. Figure

5.19 shows a *.SHP file selected for importing into 3D Studio Max. Figure 5.20 shows the shape file in the **Top** viewport. Figure 5.21 is a rendering of the *.SHP file after being extruded and two box 'sides' added to complete a 3D model in the **Perspective** viewport.

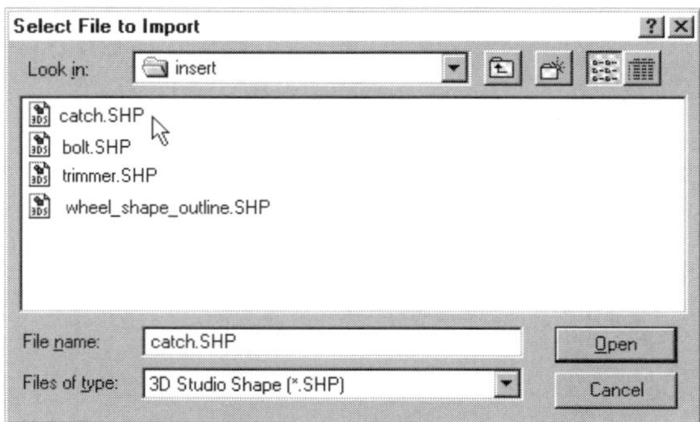

Fig. 5.19 A 3D Studio *.SHP file selected for importing into 3D Studio Max

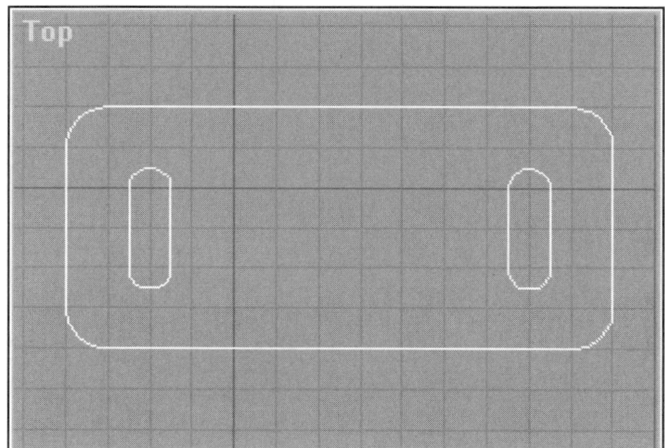

Fig. 5.20 The shape file as seen in the **Top** viewport in 3D Studio Max

Fig. 5.21 The 3D model created from the shape file

Exporting files

Models created in 3D Studio Max can be exported in one of three formats – 3D Studio (*.3DS); AutoCAD (*.DWG) or AutoCAD DXF (*.DXF) formats as indicated in Fig. 5.22. The DXF format, although originated by Autodesk, the manufacturers of AutoCAD, is used very widely in CAD (Computer Aided Design) software packages. This means that no matter what CAD package you are using, it is usually possible to export 3D Studio Max model data to a CAD package in DXF format.

Example – exporting to *.DWG format

1. Create the model to be exported in 3D Studio Max.
2. Select **Export...** from the **File** pull-down menu. The **Select File to Export** dialogue box appears (Fig. 5.22).

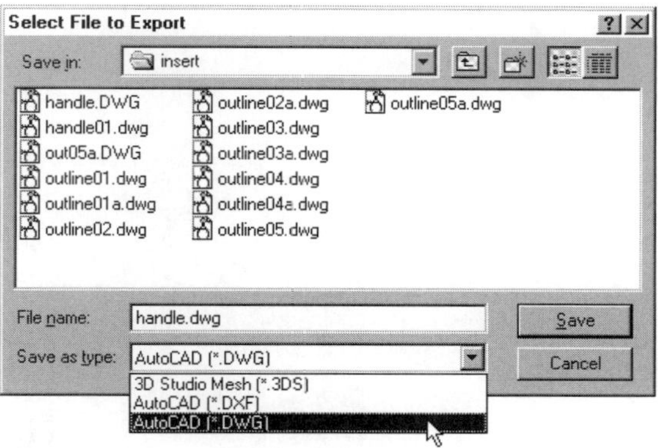

Fig. 5.22 The **Select File to Export** dialogue box

3. *Left-click* in the **Save as type:** box to bring up the popup list shown in Fig. 5.22. Select **AutoCAD (*.DWG)** from the popup list.
4. *Enter* the required filename in the **File name:** box of the dialogue box, followed by a *left-click* on the **OK** button.
5. The **DWG Export File Current 3D Studio Max Frame** dialogue box appears as shown in Fig. 5.23. Set the check circles as required. Figure 5.23 is a fairly common example of the settings required.
6. *Left-click* on the **OK** button of the dialogue box and the file is saved to the name *entered* in the **File name:** box of the **Select File to Export** dialogue box.

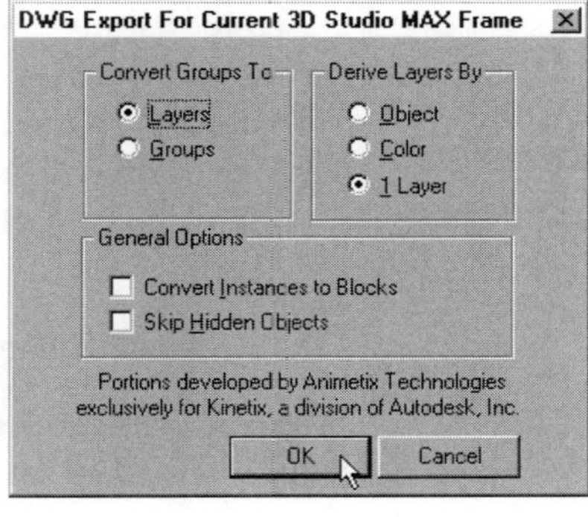

Fig. 5.23 The **DWG Export File Current 3D Studio Max Frame** dialogue box

Figure 5.24 shows the model created in Max and Fig. 5.25 the drawing which has been exported to AutoCAD Release 13, opened in Release 13. It should be noted that it is only to Release 13 that the *.DWG file data can be exported. If using other releases of AutoCAD or another software package it is best to use the export to file name of type ***.DXF**.

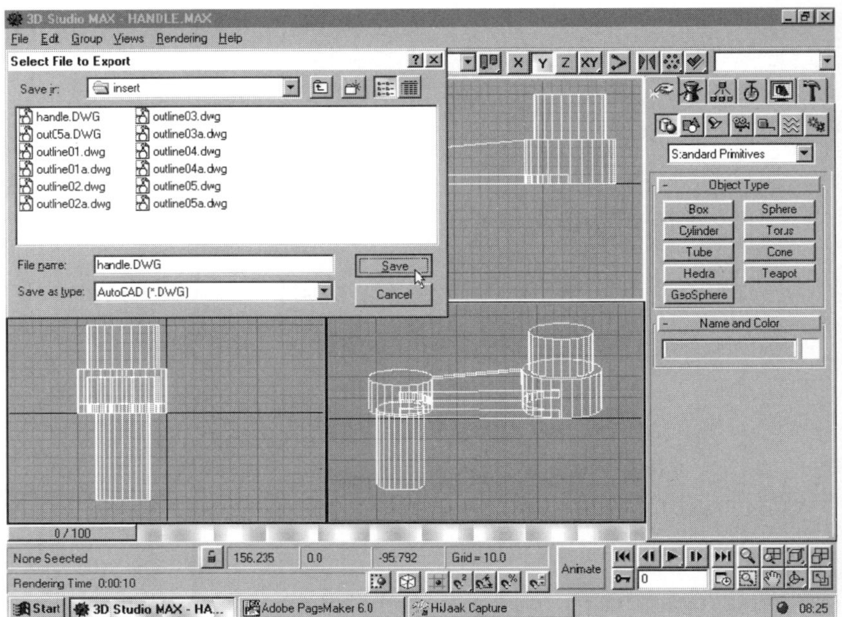

Fig. 5.24 Saving a model created in 3D Studio Max as an AutoCAD *.DWG file

Notes

1. If a DXF file is opened in AutoCAD, the AutoCAD window must be opened as a **New** drawing area. If this precaution is not observed, parts of a 3D model may not load.
2. Although a model exported to AutoCAD may look somewhat different when opened in AutoCAD to a model created in AutoCAD itself, the file so exported can be used in a similar manner, as can a native AutoCAD file, in that it can be printed, hidden lines can be hidden with the AutoCAD tool **Hide** etc.. However, the parts of the AutoCAD drawing exported from 3D Studio Max are not correct AutoCAD solids, so they cannot be acted upon by the Boolean operators of AutoCAD.

Archiving

Some 3D Studio Max files can be very large. To save disk space a drawing can be saved in an archived form. If a file is to be saved in

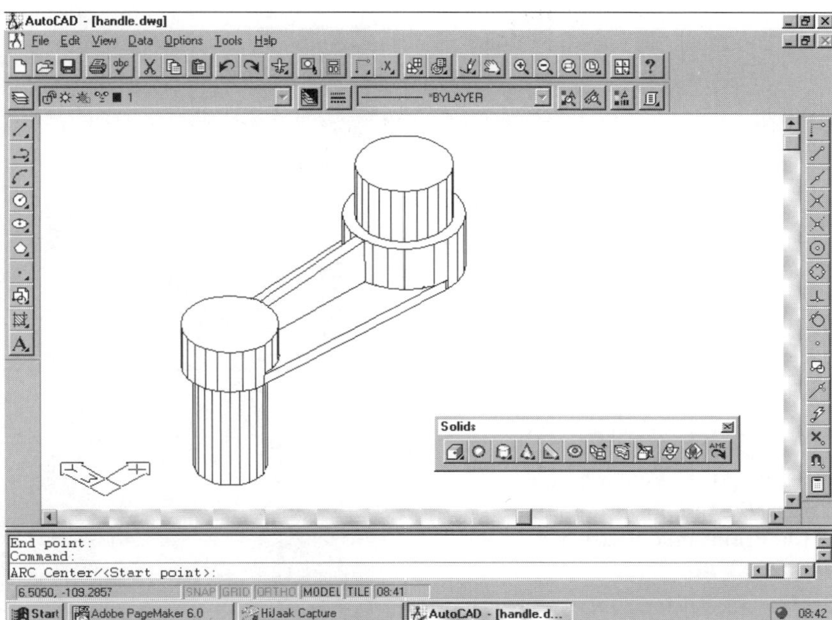

Fig. 5.25 The file created in 3D Studio Max exported to AutoCAD Release 13

a zipped form – archived to a smaller file size, then select the **Archive...** command from the **File** pull-down menu. The **File Archive** dialogue box (Fig. 5.26) appears. Select the directory in which the zipped file is to be saved from the **Save in:** box; *enter* the required file name in the **File name:** box and *left-click* on the **OK** button. The file will saved to the selected directory with the file name extension ***.zip**. The file will be considerably less in size depending upon the archiving software in use.

It must be noted that the archiving software used for this purpose must be *entered* in the **Files** dialogue box of the **Preference Settings** group of boxes. Figure 5.27 shows an example of this.

Fig. 5.26 Saving a file in an archived form

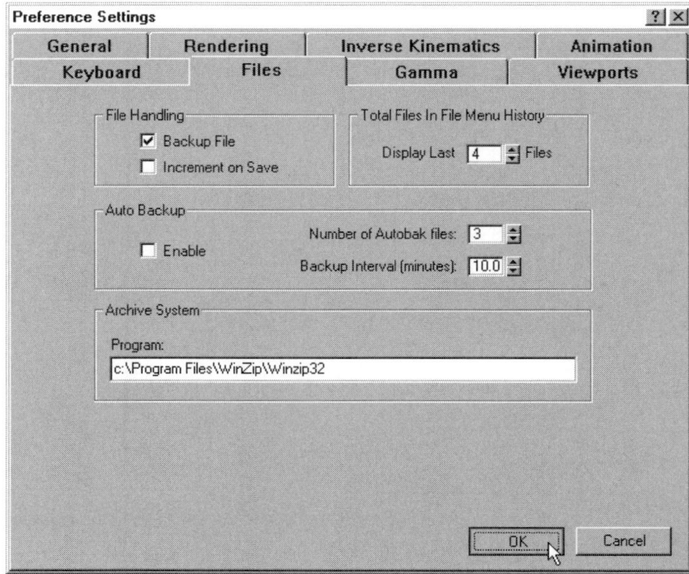

Fig. 5.27 An entry made in the **Arhive System Program** box of the **Preference Settings** dialogue box

Some experiments

Example 1 – the menu in viewports

Right-click on the name at the top left of any viewport. A menu appears showing a number of options available for adjusting features in the viewport. In Fig. 5.28 in a **User** viewport, **Smooth + Highlight** has been turned on (tick against the words) and **Show Grid** has been

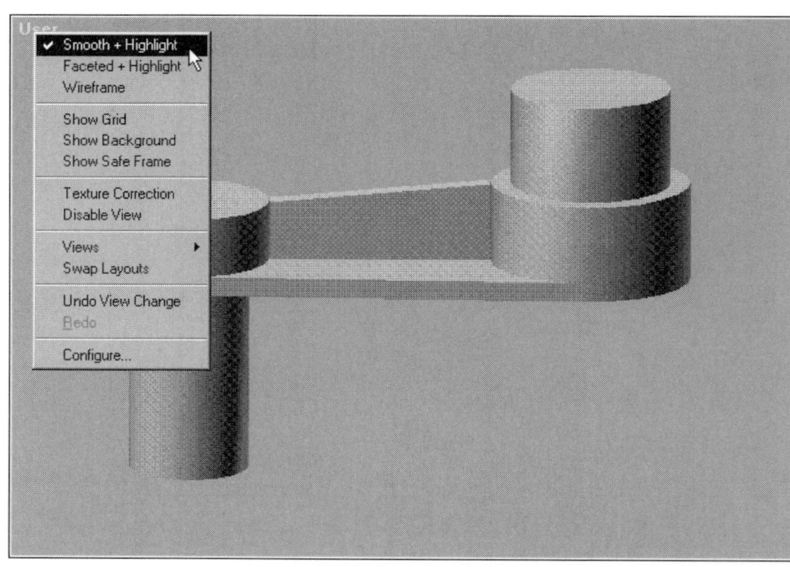

Fig. 5.28 The menu which appears with a *right-click* on the viewport name

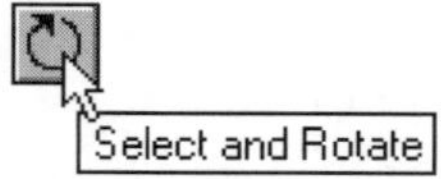

Fig. 5.29 The **Arc Rotate** icon

turned off (no tick showing). With one of your models opened in the viewports, experiment with the various commands in the menu.

Example 2 – trying out animation

With the same model opened in the viewports and with the **User** (or **Perspective**) viewport active, *left-click* on the **Select and Rotate** icon (Fig. 5.29) in the toolbar. The model can be rotated by movement of the rotate icon under mouse control. Then:

Fig. 5.30 The **Animate** button

1. *Left-click* on the **Animate** button (Fig. 5.30). It highlights red and the active viewport is outlined in red. Then move the time slider so that it shows **20/100** (Fig. 5.31) and rotate the view in the **User** viewport under the action of the **Select and Rotate** tool.

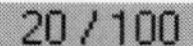

Fig. 5.31 The time slider

2. Repeat with the time slider at 40, at 60, at 80 and at 100, with a different rotation of the view in the **User** viewport at each number of the slider.
3. *Left-click* on the **Play Animation** button (Fig. 5.32). The animation plays.

Fig. 5.32 The **Play Animation** button

Example 3 – making a preview

1. With the same model in the viewports and with the **User** (or **Perspective**) viewport active, *left-click* on **Make Preview...** in the **Rendering** pull-down menu (Fig. 5.33).

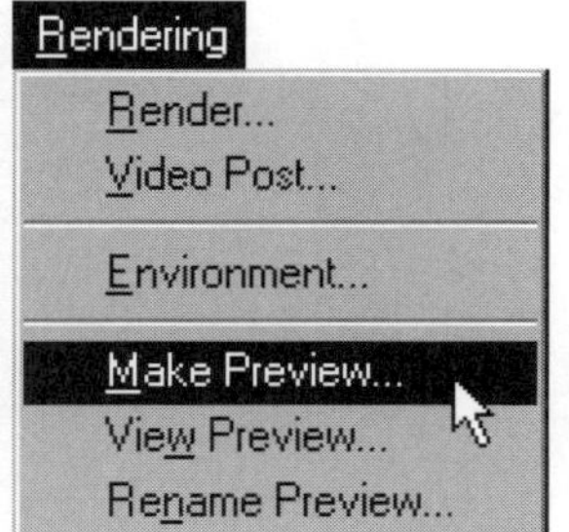

Fig. 5.33 Selecting **Make Preview** from the **Rendering** pull-down menu

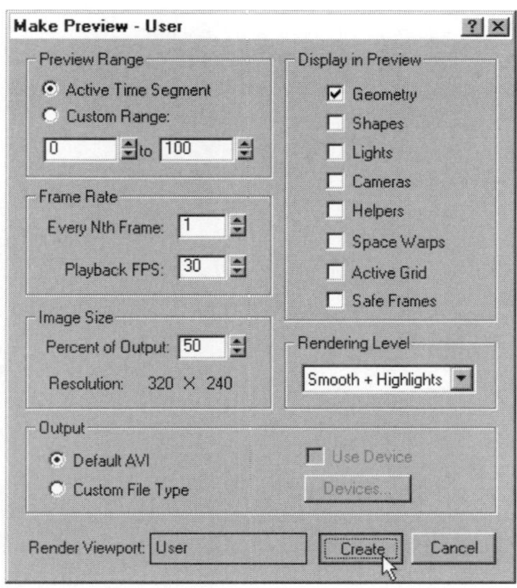

Fig. 5.34 The **Make Preview – User** dialogue box

2. The **Make Preview – User** dialogue box appears (Fig. 5.34). Accept the default values shown and *left-click* on the **Create** button.
3. The 3D Studio Max window changes as shown in Fig. 5.35 and the animation is created.

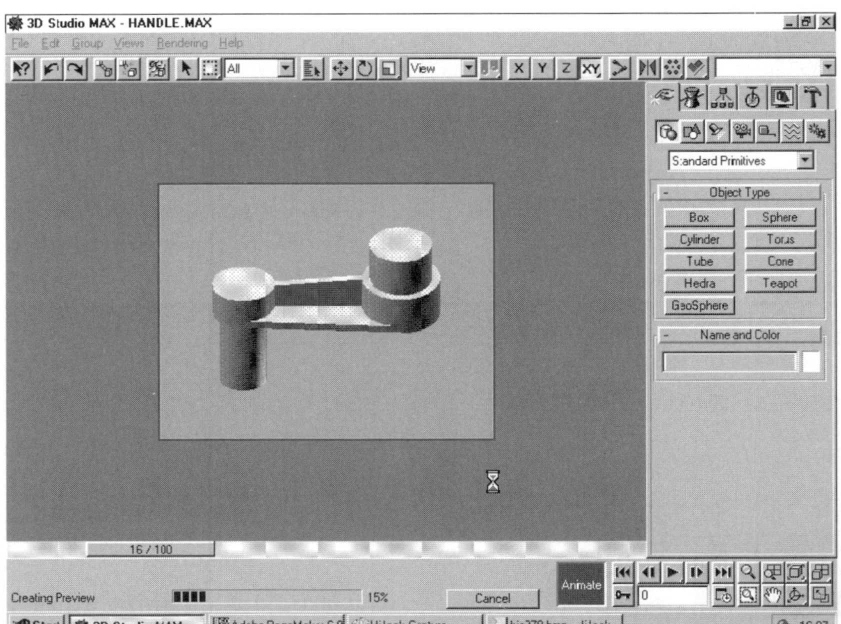

Fig. 5.35 The 3D Studio Max window as an animation is being created

4. When the animation has been completed the **Media Player** box appears as shown in Fig. 5.36. The animation can be played by a *left-click* on the **Play** icon.

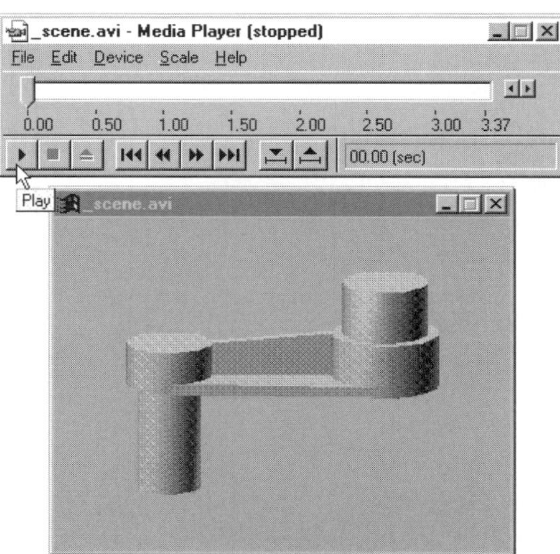

Fig. 5.36 The model in the **Media Player**

5. Experiment with other buttons in the **Media Player** box.

Exercises

It is assumed that the reader will have access to AutoCAD Release 13, or to a CAD software system that includes the saving of 3D solid model drawings in DXF format. Each of the following three exercises is based on a 3D solid model drawing being imported into 3D Studio Max.

It is also suggested that, if you have other DXF 3D solid model drawings available, you experiment with importing them into 3D Studio Max and adding to the models so imported.

1. Figure 5.37 shows the dimensions for the 3D solid model drawing for this exercise. The solid model is intended to be constructed either in AutoCAD Release 13 or in a CAD software system capable of saving a 3D model in DXF format.

   Construct the model and import it into 3D Studio Max. Render the resulting model in the **Perspective** viewport as indicated in Fig. 5.38.

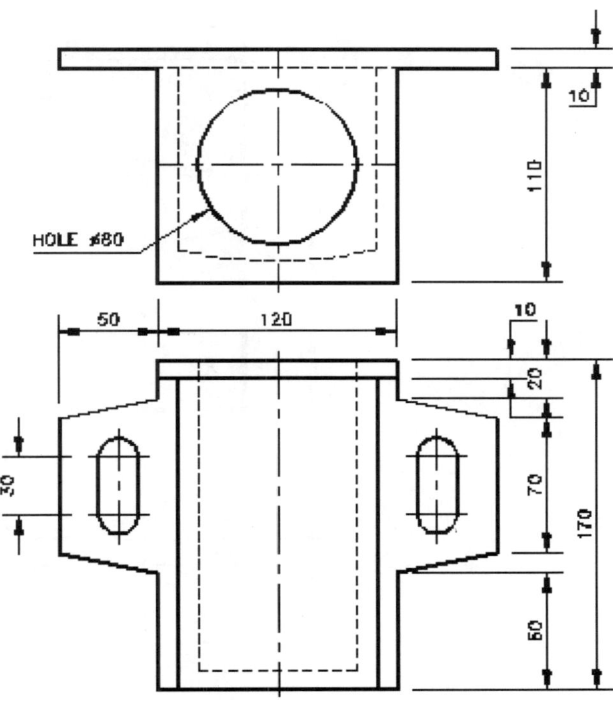

Fig. 5.37 Dimensions for Exercise 1

Fig. 5.38 Exercise 1

2. Figure 5.39 gives the dimensions for the construction of a 3D solid model drawing in a CAD system for exporting to 3D Studio Max. Construct the drawing in the CAD system and import it into 3D Studio Max. Render in the **User** viewport as shown in Fig. 5.40.

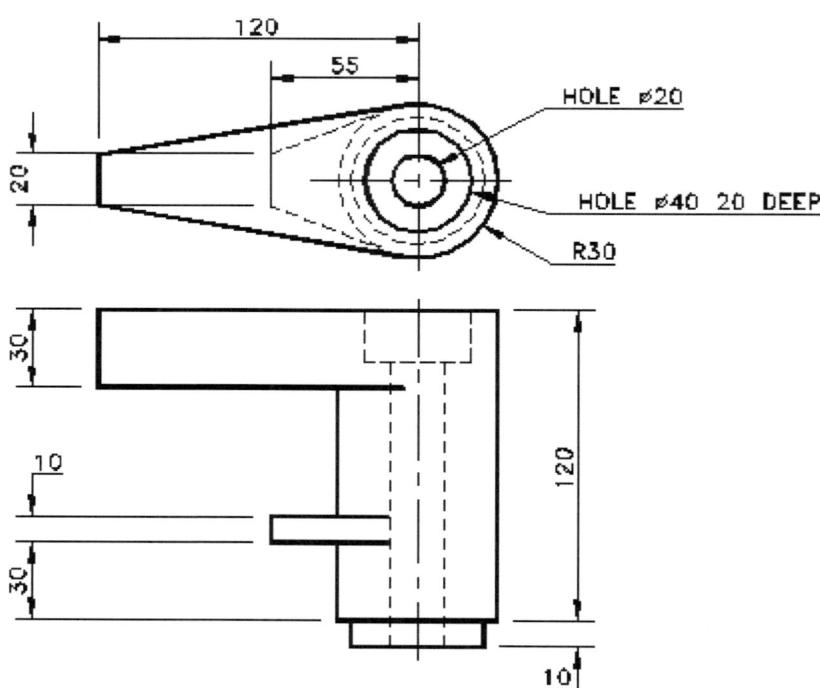

Fig. 5.39 Dimensions for Exercise 2

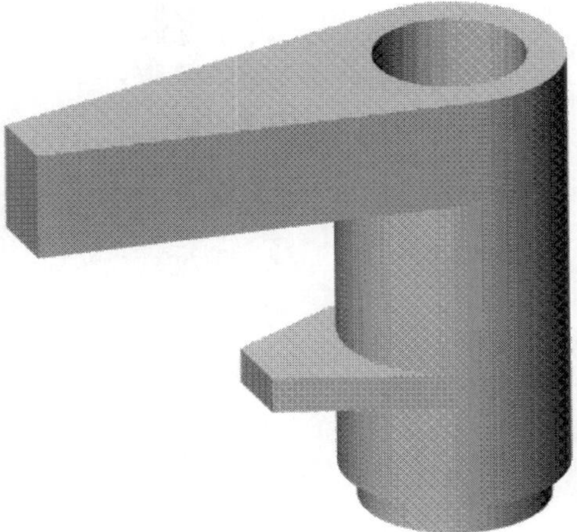

Fig. 5.40 Exercise 2

3. Construct a 3D solid model to the dimensions given in Fig. 5.41 in a CAD system. Then import the model drawing into 3D Studio Max. In 3D Studio Max add two cylinders, one of radius 30 and length 500, the other of radius 40 and length 40. Create the Boolean union of the two cylinders and move to fit in the hole of the original imported model.

   Animate the cylinder with its 'head' to move in and out of the imported model in steps of 20 movements. Figure 5.42 shows the cylinder(s) at the start of the movement and Fig. 5.43 the position at point 50 in the movement.

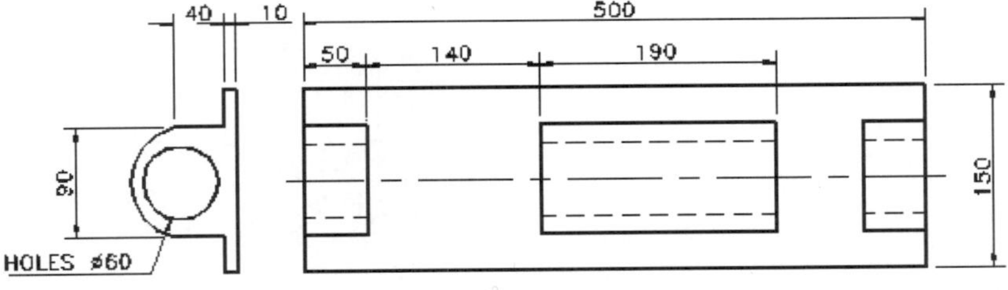

Fig. 5.41 Dimensions for Exercise 3

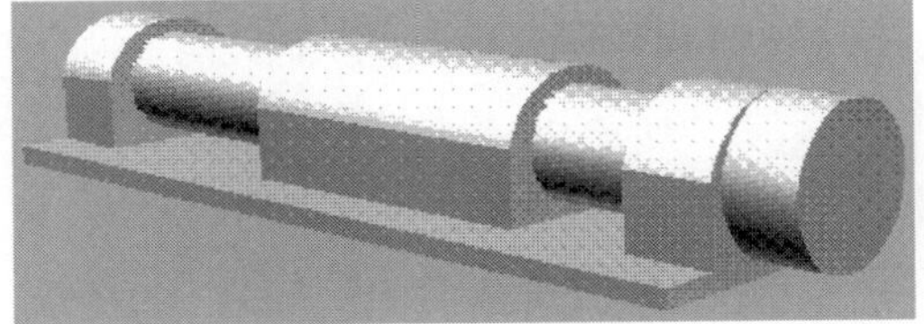

Fig. 5.42 Exercise 3 – start of animation

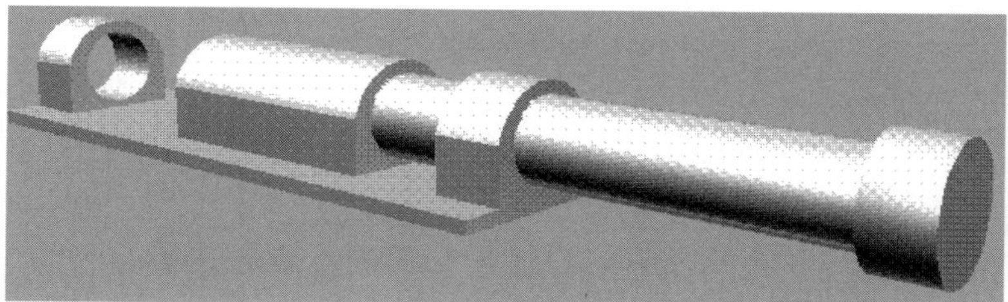

Fig. 5.43 Centre of animation

CHAPTER 6

Vertices, grids and further examples

Edit Spline

Shapes can be edited to amend their outlines by using the vertices of the shape with the tool **Edit Spline** from the moderators. In the **Front** viewport create an outline similar to that shown in Fig. 6.1 with the **Line** tool, with **Initial** and **Drag** type both set to **Corner**.

Example 1 – creating a wineglass

1. After creating the outline as in Fig. 6.1, *enter* a new name in the name box just below the icons at the top of the Command panel. Then *left-click* on **Edit Spline** in the Command panel (Fig. 6.2). Small crosses appear at each of the vertices of the outline, with a small square at the start (and in this example, the end) of the outline (Fig. 6.3).

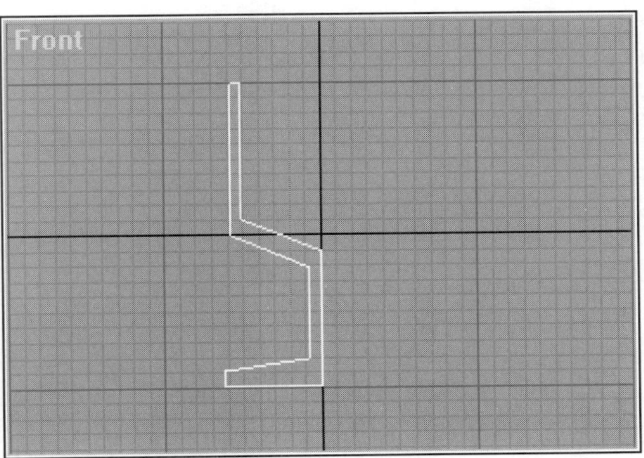

Fig. 6.1 Example 1 – **line** outline

2. A *right-click* on any of the vertices brings down a menu as shown in Fig. 6.3. At each vertex in turn, bring down the menu and select

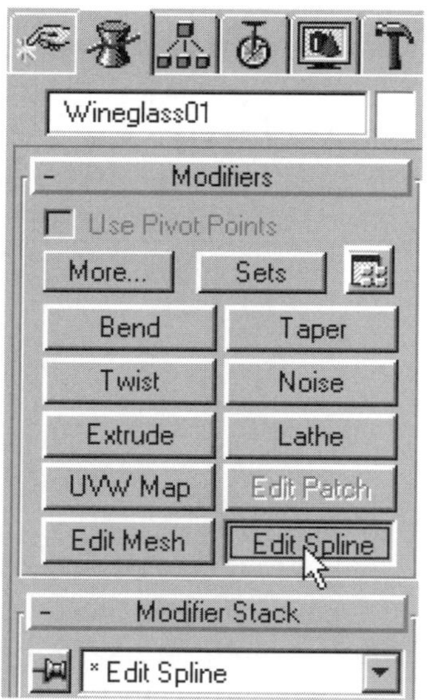

Fig. 6.2 *Left-click* on **Edit Spline**

Bezier. The vertices are now equipped with handles which allow control of the Bezier splines making up the outline. One of these is shown in Fig. 6.4.

3. *Left-click* on the **Select and Move** icon in the toolbar. *Left-click* on any of the vertices and move the vertex, or with the **Move** cursor over one of the Bezier handles move the handles. It will be found that the complete outline can be changed to whatever shape is required. In this case Fig. 6.4 shows the outline after the Bezier controls have been moved at every vertex, forming the basis for a wineglass model. Some practice and patience will be necessary until the use of the Bezier controls has been mastered.

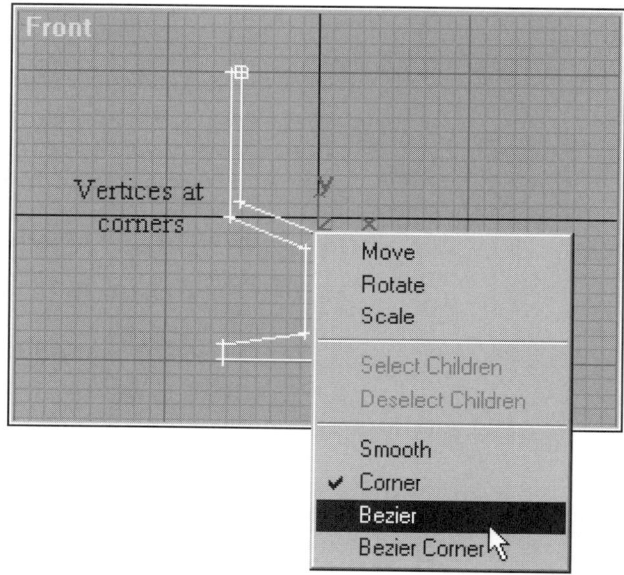

Fig. 6.3 Vertices showing, together with the menu which appears with a *right-click* on any vertex

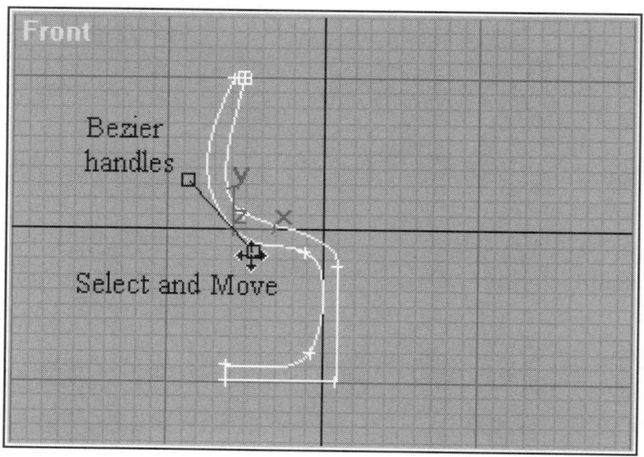

Fig. 6.4 One of the Bezier spline controllers

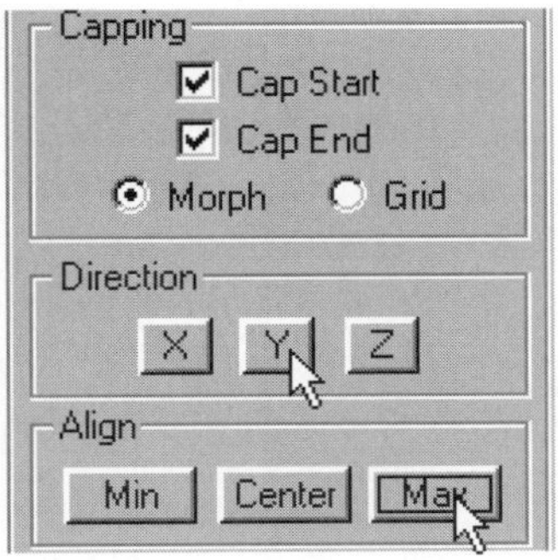

Fig. 6.5 Settings in the **Lathe** Command panel options

4. Select **Lathe** from the moderator buttons, then **Y** under **Direction** and **Max** under **Align** (Fig. 6.5). The wineglass forms (Fig. 6.6). In this illustration the scene in the **Perspective** viewport has been acted upon by **Smooth and Highlight** from the menu appearing with a *right-click* on the name of the viewport.

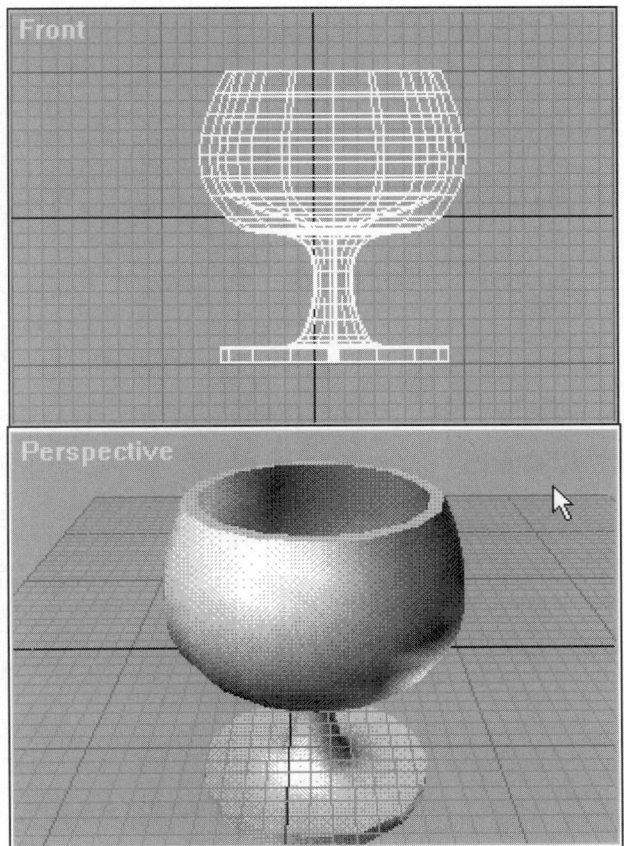

Fig. 6.6 Example 1

Example 2 – creating another wineglass

1. With **Select and Move** active, press the **Shift** key of the keyboard, then move the wineglass. A copy of the model appears and the **Clone Options** dialogue box comes on screen (Fig. 6.7). Make **Copy** active (dot in check circle against **Copy**) and a second wineglass is formed.
2. Select Wineglass02 and, from the popup list appearing with a *left-click* on **Lathe** in the Command panel, select **Edit Spline** (Fig. 6.8). The original spline reappears in Wineglass02.

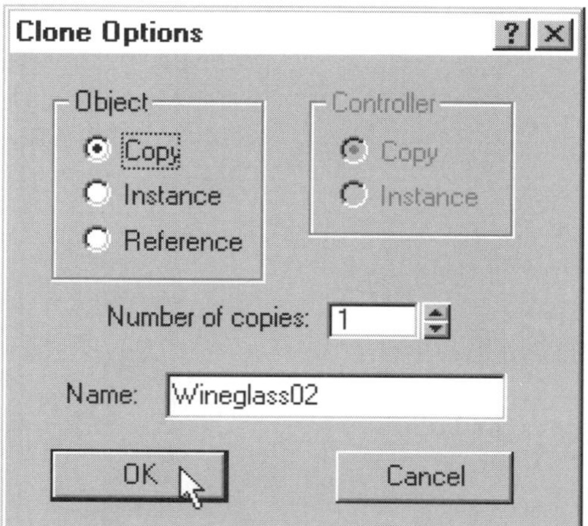

Fig. 6.7 The **Clone Options** dialogue box

3. With the aid of the Bezier controls, which are still active with the spline, change the shape of the wineglass to achieve another model.

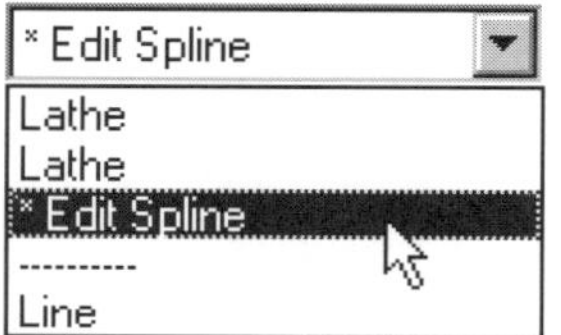

Fig. 6.8 Select **Edit Spline** from the popup list

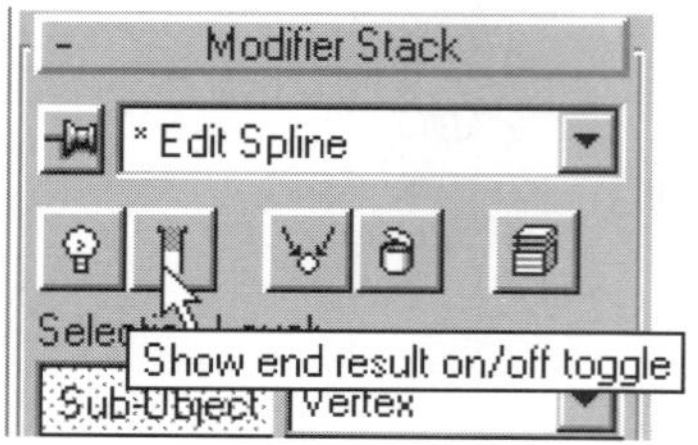

Fig. 6.9 The **Show end result on/off toggle** icon

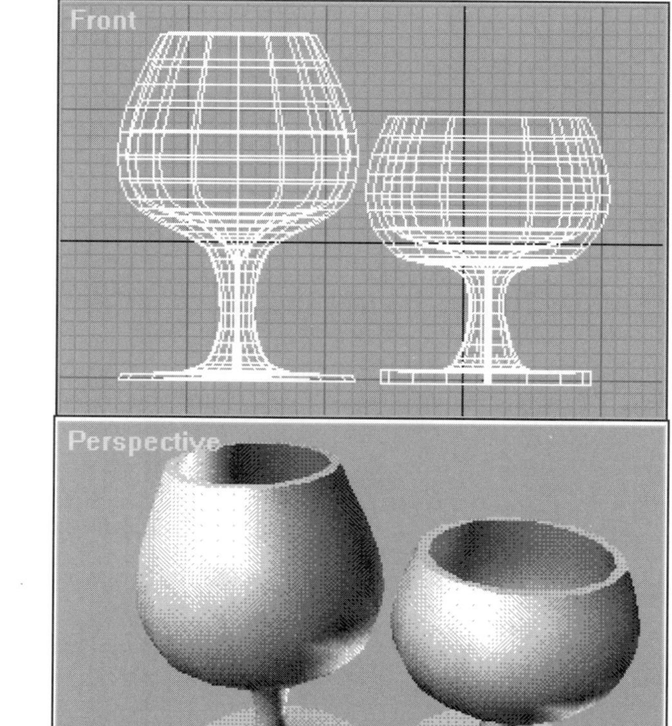

Fig. 6.10 Example 2

Check as the changes proceed by holding a *left-click* on the **Show end result on/off toggle** icon (Fig. 6.9).

4. The resulting second wineglass is shown in Fig. 6.10.

   Again some practice is required to achieve a required shape for a suitable wineglass when the outline is acted upon with the **Lathe** modifier.

Example 3 – modifying a shape

1. Create a circle – any size will do.
2. Select **Edit Spline** from the modifiers. *Left-click* at any of the four vertices which show on the circle and a Bezier controller will appear (Fig. 6.11).
3. With **Select and Move** active redesign the circle to any shape – an example is given in Fig. 6.11.

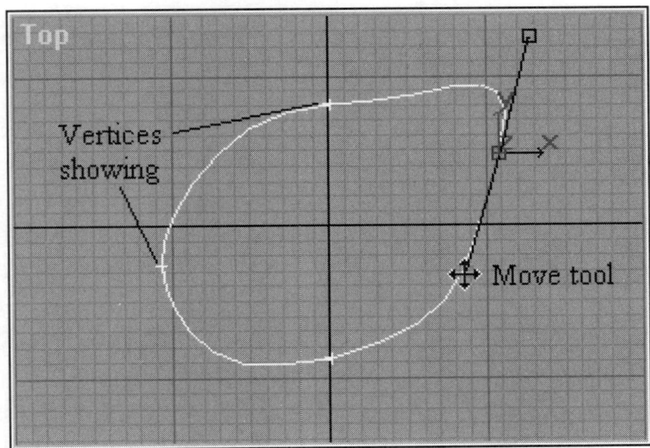

Fig. 6.11 Example 3

Example 4 – edited circle with further modifiers

1. Create a circle of radius 30 in the **Top** viewport as shown in **Stage 1** of Fig. 6.12.
2. With **Edit Spline** amend its outline as shown in **Stage 2**.
3. **Extrude** to a height of 150 as shown in **Stage 3**.
4. Using the modifier **Bend** with **Angle** set to 90 and **Direction** set at 45 to modify the model as shown in **Stage 4** of Fig. 6.12.

Grid Helper

A *left-click* on **Helpers** in the Command panel (Fig. 6.13) brings up a number of helper buttons. In this example we will be using the **Grid Helper**.

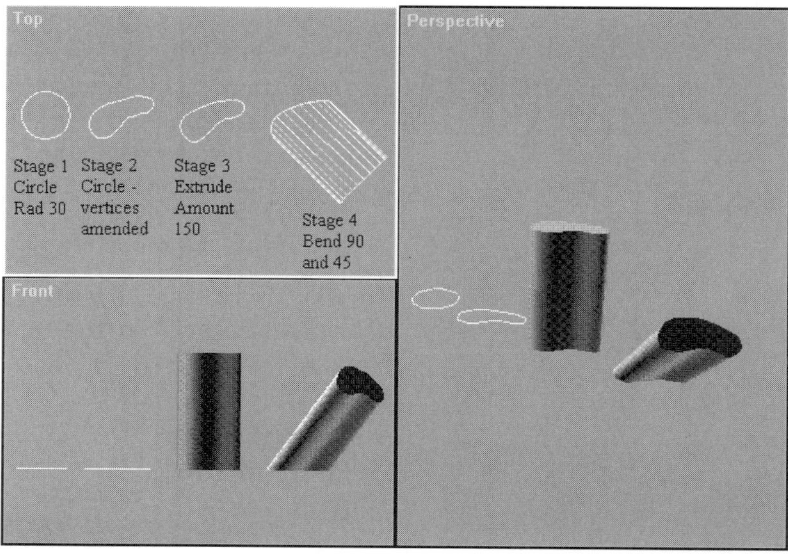

Fig. 6.12 Example 4

Example 5

Fig. 6.13 The **Helpers** in the Command panel

1. Create a **Box** of **length** 100; **Width** 200; **Height** 100.
2. *Left-click* on the **Helpers** icon (Fig. 6.13), then on the **Grid** button. A grid appears in the selected viewport – in this example, the **Top** viewport. *Drag* the grid to a reasonable size as shown in Fig. 6.14.
3. *Left-click* on the **Align** button in the toolbar (Fig. 6.15) and select the **Box**. The **Align Selection** dialogue box appears (Fig. 6.16).
4. Set the check circles in the dialogue box as indicated in Fig. 6.16. The box moves so that the grid is on its top surface as shown.
5. Any new shape or geometry created will now be placed on the new grid.

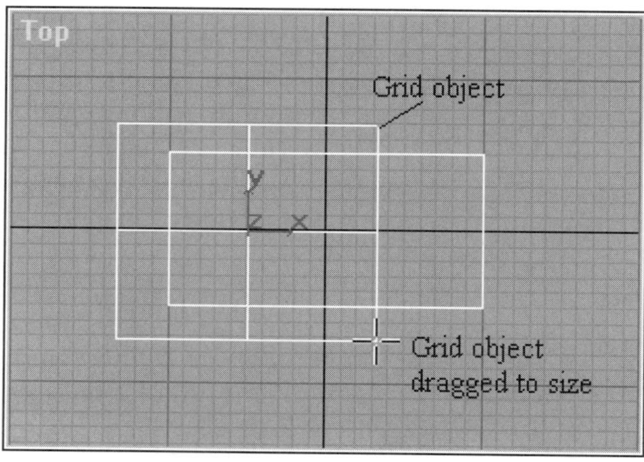

Fig. 6.14 Example 5 – placing a grid

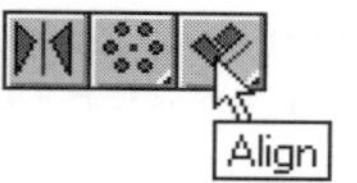

Fig. 6.15 The **Align** button

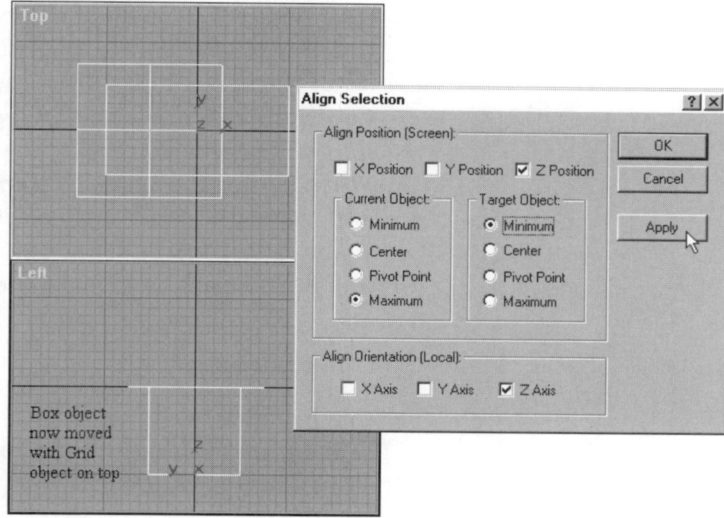

Fig. 6.16 The **Align Selection** dialogue box

Example 6

1. Create a **Star** as shown in **Stage 1** of Fig. 6.17.
2. Select **Edit Spline** and adjust the vertices as shown in **Stage 2** of Fig. 6.17.
3. **Extrude** to 120 as shown in **Stage 3**.
4. Use the modifier **Taper** set as shown in **Stage 4** to finish the model.

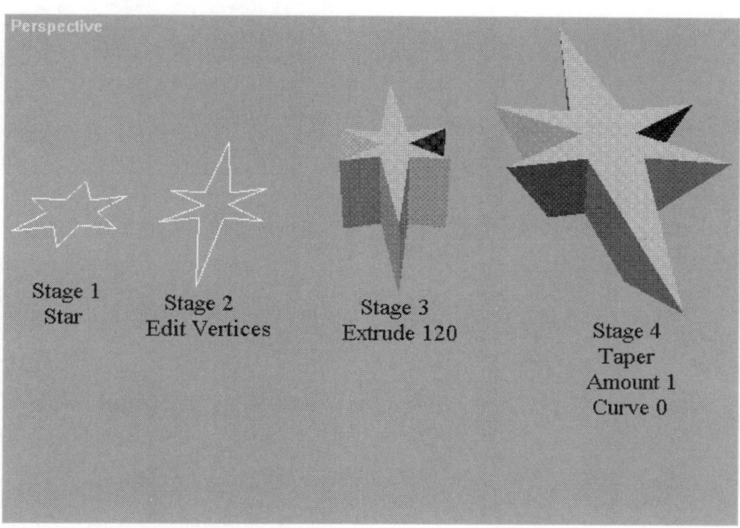

Fig. 6.17 Example 6

Notes

1. It will be seen from the **Clone Options** dialogue box that more than one copy or instance may be made if required.

2. If an **Instance** is made of an object in the **Clone Options** dialogue box, any changes made to any of the instances will be repeated in all of them, including the first from which they were copied. If **Copies** are made, they are independent of the original from which they were copied.
3. When calling the **Clone Options** dialogue box to screen the **Select and Move** tool must first be active.
4. When redesigning a shape using **Edit Spline**, the **Select and Move** tool must be active to make the necessary changes.

Exercises

1. Create a **Line** outline similar to that shown in Fig. 6.18. Then with **Edit Spline** redesign the outline to form a bowl similar to that shown in Fig. 6.19.

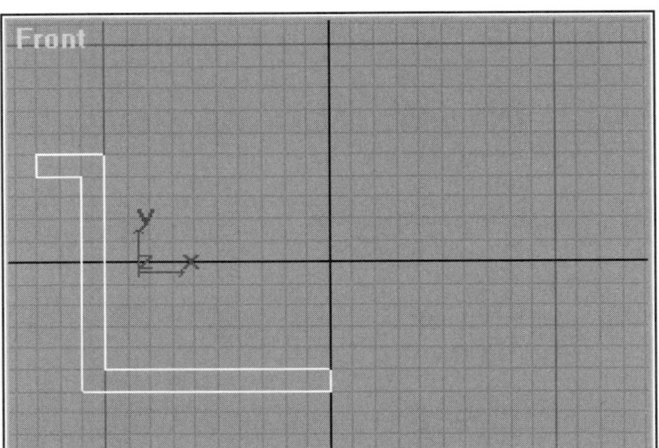

Fig. 6.18 Outline for Exercise 1

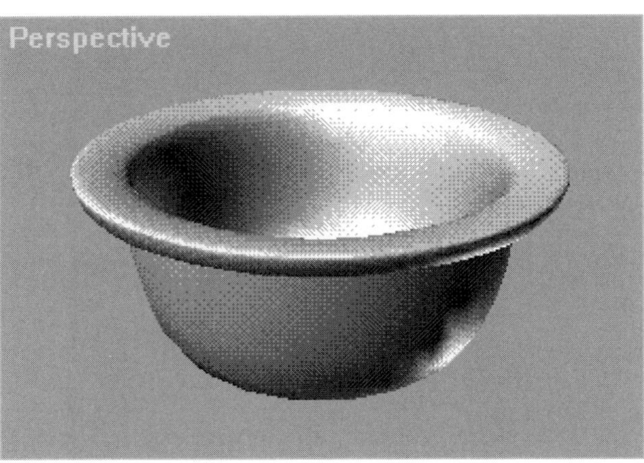

Fig. 6.19 A **Smooth + Highlighted** version of Exercise 1

2. Figure 6.20 shows a **Cylinder**, a **Cone** and a **Tube** resting on a **Box** created with the help of a **Helper Grid**. Working to any convenient sizes create a similar scene.

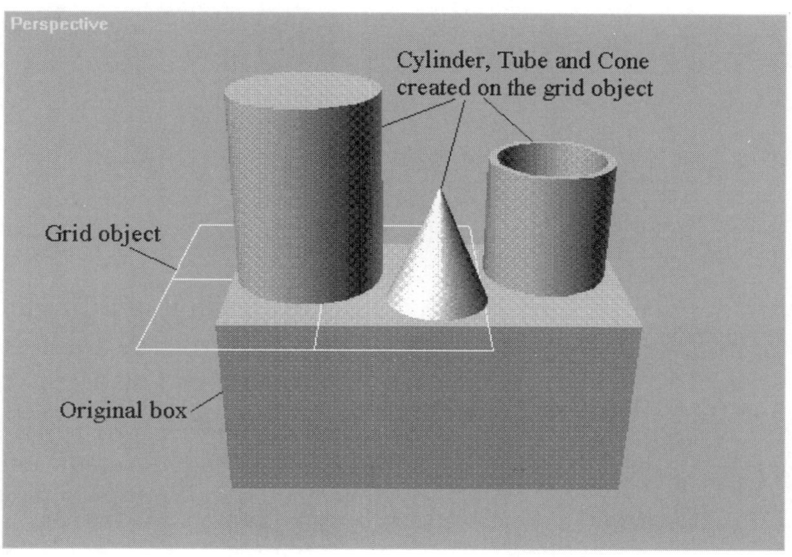

Fig. 6.20 Exercise 2

3. Figure 6.21 shows a circular table top surmounted upon a tapered **NGon** with a vase on the table.

   Create a similar scene to any suitable dimensions. Note that the grid can be hidden if it is first selected, followed by a *left-click* on **Hide Selected**.

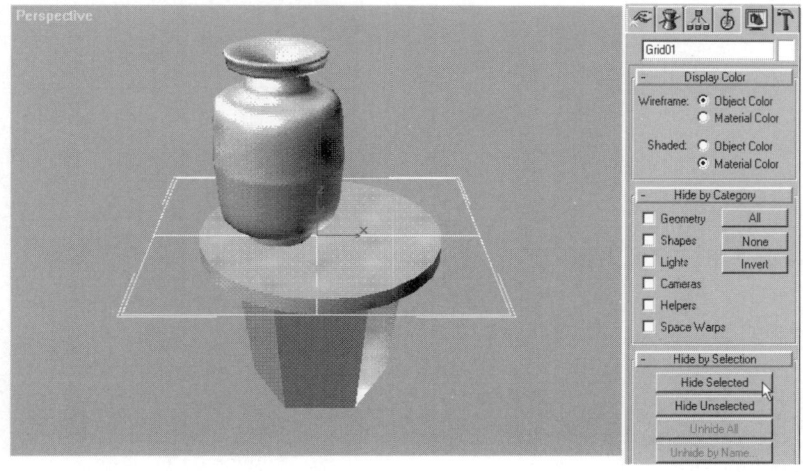

Fig. 6.21 Exercise 3

4. Figure 6.22 shows a panel formed from an extruded outline created with **Line** on which an extrusion of my name has been added. Each letter of the text was individually positioned and, if necessary rotated.

   Create a similar panel using your own name.

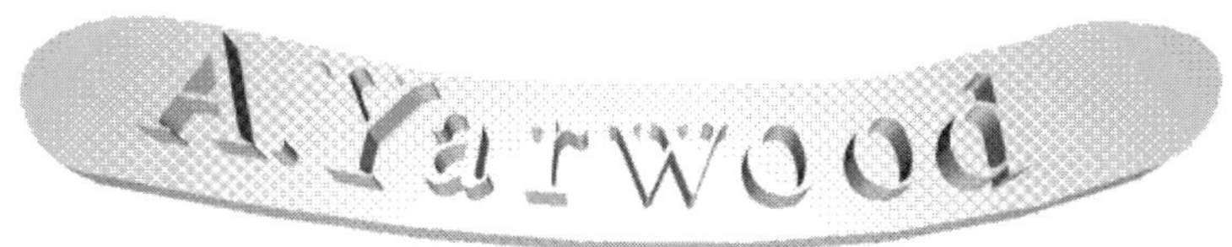

Fig. 6.22 Exercise 4

Edit Mesh and Edit Patch

Example 1 – Edit Mesh

1. Create a **Cylinder** of any radius and height.
2. *Left-click* on the moderator **Edit Mesh** (Fig. 6.23). Small crosses appear at all the vertices of the cylinder.

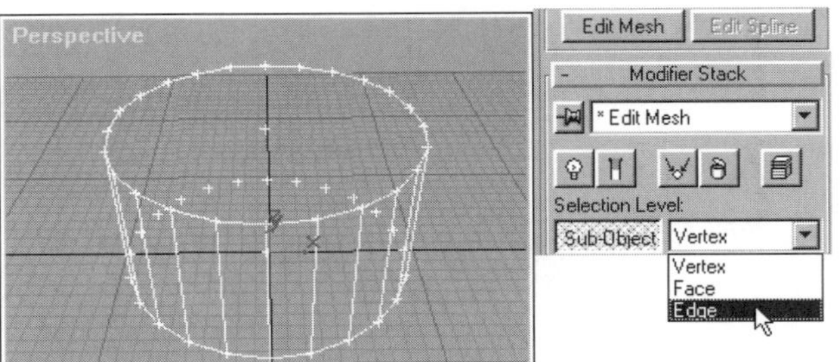

Fig. 6.23 Select **Edit Mesh** followed by **Edge**

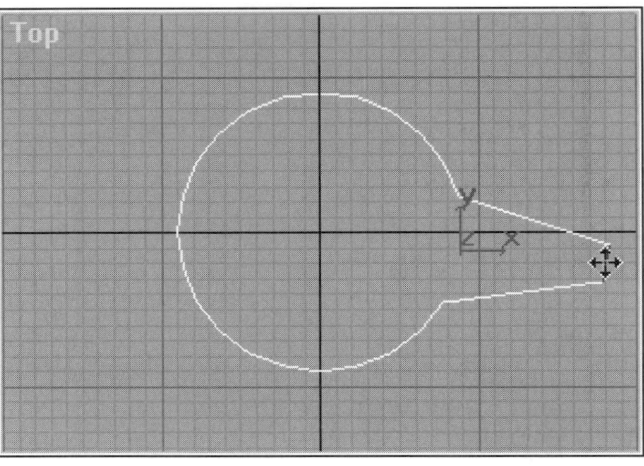

Fig. 6.24 *Dragging* an edge from the cylinder

3. In the **Sub-Object** window select **Edge** from the popup menu.
4. With **Select and Move** active, select an edge of the cylinder and *drag* it away from the centre of the cylinder (Fig. 6.24). The edge is pulled out from the cylinder as shown.
5. Now select **Face** from the **Sub-Object** popup list and move the top of the cylinder (which is a face) with the result as shown in Fig. 6.25.

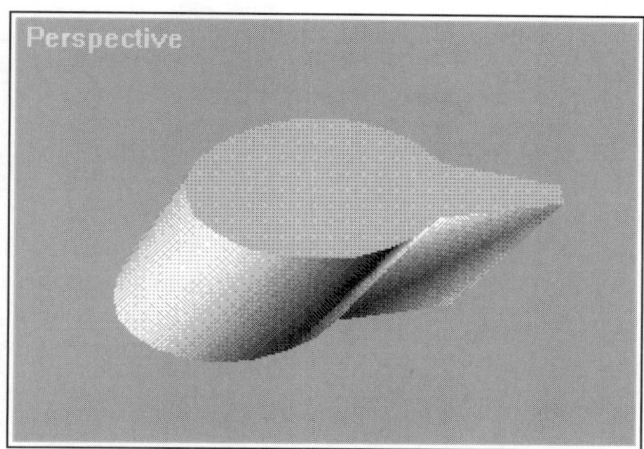

Fig. 6.25 Example 1 – *dragging* a face

Example 2 – Edit Mesh

Repeat with another **cylinder** using the **Edit Mesh** on Vector, on an Edge and on a Face as shown in Fig. 6.26.

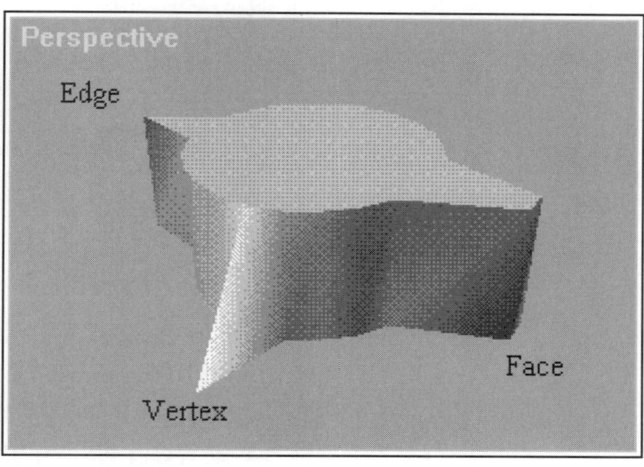

Fig. 6.26 Example 2

Example 3 – Edit Patch

1. Create a **NGon** of 8 sides and **Extrude** by 100.
2. Select the moderator **Edit Patch**. Figure 6.27 shows the patches on the extrusion.

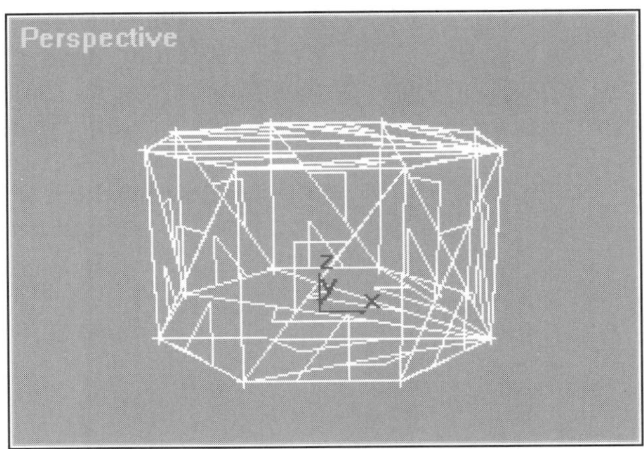

Fig. 6.27 The extrusion for Example 3 showing its patches

3. Select **Vector** from the **Sub-Object** popup menu and with **Select and Move** active, move a vector.
4. Then select **Edge** from the **Sub-Object** menu and move an edge.
5. Figure 6.28 shows the results of these two actions.

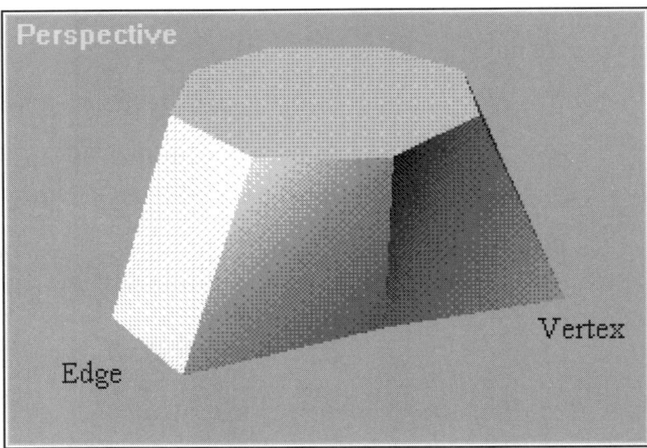

Fig. 6.28 Example 3

Further exercises

6. Figure 6.29 shows a cylinder which has been acted upon by the modifier **Edit Mesh** with **Edge** selected from the **Sub-Object** popup list. The hole is a second cylinder subtracted from the first under the action of a Boolean operator.

   Construct the given model working to any convenient sizes.
7. Figure 6.30 shows a **GeoSphere** which has been edited with the aid of **Edit Mesh** with **Vertex** selected from the **Sub-Objects** popup list.

   Construct a similar model to any suitable dimensions.

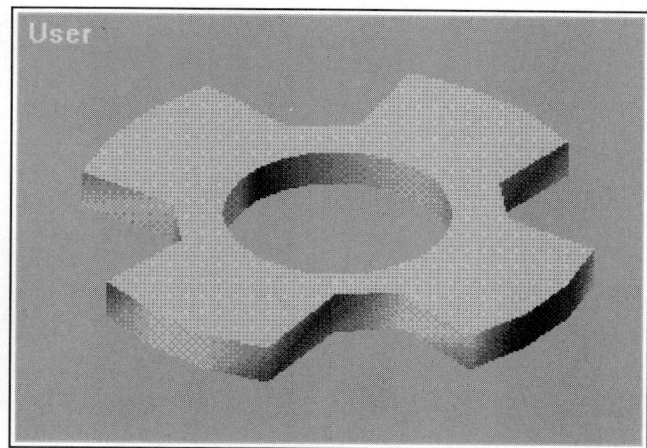

Fig. 6.29 Exercise 5

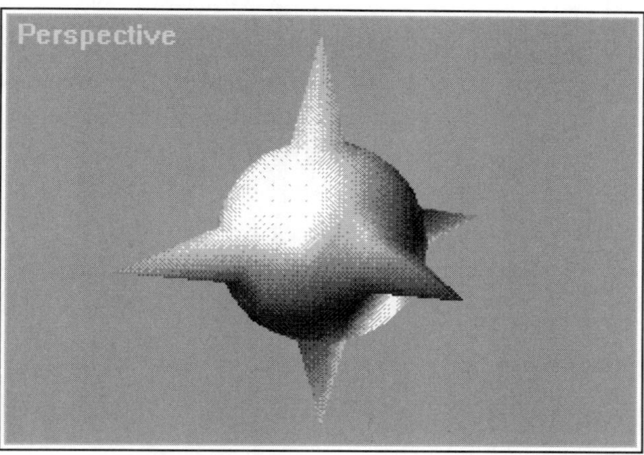

Fig. 6.30 Exercise 6

8. Figure 6.31 shows a cylinder which has been acted upon by the moderator **Edit Patch** with **Vertex** selected from the **Sub-Objects** popup list.

   Working to any convenient sizes construct a similar model.

The viewport control tools

These have been mentioned briefly before (Chapter 1). A fuller description of these eight tools, the icons for which are found at the bottom right corner of the 3D Studio Max window, is now given. Figure 6.21 gives the names of the tools associated with the icons. When the **Perspective** viewport is active, the **Region Zoom** tool icon is replaced with the **Field of View** tool icon (Fig. 6.33).

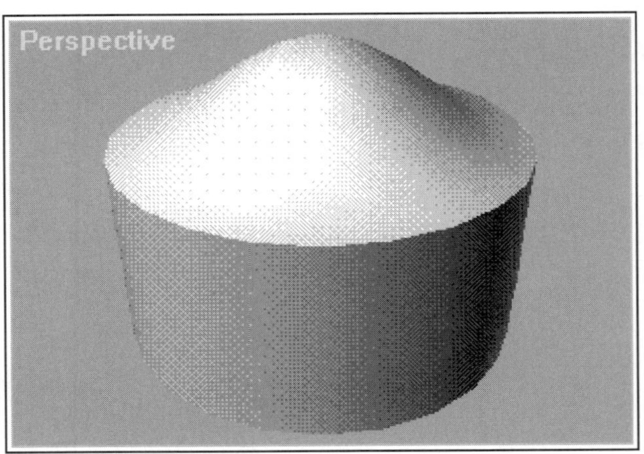

Fig. 6.31 Exercise 7

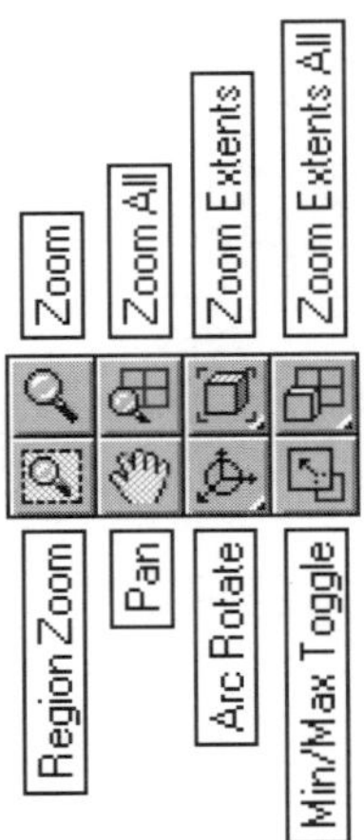

Fig. 6.32 The eight viewport control tool icons

The Viewport Configuration dialogue box

A *right-click* on any of the eight tool icons brings the **Viewport Configuration** dialogue box on screen. This is more than a single dialogue box as it has five parts, each of which is a dialogue box in its own right (Fig. 6.34).

Fig. 6.33 The **Field of View** tool icon showing when the **Perspective** viewport is active

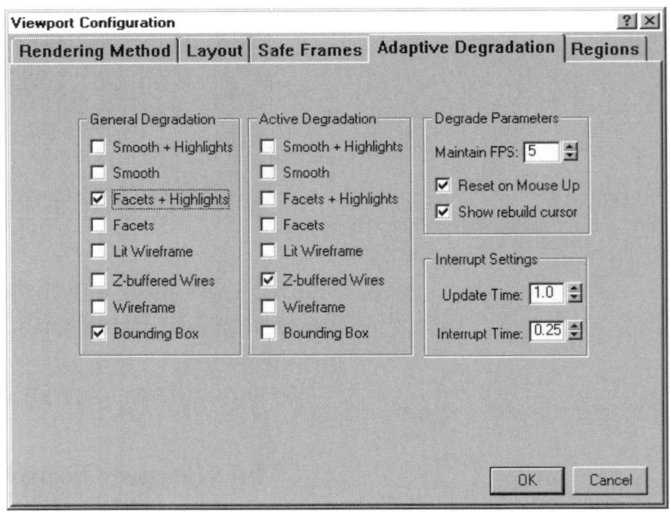

Fig. 6.34 The **Viewport Configuration** dialogue box

The Zoom tool

Left-click on the icon and the cursor changes to the icon. Move the zoom cursor into any viewport and move upwards to zoom in (make the objects in the viewport larger) or down to zoom out (make objects smaller).

The Zoom All tool

The action of this tool is similar to that of the **Zoom** tool. The icon becomes the cursor, but an upward movement in any viewport and all viewports are zoomed in and a down movement zooms all viewports out.

The Zoom Extents tool

Left-click on this tool. The icon becomes the cursor and by a *left-click* in any viewport causes the objects in the viewport to become zoomed to as large as can be fitted in the selected viewport.

The Zoom Extents All tool

Selection of this tool causes the objects to be zoomed to their extents in all viewports.

The Region Zoom tool

Select this tool icon and the icon becomes the cursor. This tool is really a zoom window tool. An area of objects in a viewport (other than a **Perspective** viewport) can be selected in a window formed by two *left-clicks* at opposite edges of the area to be zoomed. Figure 6.35 shows part of objects in a **Front** viewport in a **Region Zoom** window. The second *click* causes the area within the window to fill the viewport.

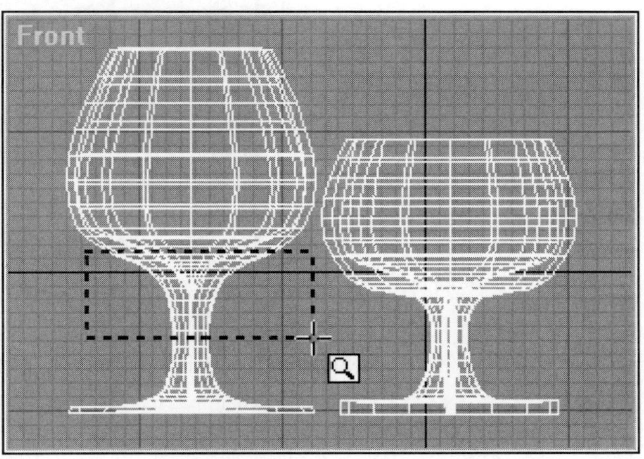

Fig. 6.35 Using the **Region Zoom** tool

The Pan tool

When this tool is selected the icon becomes the cursor and any viewport can be panned up or down, to left or to right as desired.

When used in the **Perspective** viewport, because the viewport is being panned and not the objects in the viewport, the appearance of the objects in the viewport will be changed.

The Arc Rotate tool

This tool is of value if one wishes to change the direction in which the objects in any viewport are being viewed. Note that the objects in the selected viewport are not rotated, it is the whole of the viewport. The use of this tool can often give the operator a better view of a model as it is being constructed. When in use the icon becomes the cursor and a circle appears in the viewport. As with the **Pan** tool, it is the viewport which is rotated. Note the square handles at each quadrant of the circle which appears when the tool is active. It is advisable to experiment with the tool with the cursor in the handles and also not in the handles. Figure 6.36 shows the appearance of a **Perspective** viewport when the tool is active.

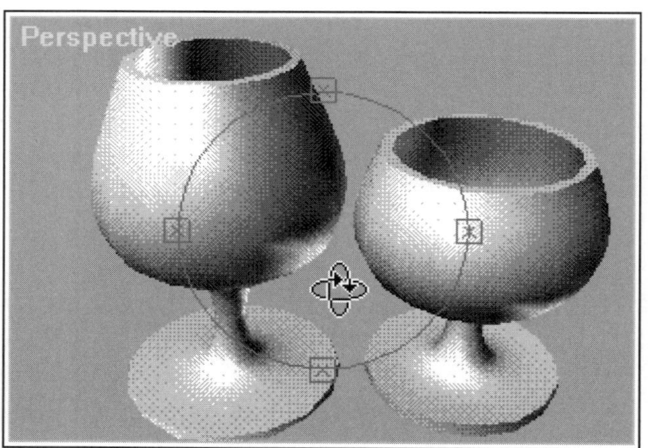

Fig. 6.36 The **Arc Rotate** tool and its associated circle and icon

The Max/Min toggle

A *left-click* causes the active viewport to enlarge and fill the area occupied by the existing viewports. A second *left-click* on the tool causes the original viewport layout to return to screen. Note that

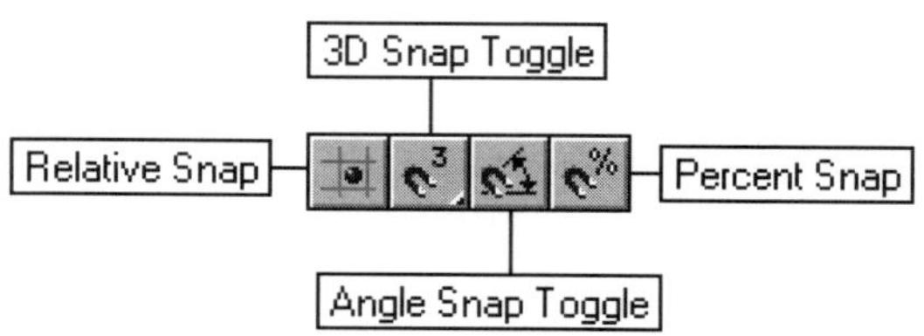

Fig. 6.37 The **Snap** tool icons

pressing the **W** key of the keyboard has the same effect. This tool is valuable when determining the exact shape of small detail in any viewport.

Other dialogue boxes opened with right-clicks on icons

A *right-click* on any one of the **Snap** tool icons in the Status bar (Fig. 6.37) brings up the **Grid and Snap Settings** dialogue box (Fig. 6.38). Settings for **Grid** and **Snap** may be made in the dialogue box(es).

A *right-click* on the **Degradation Override** icon brings up the **Viewport Configuration** dialogue box. A *right-click* on the **Spinner Snap Toggle** icon brings up the **Preference Settings** dialogue box and a *right-click* on any one of the **Play Animation** icons will bring up the **Time Configuration** dialogue box (Fig. 6.39).

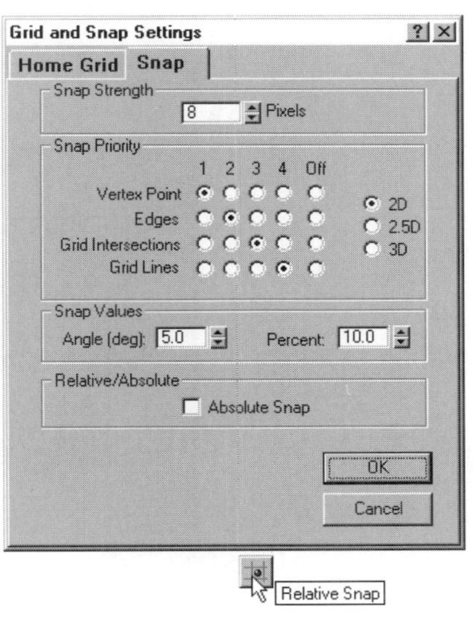

Fig. 6.38 The **Grid and Snap Settings** dialogue box

Further exercises

8. Figure 6.40 shows a ratchet wheel created from a cylinder of 48 sides, in which alternate edges have been acted upon by **Edit Mesh** to form the teeth. The central hole was Boolean subtracted from the edited cylinder.
   Working to any suitable sizes construct a similar ratchet wheel.
9. Figure 6.41 shows a form of weapon suitable for use with a game software package. The head was formed from a star of eight points, which was extruded in two segments. The extrusion was acted

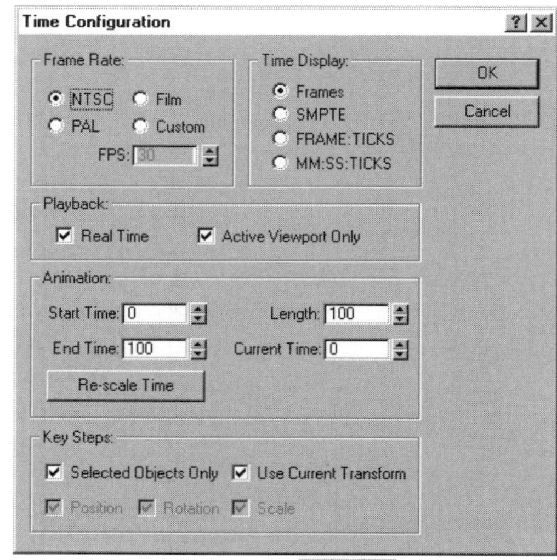

Fig. 6.39 The **Time Configuration** dialogue box

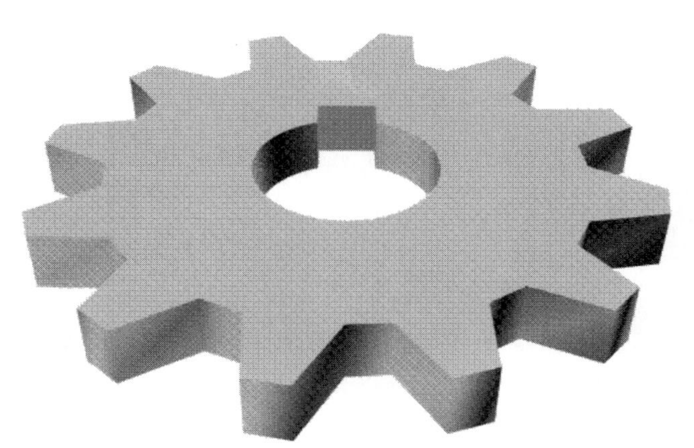

Fig. 6.40 Exercise 8

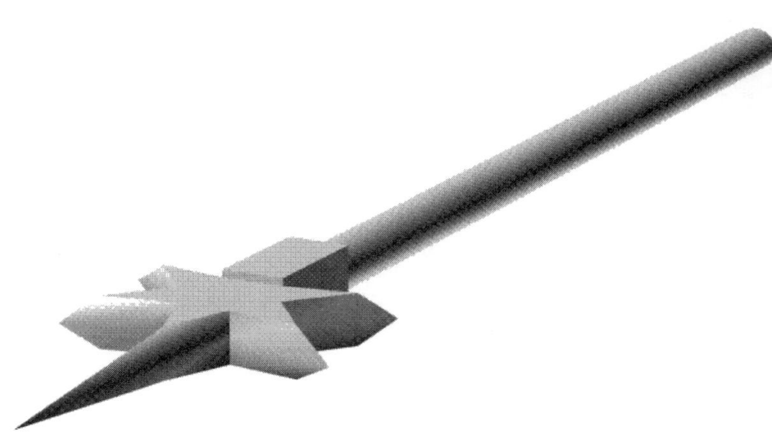

Fig. 6.41 Exercise 9

upon with **Edit Mesh** to form the points of the head. A box and cylinder handle was then added.

Construct a similar model working to any convenient sizes.

10. Figure 6.42 shows a model of a handle constructed from an extruded line outline, to which has been added two cylinders of different sizes.

    Construct a similar handle to any convenient sizes.

Fig. 6.42 Exercise 10

11. Figure 6.43 is a model of a puppet head. Working to any suitable sizes construct a similar model to that shown.

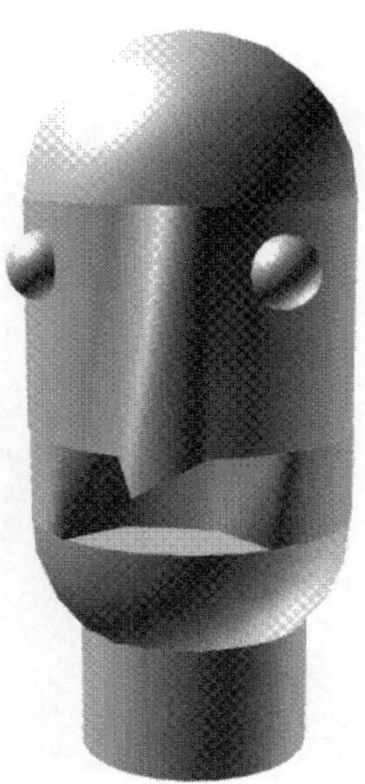

Fig. 6.43 Exercise 11

CHAPTER 7

Lights and Cameras

Lights

Two types of lights will be used in scenes described in this chapter – omni lights and target spot lights.

Omni lights

Omni light is a source of lighting which casts light in all directions. It cannot be used to form shadows, but can be coloured if required. When no lights are added to a scene two default omni lights will be present, but are not represented by any icons in the scene. These two default lights are placed so that one is in front of and above the scene and the second is placed below and behind the scene. When any lighting is added to the scene the two default lights are automatically switched off.

Omni lights can have attenuation applied – objects lit in the distance will appear darker; those nearer will appear lighter.

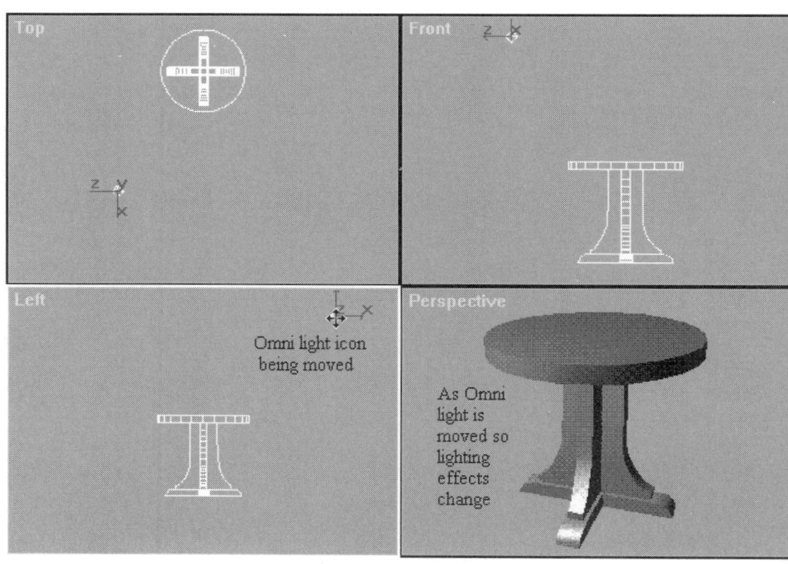

Fig. 7.1 The 3D Studio Max window with an omni light placed in position

Omni lights are placed in the scene under mouse control and are objects, which like other objects can be moved to new positions.

Target Spot lights

Target spot lights are adjustable spot lights which cast a beam of light. They can be configured so as to cause shadows to appear. To place a target spot light in a scene its icon is placed, then *dragged* to position the spot and its target area.

The Perspective viewport

If the **Perspective** viewport is in its **Smooth+Highlight** mode (*right-click* on the viewport name and select **Smooth+Highlight**), the results of placing lights in a scene will be seen in the scene showing in the viewport.

Examples of placing lights in a scene

Example 1 – placing an Omni light

A scene showing a table previously created in 3D Studio Max will be used to demonstrate the placing of lights and camera in a scene. The file containing the table (**table.max**) is first opened, then:

1. Set the **Perspective** viewport to its **Smooth+Highlight** configuration.
2. In the **Top**, **Front** and **Left** viewports zoom and pan the scene as indicated in Fig. 7.1.
3. Select **Lights** from the Command panel, followed by a *left-click* on **Omni** (Fig. 7.2).
4. *Left-click* in the **Top** viewport to position the light, then using **Select and Move** move the light to a suitable position in the **Top** and **Left** viewports, watching the lighting effects in the **Perspective** viewport. Move the light icon until the desired lighting effect is obtained.

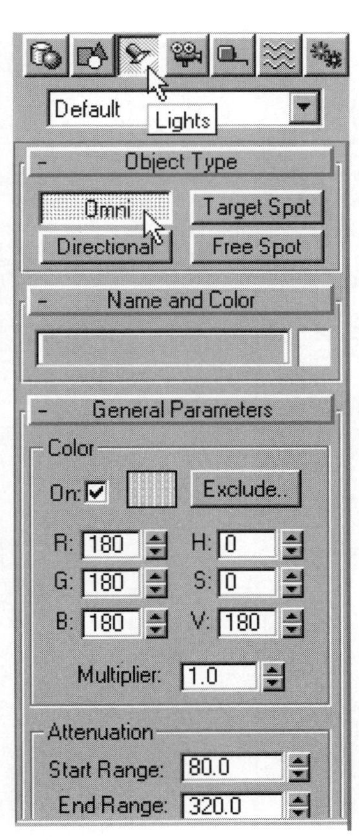

Fig. 7.2 Selecting **Omni** from the Command panel

Note: In the above example no attenuation was applied to the omni light.

Example 2 – placing a Target Spot light

1. Using the same scene, select **Target Spot** from the Command panel (see Fig. 7.2).
2. Position the Target Spot icon in a suitable position and *drag* the target cone as shown in Fig. 7.3.
3. With **Select and Move**, move either (or both) the light icon and the target icon to a suitable position.
4. Watch the lighting effect as it appears in the **Perspective** viewport.

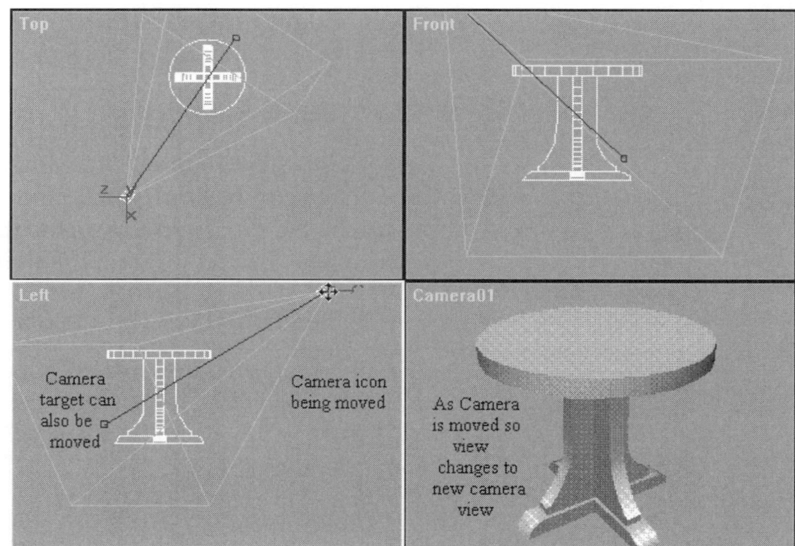

Fig. 7.3 Placing a **Target Spot** light

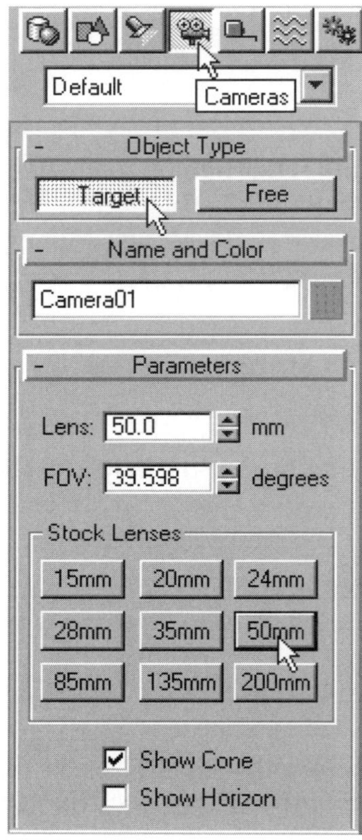

Fig. 7.4 Setting parameters for a **Target Spot** light

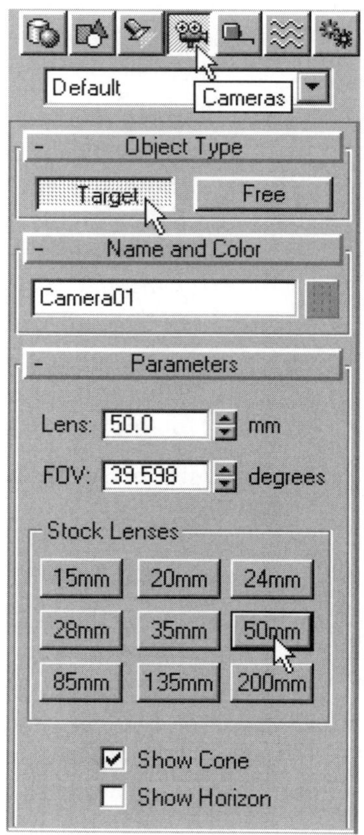

Fig. 7.5 Selecting camera parameters

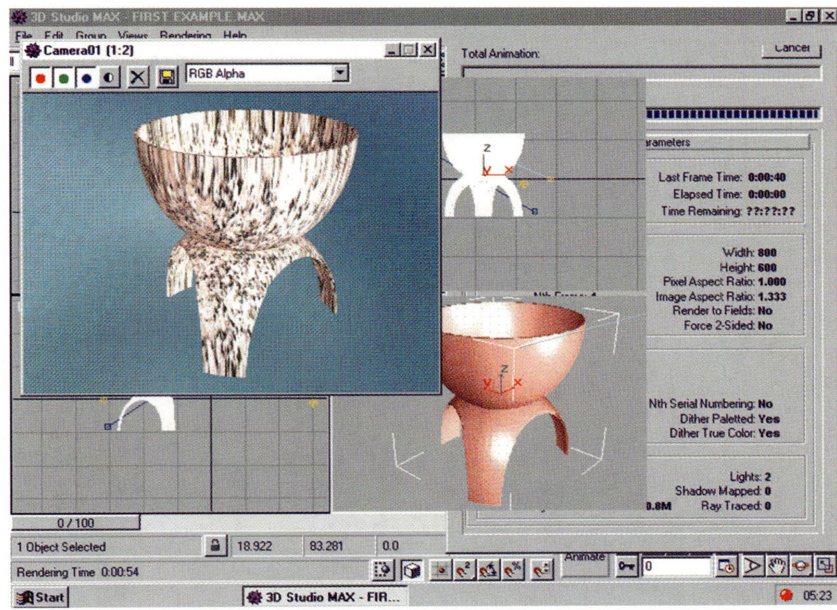

Plate I A 3D Studio Max scene being rendered

Plate II Two renderings of the scene in Plate I

Plate III Two further renderings of the scene in Plate I

Plate IV Two more renderings of the scene in Plate I

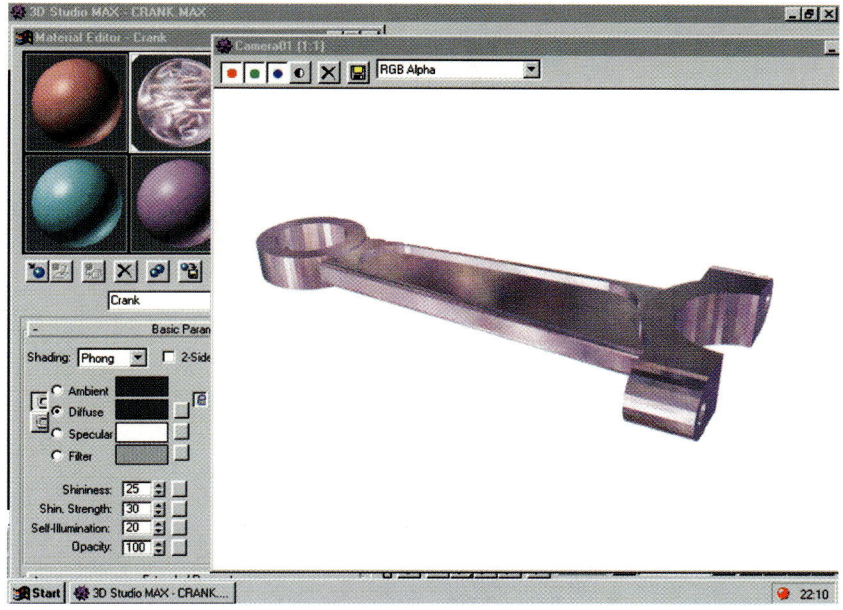

Plate V A rendering of a crank shaft showing the Material Editor on screen

Plate VI A rendered scene of a bottle of wine, its cork and two wine glasses on a table top

Plate VII A rendered scene of a kitchen shelf with saucepans and an oil bottle

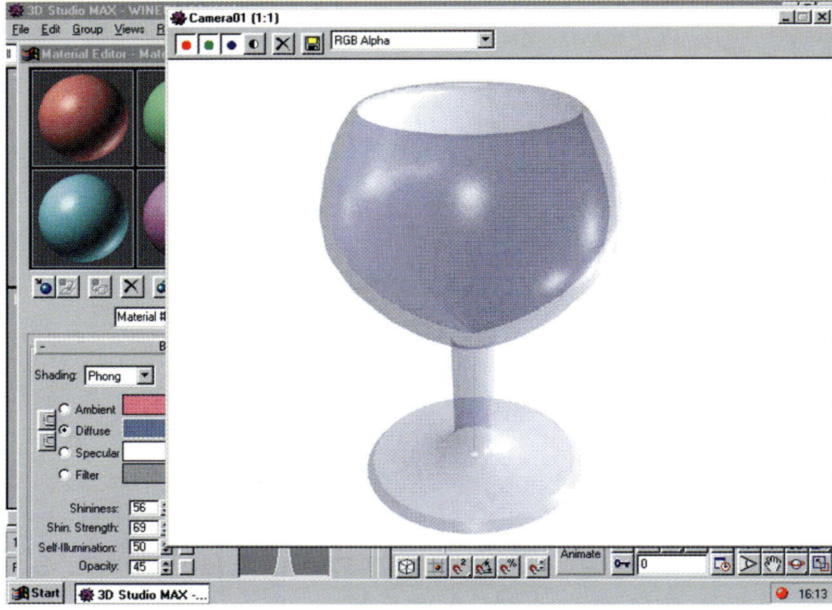

Plate VIII A rendering of a wine glass

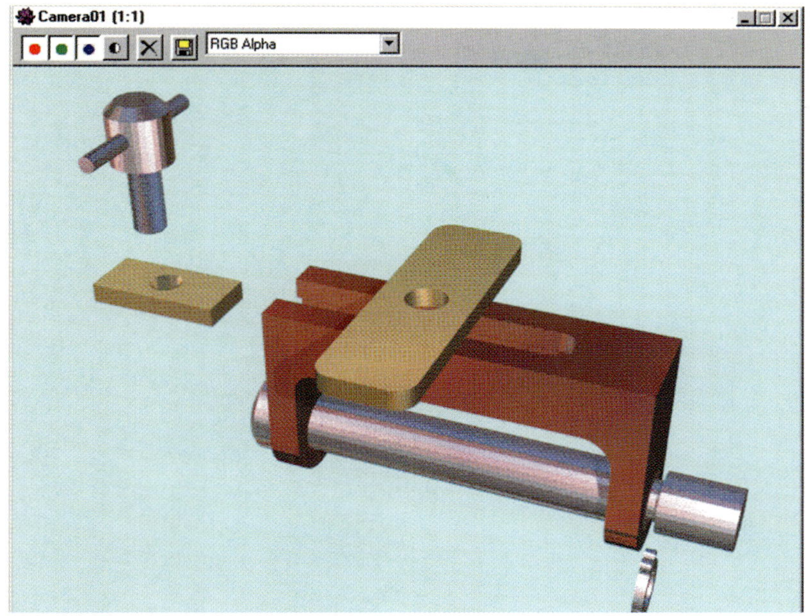

Plate IX A rendering of an engineering component, with its parts in an exploded position

Plate X A rendered scene of a corner of a room, including a table and table lamp

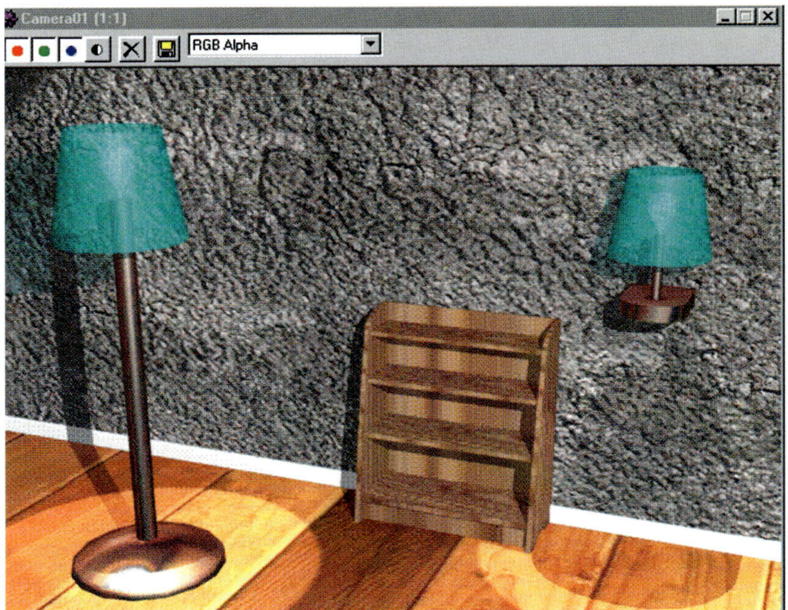

Plate XI A rendering of a room scene with a wall light and a standard lamp

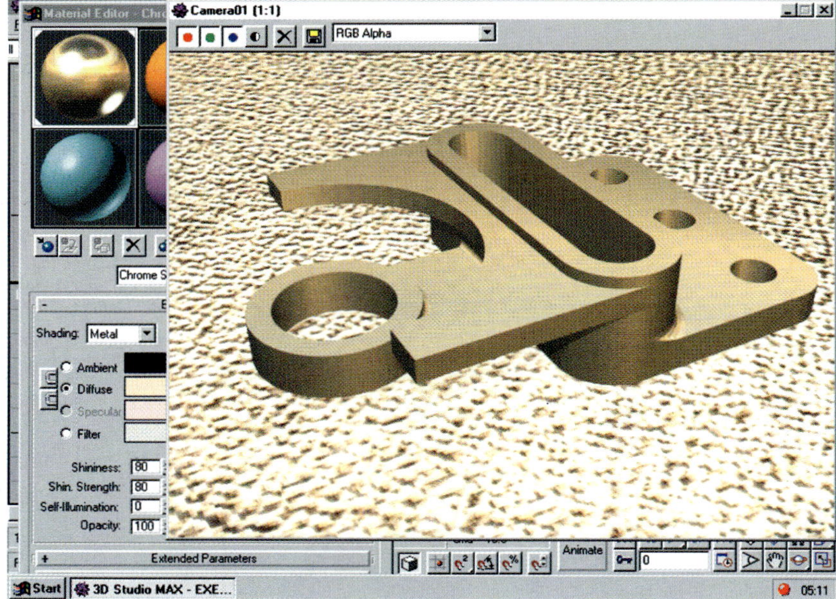

Plate XII A rendering of a microscope stand shown within 3D Studio Max; part of the Material Editor is showing

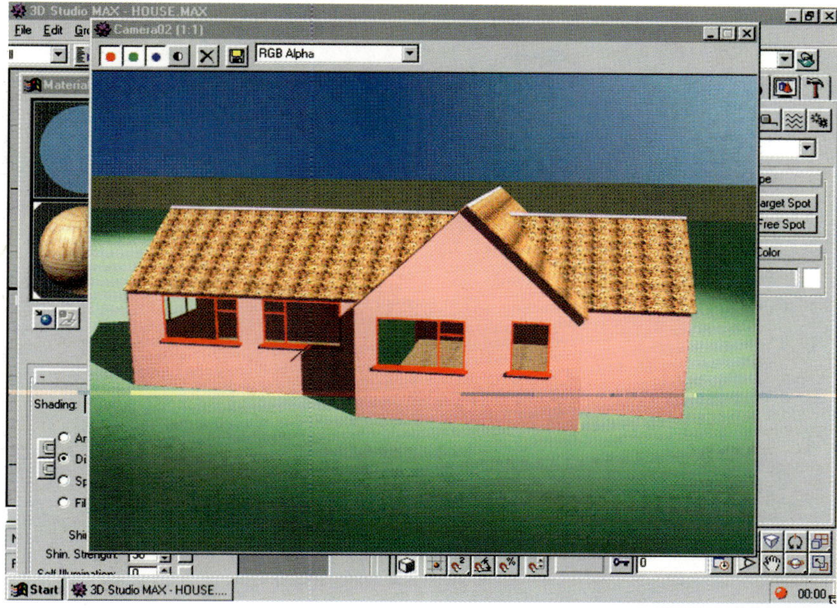

Plate XIII A rendered bungalow scene within 3D Studio Max

Plate XIV A rendering of a flask with a label

Plate XV A cube mapped using different mapping methods

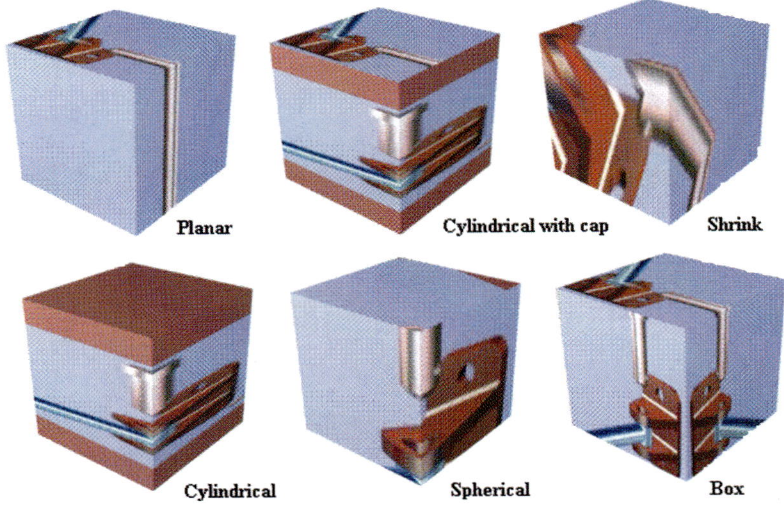

Plate XVI A rendering of a room scene showing different techniques for applying materials

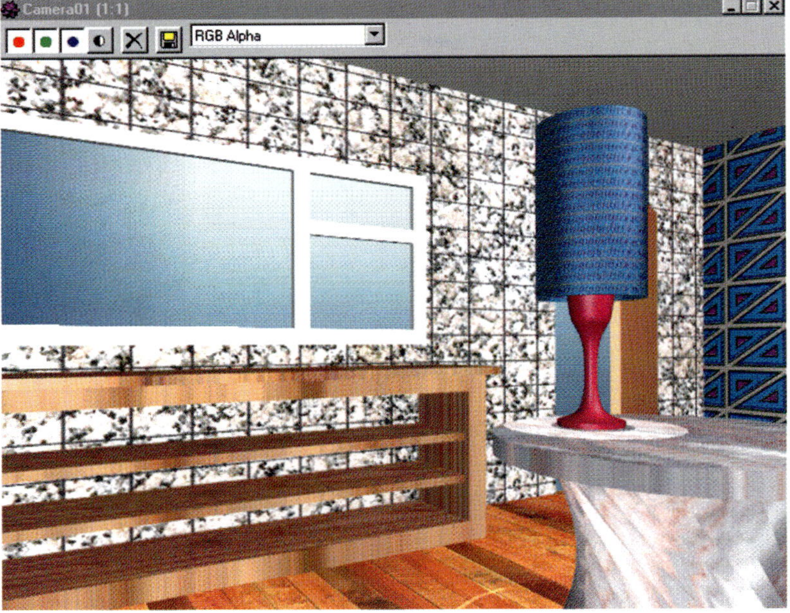

Note: Figure 7.4 shows the settings made in the Command panel for the target spot light being used in the above example. Note the check circles for **Show Cone**, **Rectangle** (cone) and **Cast Shadows** have been checked as being on.

Cameras

Example 1

1. Select **Cameras** from the Command panel and select **Target**. Then set parameters as shown in Fig. 7.5.

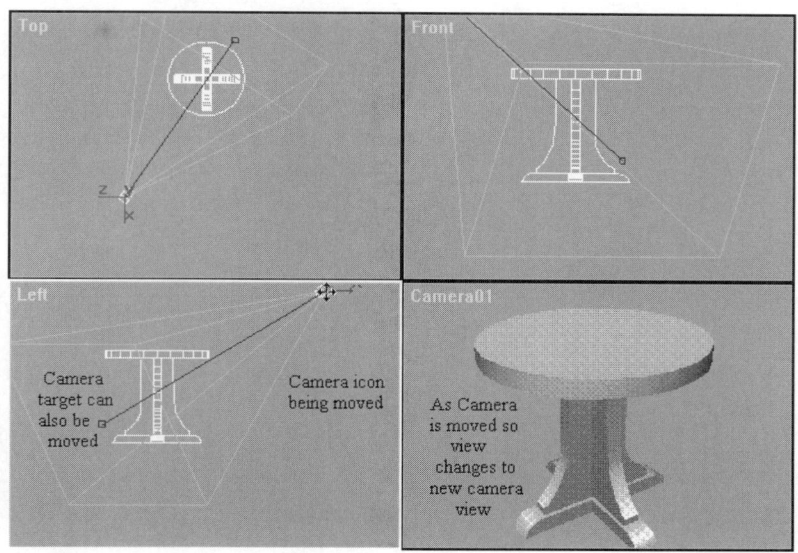

Fig. 7.6 Placing a camera in the scene

2. *Left-click* in the **Top** viewport and *drag* the target icon of the camera towards and slightly beyond the table in the scene as shown in Fig. 7.6.
3. In the **Perspective** viewport, configure the viewport to **Camera01** view (Fig. 7.7). Note that the icons at the bottom right-hand corner of the 3D Studio Max window change. More about these changes later.
4. With **Select and Move** *drag* either the camera icon or (and) the target icon of the camera until a suitable view shows in the **Perspective** viewport.

Fig. 7.7 Setting the **Perspective** viewport to **Camera01**

The Camera icons in Viewport controls

When a viewport is changed to show a **Camera** setting, the icons of the viewport controls in the bottom right of the window change. They will now show as in Fig. 7.8.

Perspective
Roll Camera
Dolly Camera
Zoom Extents All
Field-of-View
Min/Max Toggle
Truck Camera
Orbit Camera
Pan Camera

Fig. 7.8 The camera icons in the viewport control set of icons

Examples of using the camera viewport controls

Experiment with the camera viewport control tools represented by these icons as in the following examples.

Orbit Camera

Figure 7.9 shows the **Orbit Camera** tool in action. Select the icon and in the **Camera01** viewport move the icon. It will be seen that the action of the camera orbiting is reflected in all viewports.

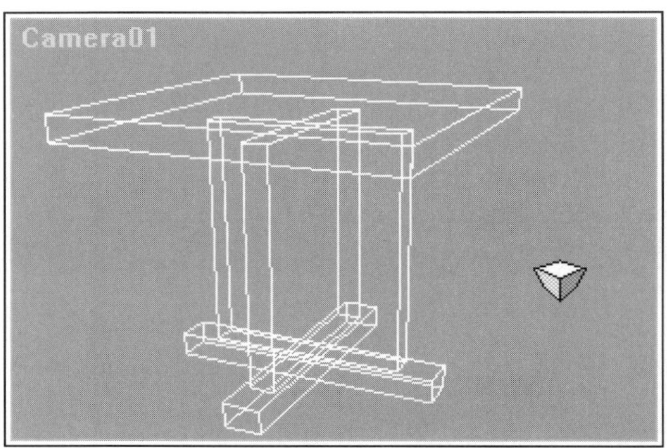

Fig. 7.9 The **Orbit Camera** tool icon in the **Camera01** viewport

Perspective

Figure 7.10 shows the **Perspective** tool in use. Again as the perspective view of the camera viewport is changed by movement of the mouse and its cursor, all viewports are affected.

Roll Camera

Figure 7.11 shows the **Roll Camera** tool in use. As the camera is rolled so its action is seen in all viewports.

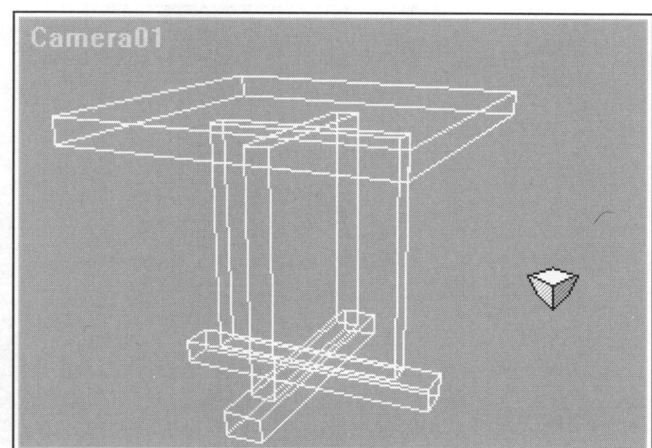

Fig. 7.10 The **Perspective** tool icon in the **Camera01** viewport

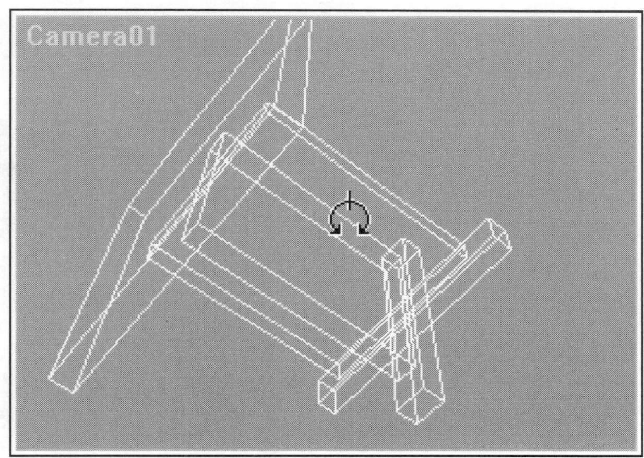

Fig. 7.11 The **Roll Camera** tool icon in the **Camera01** viewport

Example 2 – lights and a camera

A fairly standard form of lighting for a single object such as the table used in these examples can be lit with two lights – an omni and a target spot. A camera and the two lights can be placed as follows.

1. First position a camera.
2. Set a target spot light near the camera and *drag* its target icon to cover the object.
3. Set an omni light to the left (or right) and above the object(s) in the scene. Figure 7.12 shows the results of the positioning of a camera, an omni light and a target spot light.
4. Figure 7.13 shows a rendering of this example. Note the shadows cast by the target spot light.

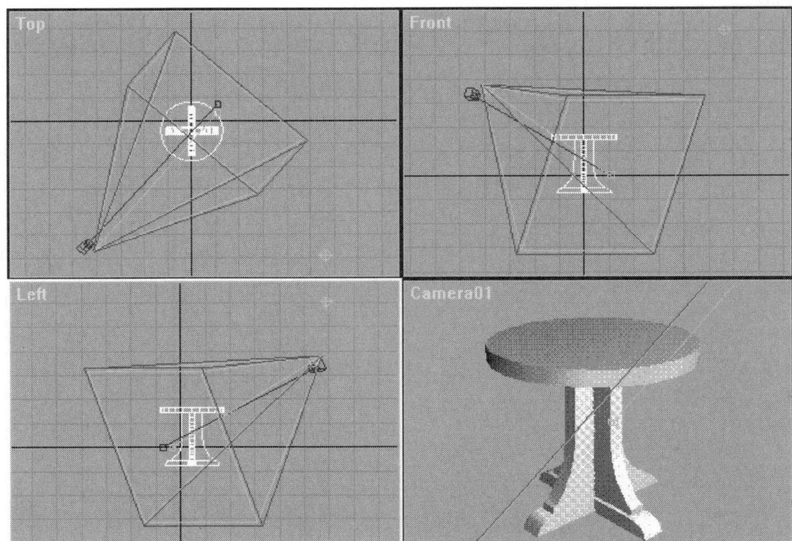

Fig. 7.12 Second example of a camera and lights

Fig. 7.13 A rendering of the table with a camera and two lights in position as in Example 2

Example 3 – adding a table lamp and its light

1. Using **Line** and **Edit Spline** followed by **Lathe**, create a table lamp, placed on the table top, such as that shown in Fig. 7.14.
2. Position a target spot light in the centre top of the lamp, with its target point just below the table top.
3. With **Target Spot Attenuation** at the default settings render the **Camera01** viewport. The results are as shown in Fig. 7.15.
4. Reset **Attenuation** to **End Range** of 500 and render again. The result is shown in Fig. 7.16.

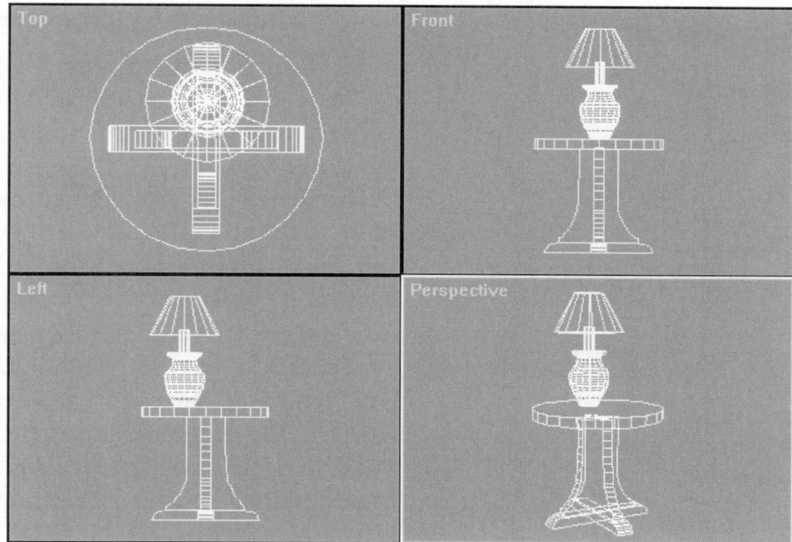

Fig. 7.14 Adding a table lamp

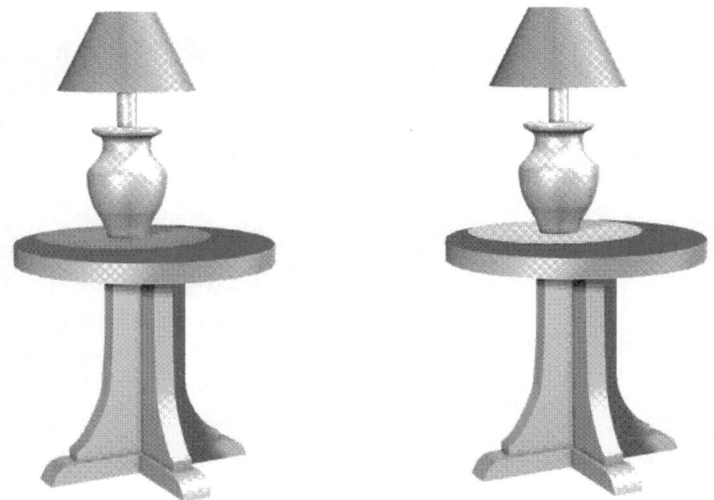

Fig. 7.15 Target spot light in lamp. Left-hand rendering at default values of **Attenuation**. Right-hand rendering with **Attenuation End Range** set at 500

Note on attenuation

With attenuation, objects at a further distance from a light source are not so well lit. Those nearer are better lit. Without attenuation this natural result does not occur. Thus with attenuation, light fall-off increases with distance from the light source.

In the last example if the **Hotspot** figure of the target spot light settings in the Command panel are decreased, the circle of the light falling on the table will be smaller. It is worth while experimenting with the **Attenuation** and the **Hotspot** and **Falloff** settings.

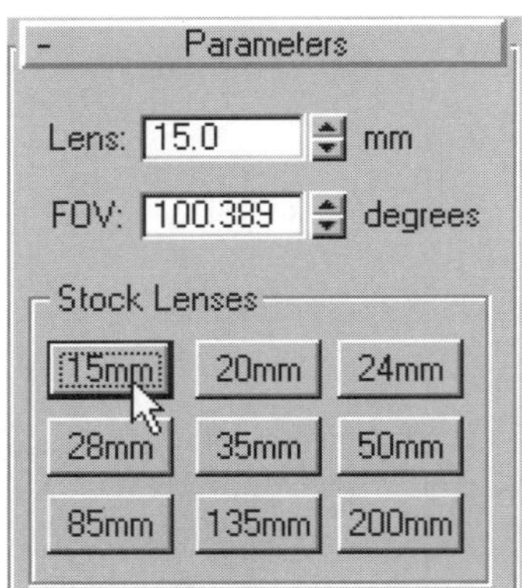

Fig. 7.16 The **Stock Lenses** buttons for a target camera

Example 4 – changing camera lenses

1. In the **Edit** pull-down menu, select **Select By Name** and in the dialogue box which appears select all the lights and the camera. When selected delete them (press the **Delete** key of the keyboard when selected).
2. Delete the table lamp in its entirety – base and shade.
3. With only the table now showing add a camera and adjust to a suitable position showing the table in the **Camera01** viewport with **Smooth+Highlight** configuration.
4. Now experiment with the appearance of the view in the **Camera01** viewport by changing the **Stock Lenses** by *left-clicks* on each of the lens buttons in turn, commencing with the 15 mm and finishing with the 200 mm lens (Fig. 7.16).
5. Then hold a *click* on the up arrow to the right of the **Lens:** window, watching the changes in the **Camera01** viewport.
6. In a similar manner hold a *click* on the up arrow to the right of the **FOV:** window and watch the changes in the viewports. **FOV** = field of view.

Note: The standard lens in most cameras is 50 mm. 15 mm is very wide angle and 200 is towards a telescopic lens. The results obtained in stages 4–6 of the above example should show you results varying from wide angle (15 mm) to telescopic (200 mm).

Free cameras

Free cameras are not usually used to 'shoot' a scene. They are used when one wishes to animate the camera, as for example when moving around a scene so as to see it from all directions. In an example such as that, a free camera would be set to view the scene at a suitable position, then moved in steps around a circle. This will be described in Chapter 10.

Directional lights

Directional lights give out beams of light in front of and behind the icon. The icon can be rotated or moved. Figure 7.17 shows a directional light in a scene.

Directional lights can be used to give lighting similar to sunlight. As with other lights, colour can be included with the light if necessary.

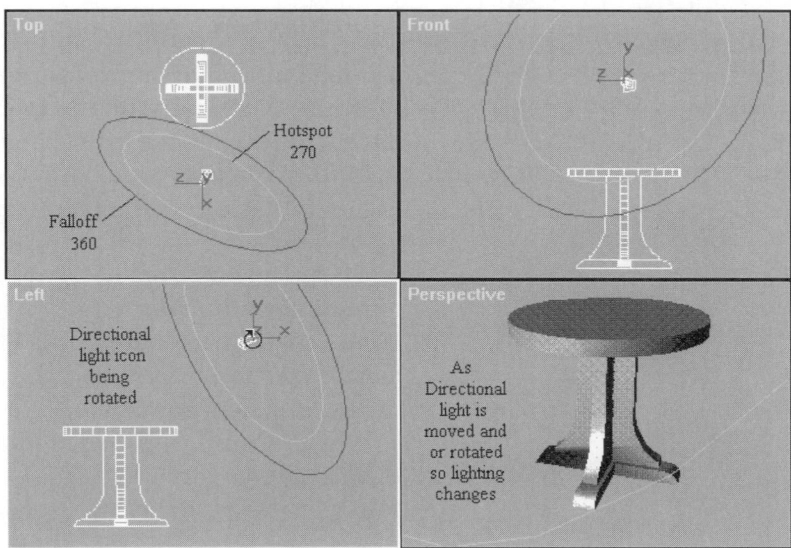

Fig. 7.17 An example of the rotation of a directional light

Free spot lights

Figure 7.18 shows a free spot light with its **Hotspot** set to 18 and **Falloff** set to 50, with the **Target Distance** set to 200. Like other lights a free spot light can be moved or rotated and as can be seen in Fig. 7.18 the hotspot and falloff are clearly differentiated. In this example also, the check circle against **Shadows** was set on.

This is useful, particularly in animations such as when a car is moving with its headlights on, or a spot is to be moved in an animation in a theatre scene.

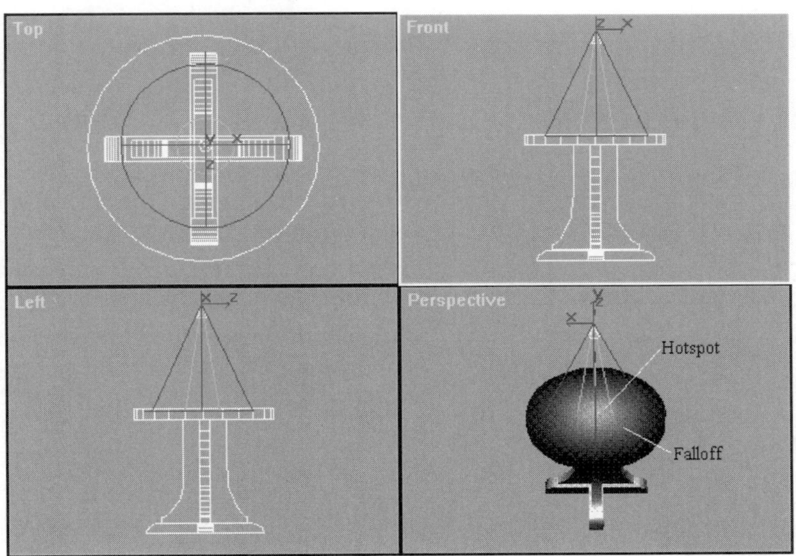

Fig. 7.18 An example of a free spot light

Exercises

1. The table and lamp shown in examples in this chapter were created in 3D Studio Max. Working to any dimensions, create a similar table and lamp stand with shade and follow the steps for adding lights and cameras detailed in the above examples.
2. Figure 7.19 is a rendering of a stand as part of a model for sending off a rocket.

   Create a similar model and add a camera and lighting before rendering your model.
3. Figure 7.20 is a rendering of a 3D model of part of a brooch, constructed in AutoCAD and imported into 3D Studio Max before having a camera and lights added and then being rendered.

   Create a similar brooch model, add a camera and lighting and then render your model

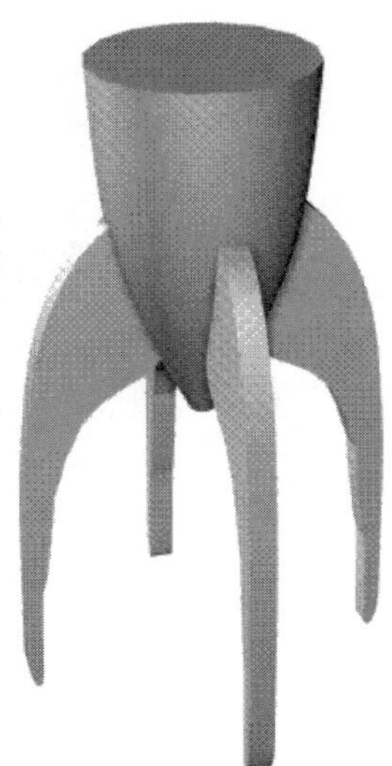

Fig. 7.19 Exercise 2

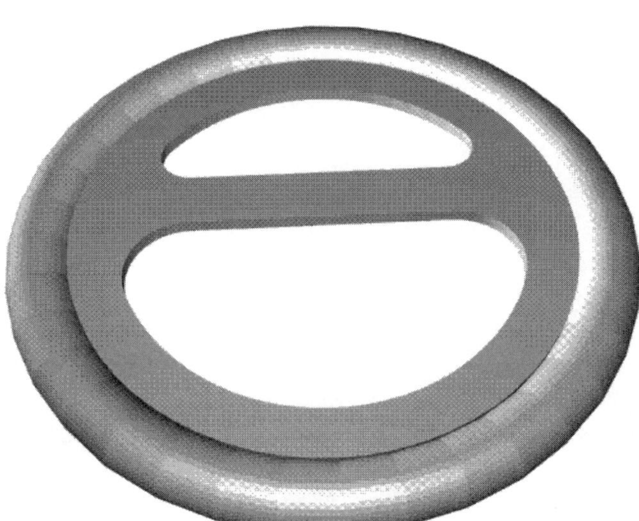

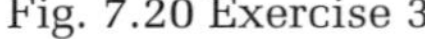

Fig. 7.20 Exercise 3

4. Figure 7.21 shows a rendering of a simple stool model created and rendered in 3D Studio Max. Figure 7.22 shows the model in four viewports prior to being rendered in the **Camera01** viewport. Note the flat surface (a box) on which the stool stands in order to show the shadows produced from the target spot light.

   Attempt to create a similar model, add a camera and lights and then render.

Fig. 7.21 Exercise 4

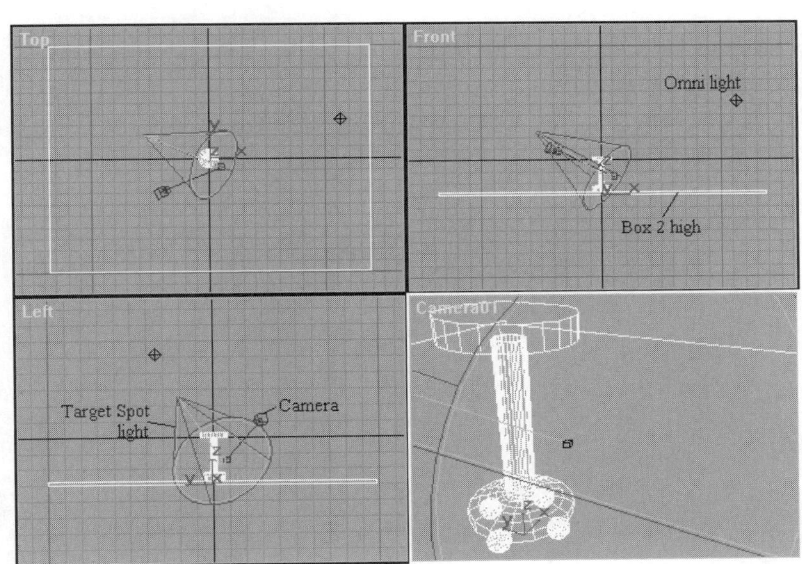

Fig. 7.22 Creating the model, a camera and lights for Exercise 4

5. Figure 7.23 shows a box with a handle which has been created and rendered in 3D Studio Max. Note the base on which the box is standing in order to bring out the shadows cast from the target spot light. Figure 7.24 shows the model being created in a four-viewport window. In this illustration the camera and lights have been hidden to show the outlines more clearly.

   Create a similar box and add a camera and lights before rendering.

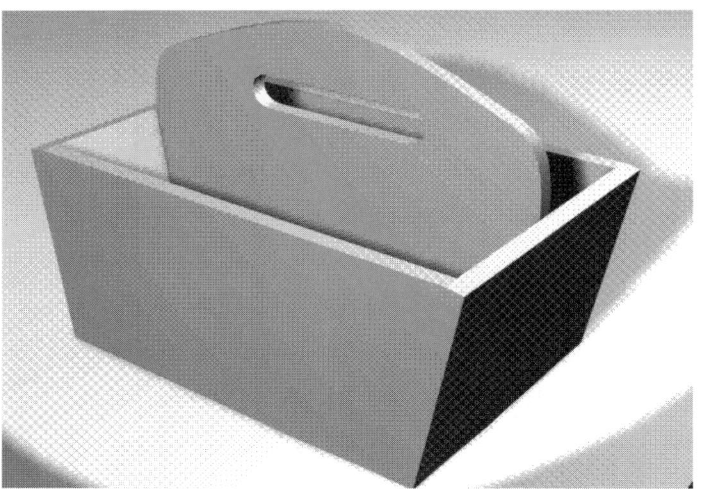

Fig. 7.23 Exercise 5

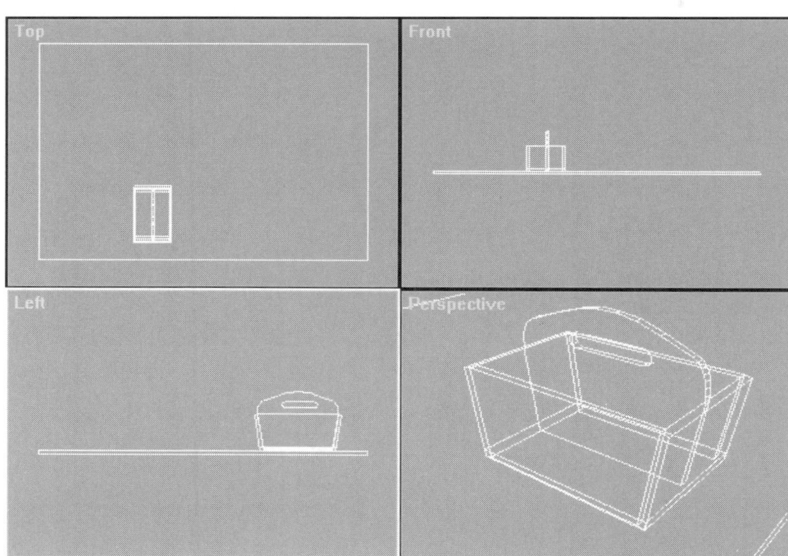

Fig. 7.24 Creating the model for Exercise 5

CHAPTER 8

Materials

The Material Editor

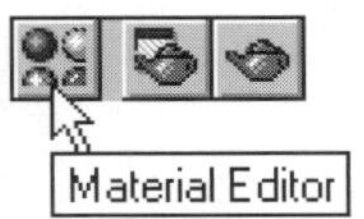

Fig. 8.1 The **Material Editor** icon

Left-click on the **Material Editor** icon in the toolbar (Fig. 8.1). The **Material Editor** dialogue box appears (Fig. 8.2). The **Material Editor** is a very complicated dialogue box as can be partly seen by reference to Fig. 8.3 in which the names of the tools below and to the right of the six sample spheres in squares in the upper part of the dialogue box are shown.

Note the following details in Fig. 8.3:

1. One of the sample spheres is surrounded by a white border, showing that this is the selected sample.

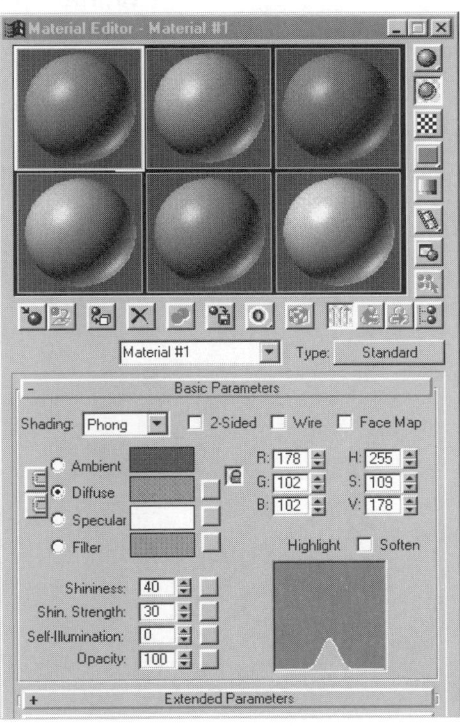

Figh. 8.2 The **Material Editor** dialogue box

2. Several of the tool icons have flyouts, which are included in Fig. 8.3. That on the left of the illustration is the flyout of the **Material Effects Channel** icon.

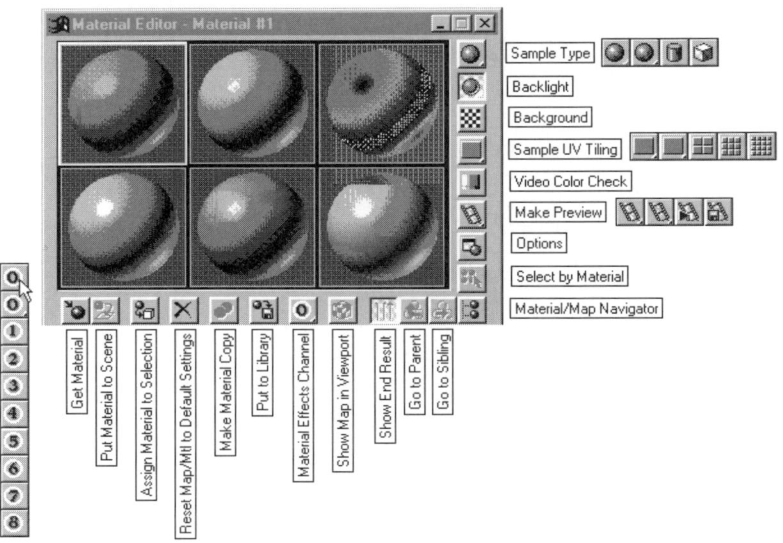

Fig. 8.3 The names of the icons in the **Material Editor** dialogue box

Examples of assigning materials in a scene

Example 1

Create a simple table scene such as that shown in Fig. 8.4. Add a camera and lighting. Set the bottom right-hand viewport to **Camera01**

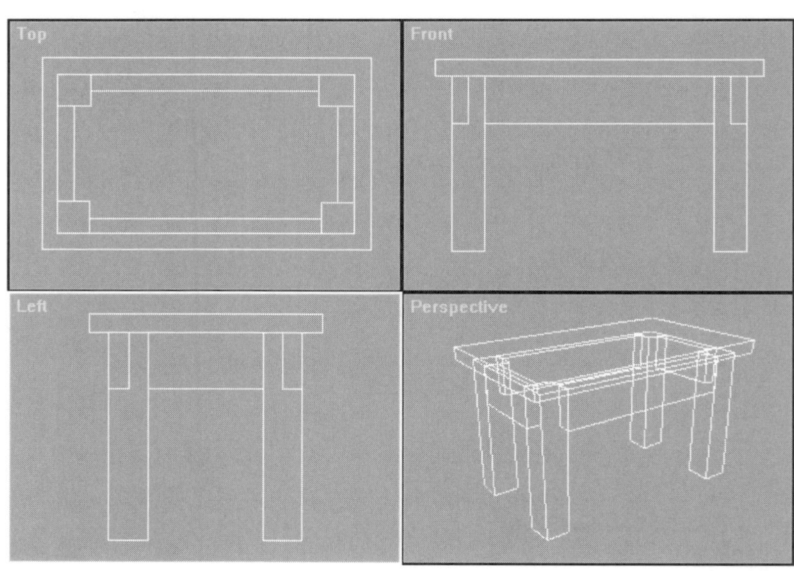

Fig. 8.4 The table model created for Example 1

and configure it to **Smooth+Highlight**. The table consists of a series of **Box**es, each a separate object. To apply simple colour materials to each of the objects making up the table:

1. *Left-click* on the **Material Editor** icon.
2. Select any one of the objects in the table such as one of the legs. Note this can be carried out while the dialogue box is on screen.
3. *Left-click* in any of the sample sphere boxes. *Left-click* on the **Assign Material to Selection** icon. The selected object changes to the colour of the sample sphere which has been chosen.
4. Continue in this way until all the objects making up the table model have been assigned a material.

Figure 8.5 shows a rendering of the result with different colours applied to legs, rails and top.

Fig. 8.5 A rendering of the table with different colour materials assigned

Changing the colours of the sample spheres

The colours in the sample spheres can be edited as follows:

1. Select any one of the sample spheres. It becomes highlighted with a white edging.
2. *Left-click* in the **Ambient** colour swathe. The **Color Selector: Ambient** dialogue appears as in Fig. 8.6.
3. Adjust the sliders **Red**, **Green** and **Blue** in the colour chart of the dialogue box (Fig. 8.6). As the sliders are adjusted, the sample sphere changes colour as does also the object to which the colour in the sample sphere has already been assigned.
4. Experiment also with the **Hue:**, **Saturation:** and **Value:** sliders.
5. Adjust the values of the **Diffuse** values.

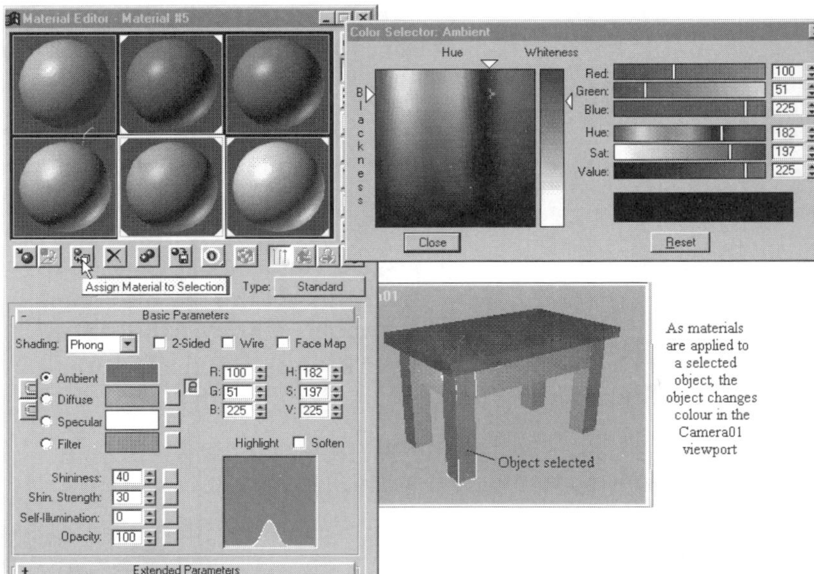

Fig. 8.6 The **Color Selector: Ambient** dialogue box

4. Adjust the colours of the objects via the sample spheres in the same way until suitable colours have been assigned to all parts of the scene.

Note: When a colour has been assigned to an object, the sample colour sphere is enclosed in small white triangles.

Fig. 8.7 The wineglass model for Example 2

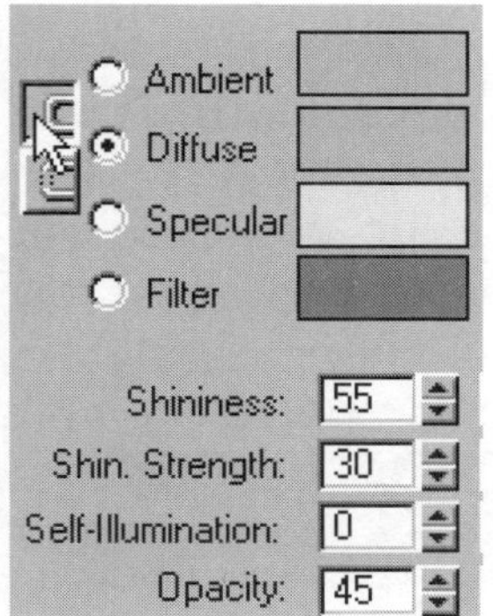

Fig. 8.8 Settings in the **Material Editor**

Example 2

Create a wineglass similar to that shown in Fig. 8.7 and add a camera and lighting. Set the **Perspective** viewport to **Camera01** and to **Smooth+Highlight**, and adjust the camera and the lights to obtain a good view of the wineglass model in the **Camera01** viewport. Then:

1. Select the wineglass model in the **Camera01** viewport.
2. Call the **Material Editor** dialogue box.
3. In the dialogue box, select any one of the colour sample spheres.
4. *Left-click* in the lock icon between the **Ambient** and **Diffuse** colours. The colours become the same. Set either of the colours to a green.
5. Set the **Shininess:** and **Opacity:** figures as shown in Fig. 8.8.
6. Render the **Camera01** viewport. It will be seen that the wineglass has become transparent as shown in Fig. 8.9.

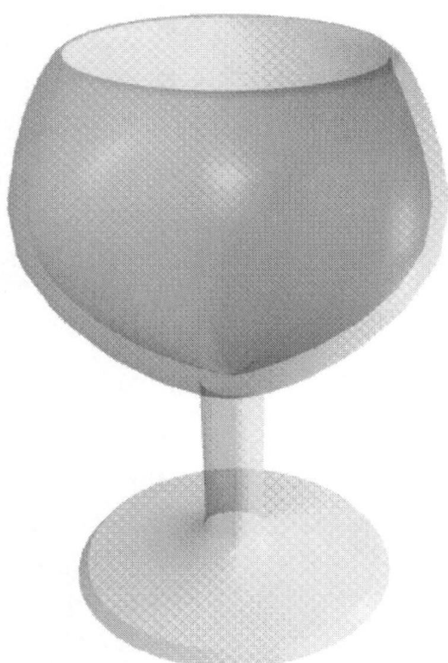

Fig. 8.9 Example 2 – a rendering

Note: Experiment with the settings:

Ambient:
Diffuse:
Shininess: and **Shin Strength:**
Self Illumination:
Opacity:

and render the wineglass model for each of your groups of settings.

Example 3

This example uses an AutoCAD drawing imported into 3D Studio Max. After constructing the 3D model of a crank in AutoCAD Release 13, the model was imported in Max (Fig. 8.10). A camera and lighting were added to the scene and the **Perspective** viewport was set to **Camera01**.

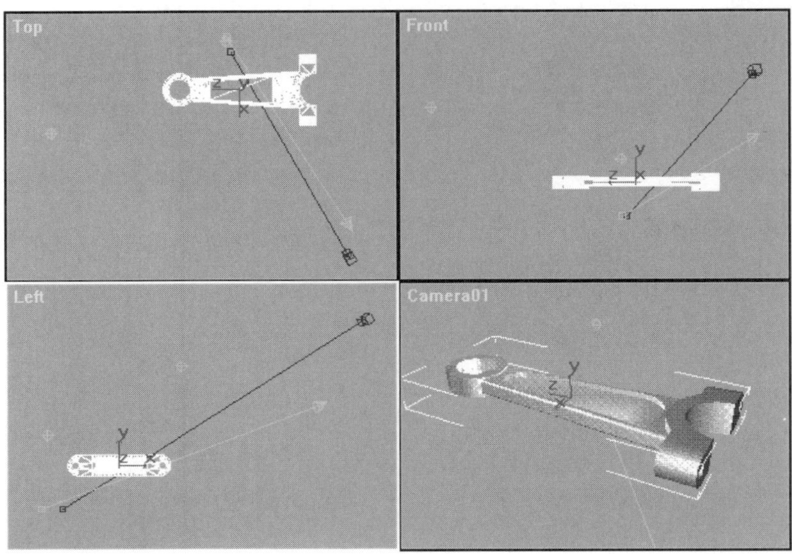

Fig. 8.10 The scene for Example 3

Then:

1. Make sure the model is selected.
2. Call the **Material Editor** dialogue box to screen.
3. *Drag* the colour sphere from the top right corner to the centre top square. It replaces the colour sphere in the centre square. Select this centre colour sphere and with **Assign Material to Selection** assign the material to the crank. You will see the name **Tex # 1** in a name box below the lower line of icons. Change that name to **Crank**.
4. *Left-click* on the **Maps** bar at the bottom of the dialogue box. You may have to close the rollouts already in the box by *left-clicks* on the bars marked with a negative sign.
5. *Left-click* in the button bar (named **None**) opposite **Reflection**. The **Material/Map Browser** dialogue box appears (Fig. 8.11). In the box select **New** at the top left-hand corner. The **Material Editor** dialogue box reappears but with The **Bitmap Parameters** area of the rollout showing (Fig. 8.12).
6. Opposite **Reflection** *enter* **Crank Material**. *Left-click* on the empty button bar marked **Bitmap:**. The **Select Bitmap Image File** dialogue

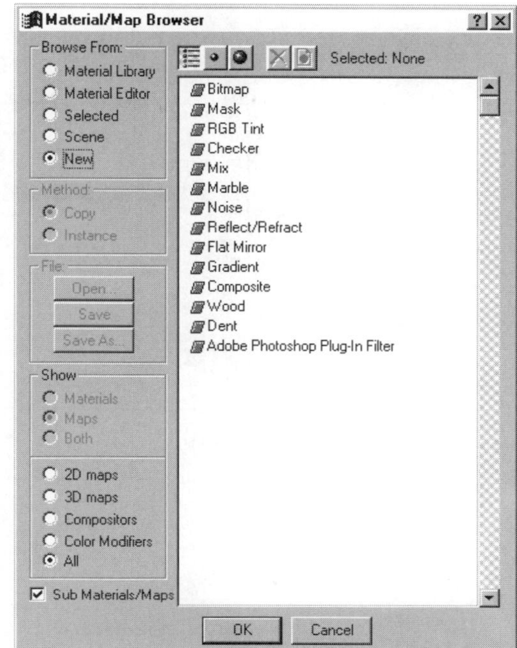

Fig. 8.11 The **Material/Map Browser**

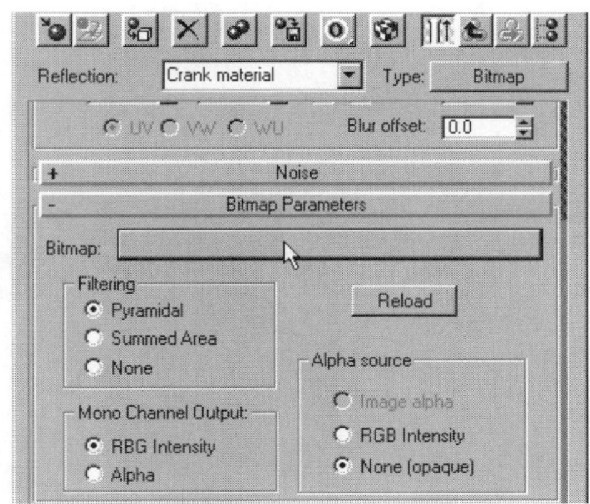

Fig. 8.12 Part of the **Material Editor** as it now appears

box appears (Fig. 8.13). The appearance of the bitmap can be seen by a *left-click* on the **View...** button as shown in Fig. 8.13.

7. Go back to the original **Material Editor** rollout with a *left-click* on the **Go to Parent** icon (see page 199). Lock **Ambient** and **Diffuse** and change their colours to black – **R:**, **G:** and **B:** all to zero (0).
8. Because the results of adding a reflection map will not show in the **Camera01** viewport, **Quick Render** the viewport. The result is as seen in Fig. 8.14.

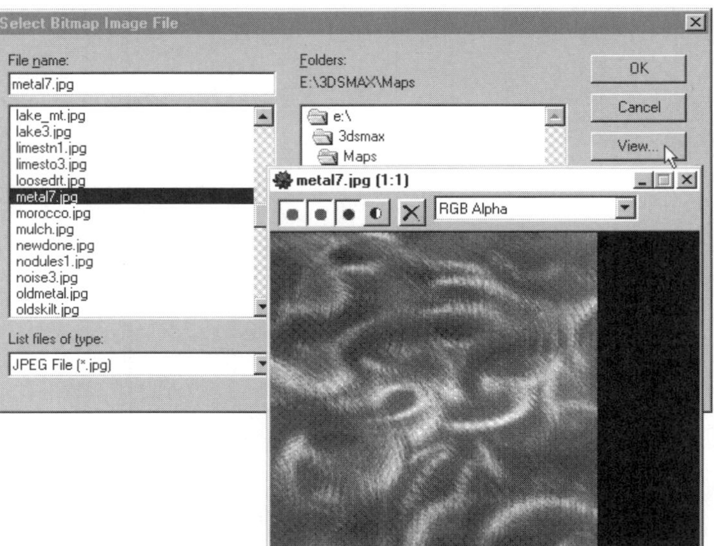

Fig. 8.13 A bitmap showing when **View...** is selected from the **Select Bitmap Image File** dialogue box

Notes

1. When in the **Material Editor**, even if its associated dialogue boxes are open, selection of parts of a scene can still take place without having to close the dialogue box.
2. Also when in the **Material Editor** the scene in a viewport can still be rendered without closing the dialogue box or its associated boxes.

Fig. 8.14 Selecting **Environment...** from the **Rendering** pull-down menu

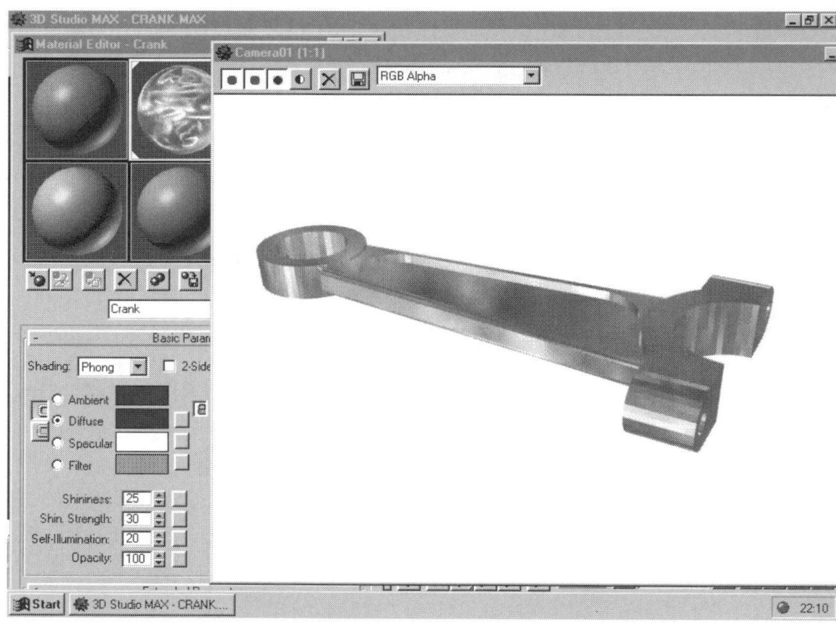

Fig. 8.15 Rendering Example 3. Note that rendering can take place even when the **Material Editor** dialogue box is open

3. The results of bringing in the reflection map does not show very well in the colour sphere from which the material was assigned to the model. This can also be seen in Fig. 8.15 from the appearance of the centre top colour sphere in the **Material Editor**.

Adding a background to Example 3

1. *Left-click* on **Environment...** in the **Rendering** pull-down menu (Fig. 8.14).
2. In the **Background** area of the dialogue box *left-click* on the **Assign...** button. The **Material/Map Browser** dialogue box appears (Fig. 8.16). In this dialogue box, *left-click* on **Material Library** and in the library list *double-click* on a bitmap icon. In this example we have chosen **SKY**.

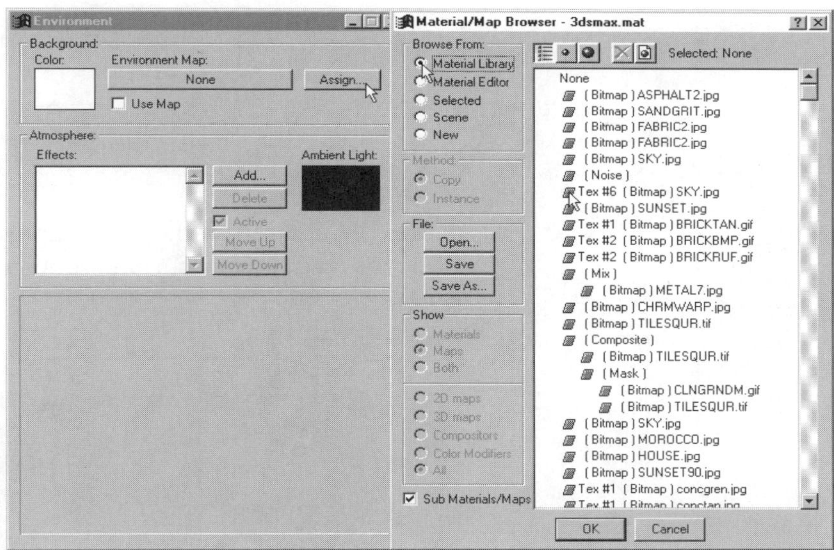

Fig. 8.16 The **Environment** dialogue box with the **Material/Map Browser** showing

3. The name of the bitmap appears on the **Environment Map** button bar. A *left-click* on that bar brings up yet another dialogue box **Put to Material Editor**.
4. In the **Put to Material Editor** dialogue box (Fig. 8.17), *click* in **Slot 2**, which shows the material already assigned to the Example 3 model. *Left-click* on the **OK** button and close the **Environment** dialogue box.
5. Now render the viewport **Camera01** and it will be seen that a sky background has been assigned to the rendering (Fig. 8.18).
6. It is advisable to experiment with backgrounds in this manner taken from the materials libraries.

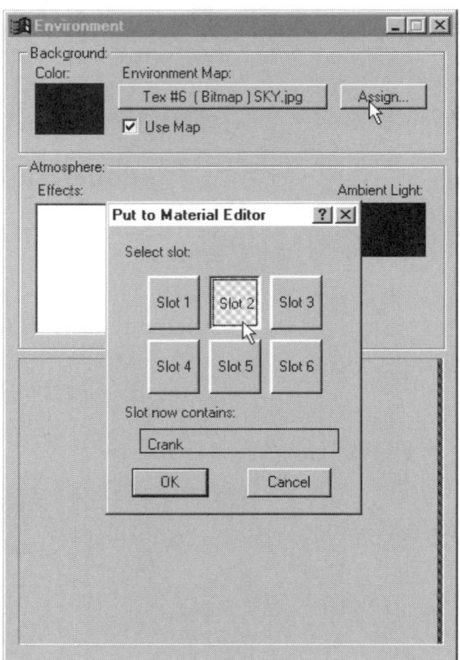

Fig. 8.17 The **Put to Material Editor** dialogue box

7. In the **Camera01** rendering window, *left-click* on each of the colour icons (red, green and blue dots) in the toolbar of the rendering

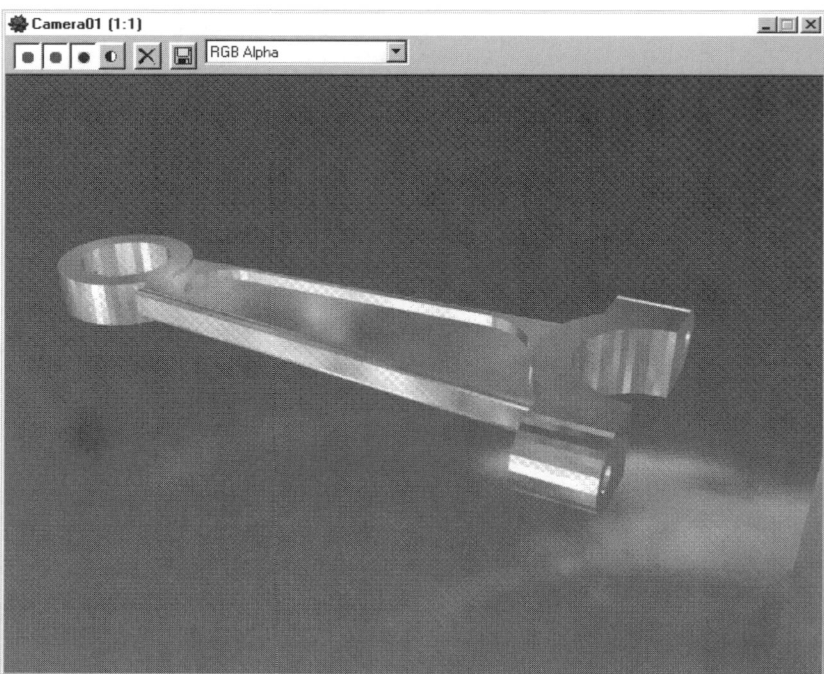

Fig. 8.18 Example 3 with its sky background

window in turn to show what happens when the selected colour is turned off. Also *click* on the **Save Bitmap** icon and in the dialogue box which appears bring up the **Files of type:** popup list to see the types of files in which a rendering can be saved.

Example 4

This is the rendering of another AutoCAD drawing file imported into 3D Studio Max.

1. Import the drawing file. Add a camera and lighting. Configure the **Perspective** viewport to **Camera01** with **Grid** not showing.
2. Make sure the object – a drill tray from a drilling machine – has been selected.
3. Call the **Material Editor** to screen and select the top left colour sphere in Slot 1.
4. *Left-click* on **Get Material** (Fig. 8.19). The **Material Map/Browser** appears (Fig. 8.20). Set the check circle against **Material Library** to on (dot in circle) and select **Metal Galvanised** from the list of materials (you will have to scroll down the list to reach this material). Then *left-click* on the **OK** button.
5. The colour sphere in Slot 1 changes to show this selected material. *Left-click* on **Assign Material to Selection**. The 3D model in the **Camera01** viewport changes colour.

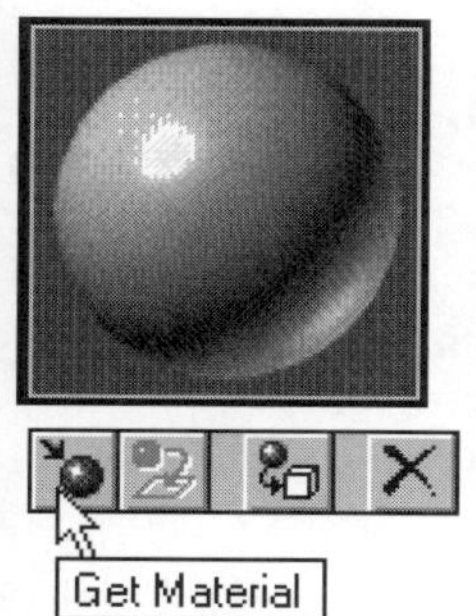

Fig. 8.19 Select **Get Material**

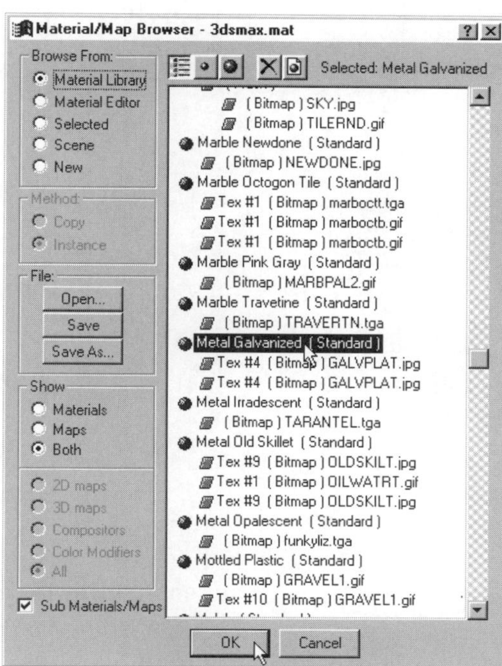

Fig. 8.20 The **Material/Map Browser**

6. Attempt to render the **Camera01** viewport. The **Render Error** message box (Fig. 8.21) appears. *Click* **Cancel** to close the message box.

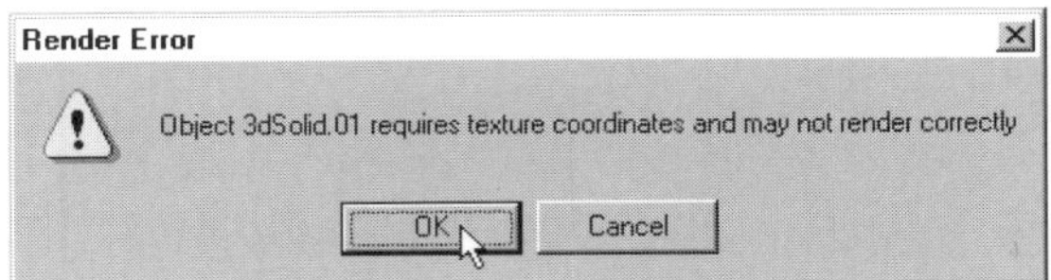

Fig. 8.21 The **Render Error** message box

7. In the **Material Editor** open the **Maps** rollout and select the bar against **Diffuse** which is showing the material name. Then *left-click* on the **UVW Map** button in the modifiers rollout in the Command panel (Fig. 8.22). A **Diffuse** map shows in the **Camera01** viewport and the viewport will now render (Fig. 8.23).

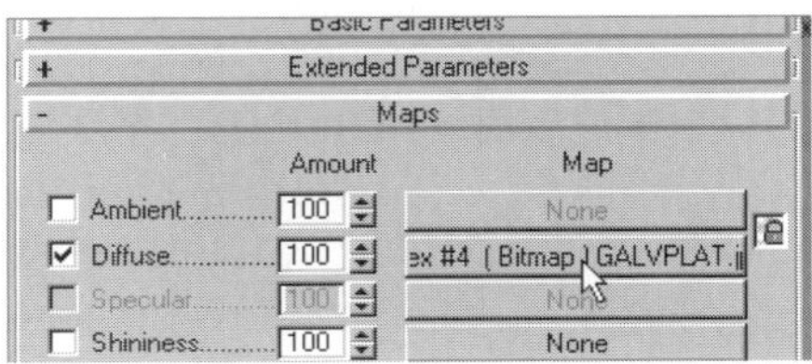

Fig. 8.22 Select the **Diffuse** bar button

UVW Map

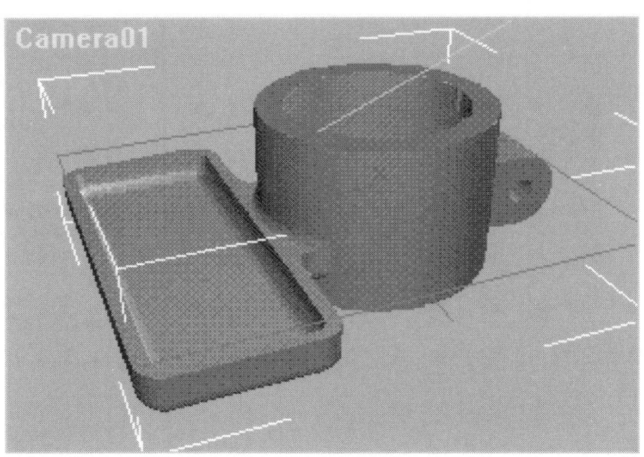

Fig. 8.23 Placing a **Diffuse** map in the **Camera01** viewport

Notes

1. **Ambient** lighting is a general light which is in every scene. It has no real source or position but should be understood as general background lighting.

2. **Diffuse** lighting is what most of us would refer to as ordinary lighting. It is the light by which a colour is seen.
3. **Specular** lighting is that form of lighting which causes highlights to appear on a model.
4. A diffuse map must be applied in the case of Example 4 above because it is the diffuse part of the material which will be seen as a material when the object is rendered.
5. Some materials will not require mapping, making the use of the **UVW Map** moderator unnecessary. As an example assign the material **Brass** from the **Materials Library** to an object. It can be rendered without using the **UVW Map** moderator. Another example, **Yellow Plastic**, does not require mapping. Figure 8.24 shows a removable plastic handle from a card packing case rendered in **Yellow Plastic**.

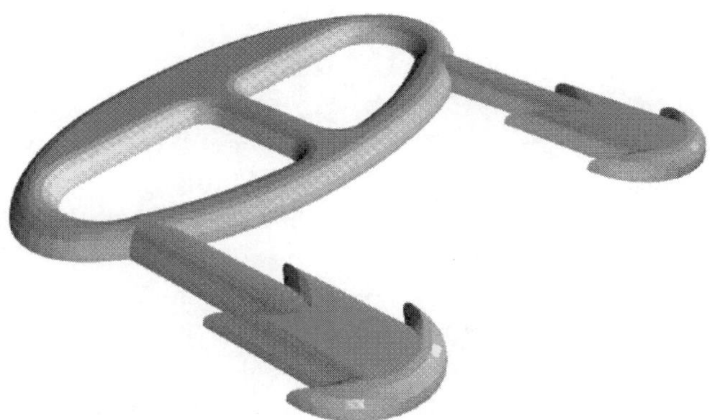

Fig. 8.24 An example of an object assigned the material **Yellow Plastic**

5. In the **Basic Parameters** for any form of material, *left-click* in the **Shading:** box to see the three forms of shading available in 3D Studio Max. **Phong** is the default. If **Metal** shading is selected, the sphere in the selected Slot will become shaded in a metallic form of shading. **Constant** shading does not provide a good quality of shading, but does allow for quicker rendering to test if lighting and materials come out as expected when rendering a scene. See Fig. 8.25.
6. Experiment with rendering an object with the check boxes against **2-Sided** and **Wire** set on (tick in check box).
7. Experiment with changing the **Basic Parameters** for different materials before assigning the material to an object.
8. When a number of objects are in a scene, it is advisable to change the names of materials to names which really describe the object to which the material has been assigned to avoid confusion if parameters need amending. This is easily carried out by deleting

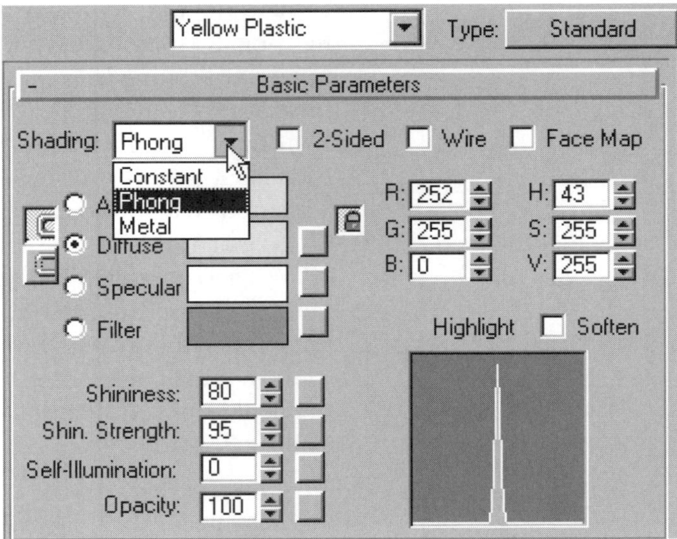

Fig. 8.25 The popup list under **Shading:** in the **Basic Parameters** rollout

the name such as **Yellow Plastic** in the material name box to (in this case) **Handle**.

9. In the **Material Map Browser** dialogue box, *click* on the **View Small Icons** and on the **View Large Icons** icons. Each material can then be seen in the form in which it will appear when assigned to an

Fig. 8.26 The **View Large Icons** display in the **Map Browser**

object. The large icons give a better representation, but take some time to appear in the browser. See Fig. 8.26. A *left-click* on any of the spheres brings up the full name of the material represented by the icon in the form of a tool tip.

Example 5

This example uses a 3D solid model drawing of a saw handle constructed in AutoCAD Release 13 and imported into 3D Studio Max. Add a camera and lighting. Set the **Camera01** viewport to **Smooth+Highlight** and with the **Grid** not showing, then:

Fig. 8.27 Selecting **Display**

1. Select the **Display** icon (Fig. 8.27) and in the **Hide by Category** rollout in the Command panel, set the check boxes against **Lights** and **Camera** on (ticks in boxes) as shown in Fig. 8.28. The lights and camera icons in the viewports disappear – they have been hidden.
2. Make sure the object (the saw handle drawing) is selected and call the **Material Editor**. Select the sphere in **Spot 1**.
3. In the **Maps** rollout set **Diffuse** on (tick in check circle), then *left-click* on the Diffuse **None** button
3. In the **Material/Map Browser** select **New** in the **Browse From:** area of the dialogue box, followed by a *left-click* on **Checker** in the list of materials.
4. Open out the **Checker Params** rollout and *click* the colour swathe next to **Color #1**. Select a colour from the **Color Selector** dialogue box. Repeat with **Color #2**. With **Color #2** you will find that the **Whiteness Selector** arrow will need adjusting before the colour appears in the swathe. The coloured sphere in Spot 1 assumes the

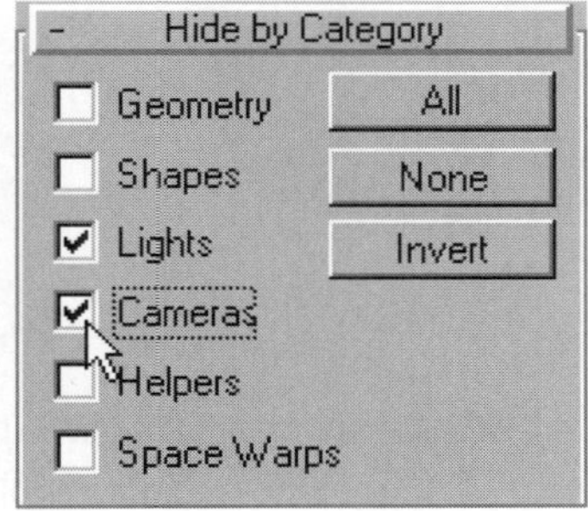

Fig. 8.28 The **Hide by Category** rollout of the **Display** Command panel

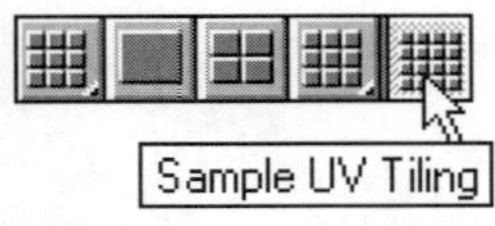

Fig. 8.29 Select the **UV Tiling** icon

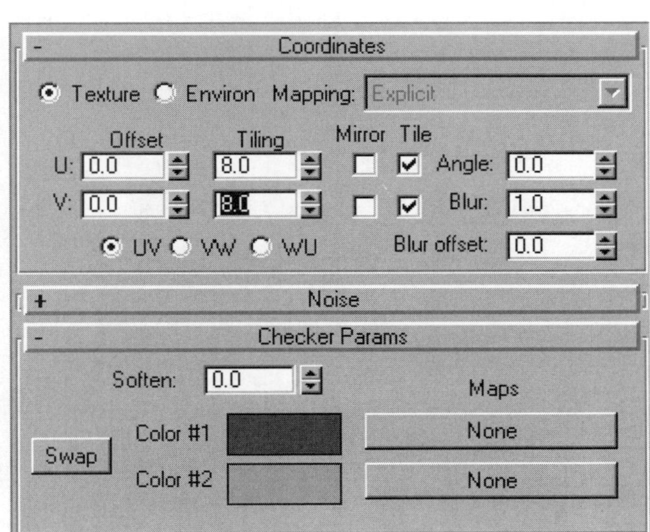

Fig. 8.30 The **Checker Params** rollout

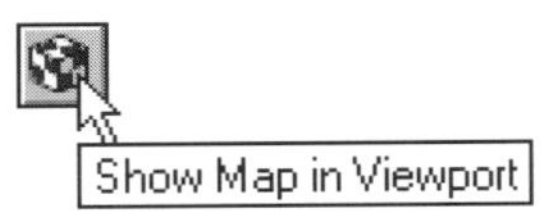

Fig. 8.31 The **Show Map in Viewport** icon

checker colours. Now *left-click* on the **Sample UV Tiling** icon at the right-hand end of the flyout (Fig. 8.29). The colour sphere changes its checker tiling. Finally set the **Tiling** figures both to 8. Figure 8.30 shows the result of these settings in the rollouts.

5. *Left-click* on the **Show Map in Viewport** icon (Fig. 8.31).
6. *Left-click* on the **Assign Material to Selection** icon and the checkered pattern appears in the **Camera01** viewport on the object there.
7. Render the resulting **Camera01** viewport. The result is as shown in Fig. 8.32.

Fig. 8.32 Example 5

Example 6

In this example all six slots of the **Material Editor** are used to assign materials to six of the objects in the scene. The scene, which was

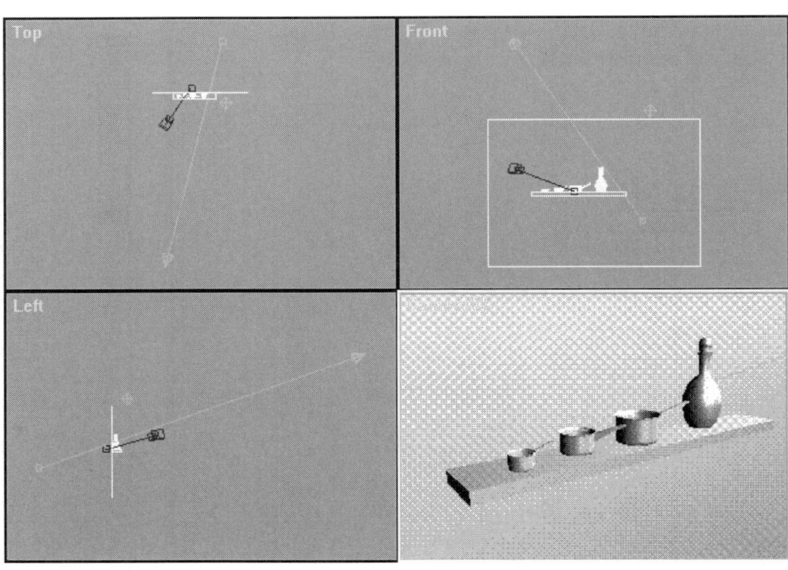

Fig. 8.33 The scene for Example 6

completely created within 3D Studio Max, comprises a shelf fitted against a wall. On the shelf are three saucepans of different sizes and a bottle made from a material appearing like granite. The bottle has a stopper. The scene is shown in Fig. 8.33.

Each of the objects in the scene was given a name as shown in Fig. 8.34. The dialogue box shown in Fig. 8.34 was brought to screen by choosing **Select By Name** from the **Edit** pull-down menu.

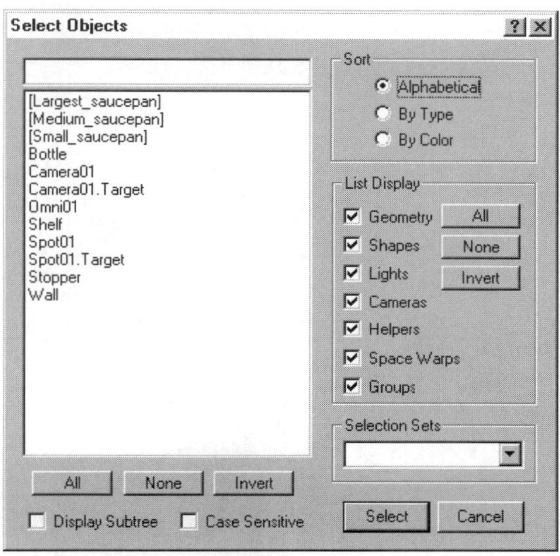

Fig. 8.34 The names of objects showing in the **Select Objects** dialogue box

Materials were assigned to the objects as follows:

Largest saucepan: Chrome Pearl (Standard).
Medium saucepan: The sphere already showing in Slot 4.
Small saucepan: Chrome Morocco (Standard).
Bottle: The default material before any material is assigned.
Shelf: Wood Ashen (Standard).
Stopper: The sphere already showing in Slot 4.
Wall: Concrete Tan (Standard).

These assignments resulted in the **Material Editor** slots appearing as indicated in Fig. 8.35.

The resulting rendering of the scene is shown in Fig. 8.36.

Note

Left-click on the **Sample Type** icon in the **Material Editor** to change the sample type from sphere to cylinder of cube (Fig. 8.37).

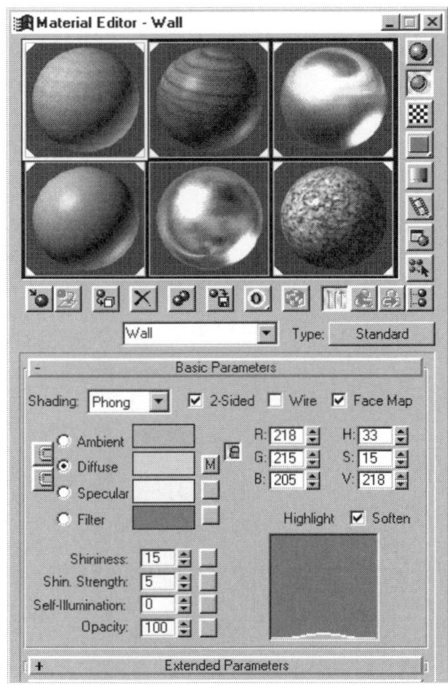

Fig. 8.35 The **Material Editor** slots showing for Example 6

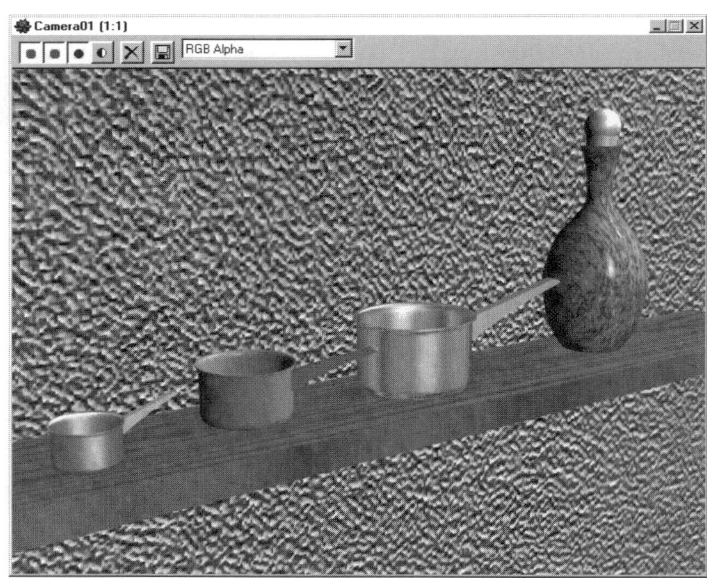

Fig. 8.36 A rendering of Example 6

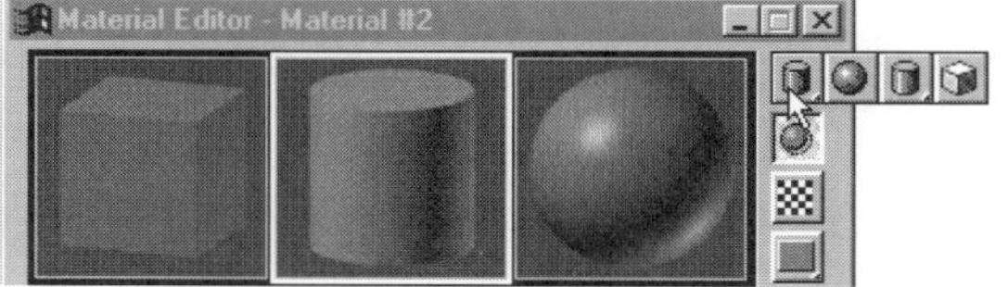

Fig. 8.37 Changing sample types in the **Material Editor**

Exercises

1. Figure 8.38 shows the dimensions to which the parts of a towing bracket, its towing and holding pins have been drawn. Figure 8.39 is a rendering of the bracket and its pins from the AutoCAD Release 13 drawing imported into 3D Studio Max. To import the drawing note the settings in the **Import Options** dialogue box (Fig. 8.39).

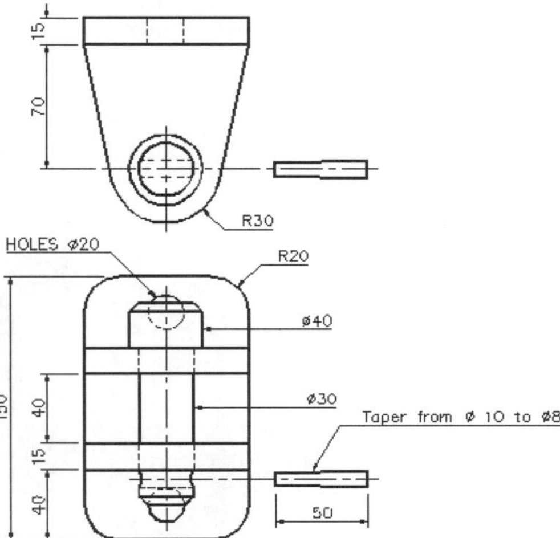

Fig. 8.38 Dimensions for Exercise 1

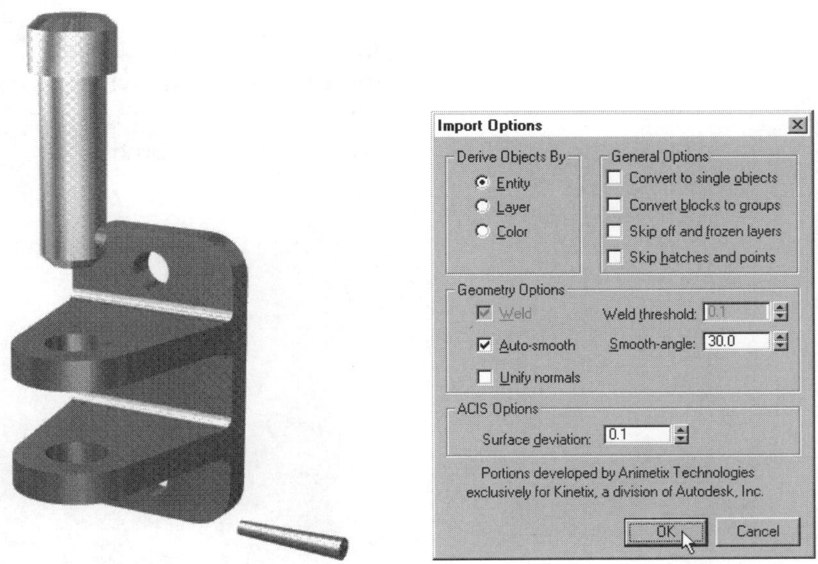

Fig. 8.39 Exercise 1 and the **Import Options** dialogue box settings

Construct a solid model drawing of the towing bracket to the dimensions given in Fig. 8.38, with the bracket and its pins as three separate solids. Import the drawing into 3D Studio Max, add lighting and a camera. Add materials:

Bracket: Chrome Morocco.
Towing pin: Chrome Pearl.
Holding pin: Chrome Sunset.

Then render your model (Fig. 8.39). Move the pins into their holding position and render again (Fig. 8.40).

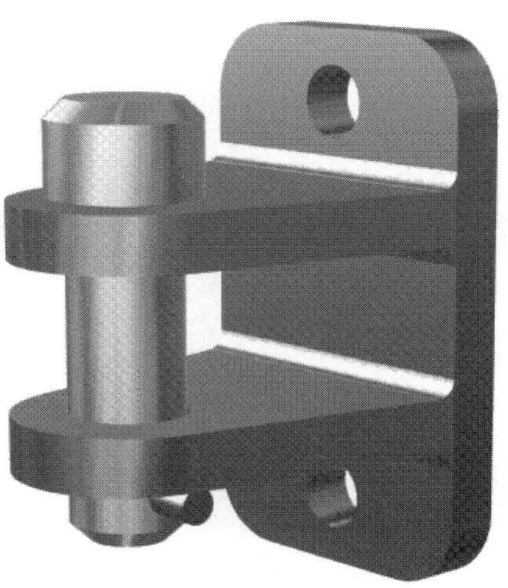

Fig. 8.40 The second rendering for Exercise 1

2. Figure 8.41 shows a rendering of a wine bottle partly filled with red wine, its cork and two wineglasses, partly filled with red wine. The bottle, cork and glass are resting on a round table top. All the objects were created in 3D Studio Max.

Fig. 8.41 Exercise 2

Create the five objects, add a camera and lighting and appropriate materials. Then render your scene.

3. Figure 8.42 shows the text **3D Studio Max** surmounted upon three blocks. Create a similar scene, add a camera, lighting and materials and render the scene you have created.

Fig. 8.42 Exercise 3

4. Figure 8.43 shows a rendering of another AutoCAD Release 13 3D solid model drawing which has been imported into 3D Studio Max. A camera, lighting and materials were included in the scene before rendering.

Fig. 8.43 Exercise 4

Fig. 8.44 shows the dimensions of the original AutoCAD drawing.

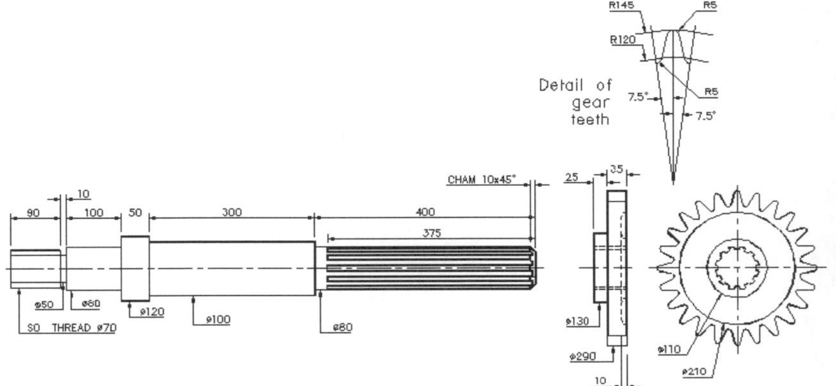

Fig. 8.44 Dimensions for Exercise 4

5. Figure 8.45 shows a rendering of a clock face with hands set at a time. Create a clock face similar to that shown to any suitable sizes, add the text for the hours and the two hands.

   Add a camera, lighting and suitable materials to all parts of the clock you have created, followed by rendering.

Fig. 8.45 Exercise 5

CHAPTER 9

Rendering

The Rendering pull-down menu

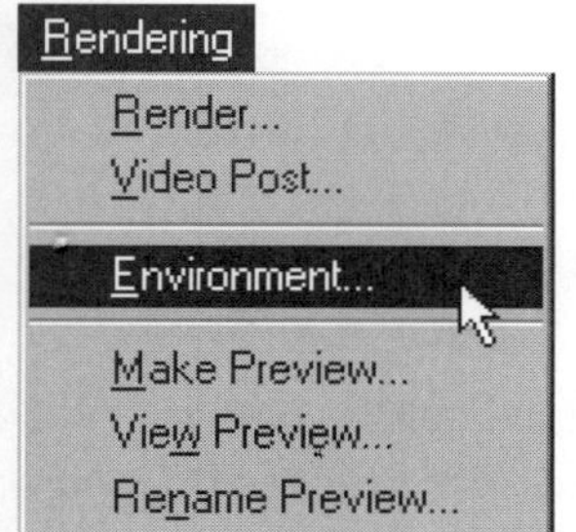

Fig. 9.1 Selecting **Environment... from the** Rendering pull-down menu

Settings in the **Environment** dialogue box are among the first settings to be made when starting a rendering. The dialogue box is called to screen with a *left-click* on **Environment...** in the **Rendering** pull-down menu (Fig. 9.1). As with many of the dialogue boxes in 3D Studio Max, the **Environment** dialogue box contains a number of sub dialogue boxes from which settings can be made. The results of some of these settings can be seen in Plates I–IV in which the parameters for backgrounds, ambient lighting, fog and coloured fog are added to a simple model created in 3D Studio.

Background colour

In the **Environment** dialogue box, *click* in the **Color:** box in the **Background** area of the dialogue box. The **Color Selector: Background Color** dialogue box appears, from which a colour can be selected. In the example shown in Fig. 9.2 the colour white has been set for background, by *dragging* the arrow on the right of the **Whiteness:** bar to the bottom of the bar. As the change is made so the **Color:** box changes to the new setting of colour. Any of the colours available from the **Color Selector** can be used as a background for a rendering.

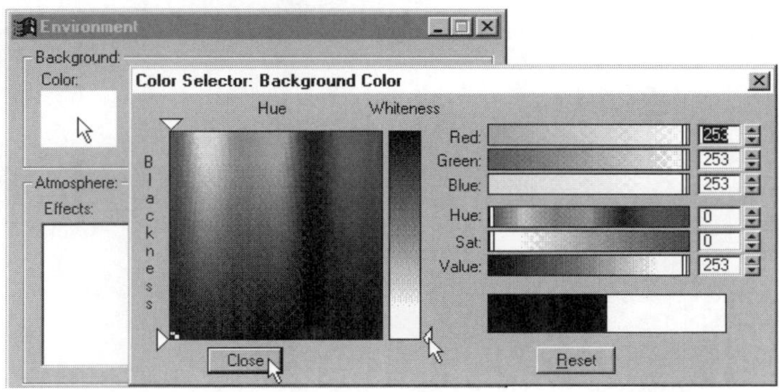

Fig. 9.2 Setting a background colour

Most of the renderings in black and white in this book have been rendered with the background colour set to white in this manner.

To make the setting shown in Fig. 9.2, first *click* in the **Color:** square of the dialogue box, then select the colour from the **Color Selector**, finally *left-click* on the **Close** button of the **Color Selector** box.

Setting an Environment map for a background

Left-click on the **Assign...** button in the **Background** area of the **Environment** dialogue box, followed by selecting **Material Library** from the **Material/Map Browser** dialogue box which appears. In the example given in Fig. 9.3 the bitmap **Sky** has been selected as a background. Plate III shows an object rendered with the **Sky** bitmap as a background.

To make the settings, first *left-click* on the **Assign...** button, then either *double-click* on the selected bitmap name or *left-click* on the name, followed by another *left-click* on the **OK** button of the **Material/Map Browser**.

Note: An environment map will take precedence over the background colour. Thus even with the background colour set to black, a blue sky environment map shows blue sky without the black interfering with the sky bitmap.

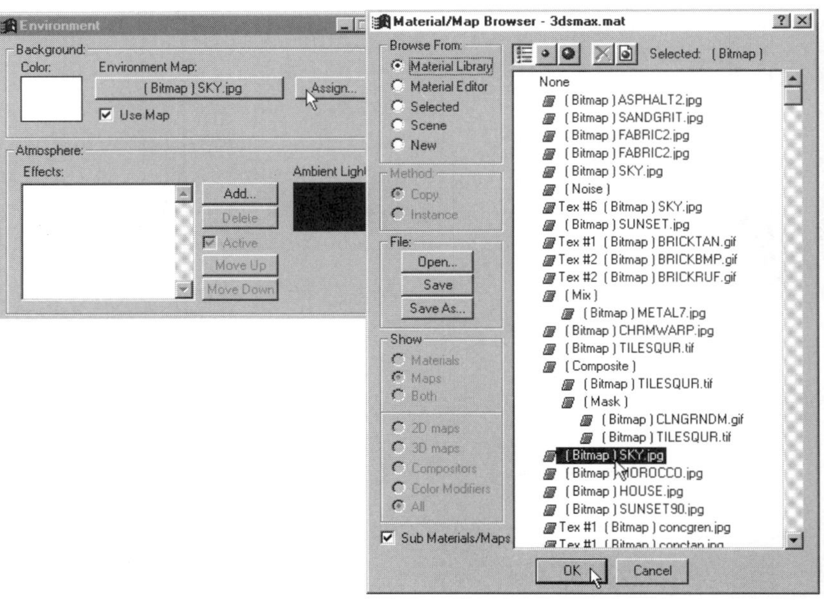

Fig. 9.3 Selecting a bitmap for background

Setting Ambient lighting

It will be remembered that ambient lighting is the general level of light permeating the area of the scene. If the general level of the ambient light is increased so will the overall lighting of the scene increase. In general it is not usually advisable to set the ambient lighting to a high a degree of whiteness.

To set ambient lighting, *click* in the square under **Ambient Light:** The **Color Selector:Ambient Light** colour chart appears. In the example given in Fig. 9.4 the arrow to the right of the **Whiteness** bar has been *dragged* to produce a grey colour in the **Ambient Light:** square. The ambient light can be set to any colour, but adjustment of the whiteness will be found to be necessary.

To set ambient light first *click* in the **Ambient Light:** square, then select the colour required and its **Whiteness** followed by a *left-click* on the **Close** button of the **Color Selector** dialogue box.

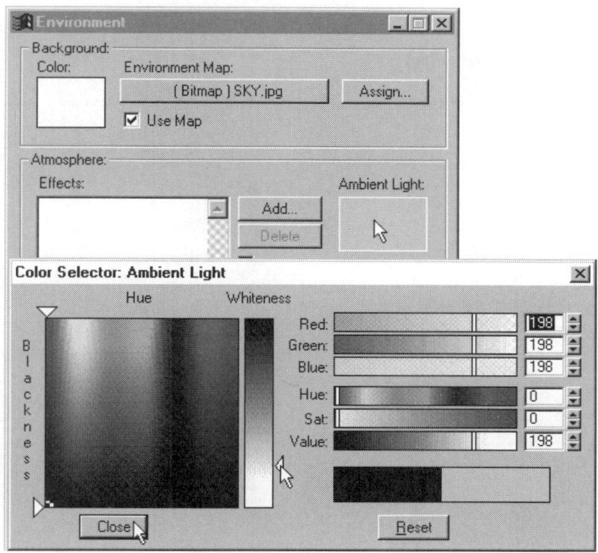

Fig. 9.4 Setting **Ambient Light**

Added Atmospheric Effects

When atmospheric effects are added to a scene they will take precedence over any background. Thus if **Fog** is added to a scene the objects in the scene will be shrouded in a fog, in which a background cannot (of course) be seen.

In the **Environment** dialogue box, *left-click* on the **Add...** button. The **Add Atmospheric Effect** dialogue box appears (Fig. 9.5). From the box, select the effect required, in this example **Fog**. Then *left-click* on the **OK** button of the **Add Atmospheric Effects** dialogue box.

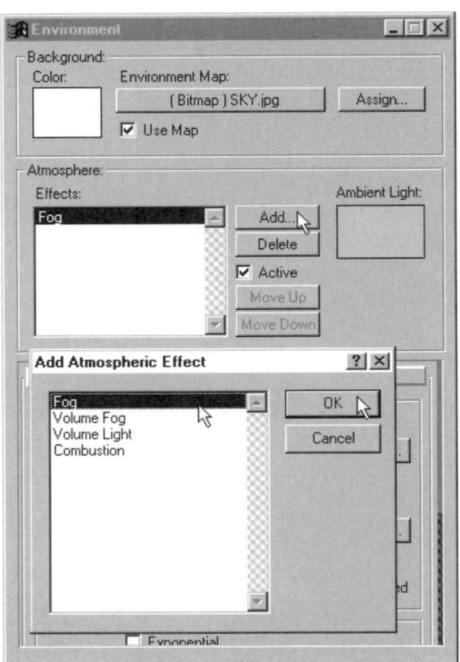

Fig. 9.5 The **Add Atmospheric Effects** dialogue box

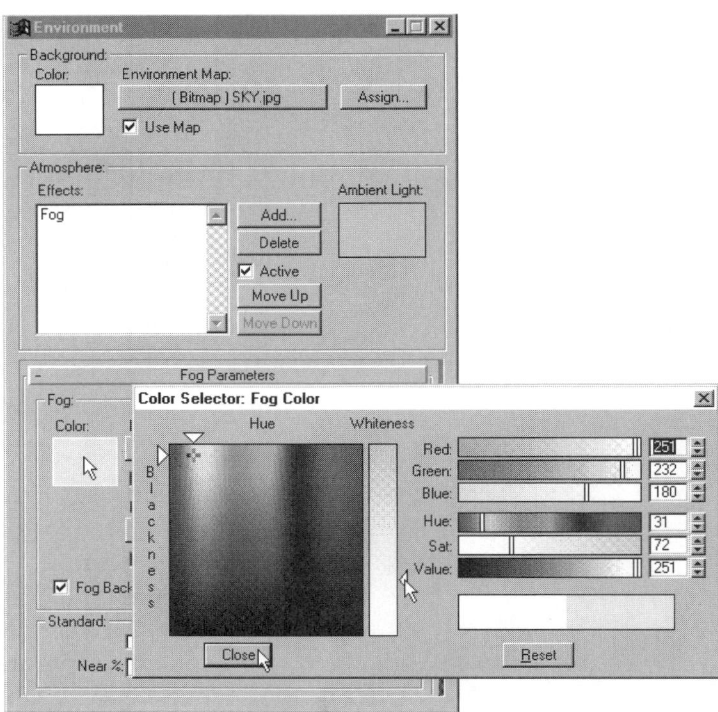

Fig. 9.6 Adding colour to fog

Fig. 9.7 Selecting **Render...** from the **Rendering** pull-down menu

Plate IV shows the effect of adding fog to a scene. The name of the atmospheric effect then appears in the **Effects:** list of the **Environment** box.

When an effect, such as fog, has been included in a scene the parameters for the fog can be set in a rollout appearing below the main part of the **Environment** dialogue box. In the example given in Fig. 9.7, a rendering of which is shown in Plate IV, colour has been added to the fog. A *left-click* on the **Color:** square of the **Fog** area of the rollout brings the **Color Selector:Fog Color** to the screen. As with previous colour selector boxes, select the desired colour from the dialogue box.

The rendering tools

We have already referred to the tool **Quick Render** in previous chapters. In the right-hand end of the toolbar there are two other render tools. Apart from the **Material Editor** tool which was referred to in the last chapter, there are three render tools – **Render Scene**, **Quick Render** and **Render Last**. When **Render Last** is called, the last scene to be rendered appears quite speedily. **Render Scene** can either be called by selecting **Render** from the **Rendering** pull down menu (Fig. 9.7) or by a *left-click* on the icon (Fig. 9.8). No matter which of these two actions is taken, the **Render Scene** dialogue box appears (Fig. 9.9).

In Fig. 9.8 the **Output Size** selected has been 800×600 and if that selection is made the rendering of the created scene will be as in Fig. 9.10 with a *left-click* on the **Render** button of the dialogue box. This particular illustration was taken from a monitor which was working to a resolution of 800×600.

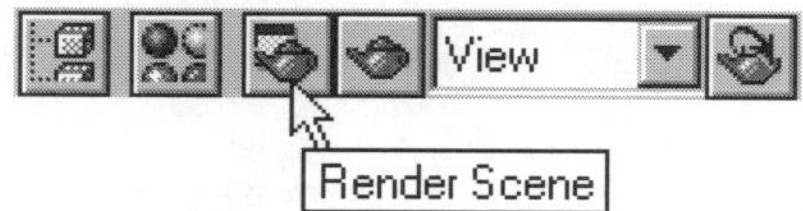

Figg. 9.8. The **Render Scene** icon

The View popup list

Left-click on the box containing the word **View** and a popup list (Fig. 9.11) appears. Selection from this list allows parts of the scene to be rendered. Figure 9.12 shows a **Region** which has been selected by *dragging* the corners of a window which appears in the scene when **Region** is selected from the popup list. Only the area within the window is rendered. Figure 9.13 shows a **Blowup** of a selected region. Figure 9.14 shows the window which appears when **Region**

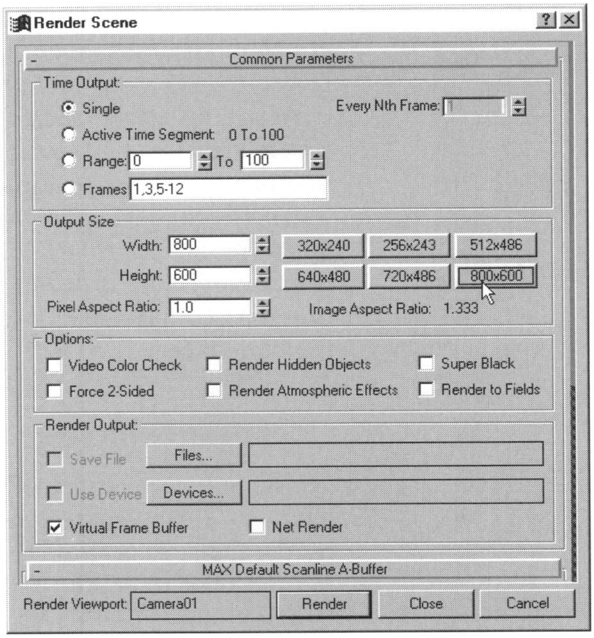

Fig. 9.9 The **Render Scene** dialogue box

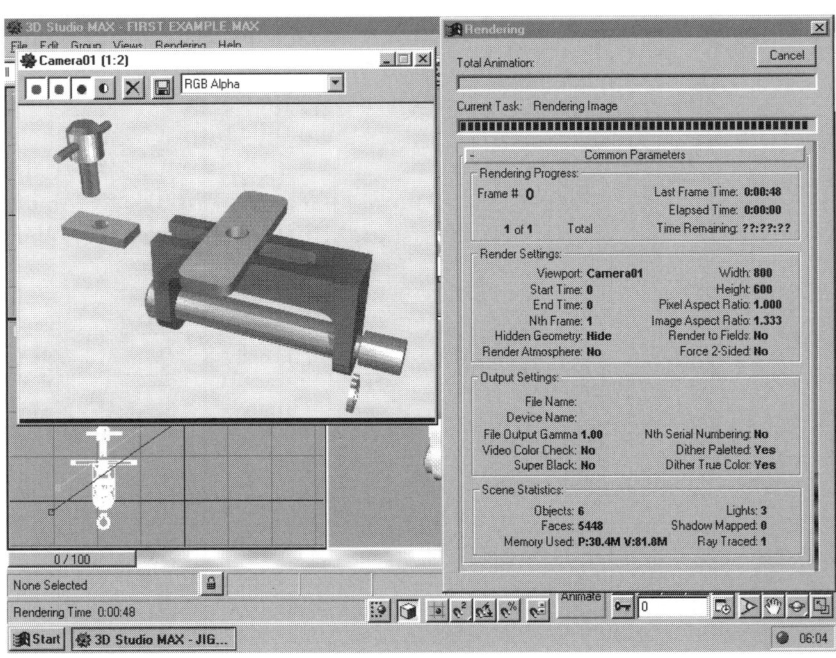

Fig. 9.10 A scene rendered to **Output** 800×600

or **Blowup** are selected from the popup list. It is by *dragging* the window to size that determines the area which is to be rendered as a **Region** or as a **Blowup**.

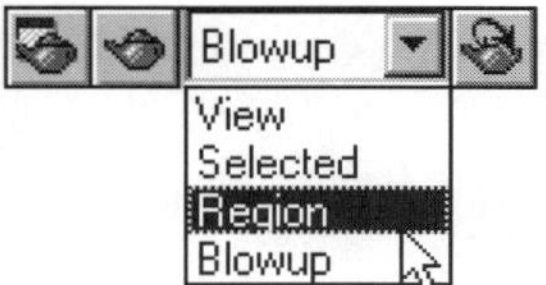

Fig. 9.11 The **View** popup list

Fig. 9.12 A rendering of a **Region** selected in a window

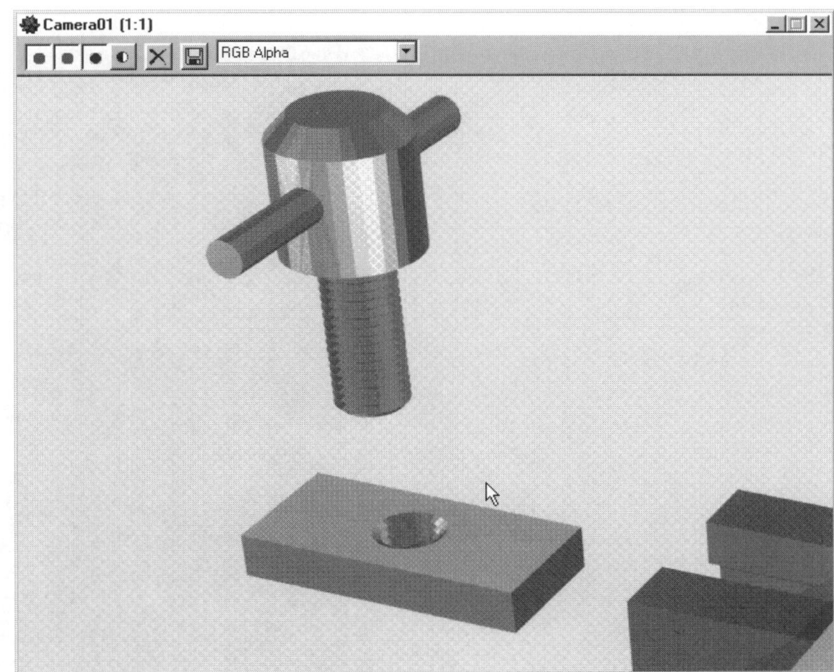

Fig. 9.13 A **Blowup** rendering of a region

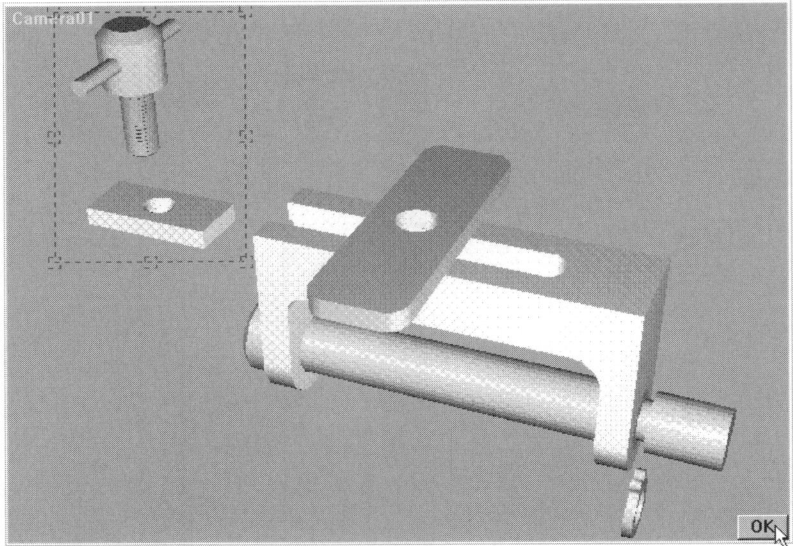

Fig. 9.14 The window appearing when **Region** or **Blowup** are selected from the popup list

The **Selected** option from the popup list refers to the rendering of any objects in a scene which the operator wishes to show being rendered. It is only the selected object which will become rendered when this option is taken.

Fig. 9.15 Rendering of a scene – Example 1

Rendering of a scene – Example 1

Figure 9.15 shows the example after rendering. The example is also shown in a colour plate (Plate X). All the objects in the scene were created in 3D Studio Max. Figure 9.16 shows the scene in its four-viewport setting before rendering.

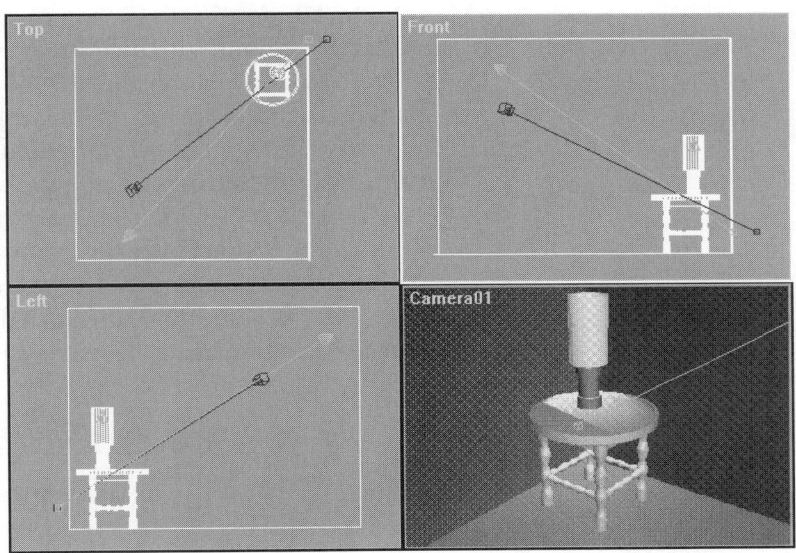

Fig. 9.16 The scene in its four viewport setting before rendering

There are seven objects in the scene – legs and rails; floor; lamp stand; lampshade; left wall; right wall; table top.

The legs and lower rails of the table were created from **Line**s which were adjusted to shape with the aid of the moderator **Edit Spline**. The upper rails of the table were created from **Box**es. The legs and rails were formed in a group. The floor and walls were created from **Box**es of 1 unit thickness. The lamp stand was created from a spline-edited **Line**. The lampshade was created from a **Tube**. The table top consists of two **Extrude**d circles, the smaller **Boolean** separated from the larger.

In addition the following have been included in the scene – a camera of lens length 50 mm; a target spot light; a free spot light; an omni light. Ambient lighting was set to a grey colour.

Materials from the **Material/Map Browser** were assigned to the objects in the scene as follows:

Legs and Rails: Oak Quarter Sawn.
Floor: Wood Ashen.
Lamp: Chrome Morocco.
Left wall: Foliage Opacity.

Lamp shade: Blue Bumpy Cloth.
Right wall: Dray Leaves.
Table top: Concrete Tan.

The **Target Spot** and **Free Spot** lights had **Shadows** and **Ray Traced Shadows** turned on before being added to the scene. The **Free Spot** light was placed inside the lamp shade so as to cast light onto the table top with the top of the lamp stand in shadow – hence the circle of light with a central circular shadow on the table top.

Note that seven objects within the scene had materials assigned to them, yet there are only six sample spheres in the **Material Editor**. In order to assign the seventh material, *left-click* on the **Reset Map/Mtl to Default Settings** icon in the **Material Editor** (Fig. 9.17) and in the dialogue box which appears (Fig. 9.18), make sure the check circle against **Affect only the mtl/map in the editor slot** is set on (Dot in circle) before a *left-click* on the **OK** button closes the dialogue box. One of the slots in the **Material Editor** can now be reused without affecting the materials already assigned to the scene.

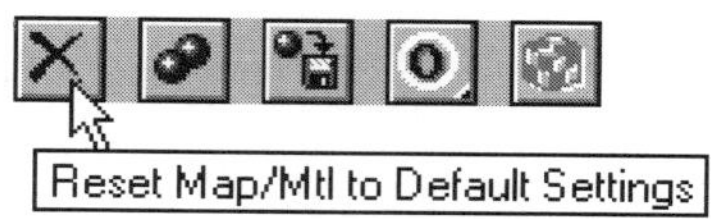

Fig. 9.17 The **Reset Map/Mtl to Default Settings** icon

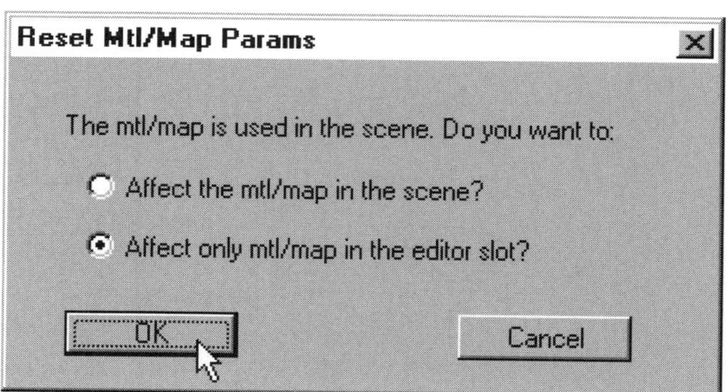

Fig. 9.18 The **Reset Mtl/Map Params** dialogue box

Saving a rendering to a graphics file

Some renderings will take a considerable time to complete depending upon the number of objects in the scene and the complexity of the lighting and materials assigned in the scene. With this in mind a rendering can be saved to a graphics file of a variety of file types. To save a rendering to file, *left-click* on the **Save Bitmap** icon in the rendering viewport (Fig. 9.19). This brings up the **Browse Images for Output** dialogue box (Fig. 9.20).

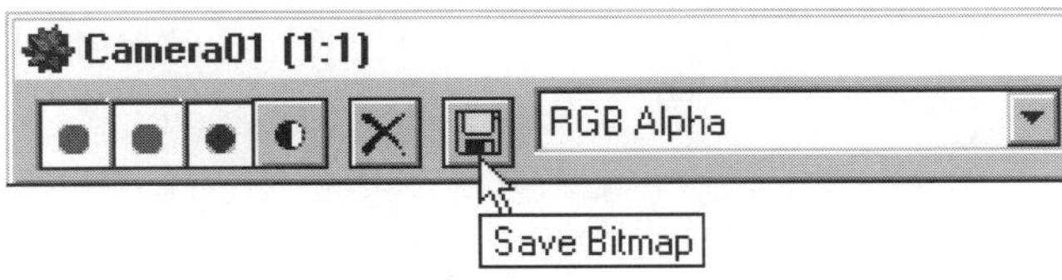

Fig. 9.19 The **Save Bitmap** icon

As can be seen a number of different types of graphics file types can be used to which the rendering can be saved. Figure 9.18 shows the rendering saved to the file name **Table-with_Lamp scene.tga**. The scene can be recalled in 3D Studio Max by using **View file...** from the **File** pull-down menu – see page 78. Graphics files so saved from renderings can also be imported into other software packages such as desktop publishers.

Notes

1. Ray-traced shadows take longer to render than shadow mapped shadows. They produce harder edges and shadows from transparent or translucent objects can be generated.
2. It will be seen from Fig. 9.20 that 3D Studio renderings can be saved in ***.BMP** format. BMP files can be opened in Windows 95 **Paint** program, which may prove to be of value for some purposes.
3. Now change the **Basic Parameters** of the material assigned to the lampshade from 100 to 20 and render the scene again. Note the changes in the way in which the lighting now affects the whole scene.

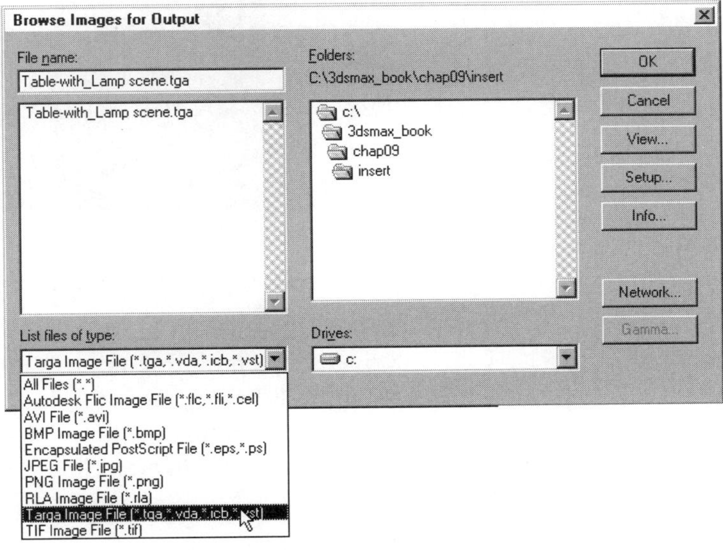

Fig. 9.20 The **Browse Images for Output** dialogue box with the **Files of type** popup list showing

The same example using a Free Camera

Now place a **Free** camera – which will become **Camera02** – with a lens length of 50 mm, in a position near to the **Target** camera. Note the difference in viewing between the two cameras. Without altering the lighting or the assigned materials, render the **Camera02** viewport and a type of 'fly-on-the-wall' view of the scene will appear. Figure 9.21 shows the results of rendering such a **Camera02** viewport.

The **Free** camera is mostly used for animations, where the camera is animated to show an all-round animation of a scene or a flyover animation of a scene. More about this in the chapter on animations (Chapter 10).

Fig. 9.21 The scene rendered using a **Free** camera

Rendering of a scene – Example 2

This second example was created from the objects described in the **Select Objects** dialogue box (Fig. 9.22) – select **Select By Name...** from the **Edit** pull-down menu.

The completed rendering is shown in Fig. 9.23 and also in Plate XVI. The following materials were assigned to the various objects in the scene:

Bookrack: Wood Ashen.
Floor: Wood Cedar Boards.

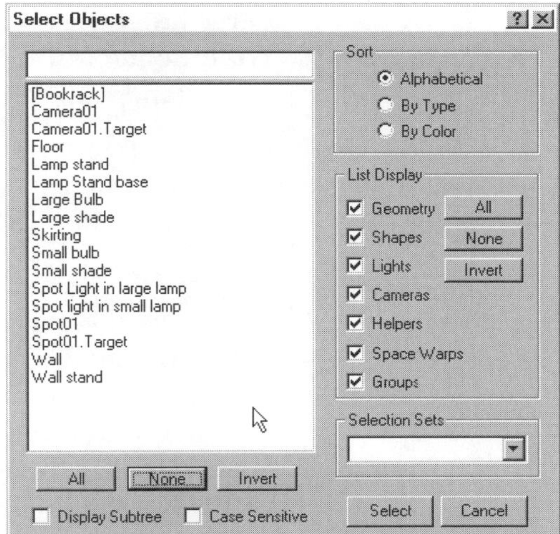

Fig. 9.22 The objects in Example 2

Fig. 9.23 Example 2 – a rendering

Lamp stand: Chrome Morocco.
Lamp stand base: Chrome Morocco.
Skirting: White Plastic.
Small shade: Cyan Plastic with Opacity changed to 40.
Large shade: Cyan Plastic with Opacity changed to 40.
Small bulb: Glass edited to give more blue.

Large bulb: Glass edited to give more blue.
Wall: Concrete Tan.
Wall stand: Chrome Morocco.

Ambient lighting was increased to grey. The two free spot lights and the target spotlight were set to show shadows and ray tracing. An additional omni light was included in the scene.

Notes

1. Remember that it is easier to identify objects in a scene if they are named as they are created.
2. It is much easier to select an object by name than by selecting from a scene if the objects are small or partly hidden by other objects.
3. If a material includes a diffuse colour map, then the moderator **UVW Map** should be called before rendering. A scene will render without mapping such materials, but may not render correctly. In any case if a map is required a warning box will appear before rendering starts.
4. It is advisable to experiment with a variety of settings when assigning materials – features such as tiling to reduce the size of details such as bricks; additional bitmaps which can be called from the rollouts of some material parameters; settings for ambient lighting; whether to use shadow mapping or ray tracing etc..

Selecting objects

When a scene is crowded with objects it may be difficult to select one of them. As a revision of notes on the selection of objects given in earlier pages, it is pointed out that selection can be carried out by any of the following means:

1. Use the **Select object** tool from the toolbar. Place the cursor on the object – the cursor changes shape to a cross – then *left-click*. The object changes colour to white and its axis arrows appear. If in a **Smooth+Highlight** mode white lines appear around the object.
2. When a number of objects are in a viewport, to select several objects, hold down the **Ctrl** key of the keyboard and *left-click* on all those objects to be selected. They become selected in turn.
3. When selecting with the aid of the **Ctrl** key, the **Crossing Selection** tool in the prompt bar controls whether the window selects within or by a crossing window.
4. All selected objects are deselected by *left-clicking* in an area of a viewport which is free of objects.
5. Holding down the **Alt** key and *dragging* a window around a group of objects deselects selected objects within the window.

6. Selection of **All**, **None**, **Invert**, **Select by** (**Color** or **Name**) and **Region** (**Window** or **Crossing**) can be carried out from these tools in the **Edit** pull-down from the menu bar.
7. To select and move, rotate or scale, *right-click* on an object or a group of objects and select the required action from the popup list which appears.
8. The same three operations can be performed from the use of the **Select and Move**, **Select and Rotate** and **Select and Uniform Scale** icons in the toolbar.
9. Selected objects or a group of selected objects can be locked to prevent accidental deselection with the use of the **Lock Selection Set** tool in the Status bar (Fig. 9.24).

Fig. 9.24 The **Lock Selection Set** icon

10. When a group of objects have been selected, they are all affected by the **Select and Move**, **Select and Rotate** and **Select and Uniform Scale** tools.
11. The problem with locking a selected object or group of objects is that no other objects can then be selected. If this causes a problem, press the **Space** bar of the keyboard and *click* in a viewport. This action deselects a selection set.

Exercises

1. Figure 9.25 shows a rendering of a garden seat model which was created entirely in 3D Studio Max. The sizes of the end frames of

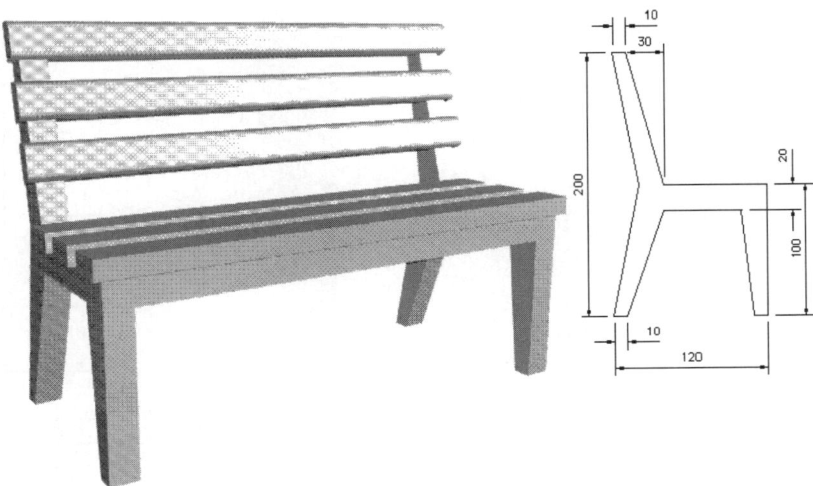

Fig. 9.25 Exercise 1

the seat are included in Fig. 9.15 to the right of the rendering.

Construct a garden seat of the same (or similar) design and create a scene showing part of a garden area which includes your seat model. Add lighting, a camera and appropriate materials and then render your garden scene.

2. Figure 9.26 is a rendering of a model of a settee. Create a settee model to a similar design and then create a scene in a room which includes the settee, a matching easy chair, a lamp and a coffee table.

   Add lighting, a camera and appropriate materials to your scene and then render.

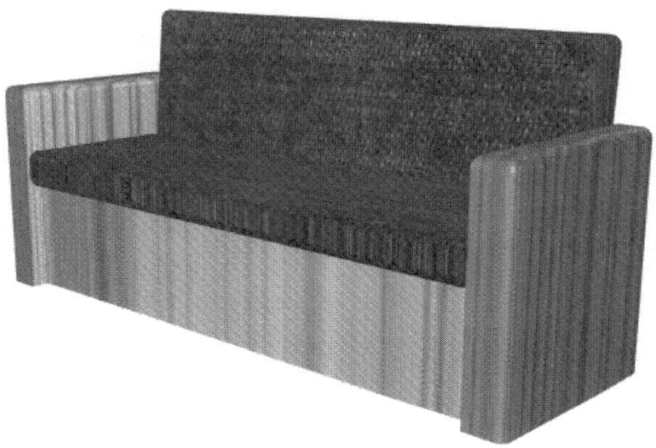

Fig. 9.26 Exercise 2

3. Figure 9.27 shows the dimensions of a part from a microscope stand, a 3D model of which was constructed in AutoCAD Release 13 and then imported into 3D Studio Max. Figure 9.28 is a rendering of the model.

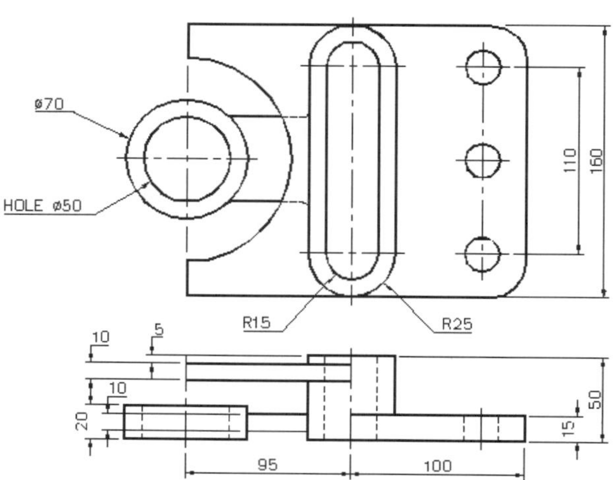

Fig. 9.27 Dimensions for Exercise 3

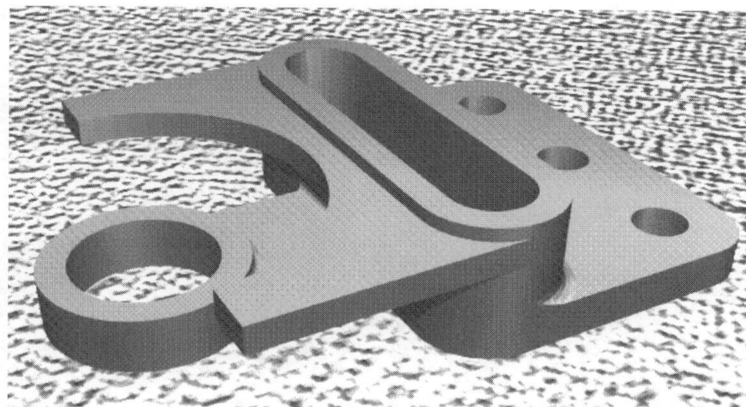

Fig. 9.28 Exercise 3

Construct a 3D model drawing of the part in AutoCAD, import the model drawing into 3D studio Max. Add lighting, a camera and materials and render the model.

4. Figure 4.29 is a rendering of a 3D model of a frying pan created in 3D Studio Max. Create a similar model and use it as part of a scene of an area of a kitchen.

Fig. 9.29 Exercise 4

5. Figure 9.30 shows a 600 unit length of H girder which is to be placed in the jig fixture shown in the rendering (Fig. 9.31) in place of the piece of strip extrusion already shown in position in that rendering.

   Working to what you consider to be suitable sizes, create the model of the stand and its two sliders as shown in Fig. 9.31, and place it in a scene on a suitable bench top with the H girder in position rather than the extrusion already held in the jig.

Fig. 9.30 Part of Exercise 5

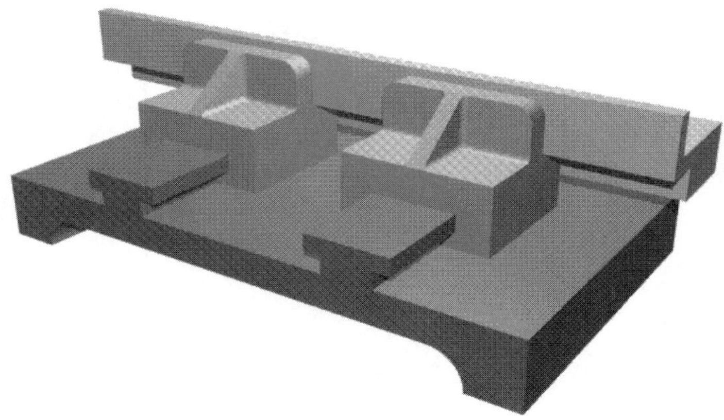

Fig. 9.31 Exercise 5

CHAPTER 10

Simple animations

Introduction

Coordinate axis constraints

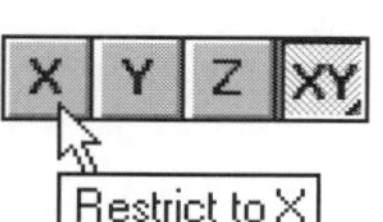

Fig. 10.1 The axis restraint icons

The axis restraint tools – **Restrict to X**, **Restrict to Y** and **Restrict to Z** (Fig. 10.1) – may prove important to ensure that the movement of objects when creating an animation are restrained to move only along selected axes – **X**, **Y** or **Z**.

Coordinate Systems

Fig. 10.2 The popup list from **View**

The settings from the popup list which appears with a *left-click* on **View** in the toolbar (Fig. 10.2) may also prove to be of value when creating an animation.

Examples of animations

Example 1

Figure 10.3 shows a rendering of a bowl with a lid. Both parts of this example were created from lines modified with **Edit Spline** and then acted upon by the **Lathe** modifier. This example shows the animation of the lid to close and open from the bowl. The lid is constrained to move only along the **Z** axis, thus during the animation, the **Restrict to Z** axis restraint is set on – *left-click* on the icon and it highlights. As the movements of the animation will be determined by movements in the **Front** viewport, the **World** coordinate system must also be set – *left-click* on **World** in the **View** popup list to set the coordinate system to **World**. After creating the two parts of the scene:

1. *Left-click* on the **Restrict to Z** icon. *Left-click* on **World** in the **View** popup list.
2. In the **Top** viewport move the lid to a position 100 grid units above the bowl (Fig. 10.4).
3. *Left-click* on the **Animate** button in the Status bar (Fig. 10.5).

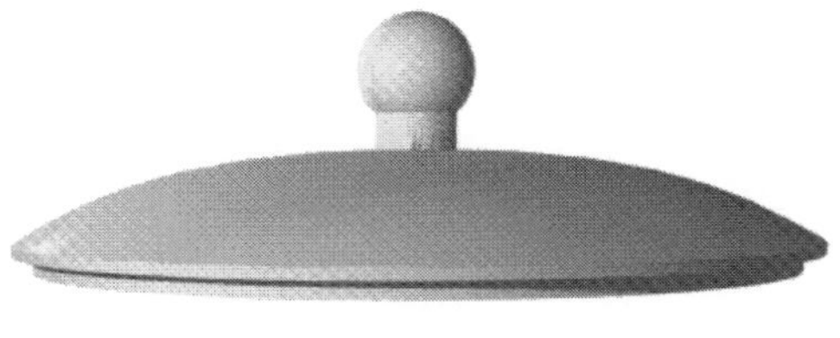

Fig. 10.3 The two parts for the Example 1

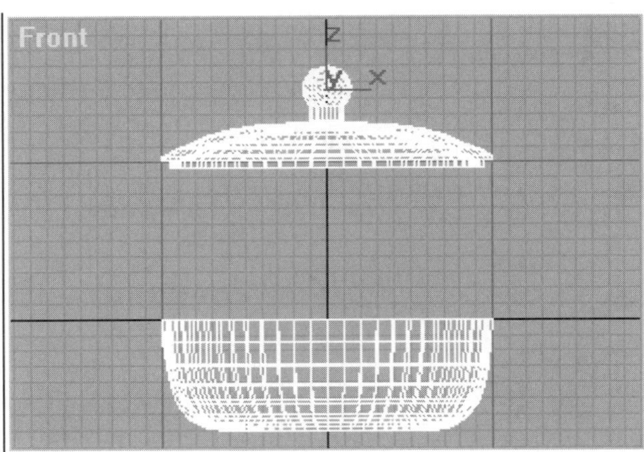

Fig. 10.4 Example 1 – primary position for the lid

4. Either *drag* the number slider frame to 20, or *enter* 20 in the number window near the **Animate** button. In the **Front** viewport move the lid (now restrained to move only along the **Z** axis) downwards by 20 grid units. Note the viewport is highlighted with a red surround when it is the active viewport with the **Animate** button set on.
5. Set the number slider to 40. Move the lid down another 20 grid units.
6. Set the number slider to 60. Move the lid down another 20 grid units.
7. Repeat items 5 and 6 with the number slider frame set to 80, then 100. Figure 10. 6 shows the slider at frame 100.

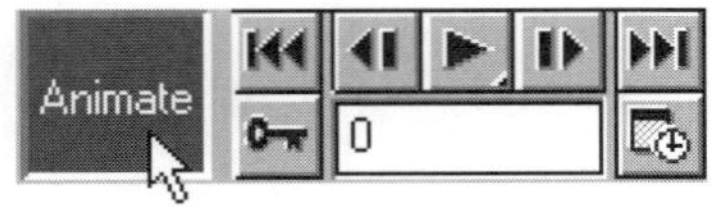

Fig. 10.5 The **Animate** button

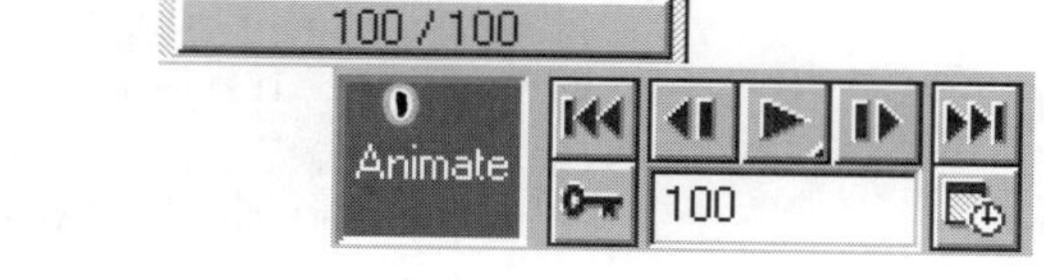

Fig. 10.6 The number slider at frame 100

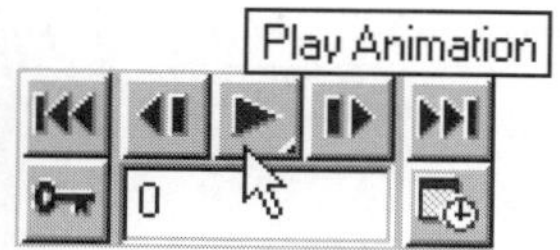

Fig. 10.7 The **Play Animation** icon

Fig. 10.8 The **Go to Start** icon

8. *Click* in the **Camera01** viewport followed by another on the **Play Animation** icon (Fig. 10.7). The viewport becomes surrounded by a red highlighting line and the animation plays. Note that the lid closes from its highest position down on to the bowl and then goes immediately back to its original position. The lid closes and opens in this manner until a *right-click* in the active viewport or a *left-click* on the **Go to Start** icon stops the animation.
9. *Right-click* on any of the timing icon buttons. The **Time Configuration** dialogue box appears (Fig. 10.9). Set the **Length:** and **End Time:** both to 200, followed by a *left-click* on the dialogue box **OK** button.

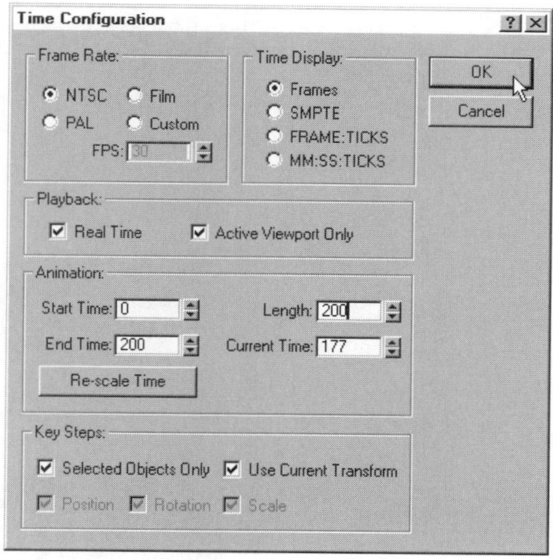

Fig. 10.9 The **Time Configuration** dialogue box

10. Set the number slider frame to 120 and move the lid 20 grid units upwards in the **Front** viewport. Repeat at 140, 160, 180 and 200. At 200 the lid should be back in its original position before the animation was created.
11. Make the **Camera01** viewport the active viewport and *left-click* on the **Play Animation** icon and the lid will move smoothly up and down in its closing and opening animation sequence.

Example 2

In this example the **Restrict to X** icon was selected as well as **World** from the **View** popup list. Only 100 frames were set as follows:

1. At frame 0, the bolt was set in position as shown in Fig. 10.10.
2. At frame 50, the bolt was moved to the position as shown in Fig. 10.11.
3. At frame 100, the bolt was moved back to the position as shown in Fig. 10.10.
4. A *left-click* on the **Play Animation** icon button caused the bolt to move out and in from its beginning position to its full movement position.

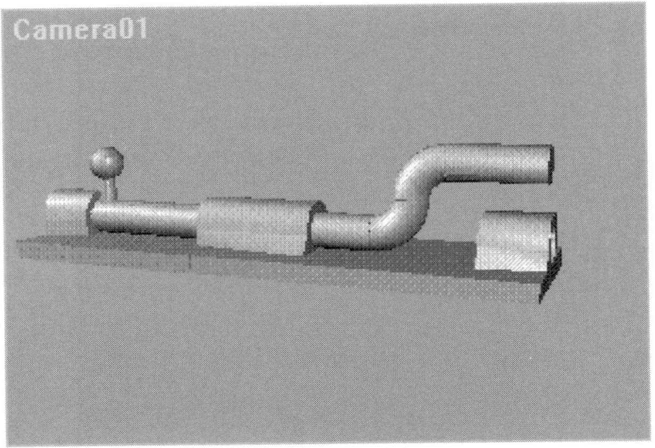

Fig. 10.10 Example 2. The bolt in position at frames 0 and 100

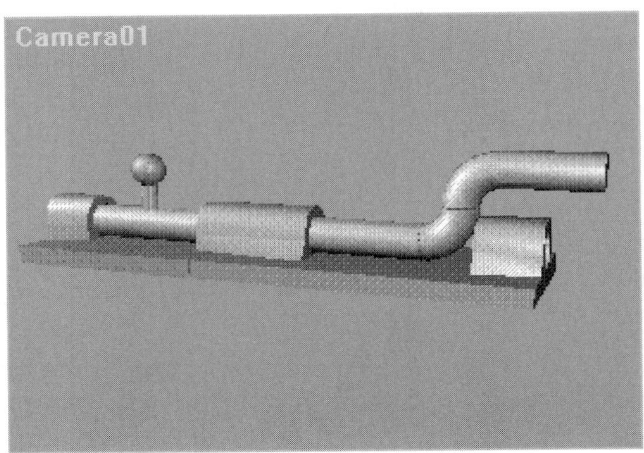

Fig. 10.11 Example 2. The bolt in position at frame 50

In this example the shape of the bolt was achieved using the **Standard Primitive Torus**, the bends being created with 90° tori. **Cylinders** were then created and the four parts joined with the aid of Boolean union. The bolt container was created from extrusions and a cylinder was subtracted from the extrusions with Boolean subtraction.

A camera and lights were added to the scene and materials assigned to each of the two parts before setting the positions for the animation.

Example 3

This example involves the animation of rotating objects – the hands of a clock as the hands rotate from 12:00 noon to 12:00 midnight. The hands were constructed from **Tube**s and extruded outlines formed from **Line**s. The Boolean union was then formed of the tube and extrusion of each hand. The two hands were mounted on a spindle created from two cylinders, of the same radius as the holes in the hands. The Boolean union was then formed of the two cylinders. The clock face was a **Cylinder** 20 units high and the numerals extruded outlines which were arrayed 12 times and then moved and rotated in position.

When the hands, its numerals and the clock face had been created, the parts were assigned materials. To create the animation:

1. The hands were renamed **Large hand** and **Small hand** to enable them to be easily selected form the **Edit** pull-down menu if necessary.
2. In order to ensure that the hands were rotated about the centre of their rings which allowed them to revolve around the clock spindle, their pivots had to be changed:
   (a) Set the **Restrict to Z** icon in the toolbar (can also be set by pressing the **F7** key).
   (b) Select the large hands. *Left-click* on the **Hierarchy** button and when its rollout appears, *left-click* on the **Pivot** button (Fig. 10.12). Then in the **Adjust Pivot** rollout *click* on the **Affect Object Only** button (Fig. 10.13).

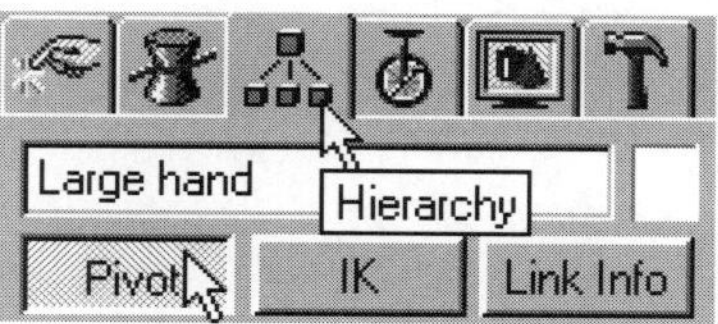

Fig. 10.12 First step in changing the pivot centre of the large hand

   (c) An enlarged set of **X,Y** axis arrows appears in place of the axis tripods on the large hand. *Click* on the **Affect Pivot Only** button in the rollout and with **Move** move the **X,Y** arrows to the centre of the large hand ring (Fig. 10.14). Repeat for the small hand. Note that the pivot has only **X** and **Y** axes showing – they are to rotate around the **Z** axis.

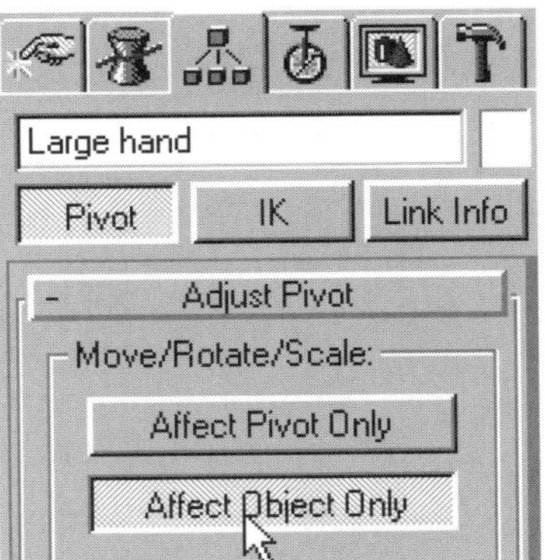

Fig. 10.13 The rollout of **Adjust Pivot**

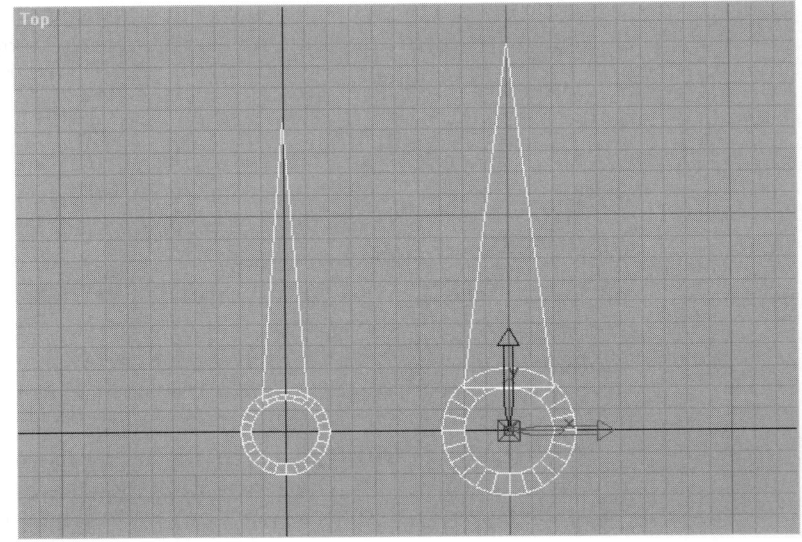

Fig. 10.14 The pivot moved to the centre of the large hand

3. Fig 10.15 shows a rendering of the two hands and their spindle. Move the hands so that they are exactly on the spindle and in the **Left** viewport move the small hand so that it is above the large hand.

Fig. 10.15 A rendering of the hands and their spindle

4. Assign materials to the various parts of the scene. A rendering of the scene is given in Fig. 10.16.

5. Commence the animation by setting the animation number frame to 0 and *left-click* on the **Animation** button.

Fig. 10.16 A rendering of the completed scene

6. *Right-click* in any of the time icons to bring up the **Time Configuration** dialogue box. Set **Length:** and **End Time:** both to 96 (i.e. 12×8, so as to use 8 frames for each hour).
7. Set the number frame to 2. Rotate the hour hand to about one quarter of the way between 12:00 and 1:00. Rotate the minute hand to the 3 on the clock face.
8. Set the number frame to 4. Rotate the hour hand to one half the distance between 12:00 and 1:00. Rotate the minute hand to 6 on the face.
9. Set the number frame to 6. Rotate the hour hand to three-quarters of the way between 12:00 and 1:00. Rotate the minute hand to 9 on the face.
10. Set the number frame to 8. Rotate the hour hand to 1 on the face. Rotate the minute hand to 12 on the face.
11. Continue in this manner at every two number frames until the hands have been set to rotate from 12:00 noon to 12:00 midnight.
12. Make the **Camera01** viewport active and then select **Make Preview...** from the **Rendering** pull-down menu (Fig. 10.17). The **Make Preview Camera01** dialogue box appears (Fig. 10.18). Make settings as shown in Fig. 10.18 and *left-click* on **Create**.
13. Depending on the **Image Size:** set in the **Make Preview** dialogue box, the frames of the preview start rendering. In the example shown in Fig. 10.19, the **Image Size:** has been set to 50%.
14. The preview can now be saved. Select **Rename Preview...** from the **Rendering** pull-down menu. The **Save Preview As** dialogue box (Fig. 10.20) appears. The preview was saved to the filename **clock.avi**.

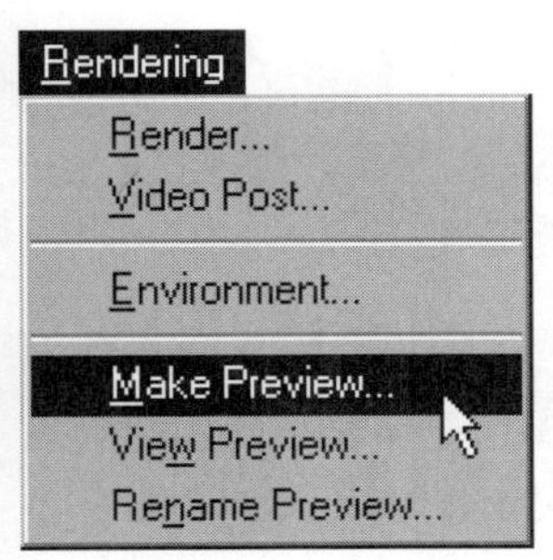

Fig. 10.17 Select **Make Preview...** from the **Rendering** pull-down menu

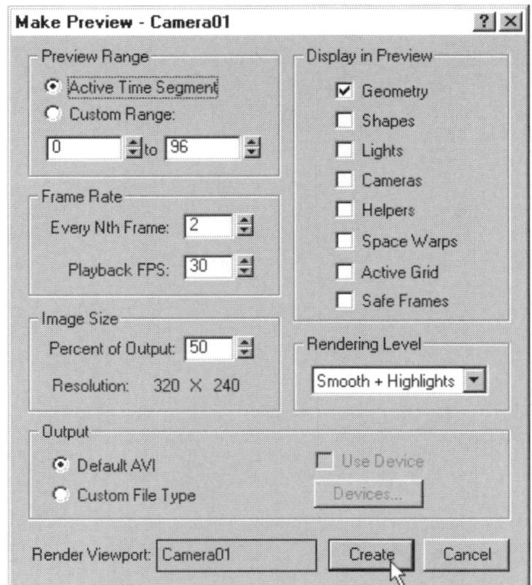

Fig. 10.18 The **Make Preview** dialogue box

Fig. 10.19 Making the preview rendering

15. To see the animation, select **View File...** from the **File** pull-down menu and from the **View File** dialogue box which appears (Fig. 10.21), select the filename **clock.avi**.
16. The **clock.avi – Media Player** appears. A *left-click* on the **Play** button starts the animation running (Fig. 10.22).

Fig. 10.20 Saving the preview

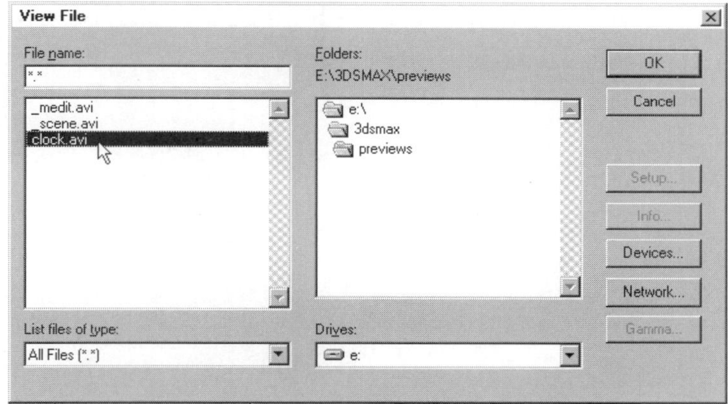

Fig. 10.21 The **View File** dialogue box

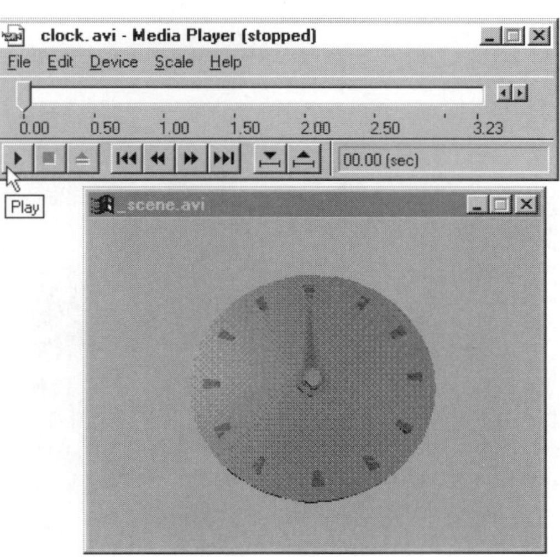

Fig. 10.22 The **Media Player**

Example 4

Not only can scenes be animated by movement and rotation, but objects or parts of a scene can be animated by modification with the modifiers such as **Bend** and **Twist**. This example shows:

1. **Frame 0** – a tube (Fig. 10.23).
2. **Frame 20** – the tube modified by **Twist** (Fig. 10.24) at **Angle:** 90.

Fig. 10.23 Example 4 – frame 0

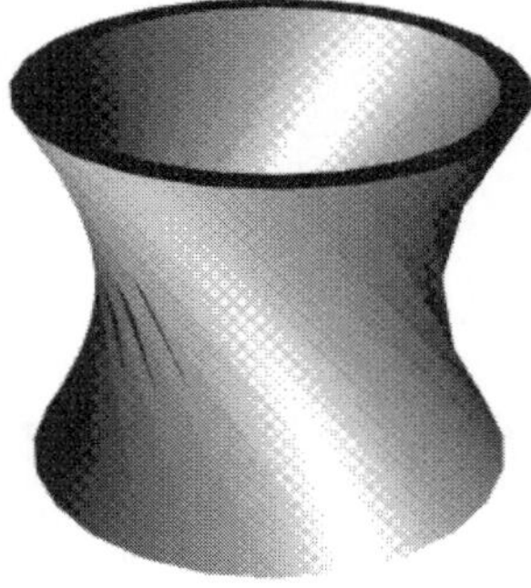

Fig. 10.24 Example 4 – frame 20

3. **Frame 40** – the twisted tube further modified by **Twist** (Fig. 10.25) at **Angle:** 135.
4. **Frame 60** – The twisted tube acted upon by **Bend** (Fig. 10.26) at **Angle:** –30.

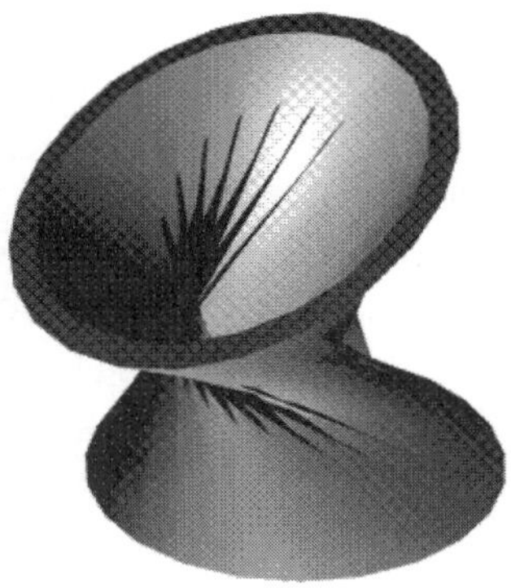

Fig. 10.25 Example 4 – frame 40

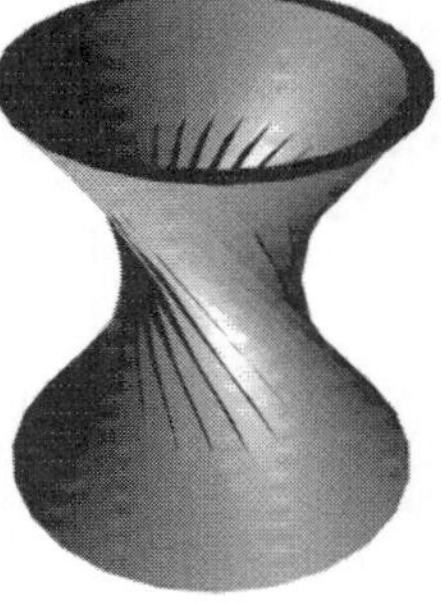

Fig. 10.26 Example 4 – frame 60

5. **Frame 80** – the twisted and bent tube further acted upon by **Bend** (Fig. 10.27) at **Angle:** –90.
6. **Frame 100** – further modification by **Bend:** (Fig. 10.28) at **Angle:** 0. A **Preview** was made and saved, then run.

Fig. 10.27 Example 4 – frame 80

Fig. 10.28 Example 4 – frame 100

Example 5

Not only can the moving, rotating moderation of parts of scenes be animated, so also can the scaling of objects or scenes using the **Select and Uniform Scale** tool. In addition cameras and/or lights can be animated. No examples of the animation of lights is given here, but an example would be to illuminate a scene changing lighting from dawn to dusk by animation of the lighting, or the animation of a spot light lighting objects such as a moving person in a scene from a theatre play. This fifth example is of the animation of a simple bungalow scene by moving a camera as if the camera were in an aeroplane flying above the bungalow in a more or less circular movement.

The shots were taken with a **Free** camera. Care must be taken to ensure that either the path is circular or perhaps elliptical, or that frequent frames are taken in order to obtain a smoothly running animation as the aeroplane flies over the house. At each frame the camera will need moving and rotating. If the **Perspective** viewport is configured to be the **Camera** viewport, the scene viewed from the plane can be identified as each frame taken.

The original scene represent a bungalow with the early morning sun shining on the scene. Figures 10.30–32 show camera shots at some animation frames in the sequence.

Figure 10.29 shows the scene in the **Camera02** rendering window as it appeared when taken with a **Target** camera of lens length 50 mm.

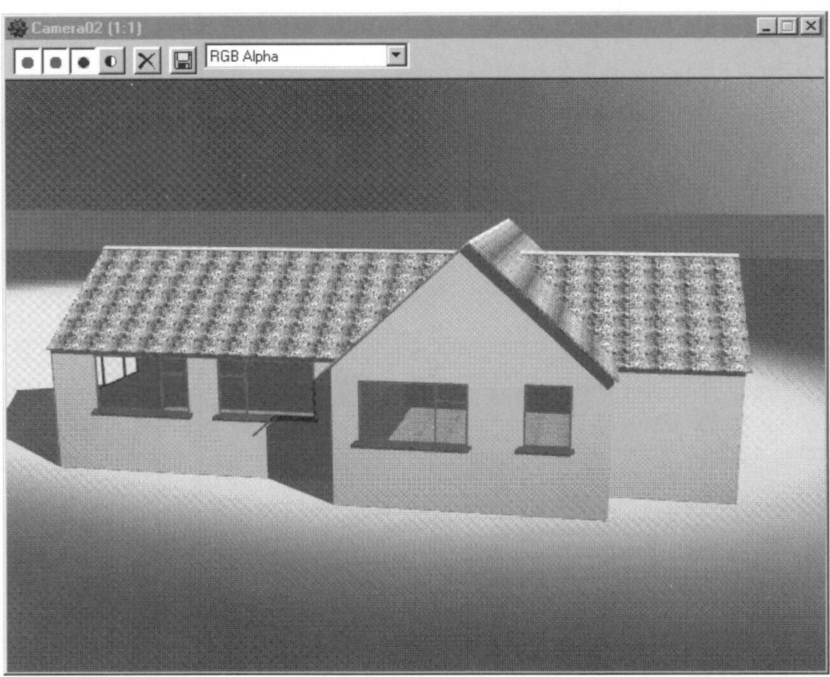

Fig. 10.29 Example 5 – frame 0

Figure 10.30 shows the scene at the 25th animation frame taken with a **Free** camera of 85 mm lens length.

Figure 10.31 shows the scene with the **Free** camera at frame 50.

Figure 10.32 shows the scene from a **Free** camera at frame 75.

Many other frames had to be taken to achieve a smooth animation.

Fig. 10.30 Example 5 – frame 25

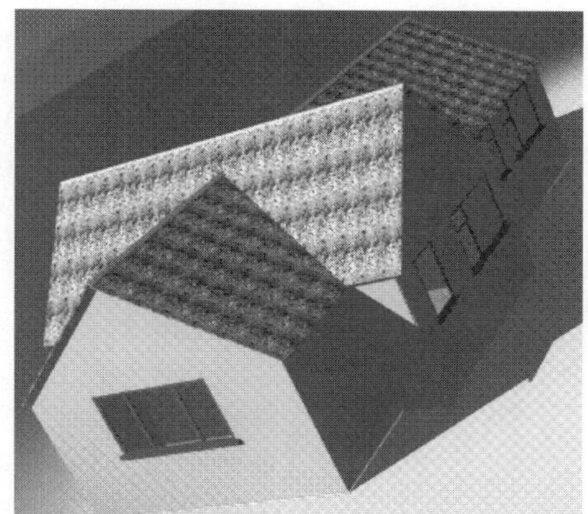

Fig. 10.31 Example 5 – frame 50

Fig. 10.32 Example 5 – frame 75

Notes on animating

1. Animations can be by **Select and Move**, **Select and Rotate**, **Select and Scale,** using the **Moderator** tools, movement and rotation of cameras, movement and rotation of lights.
2. It is advisable to name each object in a scene so that they can be easily identified for selection from the **Edit** pull-down menu.
3. When placing lights in a scene, shadows and ray tracing must be set before lights are placed – if shadows and ray tracing are required in the scene.
4. It may be necessary to set the **Environment** from the **Rendering** pull-down menu before rendering. This includes the degree of **Ambient** light, background colour and background bitmap.
5. The types of lights are for:

Ambient – general overall lighting with no definite source. Strength of light determined from the **Environment** dialogue box.

Omni – general all-round lighting from a placed source. Light shed in all directions.

Target Spot – light from a placed position directed according to the way the light is moved or rotated. Can be set so as to cast shadows and produce ray traced lighting. Forms a spot area on the scene which can be reduced or enlarged by settings in the light's rollout.

Directional – light directed from a source, the direction determined by the operator moving and/or rotating the light source. Often used in scenes to display sunlight.

Free Spot – light directed from a placed source so as to form a circular or rectangular spot of light in a scene. Movement and/or rotation under operator control once the light has been placed.

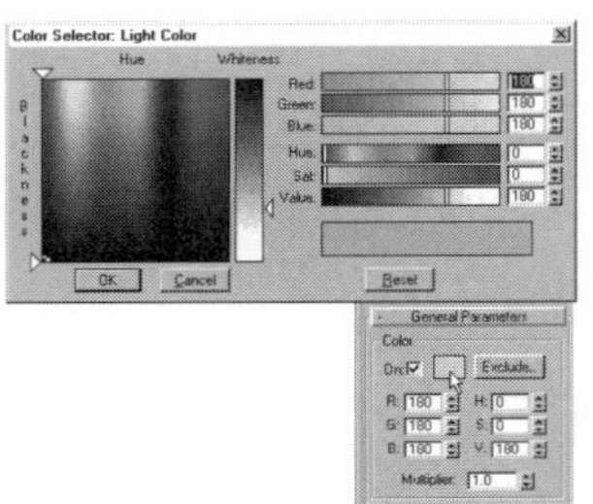

Fig. 10.33 Selecting a colour for a light

6. Colour can be added to lights if required. Figure 10.33 shows the **Color** rollout which is common to all types of lighting. A *left-click* on the colour swathe in the rollout brings up the **Color Selector** dialogue box.
7. When rotating any object for an animation, the **Pivot** centre may have to be reset by moving or rotation.
8. Also when rotating an object the **Restrict to X**, **Restrict to Y** and **Restrict to Z** tools must usually be used. Note that these can be called either from the toolbar or by pressing the **F5** (for **X**), **F6** (for **Y**) or **F7** (for **Z**) keys from the keyboard. Failure to set the resets may result in a rotation which is not the desired one. Note the changes in the axis tripods in the viewports when the resets are chosen, with the chosen axis direction highlighting to red.
9. It is useful to be able to toggle **Snap** on/off. This is best achieved by pressing the toggle key **S** on the keyboard.
10. When moving or rotating objects in a scene it is sometimes easier if the **Degradation Override** icon is set on. When the tool is on (highlighted) selected objects are enclosed in a white line box and when moved, rotated etc. only the box moves, enabling a much faster response to the movement etc. than if the whole object is acted upon.

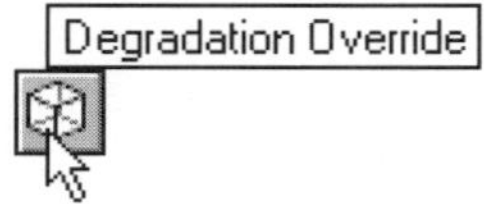

Fig. 10.34 The **Degradation Override** icon

11. The settings of the number of frames required in an animation is carried out in the **Time Configuration** dialogue box, brought to screen with a *right-click* on any of the time icons. The reader is advised to experiment with other settings in this dialogue box when creating animations.

Hierarchical linkage

When an animation is to include several objects to be animated by different methods – e.g. one part moving as a second part rotates – the objects in the animation will need to be linked. The main moving object is regarded as the parent object and the part moving differently but with the main object is regarded as the child object of the parent object. This hierarchy can be built up into several generations. As an example a puppet might be linked as follows:

Body: great grandparent.
Arms: grandparent.
Hand: parent.
Fingers: child.
Upper parts of legs: child of body.
Lower part of legs: parent of feet.
Feet: child of lower part of legs.
Head: child of body.

This hierarchy could be extended further to joints in the feet and hands; to ears, eyes, tongue etc.

When linking in a hierarchy, it is important to link the child to its parent and not the other way round. A parent is, of course, the child of a grandparent and after linking the parent's child to its parent, the parent must be linked to its parent, which is the grandparent of the child. Two simple examples follow to demonstrate linkage in an animation.

Example 1

This example is the animation of a simplified space vehicle circling around in the sky driven by a helicopter type propeller trying to find a landing place. The body of the vehicle is a **Lathe**d ellipse and the propeller is made up of four parts joined to each other by Boolean union. The propeller blades, which are slightly rotated, were created from an extruded **Line** which was **Mirror**ed to form the second blade. The two blades were joined by a **Cylinder**. The resulting propeller was joined to a spindle created from a **Cylinder**. A rendering of the completed 'space vehicle' is shown in Fig. 10.35.

As the vehicle circles around, its propeller turns in order to drive the vehicle in its circle. To create the animation:

1. Set **Snap**. In the **Top** viewport create a circle and two **Line** diagonals. This gives eight positions around the circle.
2. Create the vehicle and its propeller. The result is shown in Fig. 10.36 as seen in the **Top** viewport.

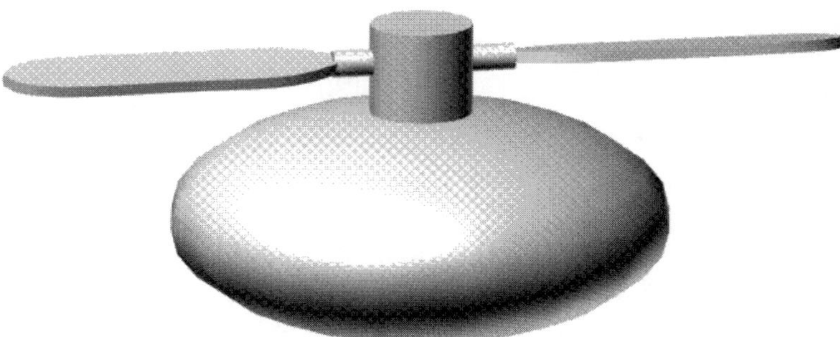

Fig. 10.35 The 'space vehicle' for Example 1

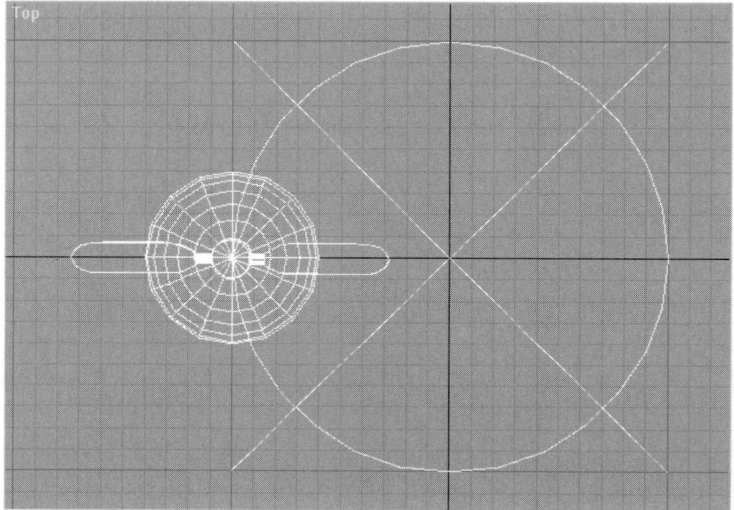

Fig. 10.36 The scene set for Example 1

3. In the **Top** viewport select the **Body**. Move the **Pivot** to the centre of the circle after selecting the **Pivot** button and **Affect Pivot Only** from the **Hierarchy** Command panel. Then reset to **Affect Object Only**.
4. In the **Top** viewport select the **Propeller** to check that its pivot is central to the blades and its spindle. Reset the **Pivot** to **Affect Object Only**.
5. *Left-click* on the **IK** button of the **Hierarchy** Command panel, select the **Propeller** and *click* on the **Child->Parent** button (Fig. 10.37). Select the **Body** and *left-click* on the **Parent->Child** button.
6. *Left-click* on the **Select and Link** icon in the toolbar (Fig. 10.38). The **Select and Link** cursor appears. *Click* on the propeller (the child) and *drag* the cursor on the body to link the child to its parent (Fig. 10.39).
7. Now set up the animation. In the **Top** viewport:
   (a) In the **Time Configuration** set **Length:** to 160 and press the **Return** key of the keyboard. The **End Time:** changes to 160.

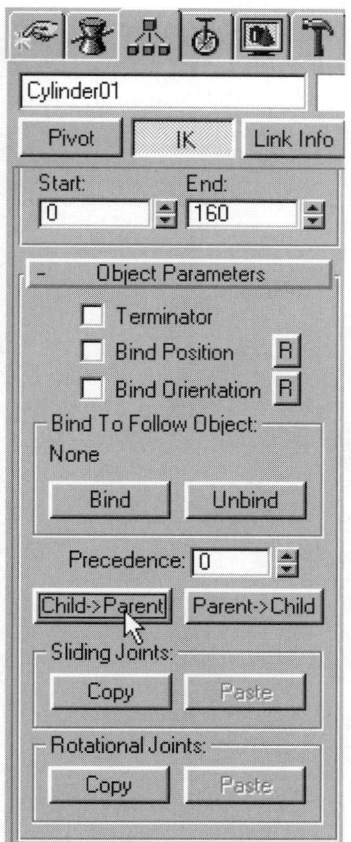

Fig. 10.37 The **IK** rollout from the **Hierarchy** command panel

(b) *Left-click* on the **Animation** button and set the time number slide to 20.

(c) Rotate the body clockwise to the first of the eight circle divisions (line crossing circle). The propeller being linked follows the body. Rotate the propeller clockwise through 360°.

(d) Set the time number slide to 40. Rotate the body to the second of the eight circle divisions. Rotate the propeller again through 360°.

(e) Continue in this manner at every 20th time number frame until the space ship is back to its start position.

8. A **Preview** of the animation from the **Perspective** viewport can now be made and saved to file. The animation can then be played, showing the space ship flying in circles with its propeller rotating with a clockwise rotation.

Example 2

This example shows the use of a hierarchy from great grandparent (Body), through grandparent (Thigh), parent (Lower Leg) and child (Foot).

The model used is a crude puppet, the parts of which were created from **Line**s which were first **Edit Mesh**ed, then **Extrude**d. Figure 10.40 is a rendering of the model before it was animated. Careful placing of links with **Select and Link** and determining the **Child Parent** relationship between each part of the body of the puppet was necessary before the animation could be created. Figure 10.41 shows the **Subtree** of the hierarchy of the model. To see such a subtree, select **Select By Name** from the **Edit** pull-down menu and set the check box against **Display Subtree** on (tick in box).

Once the puppet had been created and its linkage settled, animation could begin. The idea was to animate the puppet walking in a

Fig. 10.38 The **Select and Link** icon from the toolbar

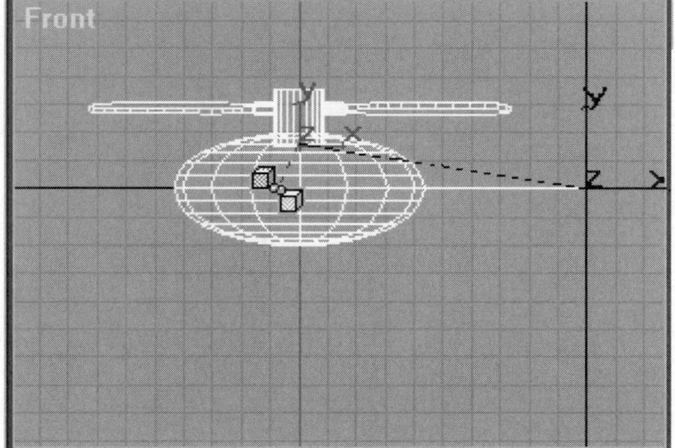

Fig. 10.39 Linking propeller (child) to the body (its parent)

straight line. With the **Animate** button on (highlighted in red), the body (carrying all its parts) was **Moved** forward 100 grid units at each 10 number frame. At each 10th frame, the arms (and their parts) and legs (and their parts) were rotated so as to assume an animation of the puppet walking.

Figure 10.42 shows renderings of the puppet at four frames of the total of 100 frames – at 0, 20, 40 and 60.

Fig. 10.40 The puppet model for Example 2

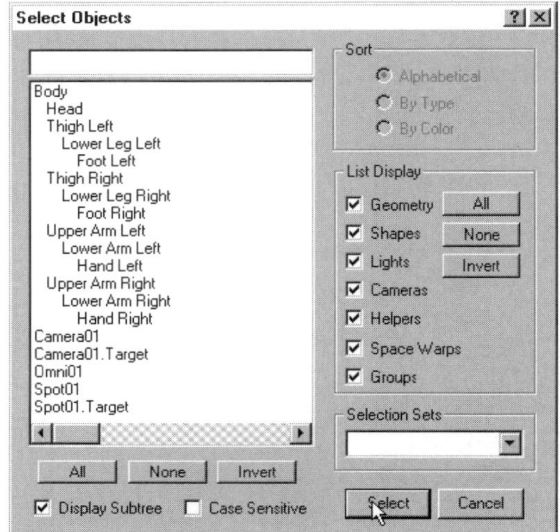

Fig. 10.41 The subtree for Example 2

Fig. 10.42 Renderings taken at four animation frames at frame 0, frame 20, frame 30 and frame 40

Exercises

The following five exercises all involve the creation of objects, their joining together as Boolean unions, or as groups, then animating them in various ways. Use your own judgement about sizes and dimensions.

1. Figure 10.43 is a rendering of a paper clip. After creating the clip, animate in such a manner that one after another pieces of paper are being placed in the clip up to a total of ten pieces.

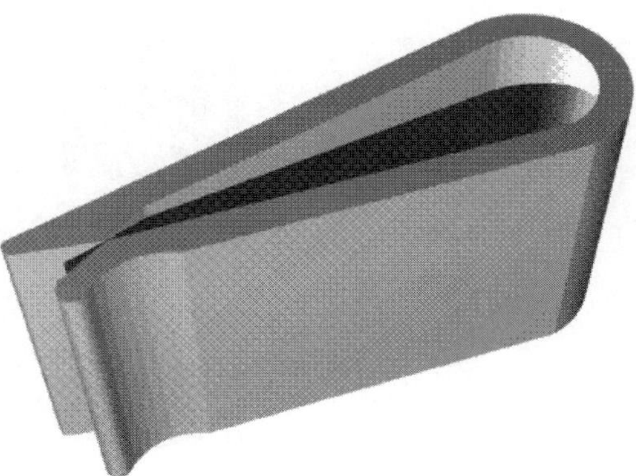

Fig. 10.43 Exercise 1

2. Figure 10.44 is a rendering of another paper clip. After creating the clip, animate in such a manner that the clip becomes larger by about a scale of 2 times, then reverts back its normal scale.

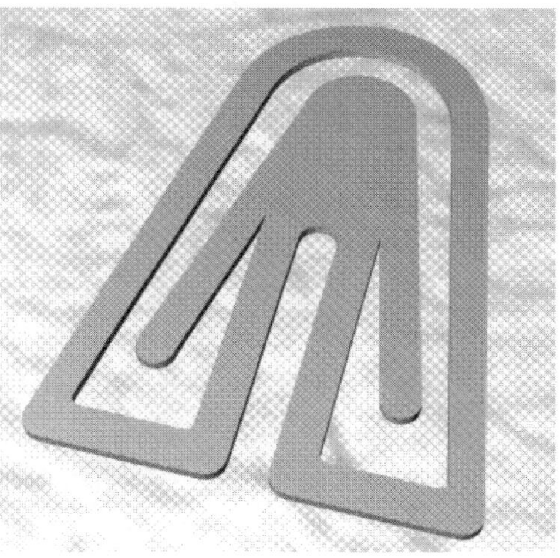

Fig. 10.44 Exercise 2

3. A model wind vane such as is used for the pumping of water is shown in the rendering Fig. 10.45.

   Create the model to your own dimensions and then animate in such a manner that the vanes rotate through 720° as the vane swings between a south-west wind and a west wind.

Fig. 10.45 Exercise 3

4. In the model shown in Fig. 10.46, as the crank is turned clockwise through 360° so the elliptical solid from the box on its cylindrical holder moves vertically through one-quarter of the cylinder's height. It then moves vertically back into the box until the bottom of the elliptical solid is in its original position.

   Create the model and the animation.

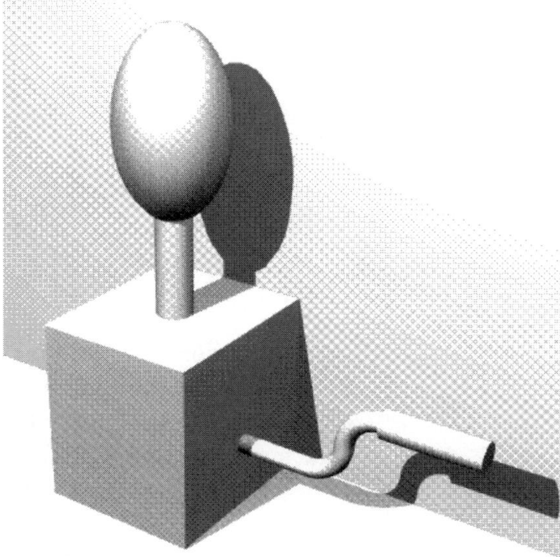

Fig. 10.46 Exercise 4

5. Figure 10.47 is a rendering of two model gears, one with 25 gear teeth, the other with 15 gear teeth. You will probably need to import the 3D model from a CAD software package.

   Add spindles to the gears and then cause the larger gear to rotate through two revolutions with the smaller gear meshed with the first.

Fig. 10.47 Exercise 5

CHAPTER 11

More about materials and rendering

Notes on the Material Editor

Assigning a material to an object is carried out via the **Material Editor**, called by a *left-click* on its icon in the toolbar. This dialogue box was first introduced in Chapter 9. Some further features from the dialogue box are given in this chapter.

1. A *left-click* on the **Get Material** icon in the dialogue box brings the **Material/Map Browser** onto screen (Fig. 11.1). In the **Browser** another *left-click* in the check circle to the left of **Material Library** brings up the 3DS Max default library of available materials. In the

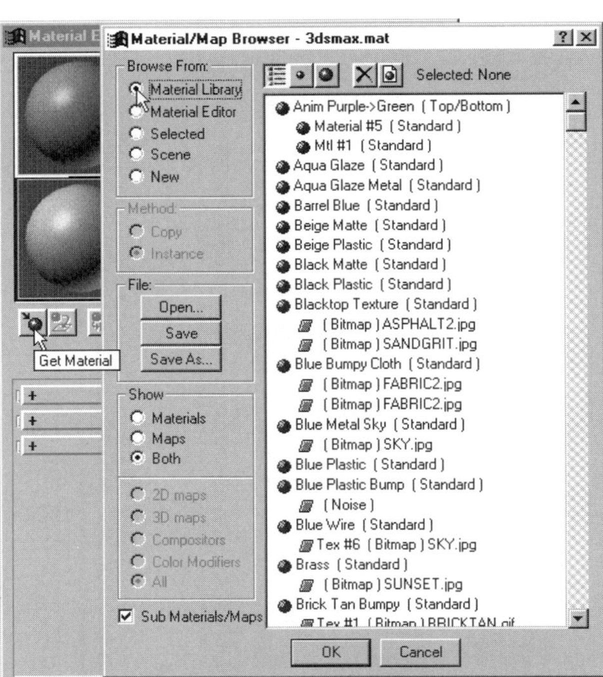

Fig. 11.1 The **Material Editor** dialogue box and the **Material/Map Browser**

Browser, a *left-click* on the **View Large Icons** causes the names in the dialogue box to change to the materials showing on rendered spheres (Fig. 11.2), making it easier for the operator to choose the material he/she wishes to assign.

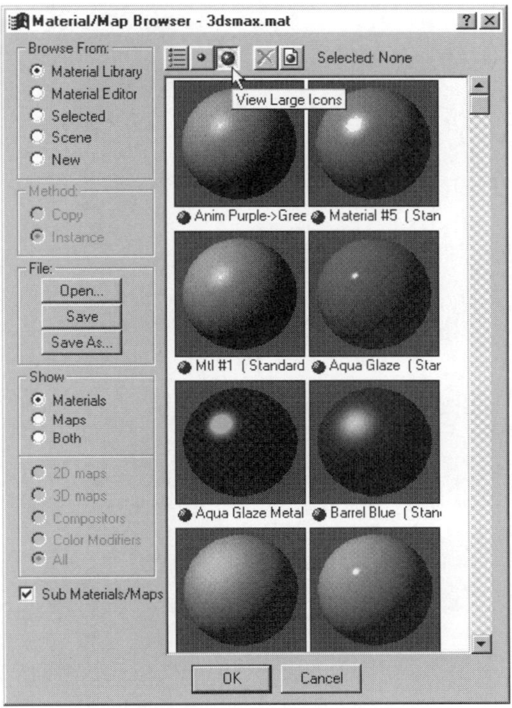

Fig. 11.2 The result of selecting the **View Large Icons** icon

2. A *left-click* on the **View Small Icons** icon and a series of smaller rendered spheres will be seen (Fig. 11.3).
3. There are four forms of rendering – **Wire**, **Constant**, **Phong** and **Metal**. To set the form of rendering *click* in the **Shading:** area of the **Material Editor** and a popup list appears showing three of the grades (Fig. 11.4). The fourth **Wire** is set by a *click* in the check box against **Wire** as seen in Fig. 11.4. If **Wire** rendering is selected, a further modification can be achieved by setting the **Size** number in the **Wire** area of the **Extended Parameters** rollout as shown in Fig. 11.5. When setting wire size, the thickness of the wire is shown in the specimen sphere of the dialogue box.

   Fig. 11.6 shows five spheres rendered as indicated in the illustration. The default method of rendering is **Phong**, which has a good degree of anti-aliasing in which the pixels at the edges of the various parts of a scene are shaded in varying degrees of grey or colour so as to sharpen up the outlines of the parts of the scene.

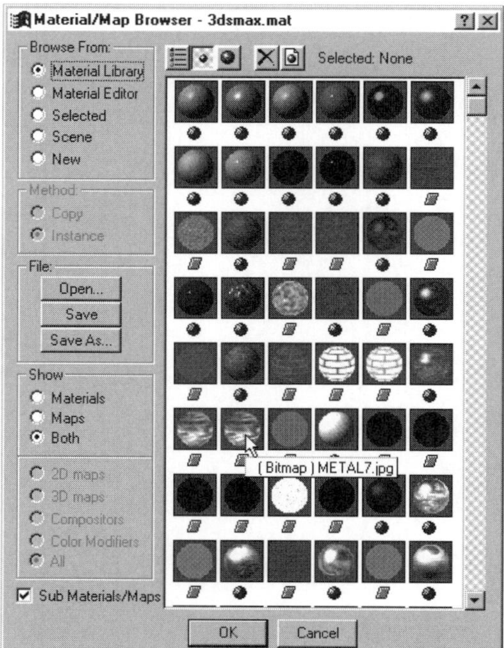

Fig. 11.3 The result of selecting the **View Small Icons** icon

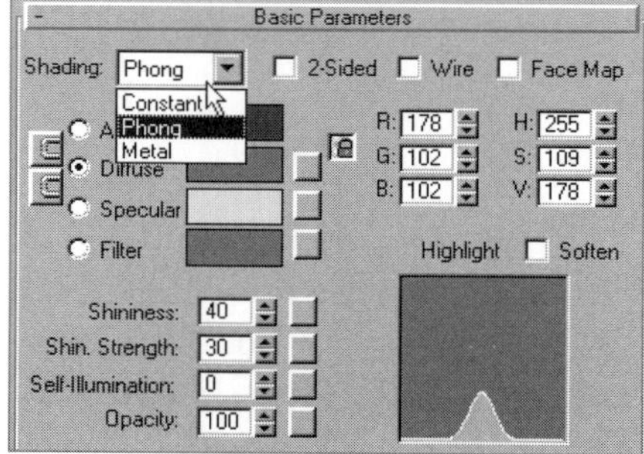

Fig. 11.4 Selecting rendering method

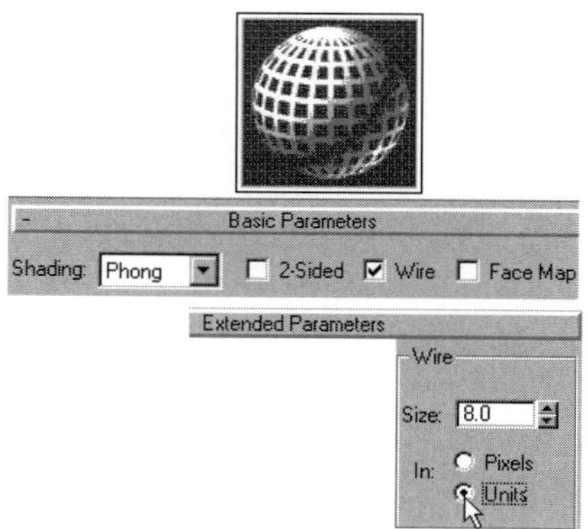

Fig. 11.5 Setting **Wire Size**

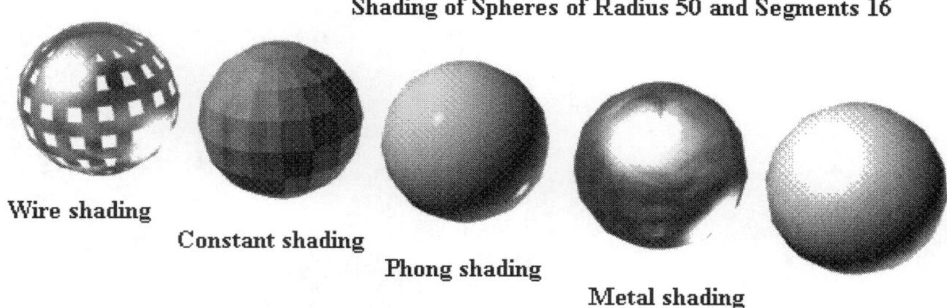

Fig. 11.6 Spheres rendered in the different forms of shading

Metal method is employed mainly for the rendering of metals and produces highlights showing the reflection normally associated with polished metals.

4. **Wire** rendering is much faster than **Constant**, which is faster than the remaining two other methods of rendering.
5. Some materials from the 3D Max default library of materials will require **UVW Mapping** to be applied to the object to which the material is being assigned. When assigning such a material unless mapping has been applied a warning box appears on screen advising the operator to apply mapping. The selection of the type of mapping is made from the **Parameters** rollout when **UVW Mapping** is chosen from **Modify** (Fig. 11.7). When mapping is to be applied it is important to use the correct form of mapping coordinates. Figure 11.8 shows a material derived from a rendering of a scene shown in Chapter 8 and used as a material. More about the method of using a rendering in this way is given in later pages of this chapter.

   The rendering from which the material was taken is shown centrally in Fig. 11.8 and the various methods of applying the material with mapping shown surrounding the rendering. In this example, no tiling was used, the default tiling figures of 1 being accepted throughout.

   Fig. 11.9 shows another set of cubes with the material **Wood Ashen** assigned and with different methods of mapping used.

Fig. 11.7 The **Mapping** types as selected from the **Parameters** rollout of the **UVW Mapping** modifier

An example of creating a material to be used as a label

Because this example involves the use of **Text**, note that text from the **Windows/Font** directory can be used in 3D Studio Max. In fact, any fonts from other sources, such as AutoCAD fonts, could also be used. Before using the Windows fonts, however, the **Path** from which the fonts files are to be taken must first be set by selecting **Configure Paths...** from the **File** pull-down menu and in the **General** section of the resulting dialogue box set the **Fonts** path as shown in Fig. 11.10.

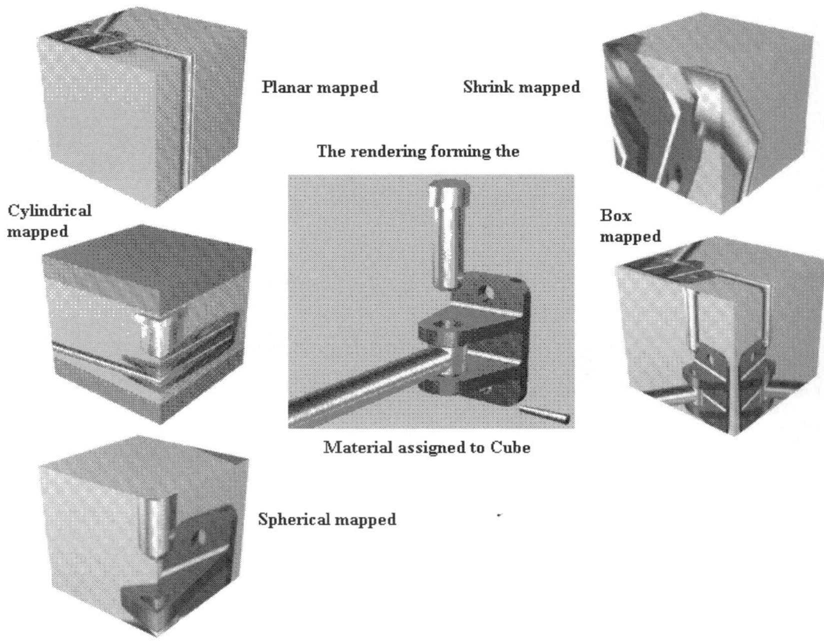

Fig. 11.8 Examples of applying a material to different mapping coordinates

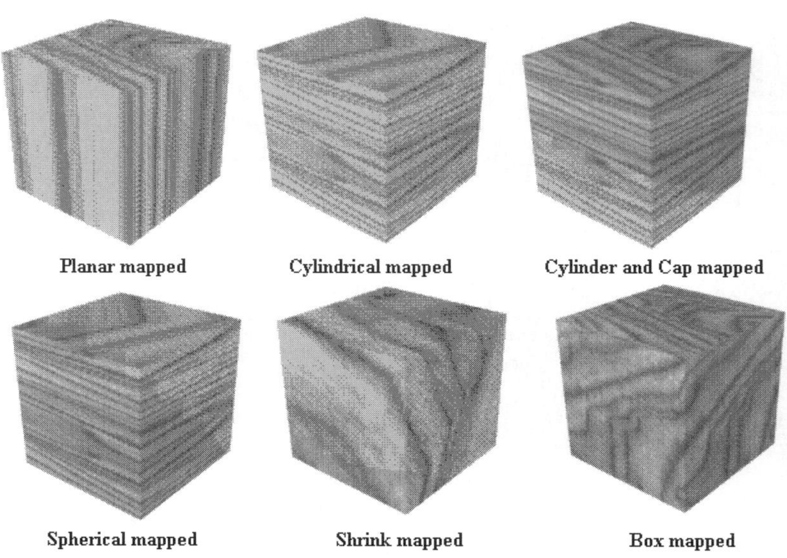

Fig. 11.9 A second example of using different methods of mapping

To create the required label:

1. Construct the label as shown in Fig. 11.11. This involved two boxes of height 0.01 units, with text in the smaller box extruded to 0.02 units. The larger box was assigned the material **Granite**

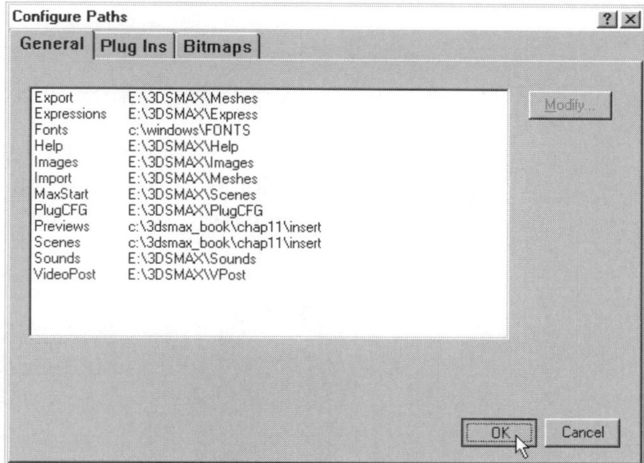

Fig. 11.10 Setting the **Fonts** path in the **Configure Paths** dialogue box

Pink Gray, the smaller box the material **Paper** and the text the material **White Plastic**.

2. You may find it necessary to involve a camera and lights. These are not shown in Fig. 11.11 because they have been hidden by using the **Display** rollout (its icon is to the right of the **Modify** icon). Then render the scene from the **Front** viewport. It is better to render to 320×240 format, set in the **Render Scene** dialogue box.
3. Save the rendering in *.tga or *.ipg format (both if you wish). This is carried out by a *left-click* on the **Save Bitmap** icon in the rendering window (Fig. 11.11).

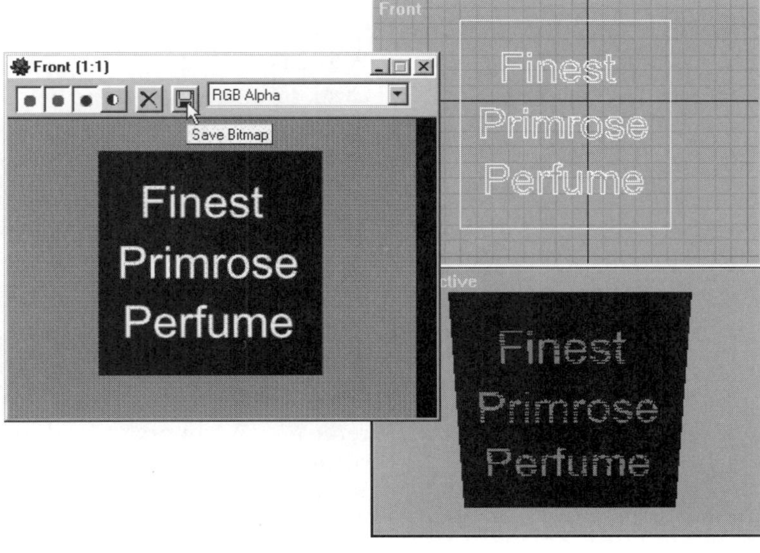

Fig. 11.11 Creating the label

4. Create the scene including the vase (the finished rendering is shown in Fig. 11.13). The vase was created from a **Line** which was amended with the aid of the modifier **Edit Spline** and then acted upon with **Lathe**.
5. Open the **Material Editor** (Fig. 11.12). Select the first of the sample spheres and assign the material **Paper** from the **Material/Map Browser** to the sphere.

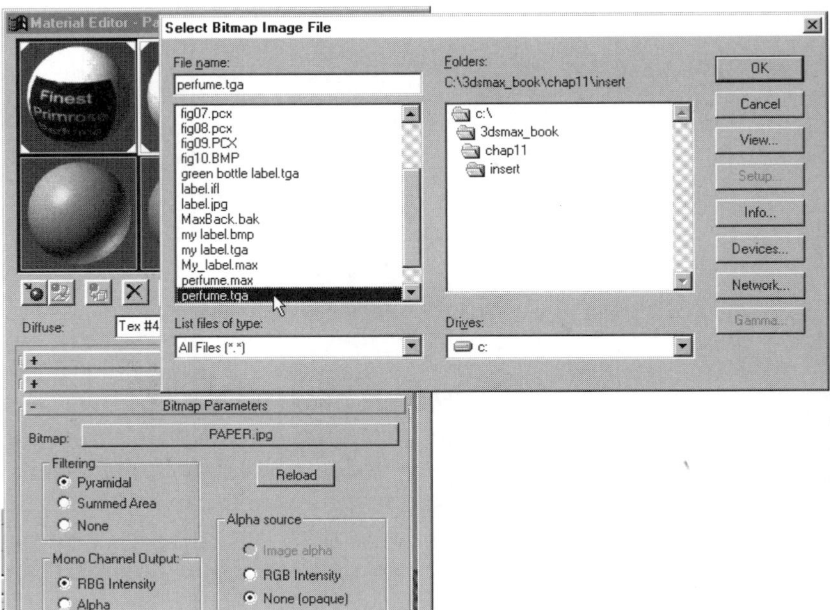

Fig. 11.12 Selecting the rendered label from the **Select Bitmap Image File** dialogue box

6. Open the **Maps** rollout for **Paper**. In the **Diffuse** bar the bitmap for **Paper** is named.
7. Click on the name in the bar. The **Select Bitmap Image** dialogue box appears. From the dialogue box select the perfume.tga file.
8. The sample sphere will now show the label as the required material. **Assign** the material to the vase object.
9. The material must also be mapped with the **Planar** type of mapping – *left-click* on **Modify** and on the **UVW Mapping** button. Then select the appropriate type of mapping – in this case **Planar**.
10. Render the scene – the result is shown in Fig. 11.13. In this scene the vase was 'placed' in a crate created from four **Box**es which were assigned the material **White Plastic** with the shininess removed. A camera was added to the scene and light added. The resulting rendering was taken from the **Camera01** viewport.

Fig. 11.13 A rendering of the completed scene

Changing of objects after materials have been assigned

Any object created in 3D Studio Max can have its dimensions and/or modifications amended even after materials have been assigned to the objects. Assigned materials conform to the new sizes and/or modifications.

Two examples are given, the first the amending of the sizes of a table top from the simple table shown previously on page 129, the second the changing of the shape of a spline of a bowl shown previously on page 168.

Fig. 11.14 A rendering of the table before changing the size of its top

Example 1 – changing sizes

Figure 11.14 shows a rendering of the table before the sizes of its top have been changed. To make the changes:

1. Select the table top. Its name appears in the window just below the tool icons at the top of the Command panel.
2. Move the Command panel until the **Parameters** rollout appears (Fig. 11.15). The sizes of the table top will show in the **Length:**, **Width:** and **Height:** boxes of the rollout.
3. *Enter* new figures for the revised sizes for the table top. In the example given, the length has been changed from 120 to 140, the width from 200 to 250 and the height from 10 to 15. Press the **Return** key of the keyboard after each entry. The changes are shown in Fig. 11.16.

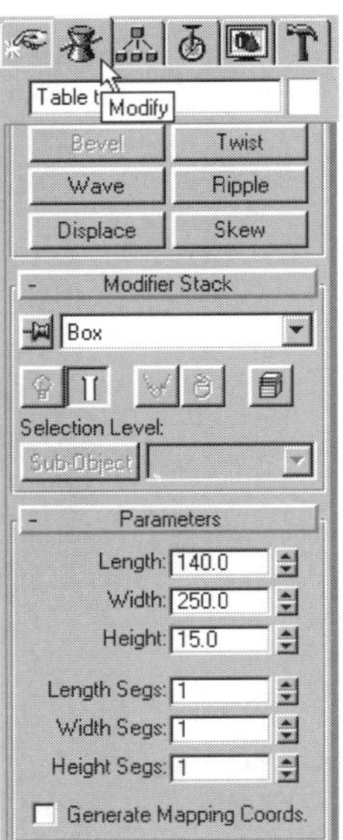

Fig. 11.15 The rollout from **Modify** showing the changes in the Length, Width and Height of the table top

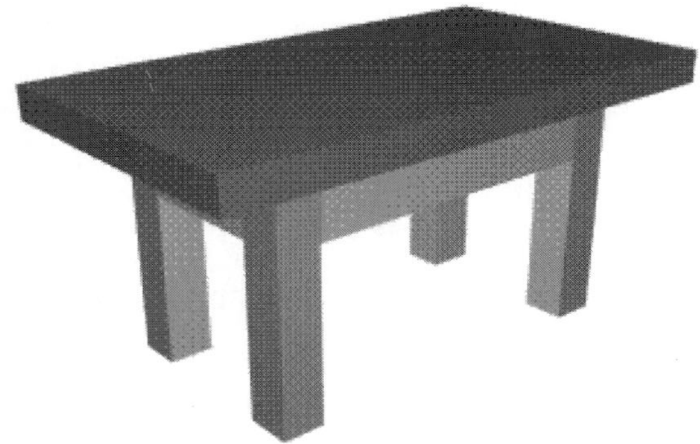

Fig. 11.16 A rendering of the table after its top has been re-sized

Example 2 – changing a modification

Figure 11.17 shows the bowl and its lid. The example demonstrates how the shape of the bowl can be changed.

1. Select the bowl.
2. Select **Modify** from the modifier icons. The name of the object appears in the window at the top of the Command panel.
3. Open up the popup list showing (in this example) **UVW Mapping**. The popup list will show the modifications used to change the **Line** into a **Lathe**d object.
4. *Left-click* on the name **Edit Spline** in the popup list. The original spline from which the bowl was formed appears.
5. In the **Front** viewport, change the shape of the spline.
6. In the popup list, select **Lathe**. The new, enlarged bowl object appears in place of the spline.

It will be noted that the assigned material has assumed the new shape of the amended bowl.

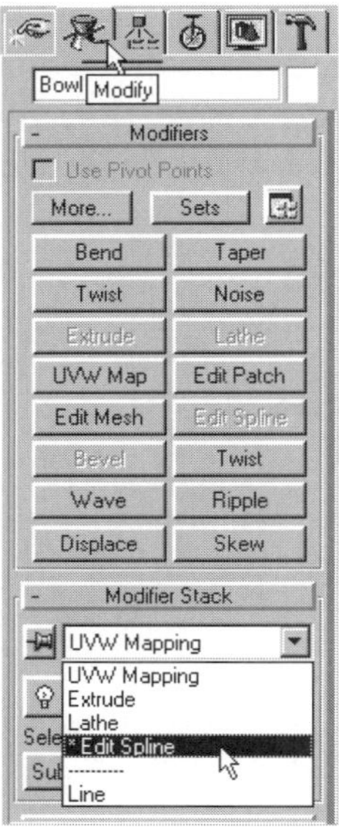

Fig. 11.17 Selecting **Edit Spline** from the popup list

Fig. 11.18 A rendering of the the original bowl before editing its spline

Fig. 11.19 A rendering of the bowl after its spline has been changed

Notes

1. It can be seen from the two examples that the materials assigned to the objects have fitted to the sizes of the enlargements of the objects.
2. Whether a material has been assigned to an object or not, an object can be amended in the same manner as in the two examples given above. This means that if an object has been given incorrect sizes or modified in a manner not as desired, changes can take place, even after an object has had material assigned and been rendered.
3. If an object has been enlarged, lighting and camera positions may have to be moved or rotated.

An example of assigning a face map

1. Create a tube and in the **Perspective** viewport adjust the viewing position of the tube so that it shows to best advantage. Set the viewport to **Smooth+Highlight** and turn off the grid.
2. Call the **Material Editor** and assign one of the sample spheres to the tube.
3. In the **Material Editor** *left-click* on the button near to **Diffuse** (Fig. 11.20).

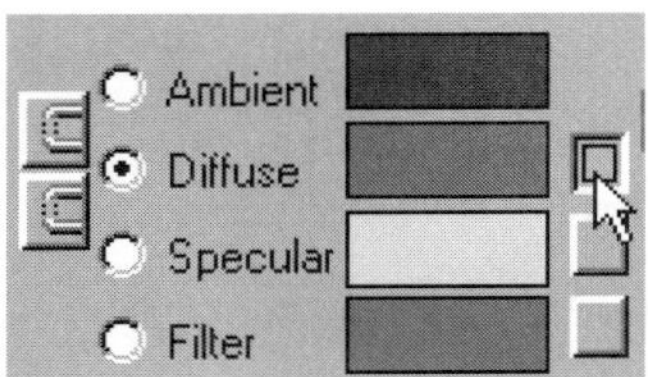

Fig. 11.20 *Click* the button next to **Diffuse**

4. The **Material/Map Browser** appears. Select **New** and **Bitmap** (Fig. 11.21).
5. *Left-click* on the button next to **Diffuse** (Fig. 11.20).
6. The **Material/Map Browser** appears. Select **New** and **Bitmap** (Fig. 11.21).

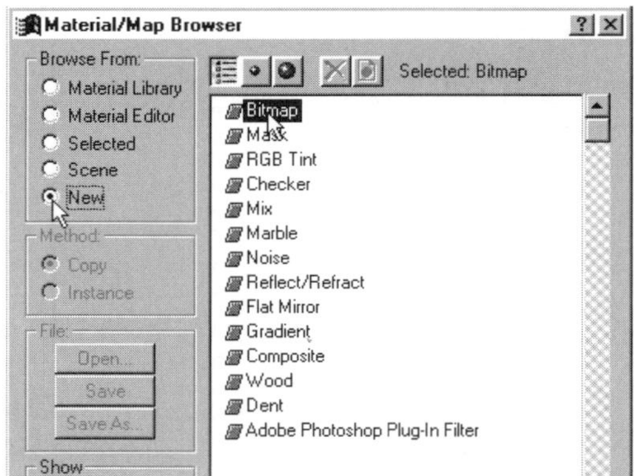

Fig. 11.21 Select **New** and **Bitmap**

7. *Left-click* on the button bar in the **Bitmap Parameters** rollout (Fig. 11.22). The **Select Bitmap Image File** dialogue box opens. From the file list *double-click* on **pat0127.tga**. The sample sphere is covered with a number of the patterns from the pat0127.tga file.

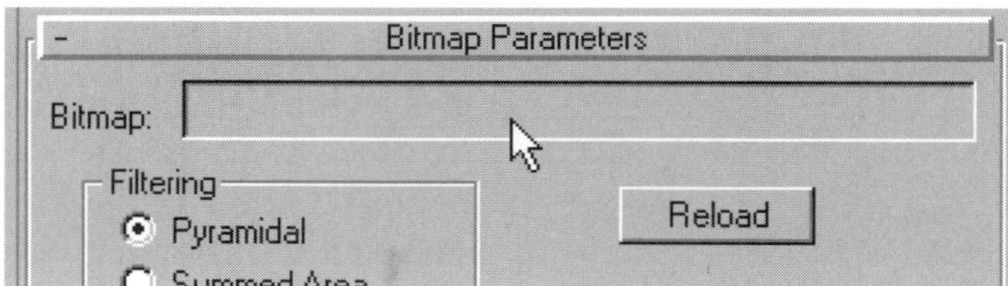

Fig. 11.22 The button bar in the **Bitmap Parameters** rollout

Fig. 11.23 Select the **Go to Parent** icon

Fig. 11.24 The finished tube

8. *Left-click* on the **Go to Parent** icon (Fig. 11.23) and set the check box for **Facemap** on (tick in the box).
9. Render the **Perspective** viewport (Fig. 11.24).

Exercises

1. Figures 11.25 and 11.26 show two frames from the animation (at frame 0 and frame 40) of a camera inside a room scene.

   The walls, ceiling, floor, window and door for the scene were created with the use of **Box**. The central table was created from a pair of **Cylinders**, the lamp stand is a **Line** modified with **Lathe** and the lamp shade a **Tube**. Materials were added to the parts of the scene as follows:

   Wall with Windows and the opposite wall – **Granite Pink Tile** with the **UVW Mapping** tiled U × 8 and VC × 8.
   End walls – **tripat.gif** tiled U × 8 V × 8.
   Also light shade – as end walls.
   Ceiling – **White Plastic.**
   Floor – **Wood Cedar Board** tiled U × 4 V × 4.
   Shelves – **Wood Ashen**.
   Table – **Granite Pink Gray**.
   Background – **Sky**.

Fig. 11.25 Exercise 1 – animation at time frame 0

Some parts were joined or subtracted with the aid of the Boolean operatives.

Lights were added and a short focal length camera, which was animated for each 10 time frames.

Create and animate a similar scene.

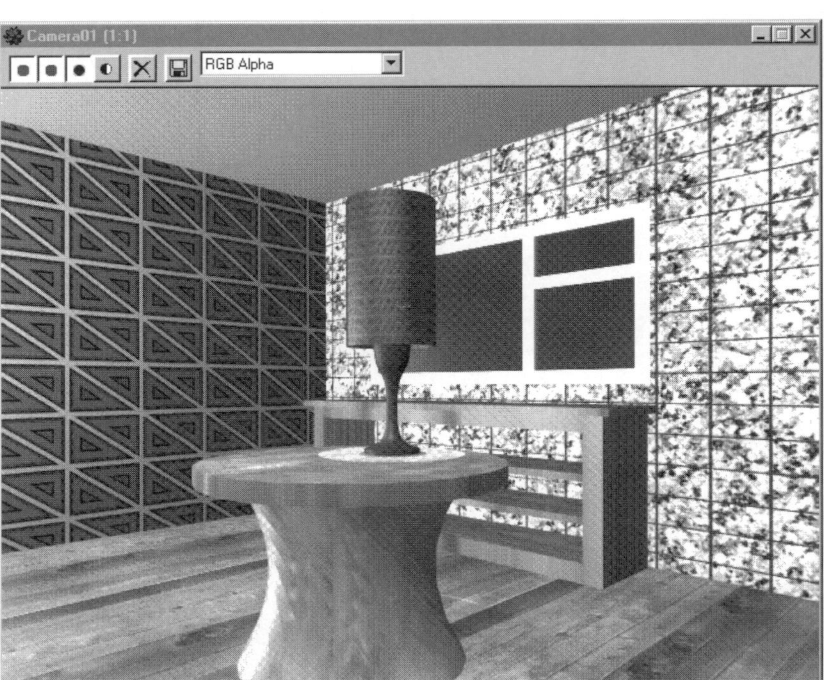

Fig. 11.26 Exercise 1 – animation at time frame 40

2. Figure 11.27 shows stages in the animation of the text **From here** from a billboard into a waste container. The path of the animation takes place along a semi-elliptical route.

   Create a similar animation of a simple phrase containing text. Choose any text phrase for the animation The purpose of this exercise is to show that text can be animated as easily as any other set of objects in 3D Studio Max.
3. Figure 11.28 shows the stages in the animation of the material **pat0153.tga** assigned to an object created form two **Box**es Boolean separated from each other.

   The total number of frames is 120. Figure 11.28 shows the tiling of frames at 20 frame intervals. The tiling was amended at each 20th frame from the **Material Editor** after the material had been assigned to the object.

   The purpose of this exercise is to demonstrate that, as with other features of 3D Studio Max, materials can be animated.

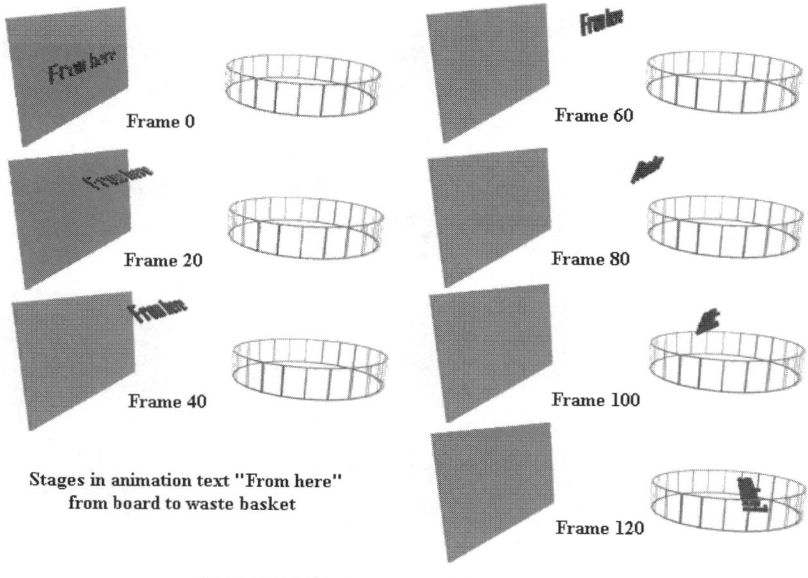

Fig. 11.27 Exercise 2

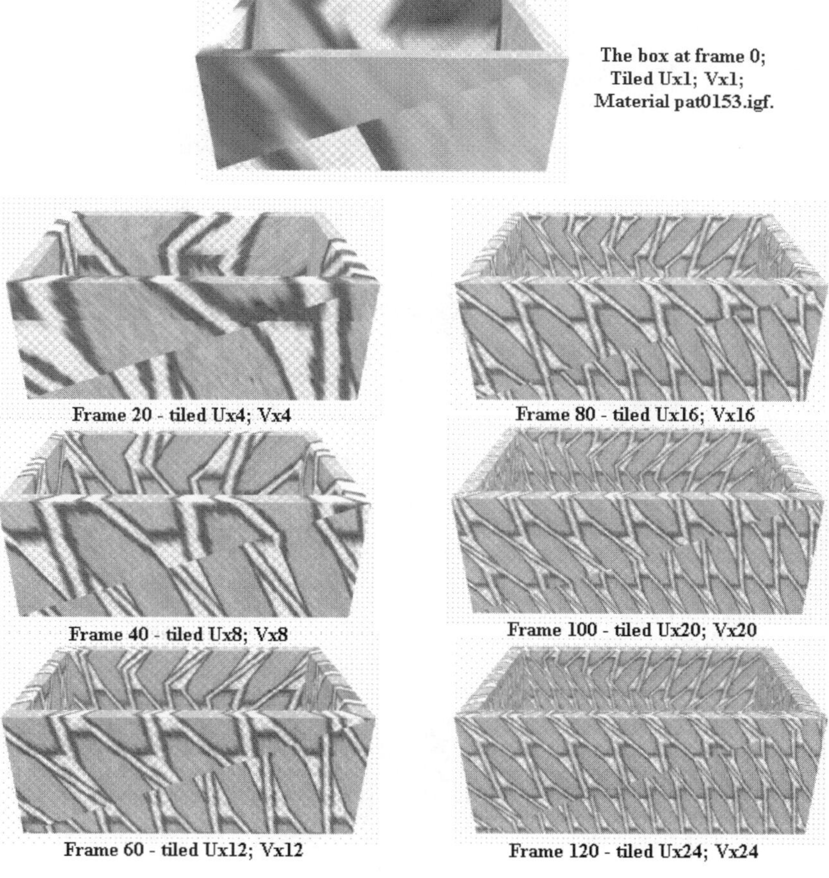

Fig. 11.28 Exercise 3

Create a similar object and assigning any one of the pattern materials from the **Select Bitmap Image** file, assign and animate a material to your object.

4. Figure 11.29 shows a rendering of a basket created from cones and assigned a material of **Wire** type.

   Working to any convenient sizes create a similar basket and then render the result.

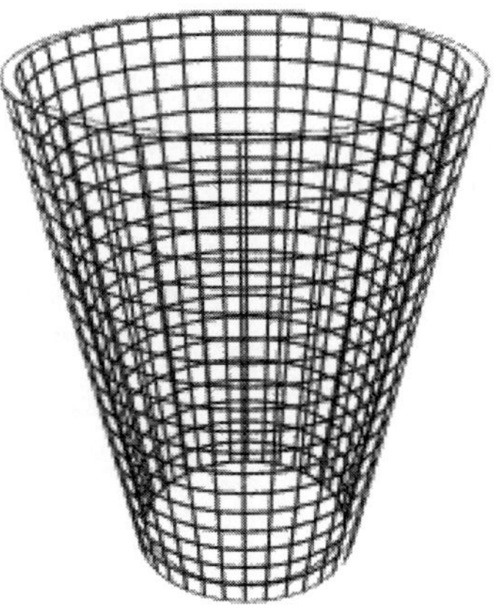

Fig. 11.29 Exercise 4

5. Using your drawing from Exercise 4 as the basket, create an animation describing the throwing of some litter into the basket from some distance to the left of the basket.

CHAPTER 12

More about creating and animating

Lofting

1. In the **Front** viewport and with **Snap** on, create an **Arc**.
2. Anywhere in the **Front** viewport, create a **Circle** of radius 20 (Fig. 12.1).

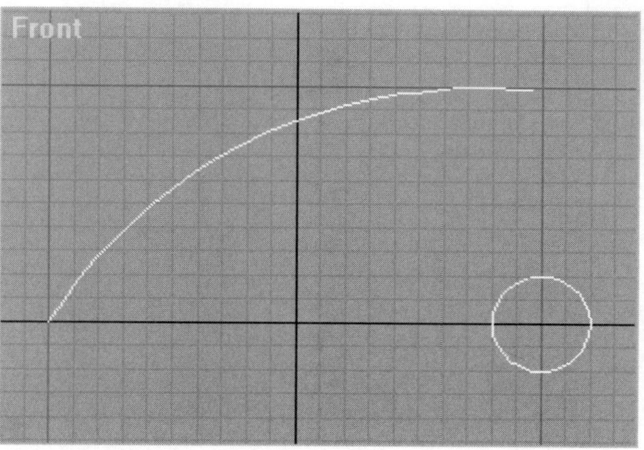

Fig. 12.1 Create an arc and a circle in the **Front** viewport

3. Select the **Arc**.
4. Select **Loft Object** from the **Geometry** popup list (Fig. 12.2).
5. Select the **Loft** button from the rollout which appears (Fig. 12.3).

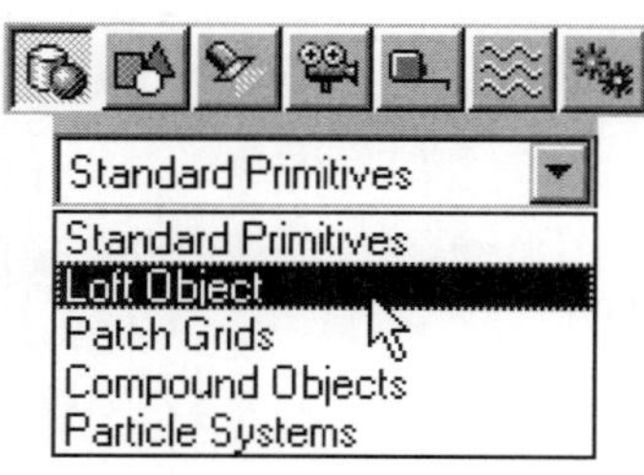

Fig. 12.2 Select **Loft Object** from the popup list

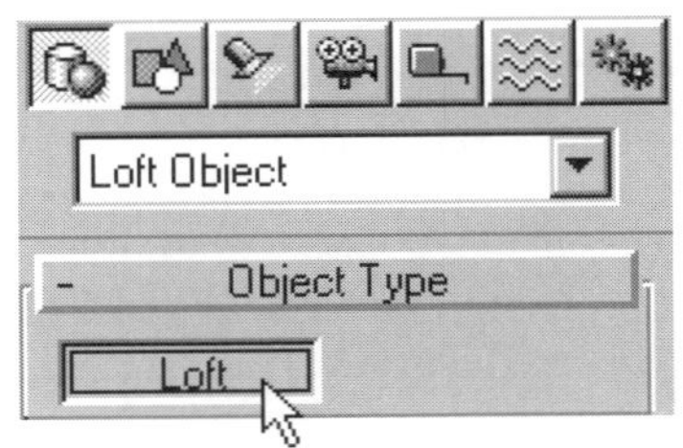

Fig. 12.3 Select the **Loft** button from the **Loft Object** rollout

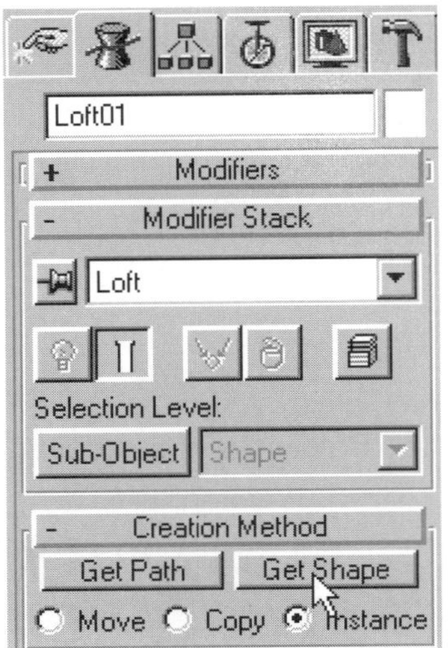

Fig. 12.4 *Left-click* on the **Get Shape** button in the rollout

6. Select the **Get Shape** button from the rollout (Fig. 12.4). Check that the **Instance** check circle is on (dot in circle).
8. Select the **Circle** as the shape.
9. In the **Skin Parameters** rollout set the check box against **Skin** on (tick in check box). The loft object now appears as in Fig. 12.5.

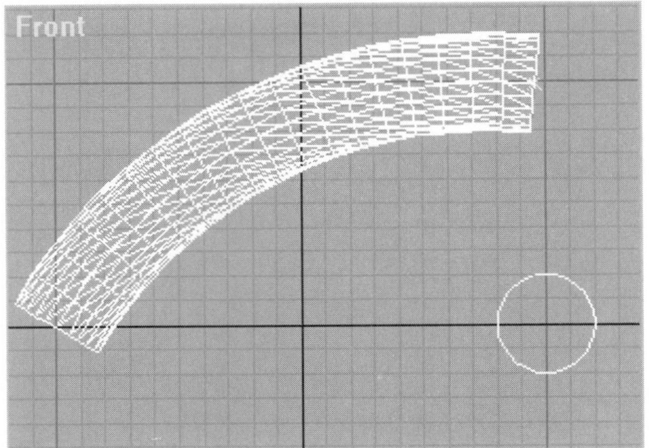

Fig. 12.5 The loft object with its 'skin'

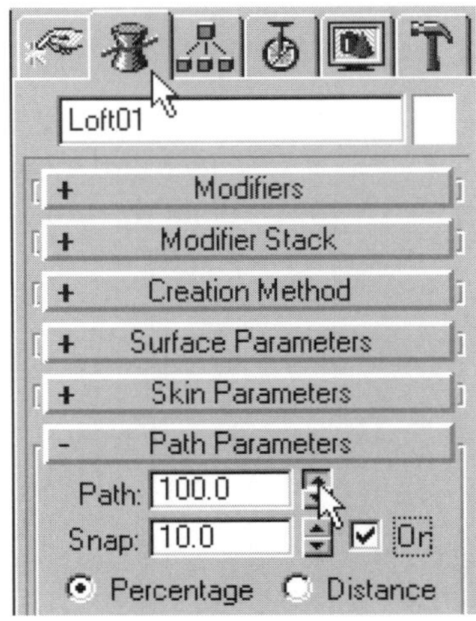

Fig. 12.6 With the **On:** check box set on, spin the **Path:** number to 100

10. Anywhere in the **Front** viewport create a **Rectangle** of side lengths 50.
11. With **Select and Move** active *left-click* on the loft object.
12. *Left-click* on the **Modify** button.
13. In the **Path Parameters** rollout of the command panel set the **On:** check box on (tick in check box). See Fig. 12.6.
14. Adjust the **Path** spinner to 100. A small cross moves along the loft object to the other end.
15. In the **Creation Method** rollout *left-click* on **Get Shape** and again on the **Rectangle** in the **Top** viewport. The **Get Shape** icon appears on the **Rectangle** and the other end of the loft object takes on the shape of the rectangle (Fig. 12.7).

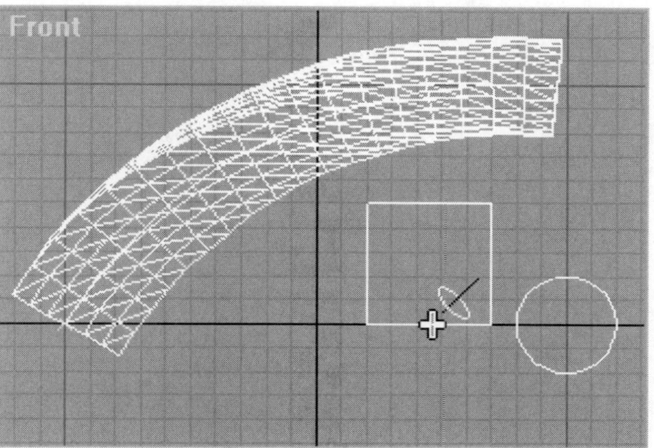

Fig. 12.7 The **Get Shape** icon on the rectangle

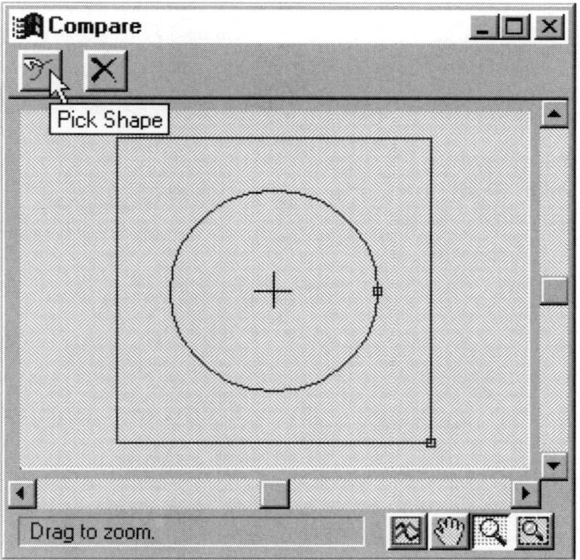

Fig. 12.8 The **Compare** dialogue box with the two shapes showing

16. It will now be noted that the loft object is twisted. This is because the start point when creating the circle is at a different position from that when creating the rectangle.
17. In the **Modifier Stack** rollout *left-click* on the **Sub-Object** button and again on the **Compare** button which appears in a rollout. The **Compare** dialogue box appears (Fig. 12.8).
18. *Left-click* on the **Pick Shape** icon in the dialogue box, followed by another on the circle at one end of the loft object. Repeat for the rectangle at the other end. Both shapes appear in the dialogue box as shown in Fig. 12.8. Note the small square at the create start point of the two shapes. To get them to coincide:
    (a) With **Restrict to Y** active, in the **Front** viewport, **Rotate** the rectangle until, in the **Compare** dialogue box, the start square of the rectangle is in line with that of the circle (Fig. 12.9).
    (b) The twist in the loft object has now been remedied. Delete the **Compare** dialogue box

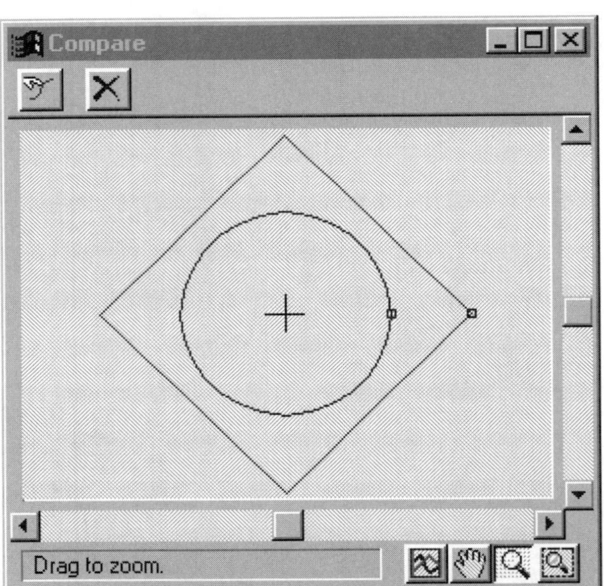

Fig. 12.9 The start point of the rectangle rotated to bring it into line with that of the circle

Figure 12.10 is a rendering of the loft objects in the **Perspective** viewport.

Three examples of lofting

Example 1

Figure 12.11 shows the loft resulting from a semicircular arc as the path with a radius of 100 units, a 6-sided NGon, with a radius of 15

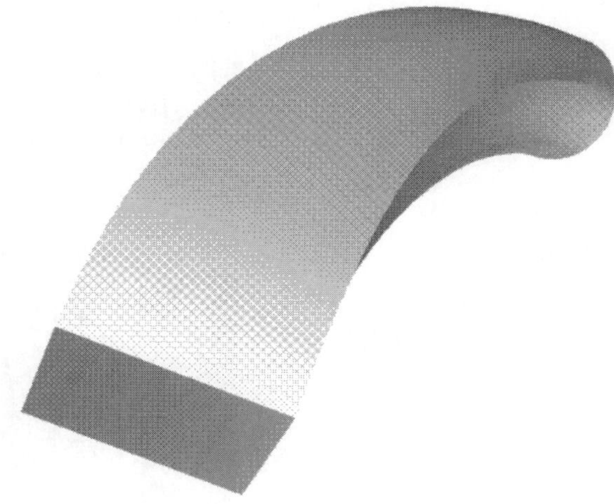

Fig. 12.10 A rendering of the loft object

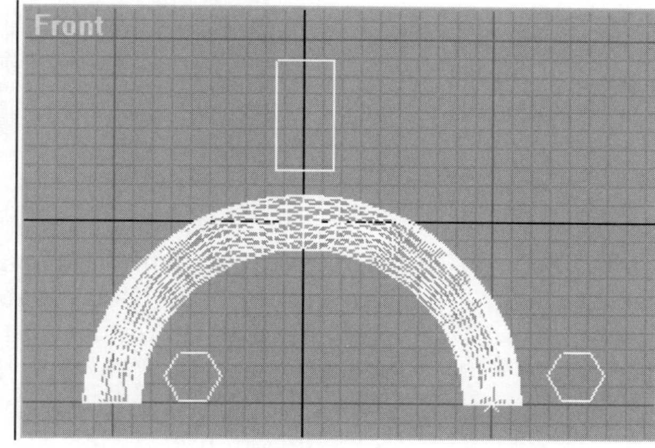

Fig. 12.11 Example 1– **Front** viewport

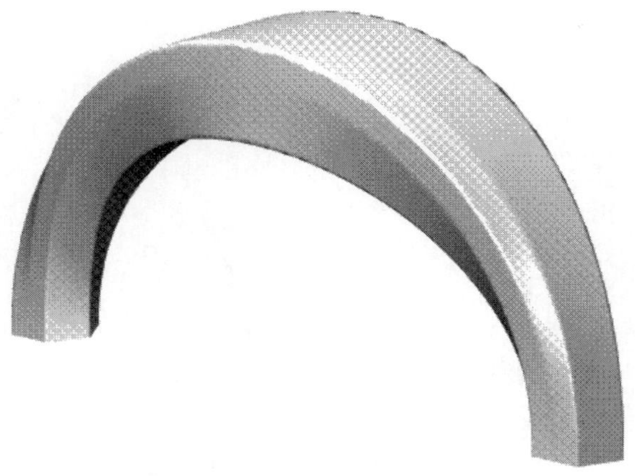

Fig. 12.12 Example 1 – a rendering from the **Camera01** viewport

as the shape at both ends (at 0% and 100%) and a rectangle (60 × 30) 50% along the length of the arc. Figure 12.12 shows a rendering of the loft object after a camera and lights have been added to the scene.

Example 2

Figure 12.13 shows the path for the frames of a picnic table created from a line which had been amended by using the **Bezier** option when modifying with the **Edit Spline** tool. The shape for the frame – a circle of radius 5 units – is included in Fig. 12.13.

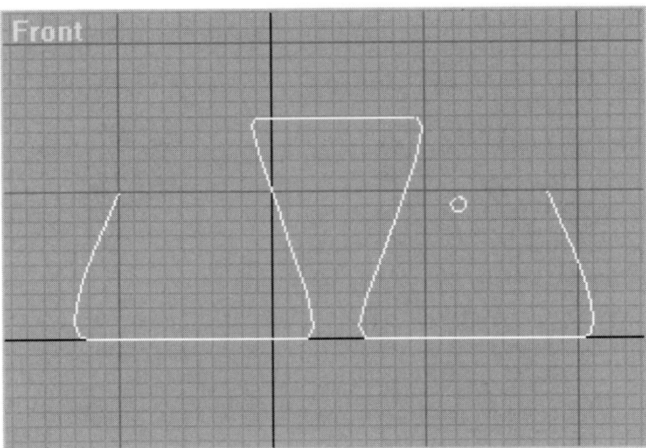

Fig. 12.13 Example 2 – the path created from an edited line spline

Figure 12.14 shows a rendering of the loft object obtained from lofting the path with its shape. In order to achieve smooth curves for this loft object the **Shape Steps** and **Path Steps** under **Options** in the **Skin Parameters** rollout for the loft were each increased to 15 (the default is 5). This, however, tends to slow down future additions to the scene in 3D Studio Max, unless extra memory is available for the computer in use.

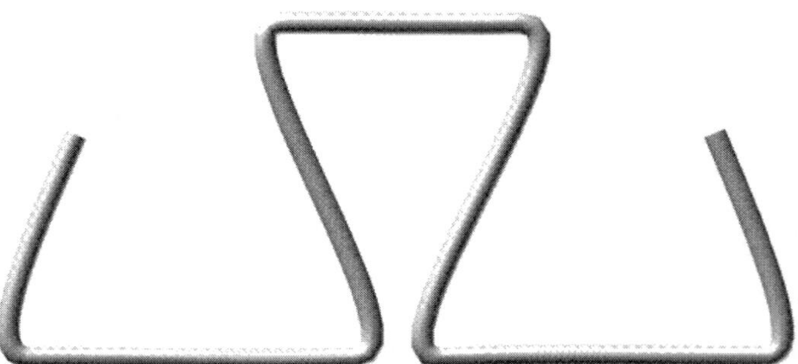

Fig. 12.14 Example 2 – a rendering of the lofted frame

After adding table slats and seats (**Box**es), a camera and lights were included in the scene and the result rendered as shown in Fig. 12.15.

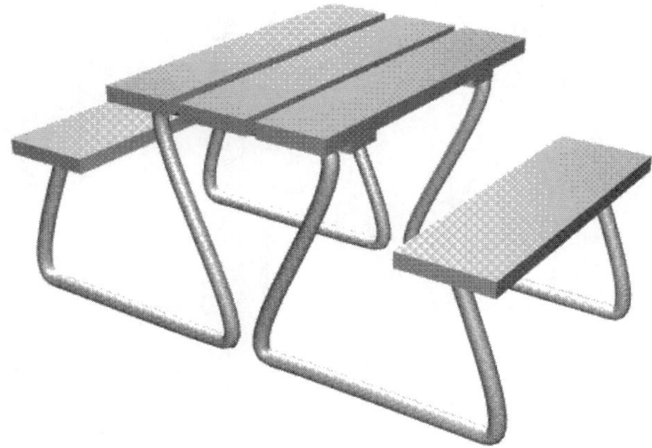

Fig. 12.15 Example 2 – the completed table

Example 3

Figure 12.16 shows the loft object resulting from a path – a 300 unit radius arc – and the shape for this example.

In order to achieve smooth curves in the rendering of this loft object the **Shape Steps** and **Path Steps** under **Options** in the **Skin Parameters** rollout for the loft were each increased to 10.

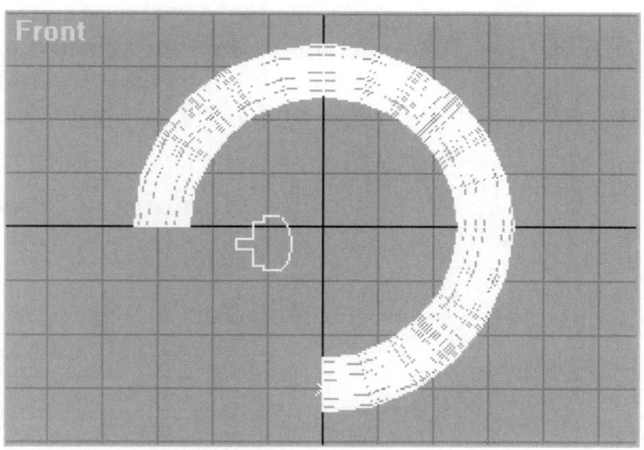

Fig. 12.16 Example 3 – the path and shape in the **Front** viewport

Note: Experiment with the various settings in the **Modify** rollouts when a lofted object has been selected – **Surface Parameters**, **Skin Parameters**, **Path Parameters** and **Deformation**. The best method of observing the action of the various settings is to create a lofted object, set the **Perspective** (or **Camera**) viewport to **Smooth+Highlight** and note the changes as the settings are varied.

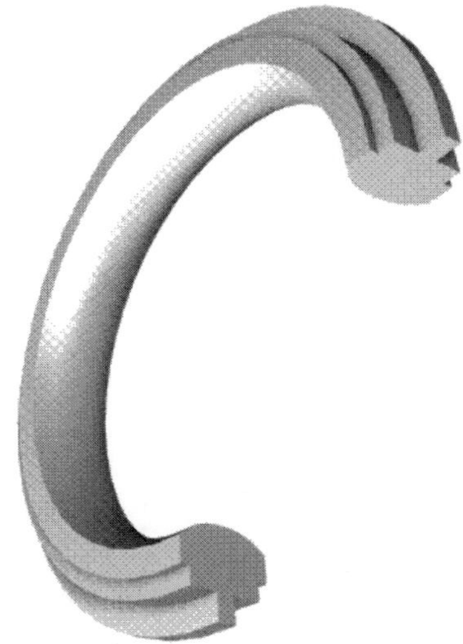

Fig. 12.17 Example 3 – a rendering

Copying objects

It is often necessary to make a copy (or copies) of an object which has been created. Copies of objects can either be truly copied, making them independent of any modification made to the copied object or its original, or they can be **Instances**, in which any modifications made to any one of the copies is automatically repeated in all the copies (or instances) including the original from which instance(s) have been created.

Examples of copying

Example 1

1. In the **Top** viewport create a cylinder of radius 30 and height 200.
2. Select the **Select and Move** tool from the toolbar.

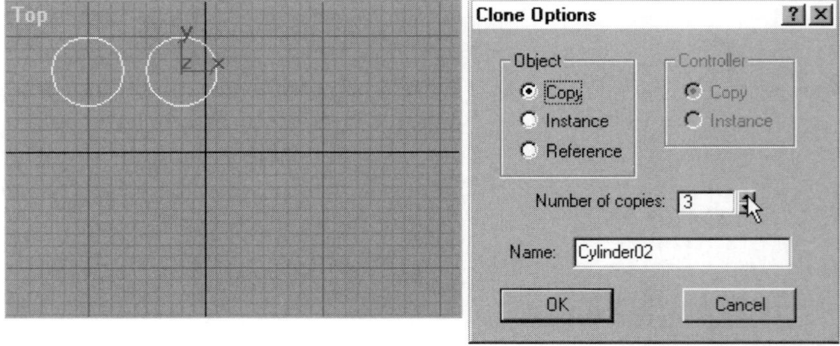

Fig. 12.18 The **Clone Options** dialogue box

3. Press the **Shift** key of the keyboard; select the cylinder. The **Select and Move** icon appears on the cylinder. With the **Shift** key still pressed, *drag* the cylinder to the right and then release the mouse button. The **Clone Options** dialogue box appears.
4. Make sure the **Copy** check circle is on (dot in circle) and *left-click* on the **Number of Copies:** spinner until the number 3 appears in the **Number of Copies:** box (Fig. 12.18). Then *left-click* on the **OK** button of the dialogue box. The result is as shown in Fig. 12.19.
5. Select any one of the cylinders and with the **Taper** modifier active, taper the selected cylinder by the amount of –1 (minus 1). The result is shown in the rendering of the **Perspective** viewport (Fig. 12.20).

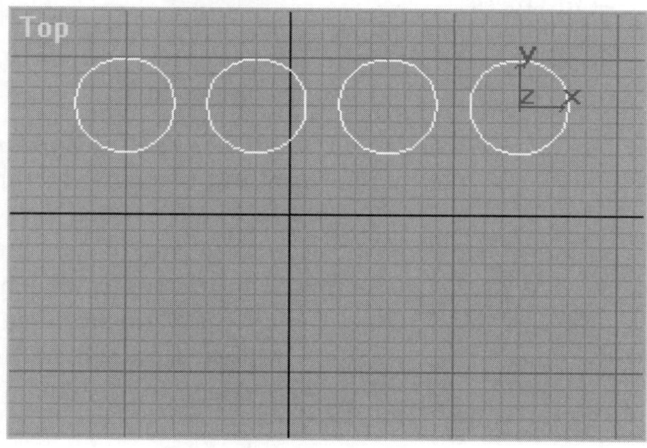

Fig. 12.19 The result of making three copies

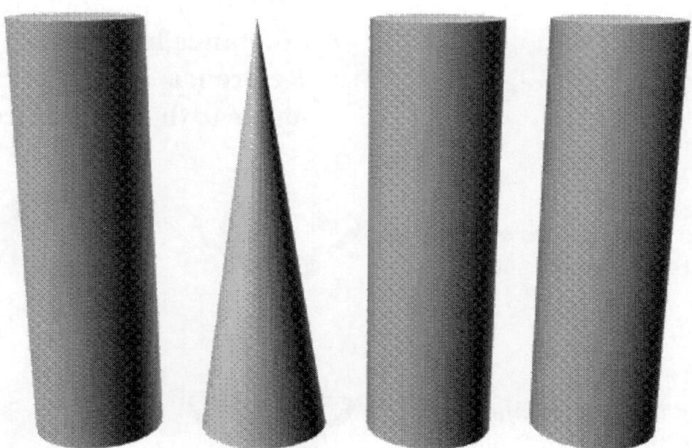

Fig. 12.20 The four copies after the action of the **Taper** modifier

Example 2

1. Create a tube of **Radius 1:** 40; **Radius 2:** 35; **Height:** 150.
2. Copy the tube three times, but this time with the **Instance** check circle set on (dot in its circle).

3. Select the modifier **Taper**. All the instances will be selected. Set the amount again to –1 (minus 1). All the instances become modified (Fig. 12.21).

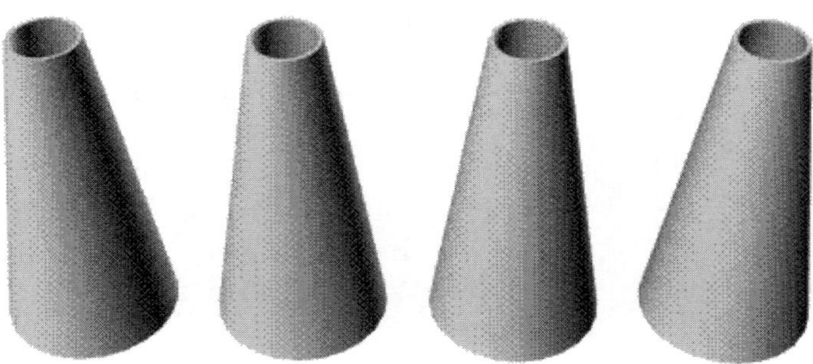

Fig. 12.21 **Taper** applied to copies made as **Instances**

Example 3

1. Create a **Teapot** of **Radius:** 40.
2. Copy the teapot with the **Reference** check circle set on (dot in circle). The result is shown in Fig. 12.22.
3. Select the first of the three reference copies and apply the **Bend** modifier to **Angle:** 20. The result is shown in Fig. 12.23.
4. Cancel the **Bend** and then apply the same bend to the first teapot – i.e. the one from which the reference copies were made. The result is shown in Fig. 12.24.
   From these three examples it will be seen that:

   A **Copy** is independent of the original from which it was copied.
   An **Instance** has no such independence.
   A **Reference** is an individual except when modifications are made to the original from which the reference copy was made.

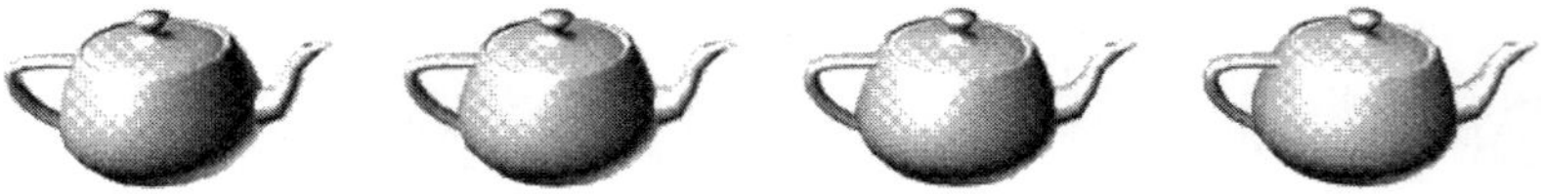

Fig. 12.22 Three copies of a teapot with **Reference** set on

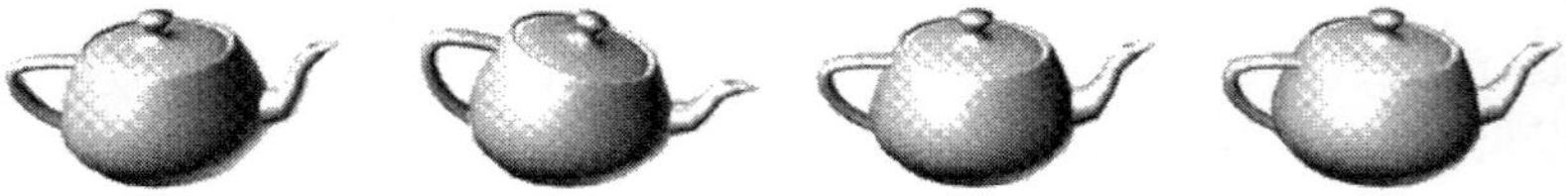

Fig. 12.23 The first of the copies modified with **Bend**

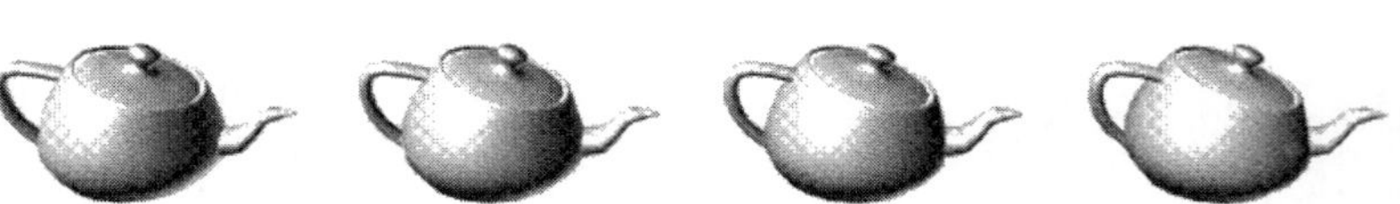

Fig. 12.24 The original has been modifed with **Bend**

Animation of modifiers

The modification of objects can be carried out in the same manner as any other animation.

Example 1

1. Create a **Box** 200 × 8 × 1.
2. Copy as **Instances** six rows each with six instances of the box (Fig. 12.25).
3. Apply the modifier **Taper** to an **Amount:** –2.5 (minus 2.5). Because the boxes are instances all the boxes will become tapered (Fig. 12.26).

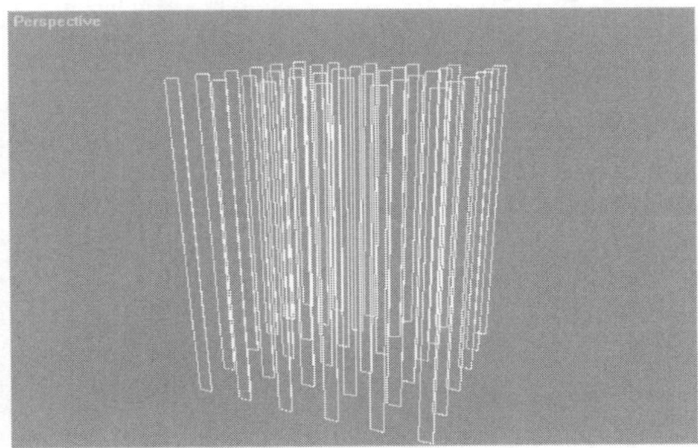

Fig. 12.25 Example 1. Create six rows of boxes with six in each row

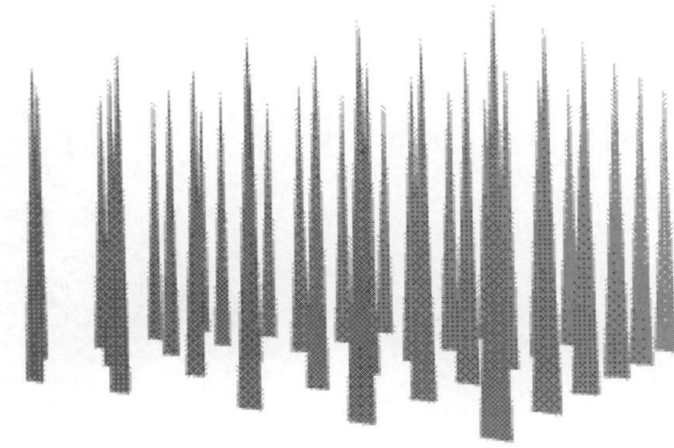

Fig. 12.26 The boxes after **Taper** at time frame 0

4. *Left-click* on the **Animation** button and set the time frame to 20.
5. **Twist** to **Angle:** 10.
6. Set time frame to 40, then 60, then 80, then 100, increasing the **Twist** by 10 each time, so that at time frame 100 the twist angle is 50.
7. Play back the animation.

Figures 12.27–29 show the animation at time frames 20, 60 and 100.

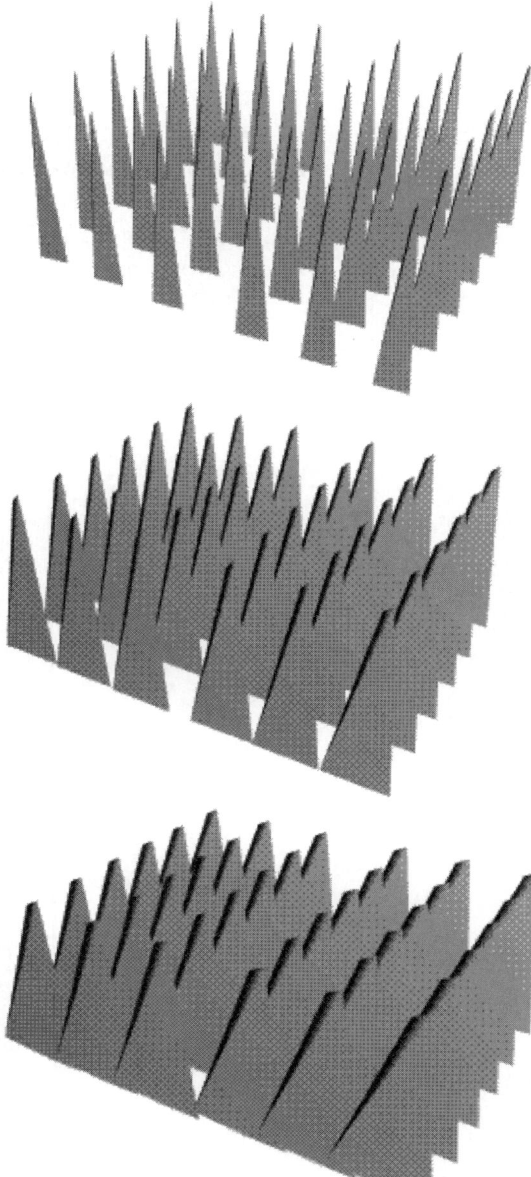

Fig. 12.27 The boxes at time frame 20

Fig. 12.28 The boxes at time frame 60

Fig. 12.29 The boxes at time frame 100

Example 2

1. Create a **Sphere** of radius 40 at the top of the **Front** viewport.
2. In the **Top** viewport create a **Box** 300 × 300 × 1 and in the **Front** viewport move it to the position the sphere will reach at frame 100.

3. *Left-click* on the **Animate** button and move the time frame to 20. Move the sphere vertically down in the **front** viewport by 50 units.
4. Move the time frame to 40 and the sphere vertically down 60 units.
5. Move the time frame to 60 and the sphere vertically down 70 units.
6. Move the time frame to 80 and the sphere vertically down 80 units.
7. Move the time frame to 97 and the sphere vertically down 90 units.
8. Move the time frame to 100 and the sphere vertically down 5 units.
9. *Left-click* on the **Modify** button and then on the **More...** button. From the **Modifier** dialogue box which appears, *left-click* on **Stretch** followed by another on the **OK** button. The **Stretch** modifier appears in the **Modify** rollout.
10. Set the **Stretch** figure to 0.4 in the **Y** direction. The sphere compresses along its Y axis.
11. Run the animation in the **Front** viewport.

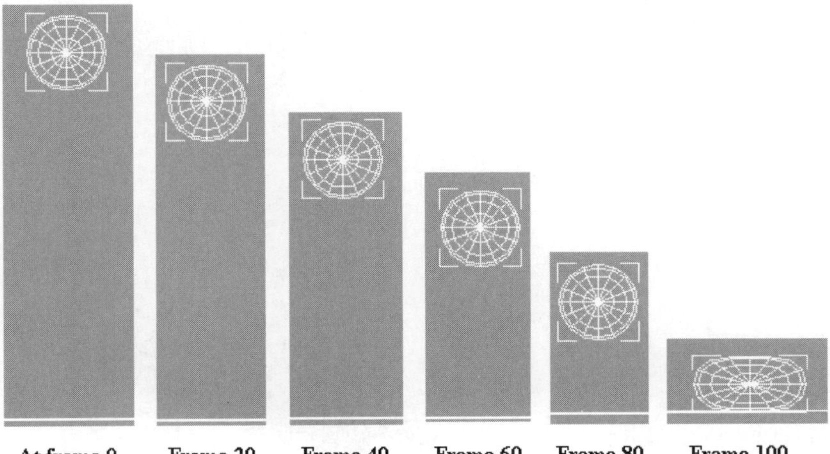

Fig. 12.30 Example 2, showing the sphere at intervals of 20 frames

A note about UVW mapping

The letters U, V and W will be seen in such terms as **UVW Mapping** – as seen in the Command panel rollout when **UVW Mapping** is to be mapped onto objects in a scene (Fig. 12.31). In fact the three letters are those which precede X, Y and Z in the alphabet and have the same significance in 3D Studio Max as X, Y and Z. Thus U stands for X, V for Y and W for Z.

Exercises

1. Figure 12.32 is a rendering of a syringe, with the plunger outside the syringe body. The scene was made up from cylinders and tubes with the injection part created from a tube which had been tapered.

Fig. 12.31 The **UVW Mapping** rollout from the **Modify** Command panel

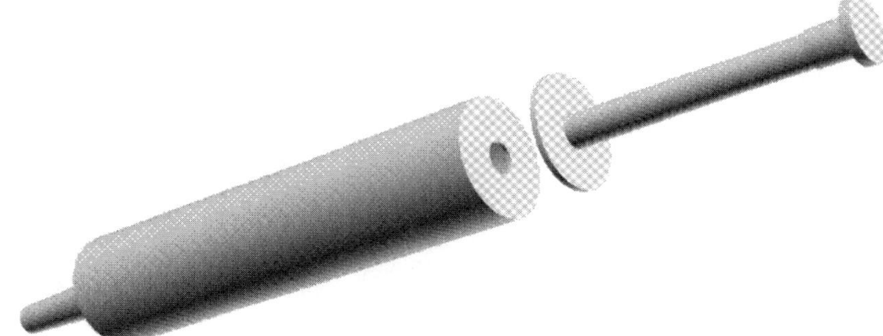

Fig. 12.32 Exercise 1

Create a similar scene, but with the plunger inside the body at its upper position. Then animate the plunger to work in and out of the body. Attempt showing a coloured liquid being squirted from the syringe as the plunger is lowered into the body.

2. In Chapter 8 a scene depicting a wine bottle and some wine glasses is shown.

   Using a similar scene, animate a wine bottle full of wine pouring the wine into a wine glass.
3. Figure 12.33 shows a pylon which has been created in 3D Studio Max from a series of boxes each of 5 units square but of varying lengths. The pylon is topped with a box onto which it is intended to create a dynamo with a three-bladed wind-generating propeller. The dynamo and its propeller are not shown in Fig. 12.33.

Fig. 12.33 Exercise 3

Create a similar pylon and add the dynamo and its propeller. Then animate the propeller to show it turning in an imaginary wind.

From your single wind generator on its pylon, set up a scene which includes a number of generators against a blue sky as if on a field and animate the scene so that all the propellers are rotating in the wind.

4. Figures 12.34 and 12.35 show three stages in the animation of four cylinders which have been tapered and then acted upon with the **Bend** modifier at each 20 time frames through **Angle:** 20, 40, 60, 80 and 100 and **Direction:** 45, 135, 225 and 315.

   The objects were assigned the material **Foliage Opacity**, a **Sky** background was included in the scene and the objects were shown as standing on a flat area created from a thin box. A suitable material should also be assigned to the box.

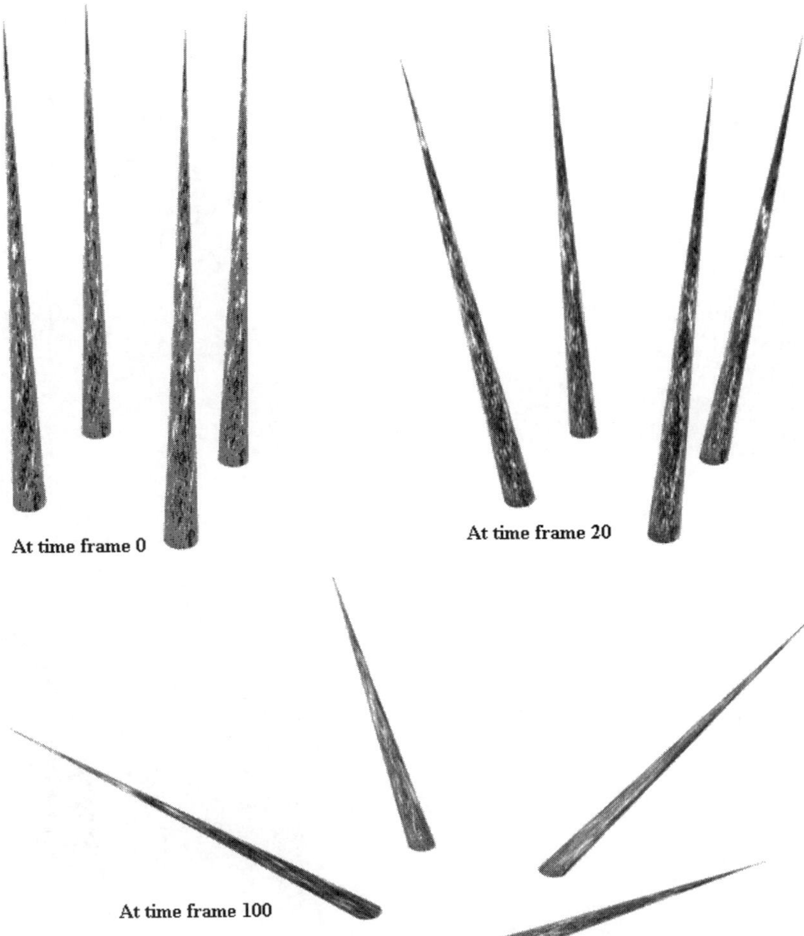

Fig. 12.34 Time frames 0 and 20 of Exercise 4

Fig. 12.35 Time frame 100 of Exercise 4

Create the scene and animate so that the four objects not only move outwards but also close inwards in a continuous animation.

5. Figure 12.36 shows a lofted object created from an arc path with a circular shape at one end and a square shape at the other. Figure 12.37 shows the same lofted object after the square shape at one end has been enlarged and rotated through 45°.

   Create a similar lofted object to that shown in Fig. 12.36 and, using it as the object for time frame 0, animate in stages of 10 frames to time frame 100 to gradually change to the object shown in Fig. 12.37. Then reduce the animation to time frame 200 to return to the original lofted shape.

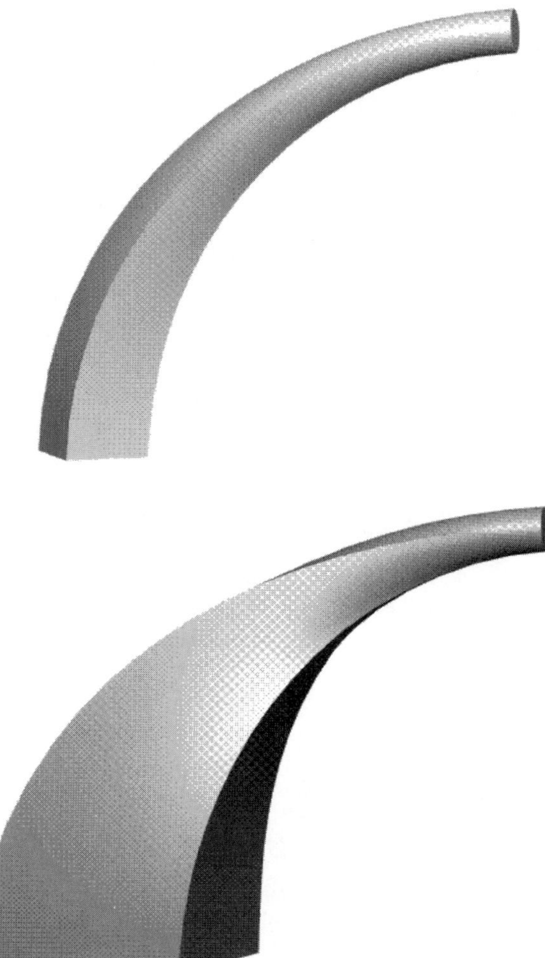

Fig. 12.36 Exercise 5. Time frame 0

Fig. 12.37 Exercise 5. Time frame 100

APPENDIX A

Keyboard shortcuts

Introduction

If the operator wishes he/she can assign a keyboard shortcut to each and every tool (command) used in 3D Studio Max. This can be carried out by following the sequence:

1. *Left-click* on **Preferences...** in the **File** pull-down menu (Fig. A.1).

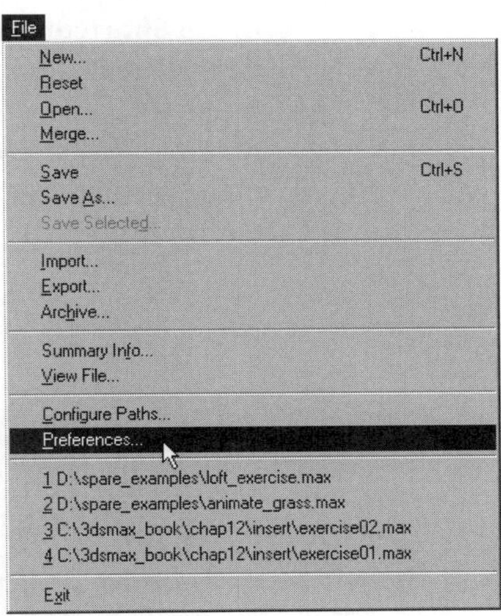

Fig. A.1 Select **Preferences...** from the **File** pull-down menu

2. The **Preference Settings** dialogue box appears (Fig. A.2). Select the **Keyboard** sub-dialogue box. In the **Command** area of the dialogue box, a list of all possible commands in the software can be scrolled. Select a command name from the list. If a keyboard shortcut has been assigned to the command the shortcut will appear below the list in the **Current Shortcut** area of the dialogue box.
3. To assign one's own shortcut to a command, select the command from the Command list. As an example the command **Array** has been selected. **Array** has not had a shortcut assigned. To assign one's own shortcut, *left-click* on **Array** in the Command list. Then

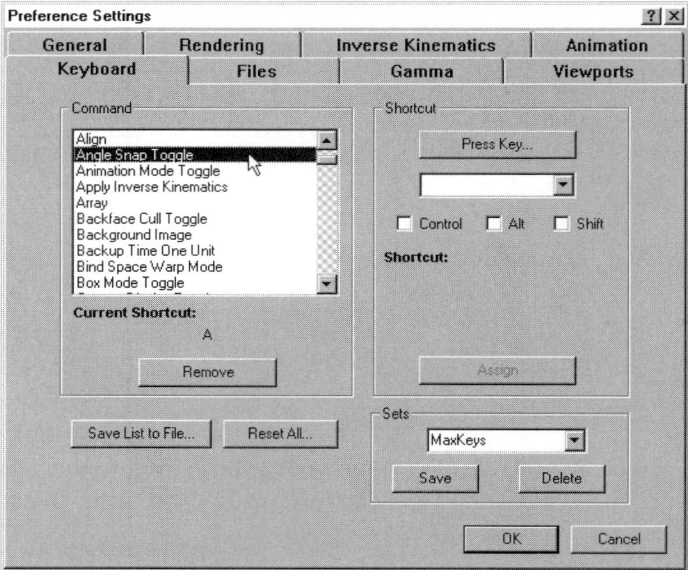

Fig. A.2 The **Preference Settings** dialogue box

in the **Shortcut** area of the dialogue box *left-click* on **Alt**, *left-click* on the **Press Key...** button, press the required key of the keyboard. Its letter (or figure etc.) will appear in the box below the **Press Key...** button. The shortcut will appear in the **Shortcut:** area of the dialogue box. It can then be assigned with a *left-click* on the **Assign** button (Fig. A.3).

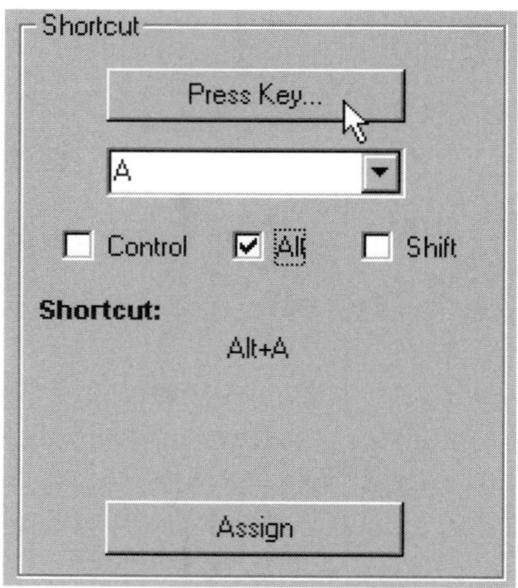

Fig. A.3 Assigning a shortcut to a command

4. If the selected shortcut has already been assigned to a command, a warning will appear in the **Currently Assigned To:** area of the dialogue box. An example is given in Fig. A.4, in which an attempt was made to assign **Shift+A** to **Array**.

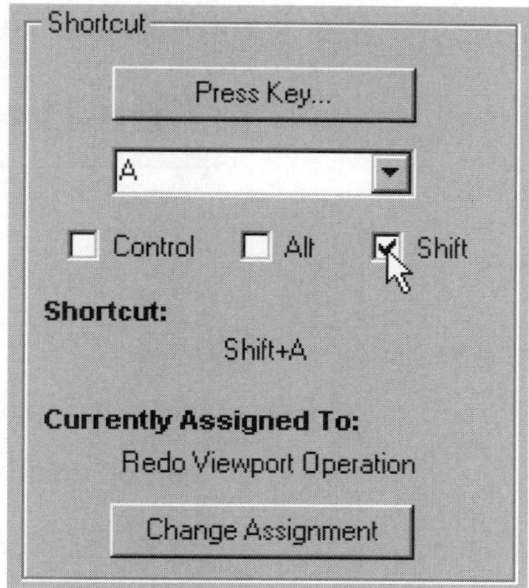

Fig. A.4 A currently assigned shortcut

Shortcuts in general use

It will be found that the following shortcuts are those an operator is most likely to use. The following lists some of the shortcuts already assigned as default shortcuts.

1. Change to Back viewport **K**
2. Change to Bottom viewport **B**
3. Change to Camera viewport **C**
4. Change to Front viewport **F**
5. Change to Grid viewport **G**
6. Change to User viewport **U**
7. Change to Left viewport **L**
8. Change to Perspective viewport **P**
9. Change to Right viewport **R**
10. Change to Top viewport **T**
11. Restrict to X **F5**
12. Restrict to Y **F6**
13. Restrict to Z **F7**
14. Delete **Delete** key
15. Open File **Ctrl+O**
16. Quick Render **Shift+Q**
17. Redraw all views **1**
18. Save File **Ctrl+S**
19. Snap Toggle **S**

APPENDIX B

File types

Introduction

3D Studio Max recognises a number of different file types, with a variety of filename extensions - the (usually) three letters preceded by a fullstop, following the filename. 3D Studio Max being a graphics form of software can load, manipulate, import, export and view a large number of graphics types of file formats which have been developed from various sources.

File types

Among the file types which can be manipulated by the software the following are included;

.exe	A file which executes a software programme. As an example the file which starts up the software is **3dsmax.exe**.
.max	Mesh file when saving a scene from 3D Studio Max.
.bak	A backup file.
.flc	An animation file.
.bmp	A bitmap image file.
.gif	A graphics bitmap file
.lft	A 3D Studio loft file.
.shp	A 3D Studio shaper file.
.3ds	A 3D Studio mesh file.
.prj	A 3D Studio project file.
.tga	A Targa bitmap file.
.fli	A file created from Autodesk Animator.
.dwg	An AutoCAD drawing file.
.dxf	An Autodesk data exchange file.
.zip	An archive file in compressed format.

APPENDIX C

Glossary

***.dxf** – A file format for drawings constructed in a CAD software package; (data exchange format). The format was originated by Autodesk, but is now in common use in many other CAD packages. 3D Studio Max can import *.dxf files.

***.gif** – A graphic file format for still images; (graphic interchange format).

***.mat** – The filename extension for a 3D Studio Max material file.

***.max** – The filename extension for a 3D Studio Max scene file.

***.prj** – The filename extension for a 3D Studio Max project file.

***.shp** – The filename extension for a 3D Studio Max shape file.

***.tga** – The filename extension for a targa graphics file.

***.tif** – The filename extension for a TIFF graphics file.

active – The viewport in which one is working is 'active' or the geometry that is being created is 'active'. To make a viewport active, click in its area.

active time segment – The number of frames in an animation that can be accessed by the time slider.

ambient lighting – An overall background lighting that affects all features in a scene.

ancestor – Describes the relationship within a hierarchical linkage between 'parents' and their 'children'.

angle of incidence – Angle at which light strikes an object. If the angle of incidence is perpendicular to a surface of an object, then it is at its brightest.

angle of reflection – Angle at which light is reflected from a surface.

animate – To animate a scene or parts of a scene. Animations can be produced when the Animate button is set on.

animation – A simulation of movement produced from a series of still images.

animation file – Files with an extension *.flc, *.fli or *.cel.

anti-aliasing – A method of sharpening up the edges of each part of a display by controlling the colours and density of pixels along the edges.

atmosphere – An effect such as fog or visible light beams produced in 3D Studio Max.

attenuation – Tthe strength of a light diminishing with distance from its source.

axis – One of the Cartesian 3D axes defining the X, Y and Z directions

axonometric – A 3D view in which up to three sides of an object are seen. In axonometric view, the sides are in parallel projection as distinct from perspective views in which parallel edges will meet in the infinite distance.

background – A flat plane behind a scene which, in 3D Studio Max, can be coloured or show a scene.

bitmap – A form of graphic file.

Boolean operation – A tool or command which results in objects in a scene being joined together (Boolean union), subtracted from each other (Boolean subtraction) or form an intersection between each other (Boolean intersection).

camera – an object representing a camera in a scene to set the direction from which the scene is to be viewed. Two types of camera are available in 3D Studio Max – target and free.

child – In a hierarchical linkage a 'child' is a subordinate object connected to a 'parent'. It should be noted that a child can itself have a child, in which case the original child also becomes a parent, but is still a child to its original parent.

clone – A copy of an object. There are three types of clone possible in 3D Studio Max: a copy, an instance or a reference.

compound object – An object made up of several objects: examples are Boolean objects, morph objects and lofted objects.

coordinate system – Objects in 3D space in 3D Studio Max are constructed along three axes: X, Y and Z. This system is based upon the Cartesian system of three-dimensional geometry.

copy – One type of object clone, separate from the object from which it was derived and which functions in its own right.

degradation – A parameter controlling a trade off between the quality and the speed of a display in a viewport.

descendant – Describes the relationship within a hierarchical linkage between a 'child' and its 'parent'; children of a child are descendants of the child, but will also be descendants of the child's parents.

diffuse light – Light that is reflected from an object when it is illuminated by directional light.

directional light – Light casting parallel rays in one direction only. In 3D Studio Max, directional light can be introduced to give the effect of lighting from the sun.

dithering – Simulating colours by mixing coloured pixels.
dolly – Moving a camera or a light along the direction in which its is pointing.

environment map – A scene from a file used as a background to a scene.
extents – The maximum boundary area of a scene. When a scene is zoomed to its extents, the scene fills the viewport in which it is placed.
eye point – The assumed position from which a scene is viewed: the camera position or user's position.

face – An area of a surface mesh formed by a triangle.
falloff – The area of the circle or rectangle at the edge of a light beam from a spot light.
falloff angle – The full angle of the beam from a spot light.
field of view – The angle of an area covered by a camera. If the field of view is large, the camera is said to be 'wide angle'. Conversely, when the field of view is small, the camera is 'telescopic'.
flat shading – A shading method in which each facet shows, making the edges between facets visible.
flic file – An Autodesk file format in which animations can be saved. Extensions for flic files may be *.fli, *.flc or *.cel.
flyout – A line of icons which appear alongside tool icons which show a small arrow in their corner.
focal length – The distance between the lens and the film in a camera. Determines the field of view of as camera. The smaller the focal length the 'wider the angle' of the camera.
frame – A single image (or 'still') from an animation.
frame rate – The number of frames per second produced in an animation.
free camera – A non-target camera.
freeze – Freezing an object is a method of preventing further editing of the object in 3D Studio Max.

gizmo – A frame surrounding an object being modified. Gizmos can be moved, scaled and rotated as if they were objects in a scene.
grid object – A helper created when a local grid is required as distinct from the grid on which an object has been created.
ground plane – The World X,Y plane on which objects are originally created.
group – A number of objects formed into a single unit, so that they can be acted upon as if they were a single object.

hedra – 3D objects with faces that are all polygons.

heirarchy – The relationship between 'parent' and 'child' objects within a system of descendents and anscestors.

helper – Objects within a scene which are only included to assist in its construction.

hierarchical linkage – A system of connected objects, described as 'parents' and 'children' in a heirarchy of descendants and ancestors.

horizon – The horizon of vision of a camera.

hot material – A material which is in both the Material Editor and the scene. Any changes in the hot material in the editor will be reflected in the material in the scene.

hotspot – The area at the centre of a spotlight. The brightest part of the beam. Also known as the beam angle.

HSV – Hue, saturation and value: terms applied to the colours used in a scene.

hue – *See* HSV. Hue is similar in meaning to 'colour' or 'shade'.

IK – *See* inverse kinematics.

image file – A file with a still image mainly used for backgrounds.

instance – One type of object clone, which reflects any changes made to the object from which it was cloned.

inverse kinematics – Animations relying upon the method of hierarchical linking.

isometric – A form of axonometric parallel projection in which perpendicular edges of an object are drawn at the same angle to the horizontal.

keyframe – The frames in an animation defining the start and end of an animation.

keys – Values for the animation of keyframes.

kinematic chain – The part of a hierarchical linkage, starting at a child and progressing up until the original ancestor of the child is reached.

light – In 3D Studio Max, three main types of light are available: omni, directional or spot. However, ambient lighting as distinct from a positioned light may be present in a scene.

light colour – The colour of a light.

link – The connection between two objects in a hierarchical linkage.

lofting – The method of creating a 3D object by moving a 2D shape along a path which defines the direction in which the lofting takes place.

map – An image which can be assigned as a material.

material – Materials are assigned to objects and define how they will look; materials have properties such as colour, reflectivity, transparency, etc.

Material Editor – A series of dialogue boxes allowing the operator to define and assign materials to objects in a scene.

material library – Material files held in a directory on disk.

matte – Describes a surface which is not shiny.

mesh object – A 3D object in 3D Studio Max made up from triangular faces.

metal shading – A form of shading associated with materials to create a realistic metallic appearance.

modal – The term applied to a dialogue box in which changes must be made before any further operations can be performed in viewports.

modeless – A term applied to dialogue boxes which can remain on screen while operations to objects in a scene can continue to be made.

modifier – Tools (commands) whose function is to change the geometry of objects: bend, twist, taper, etc.

morphing – The creation of an animation by transforming the vertices of objects.

noise – Random changing of objects based on mathematical systems.

normal – A vector perpendicular to a face.

object – Any feature created in 3D Studio Max: a geometrical shape, a light, a camera, a material, etc.

omni light – A light source which sends out light rays in all directions (omni-directional).

operand – The name given to one of the Boolean tools.

orthographic – A view seen when looking at an object in directions perpendicular to a face of the object: from the front, from a side, from the back, from the bottom, etc.

pan – The moving of a view in a viewport along an axis.

parametric – Applied to an object which changes in all its parameters when any one parameter is changed.

parent – Applied to the prime ancestor of a 'child' in hierarchical linkage.

patch – A surface in 3D Studio Max which can be deformed.

path – The route along which 2D shapes can be lofted.

perspective – Aa 3D view which attempts to simulate what a human viewer will actually see. In perspective views, edges of surfaces will eventually appear to meet in the infinite distance.

phong – A high standard of shading, in which edges will render with a relatively smooth appearance.

pivot point – The local centre for the rotation or pivoting of the transforms for an object or group.

polyhedra – *See* hedra. 3D objects with faces which are all polygons.

primitive – 3D geometric shapes used as basic building blocks in 3D Studio Max.

properties – Data about an object such as size, colour, position, etc.

ray traced shadows – Sampled rays from light sources plus reflected light from other objects. Ray traced shadows are more accurate than other shadow methods.

rendering – The production of photo- realistic models of scenes, including lighting, colours, shadows, etc.

resolution – The number of pixels in width and height of the screen monitor. In general 3D Studio Max functions reasonably well with a screen resolution of 800 (width) by 600 (height). However, higher resolutions result in clearer scenes containing more fine detail.

rollout – The extensions of the Command panel which appear when the buttons marked with a '+' sign are clicked.

saturation – A measure of the hue of a given colour.

segment – A section of a spline between two vertices.

selection set – A group of selected objects in a viewport.

shadow map – The generation of shadows providing softer edges; this method is not as accurate as ray traced shadows.

shape – A 2D object created from splines.

smooth shading – One of the shading methods in 3D Studio Max, which produces a smooth rendered surface.

snap – The cursor, under mouse control, will move only to grid points at spacings set in the Grid and Snap Settings dialogue box. Can be used to ensure accurate positioning when transforming objects.

specular highlight – The lit highlight on the surface of an object created when specular highlighting is associated with a spot light.

spline – A curve between points.

spotlight – One of the forms of lighting in 3D Studio Max. Creates a beam of light which can be focused.

sub-object – The parts of an object which are visible when in sub-object mode. The most common example is when the Edit Mesh modifier is in use.

sub-tree – That part of a hierarchical linkage tree showing only with a single parent and its descendants.

targa – A graphic file format based on a format from TrueVision.

target – The point around which a camera or a spotlight can be rotated.

TIFF – A graphic file format (tagged image file format).

toolbar – The set of icon buttons at the top of the 3D Studio Max window.

transform – The name given to actions such as move, rotate, scale.

transparency – One property of a material assigned to an object.

TrueType – The name of the most common font format used within Windows 95.

undo – A command to reverse the last action carried out by any tool.

ungroup – Reverses the action of grouping a number of objects; the group becomes a collection of single objects.

UVW – Used in mapping; an alternate name for XYZ.

vector – A control point associated with a vertex.

vertex – Control points on the outline of a shape (2D) or the suface of an object (3D).

viewport – The parts of the layout of the 3D Studio Max window in which views of a scene will appear and objects can be created.

viewport navigation controls – A series of tool icons at the bottom right of the 3D Studio Max window, representing tools used for controlling the viewports.

wireframe – One of the rendering methods in 3D Studio Max. No surfaces are rendered and only the outlines of the meshes of the scene appear.

World coordinate system – The 3D Studio Max model space.

Index